A MATTER

OF HONOUR

OTHER BOOKS BY JONATHON RILEY

History of the Queen's Royal Regiment (Canterbury, 1984)

From Pole to Pole: The Life of Quintin Riley 1905–1980
(Chippenham, 1989 and 1998)

The Monitor Mission in the Balkans (Zagreb, 1992)

Soldiers of the Queen (Chippenham, 1993)

White Dragon (Shrewsbury, 1995)

Napoleon and the World War, 1813 (London and New York,
1999 and 2007)

Regimental Records of the Royal Welch Fusiliers Vol VI, 1945–1969
(Llandysul, 2001)

Regimental Records of the Royal Welch Fusiliers Vol VII, 1969–2000
(Llandysul, 2001)

*The Life and Campaigns of General Hughie Stockwell, 1903–1986:
From Norway, through Burma, to Suez* (London, 2006)

Napoleon as a General (London and New York, 2007)

That Astonishing Infantry (with Michael Glover) (London, 2008)

Decisive Battles (London and New York, 2009)

Up to Mametz… and Beyond (ed., annotated and introduced –
original by Llewelyn Wyn Griffith) (London, 2010)

JONATHON RILEY

A MATTER OF
HONOUR

The Life, Campaigns

and Generalship

of Isaac Brock

Foreword by Donald E. Graves

ROBIN BRASS STUDIO
Montreal

Frontline Books, London

First published 2011 by Robin Brass Studio Inc., Montreal
www.rbstudiobooks.com

Published and distributed in the United Kingdom in 2011 by Frontline Books, an imprint of Pen & Sword Books Ltd,
47 Church Street, Barnsley, S. Yorkshire, S70 2AS
www.frontline-books.com

ISBN-13: 978-1-896941-65-3
ISBN-10: 1-896941-65-6

Reprinted 2012

Printed and bound in Canada by Marquis Imprimeur Inc., Cap-Saint-Ignace, Quebec

Library and Archives Canada Cataloguing in Publication

Riley, J. P. (Jonathon P.)

   A matter of honour: the life, campaigns and generalship of Isaac Brock / Jonathon Riley; foreword by Donald E. Graves.

Includes bibliographical references and index.
ISBN 978-1-896941-65-3

1. Brock, Isaac, Sir, 1769-1812. 2. Brock, Isaac, Sir, 1769-1812 – Military leadership.
3. Generals – Canada – Biography. 4. Canada – History – War of 1812 – Campaigns.
I. Title.

FC443.B76R54 2011   971.03'2092   C2011-900586-7

Contents

MAPS

Foreword

I n the nearly two centuries that have passed since Major-General Isaac Brock's death in October 1812, there have been numerous books devoted to this prominent figure in Canadian history, and the forthcoming bicentennial of the War of 1812 will undoubtedly bring forth several more. Although Brock died very early in the conflict and there were many other British generals who saw serious fighting in it, the manner of his death and its effect – not to mention the impressive memorial beneath which his remains lie today – have insured that Brock has always received a good deal of attention from biographers. *A Matter of Honour* differs, however, from previous accounts of Brock's life because it is a study of the man by a fellow general – a member of the same profession and a peer, as it were.

The irony is that, in this case, the biographer may have more military experience than his subject, for Jonathon Riley has had a distinguished military career. After joining the British army in 1973, he served in Northern Ireland (six tours with only one on the staff), Central America, the Balkans (five tours), Iraq and West Africa. In 1995 he received the Distinguished Service Order for valour after commanding The Royal Welch Fusiliers in the defence of the Bosnian town of Gorazde during a six-month siege by Serbian forces. Riley has led military forces ranging in size from a platoon to a corps and his last active assignment was deputy commander of the International Security Assistance Force (ISAF) in Afghanistan. Lieutenant-General Riley, however, is also an historian of some note, having earned a doctorate in history and written or edited thirteen books, including an assessment of Napoleon as a general. He is therefore very much a member of that distinguished line of British soldier-scholars that includes such names as General Sir John Hackett, Brigadier Richard Holmes, General Sir William Napier and Field Marshal Sir Archibald Wavell – and is thus the ideal person to examine the life of Isaac Brock.

Riley, who has personal connections in the Channel Islands, has uncovered much new information about Brock's early years and has clarified matters concerning his education and family finances. Money problems seriously affected Brock's professional career, causing him to remain in a colonial backwater where he held an important command rather than going to the Peninsula to serve with Wellington, the object of every ambitious officer. They also affected his personal life and were undoubtedly the reason for his not marrying, rather than other reasons that have been implied in recent times. We also learn much about Brock: his hat size, his physique (rather more portly than most artists or sculptors have portrayed him) and his favourite reading. Finally, Riley demolishes many of the myths that have grown up around the man, among them that of the wretched horse Alfred, whose statue adorns the battlefield of Queenston Heights, although the animal almost certainly did not have the privilege of serving there.

It is Riley's assessment of Brock as a soldier that is the core of this biography, however, and its most important aspect. It is my firm belief that historians who write about war and the military should have worn a uniform at some point in their lives – be their service ever so humble. Too often civilian historians who write about military operations are like the man who knew all the words and sang all the notes but somehow never quite learned the song. That is definitely not the case with the author of this book, as when Jonathon Riley discourses about the art of command, the principles of leadership, the conduct of operations and the effect of terrain and weapons capabilities on tactics, his words have the ring of not only truth but experience. This is actually one of the most fascinating aspects of the book that follows. When the author talks about the importance of senior commanders visiting subordinate commanders, of commanders getting out and talking to ordinary soldiers, of the difficulties of preparing for an assault crossing of a water obstacle, of the effects of fatigue and rain on morale, of the difficulties faced by a senior commander vested with both military and civil responsibilities, of the methods of encouraging resistance to the enemy by indigenous peoples, of the common experience of young officers first joining their regiments, of the necessity of leading by example and of maintaining intelligent discipline, he knows of what he speaks.

I also hold the firm belief that if one is to write about the operational and tactical level of war, there is simply no substitute for going on the actual ground. In this respect I can personally testify to Jonathon Riley's thoroughness in researching this book as I accompanied him on two battlefield tours of the Niagara Peninsula, which featured long and exhausting days followed by lengthy evening post-mortems over a comfortable dram or two. I well remember a fine April day when, having found a runnel running up the face of Queenston Heights which just might have been the way American troops took to capture the British battery, he climbed it hand over fist, grasping at branches and rocks, all the while cheerfully discoursing on the difference between an infantryman's load in 1812 and 2010. I followed faithfully only about a third of the way when I decided that I could best serve by taking photographs – for, as Milton would have it, they also serve who only stand and wait – and marked his progress by the noise of branches cracking and rocks falling from above. Where Riley could not go on the ground, as at Detroit, which is more or less buried in concrete, he made a painstaking study of all available map and pictorial material, and his account of this often-neglected operation is one of the best I have read.

These tours were always full of fascinating sidebars. A pleasant picnic lunch on the grounds of McFarland House near the Niagara River incorporated an interesting anecdotal lecture on the best way to deploy a modern infantry battalion for all-round defence, using Gorazde as a model. On another occasion, when asked to contribute to a discussion with a group of lady school teachers from Nebraska about the night assault on Fort Erie, Riley not only went through the check list a company commander must have in his head before committing his troops to such an operation but also, in response to their questions, provided them with a succinct but informative lecture on the role of the British army in Iraq. The visitors, who clearly did not meet British general officers all that often, were fascinated not only with his knowledge and erudition but also by his accent – "Don't he speak so pretty" was one not-so-*sotto-voce* comment overheard. Six months later Jonathon Riley was serving Christmas dinner to British troops in Afghanistan.

A Matter of Honour is therefore a study of a good soldier by another good soldier, but this does not mean that Riley has not been critical of Brock. For example, he makes the sound point that if Brock had faced the better trained and led American army that took the field in 1814, he might not have proved so successful. But Riley is always empathetic with his subject – having faced in his own experience many of the problems that Brock encountered – and both his praise and his criticism are sound and balanced. The result is an informative new biography of one of the major figures of the War of 1812 that will be read with profit by anyone interested in that conflict and the art of military leadership.

DONALD E. GRAVES
Day of St. Ambrose 2010
"Maple Cottage"
Valley of the Mississippi
Upper Canada

Preface

When I was eleven years old, my parents put a book in my Christmas stocking; it was Donald Goodspeed's *The Good Soldier*. Although I was partly brought up in Jersey, my parents knew nothing of Brock and they were probably attracted by the cover design, showing Brock in his cocked hat, mounted on the grey horse Alfred, waving his sword and urging British troops in red coats and 1812-pattern shakos forward into action. As an historical depiction, it contains at least three major errors, but to me it was an irresistible picture, for I had decided at an early age to be a soldier. I loved that book and because of it I became one of only a handful of British officers who even knew Brock's name, so much was it eclipsed by events in the Peninsular War at the same time. I maintained my studies of the War of 1812 for many years and tried to show its strategic connections with the wider world war of the later Napoleonic Period in my book *Napoleon and the World War*. As a result I read a number of biographies of Brock. Some were hagiographic, like Tupper or Read, and to modern scholarship somewhat lacking in rigour. Others had a reasonable basis of fact but soon drifted off into supposition, wishful thinking and romantic nonsense. On the other hand there is some good, penetrating scholarship by men like Kosche, Graves, Hickey and Malcomson on aspects of Brock's life and death, but no single-volume examination of his life, campaigns and generalship, nor its relation to his role as civil administrator. When Don Graves therefore suggested that I should write a modern biography of Brock as a general and Robin Brass said he would publish it for the bicentenary of the outbreak of the War of 1812, there was nothing on earth that was going to stop me.

My admiration for Isaac Brock as a soldier remains undimmed with the passing of the years, although I have some doubts about his grasp of strategy and the political imperatives of the time. I respect greatly his courage:

we all have a certain store of courage – some people have a great deal, some people have a little, but it is a finite resource that cannot be renewed. Brock had a great deal of it, both moral and physical, and never stinted to use it up. I also admire his sense of loyalty and in particular his loyalty to his peers, his subordinates and the families of those who had served him. It could never be said that Isaac Brock failed in his self-imposed duty to them. But I never really understood how it was that he met his death doing a captain's job. I have tried to explain this in the context of the moral compass of the late eighteenth century – since it would be meaningless to do so by today's lights. I believe that, above all, Brock was governed by his sense of honour and that the clues are there throughout his life, if we look for them. Hence the title of this biography.

As a general officer, I have held extended commands in West Africa, the Balkans, Iraq and Afghanistan. I have commanded not only British troops but those of many other nations and I have had to co-ordinate my actions closely with civil authorities: those of my own country, of our allies and of host nations. In Africa, Iraq and Central Asia I have also experienced the interplay between regular troops and indigenous tribal fighters. This being the case, I perhaps understand the problems that Brock faced in a way that no purely academic writer ever can because like him I have carried major burdens of responsibility and balanced conflicting loyalties. On the other hand, I possess two graduate degrees in history and have completed a body of published work on early nineteenth-century military history that perhaps allows me to analyze the subject matter in a way that a purely military writer might not be able to do. It is with these different but intertwined backgrounds that I approached the task of writing a biography of a deserving officer.

ACKNOWLEDGMENTS

I am very much obliged to a number of authorities. They include: the staff at the National Archives, Kew; Dr Darryl Ogier, Guernsey Island Archives; Richard Hocart of Guernsey for information on Brock's early life and on the banking house of Le Mesurier and Brock; Dr Jason Monaghan, Director, and Guernsey Museums for permission to reproduce the two authenticated portraits of Brock as a young officer in the 8th Foot and as a colonel; Library and Archives Canada for several maps, drawings and contemporary images;

the Royal Armouries for images from the records of the Board of Ordnance; the National Maritime Museum, Greenwich, for the images of the British landing at Callantsoog in the Helder, 1799, and the naval assault on Copenhagen, 1801; the curators of the regimental museums of the King's Regiment (formerly the 8th), the Royal Regiment of Wales (formerly the 41st) and the Duke of Edinburgh's Royal Regiment (formerly the 49th); Brian Leigh Dunnigan, Curator of Maps, William L. Clements Library of the University of Michigan, for his extensive knowledge and generosity in identifying the ground around Detroit and for permission to use the maps and line drawings of early Detroit; Robert Henderson for extensive help in researching contemporary images and details of military life in the early nineteenth century; Tom Fournier and Professor Ray Hobbes for their help with the movements and history of the 41st and other material; Dan Laroche and Fort George, Niagara-on-the-Lake, for the uniform of the officers of the 41st; Markus Stein for the uniform of the 8th Foot; New York Public Library for the use of the contemporary picture of a Napoleonic War period recruiting party from *The Costume of Yorkshire*; Nick Saint for permission to reproduce the image of Assistant Surgeon Faulkner; the Royal Hospital, Chelsea, for permission to reproduce for the first time the watercolour images of the Colours of the 4th U.S. Infantry, captured at Detroit; the trustees of Muckross House, Killarney, for permission to use the portrait of General John Vincent; Janet Malcomson for permission to use the photograph by the late Robert Malcomson of Brock's memorial in St Paul's Cathedral; Bob W. Scott for photographs of the Brock house and commemorative plaques at St Peter Port; Major John Grodzinski of the Royal Military College of Canada, Kingston, Ontario, for his help in unravelling British strategy and the work of Sir George Prevost; and Dr Carl Benn for his advice on aboriginal matters. Thanks to Steve Waites for his excellent maps. Finally, thanks to my good friends, and authorities on the War of 1812, Donald E. Graves and Dianne Graves for permission to use material from *Dragon Rampant* and *In the Midst of Alarms* – as well as for their endless help, encouragement, hospitality, correction and goading almost beyond endurance, without which this book would never have been written.

JONATHON RILEY

2011

ABBREVIATIONS USED IN THE TEXT

A.D.C., Aide	Aide-de-camp; a junior staff officer acting as personal assistant to a general.
A.G.	Adjutant-General; the chief personnel officer of an army or subordinate command of an army.
C.B.	Companion of the Most Honourable Order of the Bath.
C-in-C	Commander-in-chief.
G.C.B.	Knight Grand Cross of the Most Honourable Order of the Bath.
G.C.H.	Knight Grand Cross of the Royal Guelphic Order, or Order of the House of Hanover
G.O.C.	General Officer Commanding.
K.B.	Knight of the Most Honourable Order of the Bath.
K.C.B.	Knight Commander of the Most Honourable Order of the Bath.
K.G.	Knight of the Most Noble Order of the Garter.
Kt	Knight or Knight Bachelor.
L.I.	Light infantry.
P.C.	Privy Councillor.
Q.M.G.	Quarter-Master General; the chief logistic officer of an army or subordinate command of an army.

Queenston Heights

TUESDAY, 13 OCTOBER 1812, ABOUT 7 O'CLOCK IN THE MORNING

The general is a big man, over six feet tall and broad too – in fact at the age of forty-three, tending to bulk. But his movements are brisk, he is more muscle than fat and he has the tanned complexion of one who has spent his life in the open air. In his red coat and cocked hat, astride his horse, he is a conspicuous figure in the early morning light. He is the general in command of all regular troops and militia in Upper Canada and yet he is at the head of a company of less than fifty men, doing the job of a captain. Dismounting from his horse, he exchanges a word here and there with a nervous soldier in the ranks; he knows these men and they know him, for they are from the light company of the 49th Foot, the regiment he joined twenty-one years ago as a captain and which he has led into battle on the last two occasions that it has faced the enemy – in the Helder and at Copenhagen, eleven years ago. The general is Isaac Brock and although he cannot know it, this is the morning of his death.

The day is Tuesday, 13 October 1812. The place is the small village of Queenston on the Canadian side of the Niagara River. During the night, the Americans have made their second incursion into the Canadas since the declaration of war in June. They have established a precarious bridgehead on the river bank but are contained by the garrison of British and Canadian regulars and militia in the village of Queenston. But a further landing downstream has required the withdrawal of the grenadier company of the 49th from their commanding position on the heights above the village to deal with that incursion. Worse still, a body of American troops of unknown strength has managed to scramble up the heights, appear behind the British artillery redoubt just below the summit and has captured it and the gun it houses. Brock is nettled, for he was on the position when the Americans ap-

1

peared – from a direction that was supposed to have been an impossibility – and doubly nettled because he has been implicit in ordering down to the riverside the soldiers who would have stopped this gang of amateurs. More British and Canadian troops, and Mohawk warriors too, are on their way, but Brock is determined to push the Americans off the heights before they can build up their forces; his intuition tells him that a counter-attack now by a company may be worth a counter-attack by a brigade in two hours' time. And in any case, his pride has been wounded. A word of command and the men shoulder their arms. Another word and they step off in line. The advancing redcoats come under fire from American riflemen hiding in the tree-line above the redoubt almost at once.

To the Americans waiting around the position or in the trees it is obvious that a very senior officer is leading the attack; some of them, who have been on the frontier for a while, recognize Brock from their own observations or from descriptions. The sight of him causes some of the younger men to waver, but to the older fellows it is a chance not to be missed. Brock leads the light company of the 49th forward, not taking up the usual position of an officer to the right or behind the firing line as the range closes, waving his sword and encouraging the men to follow. A bullet strikes him a glancing blow on the hand but he pays no attention to it. Then, just as he makes a half turn to urge the redcoats to charge in with the bayonet, an American soldier steps out of the trees and takes deliberate aim. Some men of the light company try to bring him down before he can take his shot, but to no avail. At that range there is no mistake: the bullet takes Brock squarely in the chest and he collapses. Several of the 49th gather round him; one poor fellow is all but severed in the middle by a ball and falls across the general's body. The cry goes up: "Avenge the General!" The troops press on – but there are too many Americans and the fire is too fierce. The British and Canadians pull back, carrying their general's body, into the village of Queenston below.

CHAPTER ONE

"A Remarkable Fine Corps"

ISAAC BROCK'S EARLY LIFE AND SERVICE,
1769–1791

The Channel Islands – Jersey, Guernsey, Alderney, Sark, Herm, Jethou and Brechou – lie just to the west of the Cotentin Peninsula of Normandy and within sight of the French coast. Originally they had formed part of the Duchy of Normandy and when Duke William conquered England in 1066, the kingdom and the duchy were united. In the time of King John, during the opening years of the thirteenth century, the duchy was conquered by the King of France. The islands had the choice of staying with their king or leaving with their new duke. They chose their king. Thus the island of Guernsey, like the other Channel Islands, owes allegiance to the British *Crown*, but not directly to the British *government*. The island was governed by an assembly or parliament known as the *Etats* or States and the monarch was represented by a governor. The islands set their own laws, administered themselves and conducted their own courts under the authority of a bailiff appointed by the Crown; the bailiff was also the presiding officer of the *Etats*.

The working language of the islands was a *patois* of French, but this by no means meant that the islanders had any sympathy with France – quite the reverse. During the sixteenth century, Protestantism had become strongly entrenched, further distancing the islanders from the French on the mainland, and during the English Civil Wars the islands had for the most part declared for Parliament. In the conflicts of the late seventeenth and early to mid eighteenth centuries, the islands had been a haven for the Royal Navy and a host of privateers and were accordingly the very bane of French maritime trade. The islands all maintained militia regiments with drills every Sunday and were usually garrisoned by one or more regular British infantry regiments. The militia, like many aspects of life on the is-

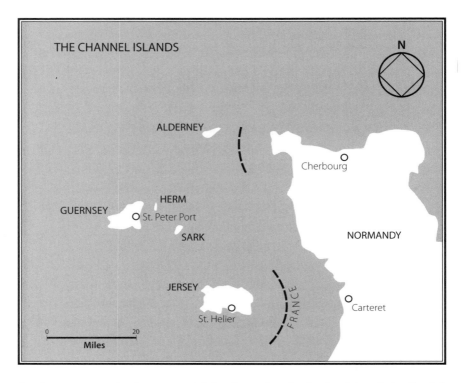

THE CHANNEL ISLANDS

N

ALDERNEY

Cherbourg

HERM

GUERNSEY
St. Peter Port

SARK

NORMANDY

JERSEY

St. Helier

FRANCE

Carteret

0   20
Miles

lands, was organized on a parish basis under the leadership of the feudal lord of the manor – the *Seigneur*.

Despite competition from France and attempts by the British government to control – and therefore tax – their trade, the Channel Islands' economies improved steadily throughout the second half of the eighteenth century. Fishing, both near home and across the Atlantic around Newfoundland, was a major source of income but the chief occupation of the population was farming. Wheat, cider and milk were the main exports and the distinctive cattle of the islands began to emerge as separate breeds about this time. Bigger incomes from agriculture and trade meant bigger properties. Many important houses were built or rebuilt about this time, including Saumarez Park in Guernsey, the seat of the Le Marchant family,[1] related by marriage to the Brocks.

The sons of notable families, especially in Guernsey, were usually sent to school in England for a few years to supplement the rather meagre education available locally. This served both to widen their outlook and improve their command of English, before they took up a career or, as many did, entered the Royal Navy or the army. Generally, estates in the Channel Islands were simply not big enough to provide the sort of existence that a gentleman's family in England would have expected. Sons of such families in the islands had no option but to go away to earn a living – hence the fact that they were over-represented in percentage terms in the Royal Navy and the regiments of the British army.

Among the notable families of Guernsey was that of Brock. Earlier biographers of Isaac Brock have identified the family as being of English ancestry, asserting their descent from various Brocks, including that Sir Hugh Brock named by Froissart in his *Chronicles* as the keeper of Derval Castle in Brittany on behalf of Sir Robert Knollys, around the middle of the fourteenth century. Certainly there are eight families of that name in various British armorial registers[2] and the Oxford English Dictionary gives the derivation as the Anglo-Saxon *Broc(e)*, for badger. However, the family of Le Brocq has been long established in the islands. In 1563 the Seigneur of St Ouen in Jersey, Helier de Carteret, took over the defence of Sark with a number of followers, one of whom was surnamed Le Brocq. The family name crops up in St Brelade, Jersey, again in 1674, and in Guernsey, a Martha Le Brocq is recorded in St Peter Port in 1668 – she appears to have been an ancestor of "Buffalo Bill" Cody. It must therefore be a strong possibility that the family was of Norman-French origin but, given the history of conflict between Britain and France, the name had become anglicised. What is certain is that the parish registers of St Peter Port, the main – indeed only – town of Guernsey show that Isaac Brock's grandfather, William, died there in 1776. William had four children: William, the eldest, who married Judith de Beauvoir; Henry, who married Susan Saumarez, sister of the famous Admiral de Saumarez;[*] Mary, who married the local magnate John Le Marchant, whose family included the general of that name;[†] and last John, born in 1729, who married Elizabeth De Lisle, the daughter of the lieutenant-bailiff of the Island. The Brock family house was large and comfortable, built of

---

* Admiral James Saumarez, 1st Baron Saumarez (1757–1836) was present at the defeat of the French in the West Indies in 1782, at St Vincent in 1797, at Aboukir in 1798 and himself defeated the French and Spanish fleets at Algeciras in 1801.

† Major-General John Gaspard Le Marchant (1766–1812) was a distinguished cavalry officer who served in the French Revolutionary and Napoleonic Wars. He founded the military college that was the forerunner of the RMC Sandhurst, at High Wycombe.

the distinctive pink granite of the islands, in the High Street of St Peter Port. It is still there, bearing a plaque identifying it, although at the time of writing it houses a chemist's shop.

John Brock died on 12 July 1777 at the early age of forty-eight at Rennes, where he had gone from Dinan, after having taken the waters because of poor health. He left eight sons and two daughters; another two sons and two daughters had died in infancy. John's estate was large enough to allow the family to live comfortably, for his daughters to marry well, and for his sons to be educated as gentlemen – this despite a large family and a long period of minority for all the children during which they would have to be supported by the estate. As they grew to adulthood there would be no question of living off the estate: the girls would have to marry well and the boys would have to embrace a profession. As one account put it,

> They were left in independent, if not affluent, circumstances; but the fond indulgence of a widowed mother, who could deny them no enjoyment, tended, notwithstanding their long minority, to diminish their patrimony.[3]

I am indebted to Dr Darryl Ogier of the Guernsey Island Archives for his work on John Brock, which reveals that he made an oral will leaving his wife 2,000 guineas, to be drawn from the Funds, that is, government bonds, or otherwise; the use for life of his house in St Peter Port; and the guardianship of his children.[4] He appointed an executor for his interests in France and two other executors for his properties outside France: his brother-in-law John Le Marchant, and Matthieu Perchard,* a financier and goldsmith with whom John Brock may have banked. From this it may be inferred that John Brock had substantial investments in the Funds; secondly that he owned more than one house; and third that he had substantial property and investments in Britain, France and the Channel Islands. According to the parish tax lists, John Brock was rated at 1,100 quarters, the sixth largest in his parish, and in 1780 his heirs were rated at 1,420 quarters,† the fourth highest.[5]

---

* Matthieu Perchard (1703–77) did not long outlive John Brock. He had goldsmithing interests in Abchurch Street, London, and in Hatton Garden. See W. Marshall-Fraser, "History of Banking in the Channel Islands and a record of banknote issue," in *Transactions of La Société Guernesiaise*, 1949, 378–443, p. 387.

† Land holdings were rated in terms of their equivalent wheat yield in quarters of a hundredweight, one quarter being therefore 28 lb (12.7 kg).

John Brock's two daughters were Mary, born in 1777, who married Thomas Potenger of Compton in Berkshire; and Elizabeth, born in 1767, who married John Tupper of Guernsey. Tupper's son Ferdinand Brock Tupper (1795–1874) was an early biographer of Isaac.[6] John Brock's two eldest sons, John, born in 1759, and Ferdinand, born in 1760 (such was the pace of child-bearing in the eighteenth century), both entered the British army. John purchased a commission in the 8th (The King's) Regiment and was killed in a duel in 1801 when a brevet lieutenant-colonel in the 81st Foot. Ferdinand, a lieutenant in the 60th Royal Americans, was killed at the defence of Baton Rouge on the Mississippi in September 1779, fighting against Spanish troops from New Orleans after Spain entered the Revolutionary War in support of the rebels. John's third son, Pierre-Henry, died aged two in 1763. His fourth, Daniel de Lisle Brock, born in 1762, was later Bailiff of Guernsey. Next came William in 1764, who subsequently made a career in banking; Pierre in 1765, who died at just one year old; Frederic in 1768; Isaac in 1769; John Savery in 1772, who later entered the Royal Navy; and finally Irving, who translated Bernier's *Travels in India.*[7] Two other little girls were born but died in infancy: an earlier Elizabeth who died in 1756 aged seven, and Rebecca, who was either stillborn or survived only a few days in 1758. These were the brothers and sisters of Isaac, John's eighth son, born on Friday, 6 October 1769, at St Peter Port, in the same year as Napoleon Bonaparte and Arthur Wellesley, 1st Duke of Wellington.[8] Their father's early death, and that of their brother Ferdinand, drew the family together.

Isaac's early life and education were spent in Guernsey, where he followed the normal pursuits of a young gentleman of the day. He mixed with his equals in island society, spoke both English and the *patois* of the island, and gained a basic education. He also learned to swim and sail a small boat in the dangerous waters around the islands. Oral tradition says that he regularly swam the half-mile along the sea wall from the harbour to Castle Cornet in St Peter Port, through waters that are notoriously prone to tide-races and sudden storms.[9] He rode, shot and fished, and he became an early devotee of the bare-knuckle ring that was almost an obsession with many gentlemen of Brock's class at that time, both as spectator and participant – indeed he was reckoned as the best fighter of his age and weight in the island.[10] By his early teens, Isaac was a big, strong lad – he grew to be 6 feet 2 inches tall, well built and broad in proportion – but despite his evident

Castle Cornet, St Peter Port, Guernsey, as it appeared in the late eighteenth century. (Author's collection)

physical prowess he had the reputation of being something of a gentle giant: slow to anger, but implacable, if cool, when roused. These physical pursuits were important in forming the character of a gentleman, especially one destined for a military career, and from an early age, therefore, Isaac learned to master, and then dismiss, physical fear and to control his emotions. He also learned that with his physical qualities he had no need to succumb to bullying or coercion.

His first school was Elizabeth College in Guernsey, which was founded in 1563 to make good the destruction of the educational system that had followed the confiscation and dissolution of the monasteries. The college was later to become a first-class public school but at this date it left much to be desired. Under the mastership of the Reverend Mr Crispin, the curriculum centred on Latin and Greek, as was usual in public schools at the time. To educate him more widely, Brock's brother Daniel had already been sent to Alderney to study privately under an *émigré* Swiss clergyman called Vallat, to prepare him for a public school in England. In 1780, at the age of eleven, Isaac went to school in Southampton, and thereafter, like his brothers Daniel and William, to Rotterdam to a French Huguenot clergyman known only as Père Jean – Father John. The rough island *patois* was not to be compared with the then internationally accepted language of diplomacy and culture, a language necessary for any gentleman of position.

In 1784, a year after Britain's humiliation in the Treaty of Versailles and the loss of her thirteen American colonies, Isaac's education came to an end. He was fifteen years old. In that year his eldest brother John purchased a captaincy in his regiment, the 8th (The King's) Regiment of Foot. His promotion opened up a vacancy lower down and the Brock family accordingly purchased a commission as ensign for Isaac in the same regiment, with seniority from 2 March 1784.

The service that young Isaac Brock joined was experiencing severe problems. At the end of the American Revolutionary War in 1783, the British army had been reduced to an authorized strength of 52,378 men, of whom 17,483 were in mainland Britain, another 12,000 in Ireland, with 3,282 allocated to the Royal Artillery for both field and garrison artillery – thus the home establishments accounted for around 50 per cent of the total. The remainder were divided between India (a mere 6,366 but augmented by the large East India Company armies); 12,421 in the remaining colonies – principally the West Indies, New South Wales and British North America; and 2,826 guarding the fortress and naval base of Gibraltar. At no time during the following decade, however, was this strength ever reached. The army varied from a low of 59 per cent of its authorized strength, 30,703 men, to a maximum of 88 per cent or 46,092. By 1792, on the eve of the outbreak of war with France, the army's actual strength was no more than 38,000 men. The reasons for these shortfalls were, first, its inability to recruit and, secondly, a very high incidence of desertion.

These failings – the results of poor pay and conditions of service, savage discipline and low popular esteem – were made worse by the enormous loss of trained and experienced soldiers at the end of the American War. Many soldiers had been engaged for the war under special acts of Parliament passed in 1778 and 1779 that allowed short three-year terms of enlistment rather than the customary longer engagement, which was generally twenty-one years with the Colours. Although bounties almost equal to a year's pay were offered as inducements to stay with the Colours, these experienced soldiers, almost to a man, returned to civilian life. Many regiments had to begin again almost from scratch. The 23rd Fusiliers, for example, were reviewed in April 1784 after their return from America having discharged many veterans and could muster only nine officers and 128 NCOs and men.[11] The establishment called for twenty-six officers and 445 NCOs and men mustered in eight companies. In addition there were two detached depot companies for recruiting and holding duties.[12] In both the regiments in which Brock served during the 1780s and 1790s, the strength never exceeded 350 men and there were always officers and men detached for recruiting duties.[13] John Houlding's investigation of the number of recruits in infantry regiments during the decade before 1793 concludes that, on the British establishment, the proportion of untrained men in regiments varied between 24 and 38 per cent, with the worst years being 1785 to 1787.[14] The period was also one of heavy losses through desertion. These losses, and also those caused by sickness, particularly in the West Indies, could only be made up by more recruiting. In the Canadas, as Brock's later service would show him, the problem of desertion was made worse by the ease with which men could slip across the border to the United States and thus escape the possibility of recapture. America was an attractive prospect to the many Irishmen who served in every regiment of the British army. In 1809, for example, 34 per cent of the 57th (West Middlesex) were recorded as Irish; the 29th (Worcestershire) reported 19 per cent of its strength in the same year as Irishmen, rising to 37 per cent in 1811.[15]

The soldier's biggest problem was his pay. Nominally a private soldier received £9 2s. 6d. per year (about £7,500 or US$11,700 in today's money when calculated using an index of average earnings)[16] but he was subjected to so many stoppages or deductions for uniforms, accoutrements, kit and rations that he often received no pay at all and, still worse, not only went deeper into debt but also could not even feed himself. John Fortescue has written with considerable justice that "It is literally true that the only alternatives open to the private soldiers were to desert or starve...."[17] This situation was only ended in 1790 by the direct intervention of King George III, whose subsequent Royal Warrant of 1792 raised the private soldier's pay to £12 0s. 3½d. per annum and, even more important, gave him a basic free bread allowance and the sum of 18s. 10½d. per year, paid every two months, free from deductions.[18]

Service life was also difficult for many officers. At the time that fifteen-year-old Isaac Brock was commissioned into the 8th Foot, about two-thirds of the initial commissions and subsequent promotions in the army were by the system of purchase. This system had started under Charles II in 1683 when the Crown, to continue the existing arrangements whereby officers, especially colonels of regiments, offset the costs of raising and equipping troops, began to sell commissions from the rank of ensign to lieutenant-colonel. Promotion to staff and general ranks beyond this was by selection or patronage. The Crown therefore held the price of an officer's commission as a bond: if he was cashiered on account of misdemeanour, he lost his investment – as the term implies. Nor did the government have to worry about pensions: if an officer wished to retire, he sold out and turned his investment into an annuity. If an officer wished to leave active service but keep some part of his pay and his investment – or indeed if there was no employment but the service wished to keep a string on him – he went on a retainer known as half pay.

Vacancies occurred when an officer retired, sold out or transferred to another regiment. An officer who wished to sell his commission was normally required to offer it first to the officer in his regiment with the most seniority in the rank immediately below his, who would then pay to the seller the difference in value between his current rank and that on offer, plus an additional sum that went to the government. For example, in order to purchase his company, John Brock would pay the price of his commission as an ensign* (his "Colours"), or £400, plus the price of a lieutenancy, £600, plus the difference – a total of £1,100, or £83,000 at today's rates using a calculation of average earnings. He would then sell on his lieutenancy, recouping all except the difference. If the officer next in seniority could not afford to purchase a vacant commission, it was offered to the next most senior, and so on. Any vacancy that occurred within a regiment would set off a chain reaction: if a lieutenant-colonelcy changed hands, that meant a majority, captaincy, lieutenancy and second-lieutenancy also became vacant, as officers moved up the ladder. The price of commissions was strictly regulated, although it varied between regiments and corps and in most cases, especially

---

* The modern equivalent is the rank of 2nd lieutenant; this rank then only existed in the 1st, 2nd and 3rd Regiments of Guards and the 7th, 21st and 23rd Regiments of Fusiliers.

in smart regiments, a sum in excess of that specified in the Regulations was always demanded. Not all promotions were through purchase, and there are examples of officers receiving promotion free of purchase either for good service or through patronage or both. When an officer purchased or received a commission, he received the rank of the seller but not his seniority and thus an officer like Brock who purchased a ensign's vacancy in the 8th Foot started at the bottom of the seniority list and worked his way up as those above him were promoted, died, transferred or left the service.

Once an officer reached the rank of lieutenant-colonel, even by brevet – a reward for bravery or meritorious service which conferred seniority on the Army List, but not within the officer's own regiment – promotion was either by merit or seniority. A lieutenant-colonel with a good record could expect eventually to be promoted to major-general (brigadier-general was an appointment at this time, not a rank) and would move up the seniority list of generals as those above him dropped off. A general in the British army, however, was only paid as such when employed as such and the Army List contained many veterans who had gained promotion by brevet, but did not hold appointments, and had therefore to subsist on the half pay of their substantive rank without brevet.[19]

The purchase system was, of course, open to abuses. Boys were routinely commissioned as a means of getting them early seniority, while incompetent but wealthy officers could gain promotion very fast; but then so too could competent but wealthy officers like Arthur Wesley (later Wellesley), the future Duke of Wellington. As there were only loose requirements for an officer to serve for any fixed period of time before promotion or a staff appointment – chiefly to prevent officers selling out in order to avoid active service – wealthy officers could rise very fast. Abuses were kept in check, although perhaps the worst corruption was prevalent in the 1780s, at the time Brock purchased his initial commission. When the Duke of York was appointed Commander-in-Chief in 1796, he began to overhaul the purchase system and root out the most flagrant abuses. This, coupled with the higher mortality rate during the war with France which began in February 1793, limited the number of promotions by purchase until by 1809 only one-eighth of promotions were gained this way.[20]

Officers were generally poorly paid, for in real terms they had not had a raise in pay since Marlborough's day. It was generally expected that, as officers were gentlemen, their families would subsidize their careers until they reached the higher ranks. In 1784 an ensign could expect to be paid just over £2 per week – comparable with a respectable shop-keeper or a minor clergyman in a poor rural parish, and about five times as much as a farm labourer. From this, however, there were deductions for the upkeep of the Chelsea Hospital, the widows and orphans fund, the army or regimental agent's fees and even deductions to pay the salaries of the officials in the paymaster's department. In peacetime this could amount to as much as a fifth of a junior officer's pay. In addition, of course, he had to pay for his lodgings, food and drink, uniforms, arms and accoutrements and augment the pay of his soldier servant. The 1780s were a time of high price-inflation and many junior officers without private means struggled to maintain the requirements of their rank and station. This financial stress was one of the reasons that regimental messes were created in the 1780s by officers who pooled their resources to be able to afford decent food and drink, and sometimes lodgings. The Regimental Mess Records for the 23rd Foot, the Royal Welch Fusiliers, for example, show that in 1787 while at Berwick, a mess was established at the Red Lion Hotel, where dinner and small beer were provided to all officers for 1s. 2d. per day, all else being paid for individually at market prices, plus 1s per week for paying staff and incidental expenses. When at Chatham Barracks in November that year, it was "the unanimous opinion of the officers … that a general mess is absolutely necessary" in the regiment.[21]

The officer corps of the army was more diverse than popular myth would suggest. In his examination of the army in the late 1780s, Houlding concluded that British officers could be grouped into four distinct classes. First were the nobility and landed gentry who, because of their station in life, possessed money and interest. This group was the most upwardly mobile through promotion by purchase, and laterally mobile through transfers between regiments in order to remain in desirable stations. The second and much larger class was the lesser gentry, families in the professions, the clergy and the respectable trades, and the sons of small independent farmers or landowners. Many of these, especially the last group, lacked the patronage needed to rise. The third group, which in some cases cut across the second class and the bottom end of the first, consisted of a significant number of officers of foreign birth or origins, such as Huguenots, who tended to form military families in which sons looked to the army from birth as their

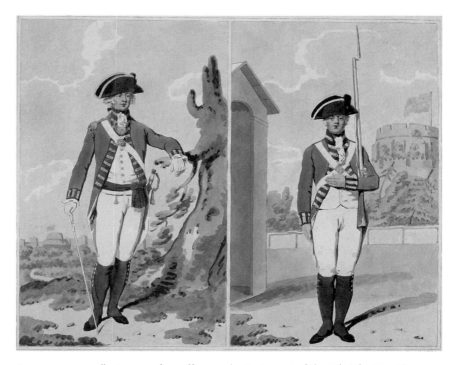

A contemporary illustration of an officer and private man of the 8th (The King's) Regiment of Foot in the 1780s. This is the uniform Brock would have worn when first commissioned into the British army. (By permission of the owner, Herr Markus Stein)

natural career. One might add Channel Islanders to this group. The fourth and smallest group, but more numerous than is commonly thought, were aging subaltern officers who had been commissioned from the ranks.[22] Having no advantages whatsoever, few of these men achieved a higher rank than lieutenant but, given their background, they were content with their lot. It is hard to identify Isaac Brock exactly within Houlding's classification, for although he was a Channel Islander, his family was clearly wealthy enough for him to enter a decent regiment and rise quickly, as we shall see.

Brock joined the service at a time when it was being greatly reduced by disbanding wartime regiments and by lowering the established strengths of the remaining regiments. That part of the army not needed to garrison the empire returned to the British Isles, where it joined the British or Irish Establishments. The British Establishment was paid for by the Parliament in Westminster, the Irish Establishment by the Irish Parliament in Dublin, with the Crown retaining control over both. Before 1793, when a barrack building programme began that went on until 1815, there were few military barracks in Britain or Ireland, and outside London, which was the preserve of the Household Cavalry and the Guards, barracks were often in a ruinous state. In the decade before the French war began in 1793, barracks outside London are known to have existed at Portsmouth, Canterbury, Chatham, Newcastle, Liverpool, Limerick, Dublin, Berwick and Winchester. There were also the old Royal Garrisons and castles whose garrisons went back into the middle ages;* more modern forts at Dover, Edinburgh, Forts William and Augustus, Deal, Landguard, Hull and Gravesend; and the Royal Arsenal at Woolwich.[23] One over-optimistic estimate in 1792 said that there was enough barrack accommodation in the British Isles and the Channel Islands for 20,000 men.[24] In that year, the authorized strength of the army was about 17,000 men on the British and Irish establishments, but the real figure was much lower than that.

In any case, even if a regiment was fortunate enough to be stationed in barracks, the army's functions in peacetime meant that much of it would be dispersed in the surrounding area. This was because the army had two major duties that militated against training: aid to the civil power and the "coast duty." Aid to the civil power was police work, usually targeted at keeping public order or putting down the riots that were fairly common in eighteenth-century Britain. The coast duty was to assist the customs and revenue services in the prevention of smuggling. Although this task fell mainly on the cavalry, some infantry regiments took part in it, requiring many small detachments in out-of-the-way coastal areas where smuggling was common. Not surprisingly, the army's involvement in police work and counter-smuggling did little to increase its popularity with its own citizens.

This general dislike of the standing army was exacerbated by the lack of barracks and the consequent need for troops to be billeted on civilians. Resistance to this throughout the eighteenth century meant that, in practice, troops were usually billeted in taverns or inns rather than private houses. This of course was bad for discipline – soldiers mixed with drink produce trouble – and usually arms had to be held centrally outside a town for fear

---

* The Tower of London, Cowes, Portland, Scilly, Pendennis, Jersey, Guernsey, St Mawes, Portsmouth, Plymouth, Upnor, Scarborough, Tynemouth, Berwick, Carlisle, Windsor, Chepstow and Hurst.

that the soldiery, once their pay was spent, would resort to armed force to extort drink.

As well as the problems that dispersion gave to good regimental officers trying to train their men, regiments were constantly being shifted from station to station. There was a loose rotation system in place between overseas garrisons and the home islands; and there was also a rotation between England, Scotland and Ireland, although regiments placed on the Irish Establishment tended to spend longer periods there, except in time of war, since the Irish regiments were held at a much reduced strength for reasons of economy. Houlding, after examining the records of seventeen regiments of foot during the period 1786–90, concluded that, on average, they spent 14.5 per cent, and in extreme cases 25 per cent, of their time during those years marching or dispersed.[25] This will be seen when Brock's service with the 8th and 49th Regiments is described.

Not only did this constant motion have an adverse effect on training regiments, but training in the late 1780s was hampered by an intense debate within the army about tactical doctrine. The substance of this debate was whether battlefield tactics should follow the practices evolved in North America during the Revolutionary War, or whether it should follow the school of Frederick the Great of Prussia, which relied on strict formations, mass and volley fire at short range, aimed at opposing an enemy who possessed mounted troops. The "American" school, which had begun with General Lord Howe's* moves to make the whole British army in the Americas adopt light infantry methods as early as the mid-1770s, developed from the experience of operating with small numbers in a continent of vast distances and heavily wooded terrain, against an often poorly-trained opponent lacking mounted troops, but who could shoot and knew how to use the terrain to advantage. As a result, the infantry had adopted loose formations and fast movements carried out by small sub-units.[26] This method counted among its chief supporters, in addition to Howe, Lieutenant-General Earl Cornwallis† and, although he was only a captain at this point, the future Adjutant-

---

* General William Howe, 5th Viscount (1729–1814) commanded the British army during the American Revolutionary War from 1775 to 1778.

† Charles, 1st Marquis Cornwallis (1738–1805) surrendered Yorktown in 1781, for which he is usually remembered. He had a distinguished and successful career elsewhere in America, during the Seven Years' War, as Governor-General of India and later of Ireland.

General of the Army, Harry Calvert* – one of many who had served in the American War and could see the benefits of the light infantry system. This school was opposed by the "German" school, led by those who had attended the Prussian army manoeuvres of 1785, principally the Duke of York, who had spent five years studying Prussian methods, and Colonel David Dundas,† a fervent proponent of Prussian methods, who had not served in America but who had turned the Dublin garrison of the early 1780s into "a bastion of reaction to the 'American style' of fighting."[27] After the Silesian manoeuvres of 1785 it rapidly became clear that it was York and Dundas who had won the battle for the soul of the British army – with consequences that would lead to some bitter defeats in the early years of the Great French War until what was actually needed, a fusion of the two schools, was achieved in the late 1790s.

Worse still was the fact that before 1784 the infantry had been using two different manuals: regiments in Britain had been training according to the Regulations issued in 1778,[28] while regiments serving in North America had followed the Regulations of 1764,[29] which were issued as a consequence of fighting the French and Indian Wars on that continent, as well as warfare in Europe. These regiments also tended to pick piecemeal from the 1778 Regulations or indeed add their own regimental standing orders.[30] The result was that the years immediately following the American war were chaotic for doctrine and training. The muddle was only solved after the Dublin garrison carried out lengthy manoeuvres in 1788 and 1789 using a drill book written by Dundas. The result was yet another interim manual, the 1789 Irish Regulations,[31] but this was a preliminary step towards the issue in 1792 of a new manual, again written by Dundas: *Rules and Regulations for the Formations, Field-Exercise, and Movements, of His Majesty's Forces* became the official manual to be followed by all infantry regiments and, despite its many shortcomings, it endured throughout the war with France and beyond.[32]

Where tactical training – still almost indistinguishable from drill except for light companies – was possible in the 1780s, the training cycle of an

---

* Lieutenant-General Sir Harry Calvert, G.C.B., G.C.H., 1st Baronet (1763–1826), Adjutant-General of the Army 1799–1818.
† General Sir David Dundas, G.C.B., 1st Baronet (1735–1820) was commissioned into the Royal Artillery and served in the Seven Years' War and the French Revolutionary and Napoleonic Wars. He was Commander-in-Chief of the Army 1809–11.

infantry regiment consisted of two major phases: basic and platoon. Basic training was for recruits and was usually conducted by an NCO with a small group. The recruit was taught military posture, movements, the various marching steps and turns, and how to look after his arms and equipment. Much emphasis was placed on the bearing and turnout of a soldier, and once he had learned to appear and move in a soldierly manner, the recruit graduated to the platoon exercise.[33]

The platoon meant something rather different in the late eighteenth century from what it means today. Today a platoon is a permanent sub-unit within a company; in the eighteenth century a platoon was a temporary fire and movement sub-unit, the strength of which varied according to the strength of the company. To avoid confusion, therefore, this level of training is best referred to as company level. The emphasis was on musketry drill. The recruit was first taught the slow drill for loading and firing his musket, with its many words of command and movements. When he had mastered this, he then underwent fire and movement training either as a company or half-company. Great emphasis was put on loading and firing, and in the British army, in contrast to most European armies, it was carried out using powder and ball and not just dumb show. Because of the limited range and accuracy of the weapon, the emphasis was always on volley fire rather than individual firing. Once the recruit had mastered this level, he was regarded as a trained soldier, although a green one, and the rule of thumb was that he was a green man until he had two years' service. Officers also had to go through basic and company level training, either individually with an instructor, in small groups or, as in some regiments, together with the recruits. The emphasis then as now was on the officer demonstrating that he knew his men's business and was as good at it as they were, or better.

In terms of organization at this time, infantry regiments had a varying number of companies, between eight and eleven, depending on the prevailing financial conditions. The ten-company battalion became standard under the 1792 Regulations. Eight of the companies in an infantry regiment were "battalion" companies and two, the light and grenadier, were "flank" companies. Nominally, the grenadier company consisted of the biggest, smartest and most experienced men and was regarded as the commanding officer's shock force, especially when assaulting a fortress or entrenched position. The grenadier companies of the several regiments in a brigade would

18

often be grouped together and operate independently of their parent regiments. The light company provided a skirmishing and scouting capability for the regiment and also provided advance, flank and rear guards. Much effort was devoted to its training and, in the same way as the grenadiers, it was often combined with the light companies of other regiments to form a specialist force.

Much of the training above company level was geared towards the regiment's annual inspection. Since 1720 infantry regiments had been inspected every year by a general officer not necessarily from their own district, who would be given the task in the previous December to prevent collusion between inspecting officers and regimental commanders. The inspecting officer would examine the regiment's interior economy, since high rates of punishment or desertion were sure indicators of problems. However, his main task was to review the battalion at drill. The annual inspection would be the one time in a year that a widely dispersed regiment would concentrate and train together and much work was devoted to preparing for this event. Copies of an inspecting officer's report were always sent to the Colonel of the Regiment, who had a far more active position at that time than now and had almost complete control over appointments, promotions and other patronage within his regiment. If a commanding officer was unsatisfactory, therefore, the Colonel had the most say in replacing him.

What of the daily routine for the soldier when Brock first joined the 8th Foot? The regime was hard, repetitive and dull. Reveille would be sounded at 5.00 a.m. in summer, 7.00 a.m. in winter, after which there would be about half an hour for perfunctory washing and shaving – although for formal parades this, especially the dressing of the hair, could take up to three hours – and a snatched breakfast of bread and small beer.* At 9.00 a.m. the old guard would fall in outside the guardroom and be inspected, a new guard would be mounted and the old dismissed. Sentries were posted and relieved throughout the twenty-four hours of duty. For the remainder not on guard, most of the day would be spent at drill, with an hour for dinner at midday,

---

* Small beer contained very little alcohol and was a widespread drink in Europe and colonial North America. In those times of poor sanitation, water-borne diseases were a significant cause of death. Because alcohol kills most water-borne pathogens and because the process of brewing beer from malted grain involves boiling the water, which also kills germs, drinking small beer instead of water was one way to escape infection.

under the discipline of the company sergeants. Tea would be taken in the late afternoon, followed by the cleaning of kit. All these meals were found from the daily rations: a pound of meat and a pound of bread per man per day plus an ounce of cheese or butter, and a pound of peas or oatmeal or potatoes, or occasionally rice. This would be cooked centrally, often by those few wives who were on the strength and who made a few shillings by cooking, washing, ironing or hairdressing. Retreat was sounded at 6.00 p.m., marking the transition to night routine, when all weapons had to be secured. Men free of duty might visit a tavern, if they had the money, until lock-up and lights-out at 10.00 p.m. During the night, the officer of the day would conduct rounds to check that the sentries were at their posts and alert.[34]

Apart from inspections, a soldier would see little of his officers in barracks, except for those on the regimental staff who were charged with administrative duties: the adjutant, responsible for discipline and manning; the quarter master, responsible for billeting and quarters, rations, ammunition and all matters of supply; the pay master; the surgeon; and the chaplain.[35] The remaining company and regimental officers – the lieutenant-colonel commanding, the two majors, the captains in command of companies and the lieutenants and ensigns – would rarely be seen in the course of a normal day when not on the march. The more diligent officers might study their profession, but otherwise they would hunt or shoot or amuse themselves in society, for the officers did not run the regiment: that was the job of the non-commissioned officers and the staff, whose task was to prepare the soldiers for the field and manage the interior economy of the regiment – its book-keeping and administration, its quarters and messing, its disciplinary record and rate of desertion. The job of the officers was to command. They would thus be seen at the head of the troops on manoeuvres or on campaign – but especially in battle. For with the possible exception of the lieutenant-colonel commanding the regiment, who would manoeuvre it and decide the battle tactics, command was synonymous with leadership; leadership meant example, and example meant being in the forefront of danger. Little else was expected of an officer other than that he should be brave in the face of the enemy, but woe betide any who was not brave: what mattered more than anything else for an officer, more even than for a gentleman in civil life, was his honour. But in the field, the officers would also take a good deal more interest in the well-being of their men. It was a long-held tradition in the

British army, and one still valid to this day, that on campaign the first priority was the horses (or in modern terms, vehicles), then the weapons, then the NCOs and men, and finally the officers. No officer would dine, then as now, without seeing his horses and men fed first.

The 8th Foot was one of the most senior regiments of the army, as its number indicated, with a proud record of service to the Crown. It had been raised by James II in July 1685 as Princess Anne of Denmark's Regiment – the future Queen Anne – during the Monmouth rebellion. After the first Jacobite War it had had the honour of being designated as The King's Regiment. It bore on its Colours the white horse, the badge of the House of Hanover, as a mark of its special favour with the King after its gallantry at the battle of Sheriffmuir in 1715. The regiment had been active throughout William III's wars, under Marlborough, and in Europe during the Seven Years' War. Throughout the American War it had served chiefly in the Canadas, repelling several attempts by the revolutionary army at invasion.[36]

The regiment contained a great deal of experience of war in the wilderness, having spent eighteen years in North America, including eight before the Revolutionary War had started. When the war began, the 8th occupied a series of forts at Niagara, Detroit, Michilimackinac and Oswego, guarding the navigation of the St. Lawrence River and the Great Lakes. The original purpose of these forts had been as a meeting place for Britain's aboriginal allies, who would gather every spring to receive presents from the Indian Department and barter furs with the Montreal traders of the North West Company. This placed the officers of the regiment close to the powerful Iroquois Confederacy and nations to the west; constant contact with native people made the officers and men familiar with the skills of their aboriginal allies. Two officers in particular were prominent in cultivating the alliance with the native peoples: Captain Arendt DePeyster* and Lieutenant John Caldwell.† DePeyster was appointed commandant of Fort Michilimackinac

---

* Arendt Schuyler DePeyster (1736–1822) was a Loyalist from New York of Dutch origins, commissioned into the 8th Foot after serving against the French in the Seven Years' War, when he was captured and imprisoned in France. After his release he joined the 8th in Germany and remained with it thereafter.

† Sir John Caldwell, 5th Baronet (1756–1830) stayed with the 8th until 1787 and would have been well known to Brock.

Arendt Schuyler DePeyster in the uniform of a lieutenant-colonel of the 8th Foot (The King's). He was in command of the 8th when Brock joined the regiment. This portrait appeared as the frontispiece of DePeyster's autobiographical *Miscellanies, by an Officer* in 1813.

in 1776 and he participated in several campaigns, notably that of Major-General John Burgoyne in New York. He took command of Fort Lernoult – later Detroit – in 1779 and effectively managed his native allies against the rebel militias of Pennsylvania and Kentucky. Although Britain ceded Detroit to the United States at the end of the war, it remained in British hands until 1796. DePeyster stayed with the regiment after the Revolutionary War and was actually in command of the 8th when Brock was commissioned on 8 March 1785.[37] He retired from the army in 1795 and then took command of the Dumfries Royal Volunteer Corps, in which the poet Robbie Burns served before his death in 1796, aged thirty-eight. Burns addressed one of his poems, "On Life," to his commanding officer as a mark of friendship. This friendship was founded both on military service and on literature, for DePeyster was something of a writer and a poet. In 1813 he published *Miscellanies, by an Officer,* a collection of speeches to the indigenous people in North America, letters and journal entries, Iroquois vocabulary, reminiscence and poetry. The two men lie buried side by side to this day in St Michael's churchyard in Dumfries. Although Brock would never have seen this book – it was published a year after his death – he would have heard much of its contents.*

There were also others with a breadth of experience in the regiment.

---

* The book contains several favourable references to Brock, including a poem, "Impromptu," (p. 77) written on hearing of Brock's death.

When the Americans attacked Canada in 1775, Captain Robert Mathews[*] and Captain George Forster both led expeditions involving large numbers of native warriors as well as detachments of the 8th Foot to cut the enemy's lines of communication and help end the siege of Quebec. During Burgoyne's campaign in 1777, Lieutenant Henry Bird of the 8th led a small force to victory at the battle of Oriskany. In that engagement British regulars, Loyalists and natives executed a classic frontier ambush, rather than engage head-to-head in European fashion. In 1780 Bird led 1,000 native warriors and 150 British regulars on a bold expedition from Fort Lernoult during what is known as Bird's invasion of Kentucky. Walter Butler,[†] son of the founder of the famous Butler's Rangers, also served in the 8th at this time. When the regiment returned from America in 1783, therefore, the vast majority of its officers had active service experience: the major, all the captains commanding companies bar one, all the lieutenants bar one, and seven out of ten ensigns. The captains in particular were highly influential in shaping the development of new officers and men joining the regiment. In addition to Robert Mathews, they included Richard Beringer Lernoult,[‡] William Potts, Andrew Parke, John Mompesson, Robert Clements, Francis Le Maitre, Samuel Willoe and Stephen Watts.[38] At least two of them, as it happened, were also Channel Islanders – Lernoult and Le Maitre – and Mompesson may have been a third. By 1789 there were still fourteen officers in the regiment with war service in America, including the commanding officer, DePeyster; the major, Andrew Parke; and Captains Francis Le Maitre, John Burnett, Thomas Bennett, John Delgano, George Clowes, Robert Bounds Brooke, Thomas Pepyat, George Armstrong, Durrell Saumarez, Joseph Wilmott and Anthony Morrison.[39]

---

[*] Robert Mathews (c.1745–1814) was commissioned into the 8th Foot in 1761. During the American Revolutionary War he caught the eye of the governor of Quebec, Frederick Haldimand, who helped him to advance. He did not accompany the 8th back to England but transferred to the 53rd Regiment. He commanded the 53rd in the Low Countries in 1793, where he might have known Brock, and although he returned later to Quebec, they would not have served there as he departed in 1801. (*Dictionary of Canadian Biography*)

[†] Walter Butler (1752–81) was from a Loyalist family from New York. His father was an Indian agent and his work with the native people during the Revolutionary War made him the most hated man in New York State. He was killed in battle in 1781.

[‡] Richard Beringer Lernoult was the commandant of the fort later known as Detroit from 1774 to 1779, but which was rebuilt by him and named in his honour.

The 8th Foot was therefore used to having a diversity of officers with unconventional mind-sets, schooled in the American way of war, who could hardly have been enthusiastic followers of the Dundas school of Prussian warfare. Moreover it had a corps of officers who were experienced and who constituted a cohesive group that would carry the regiment through the difficult post-war period. This, combined with the culture of oral history in mess life and the example of his dead brother, would surely have been a powerful influence on the young Brock, shaping his thinking about the profession of arms. He would have become familiar with the ways of the native people and with the importance of forts like Detroit and Mackinac, places which, as fate would have it, were to feature so large in his later life. Human beings of course cannot inherit knowledge or experience through their genes, in the way that they can inherit distinctive physical characteristics: we therefore have to be told things. In Brock's day this was done through oral history – story-telling. This was a very important part of an officer's early military life, the means by which the regimental folklore, history, traditions and ethos were transmitted from one generation to the next, to the junior officers from the captains and majors. This was still the case until the end of the Cold War, but in modern times the close comradeship of officers' messes has been dissipated; it seems unlikely to survive the onset of modern media, not to mention assaults on the regimental system and the severe limitations on mess life caused by government parsimony and a culture of envy made manifest in the use of catering contractors rather than regimental mess staff on one hand, and high operational tempo on the other. The absolute requirement to dine together daily, for so long a feature of mess life, has vanished.

Finally it is of note that the 8th Foot had a strong body of Freemasons in its ranks and operated a regimental lodge, No. 156. This had been active throughout the regiment's service in North America, and indeed the first Masonic lodge in Upper Canada was that at Newark (modern Niagara-on-the-Lake), which had been started by members of the regiment, including Edward Jackson, while the 8th was in garrison at Fort Niagara.[40] It is known that Brock was a member of this lodge in later life and it can therefore be safely assumed that he joined the Masonic order while a young officer in the 8th Foot.

As we have seen, these were testing times as the army shed large numbers of experienced NCOs and men. The 8th was in a particularly difficult spot in this regard, for the inspection return of 1785/6 gives the total strength of the regiment as a mere 277. Of these, 220 were English, 28 Scottish, 19 Irish and 10 "foreign" – probably locally enlisted Canadians or Americans. Many of the men were long-service veterans: 97 had only one year of service and another 21 between 2 and 8 years with the Colours. The rest, 159 out of 277, had between 10 and 30 years' service, and 105 of these had more than 20 years. This made the NCOs and men as experienced and cohesive body as their officers – but there was a down side too, for the inspecting officer noted that the NCOs were "good, diligent but many are old and worn out." The men were also "old, mostly worn out, recruits excepted." They performed the manual exercises and firing drills "well, considering the age of the men and their long service abroad."[41] There was clearly much to be done if the regiment was to be returned to the standards expected at home.

The earliest portrait of Isaac Brock that can reasonably be authenticated shows him at the time he joined the 8th Foot: a pleasant-looking young man in his late teens with an open, handsome face and quite a large head – a feature of the Brock family – wearing scarlet regimentals with a blue turned-down collar and facings, an epaulet and gold loops consistent with the uniform of the 8th at that time.[42] Earlier biographers, drawing on oral tradition, have reported that the young Isaac Brock spent much of his leisure time studying to make up for his want of formal education. F. B. Tupper said that he "devoted his leisure mornings to study, locking the door of his room until one o'clock, to prevent intrusion."[43] Brock's personal library, sold by auction on 14 January 1813, gives some clues to what he might have been reading.[44] It contained many of the classical texts that would have been standard in a gentleman's education of the day: the works of Virgil and Horace, both in four volumes, six volumes of Plutarch and twelve volumes of Rollin's *Ancient History*. Then there are the complete works of Shakespeare, Pope, Sterne and Samuel Johnson. A good deal of military history is there as well, much of it in French: Guibert's *Oeuvres Militaires,* Voltaire on Henry IV and the age of Louis XIV; the memoirs of Condé. In English there are General Wolfe's *Instructions to Young Officers*. Finally there are text books like MacArthur on courts-martial, Johnson's *Dictionary* and several French grammars. As well as these we can expect him to have read many of the standard military texts of the day: Dundas of course, Cuthbertson's *Sys-*

Isaac Brock aged fifteen or sixteen in the uniform of an ensign of the 8th Foot (The King's). This miniature portrait was authenticated by Ludwig Kosche in 1985. (© 2010 The States of Guernsey, by permission of Guernsey Museums and Galleries)

tem for the Complete Interior Management and Œconomy, Thomas Symes's *Military Guide for Young Officers,* the lives and campaigns of Alexander the Great, Julius Caesar, Frederick the Great, Gustavus Adolphus of Sweden, Vauban, Turenne, Schomberg and Marlborough. Doubtless he also read accounts of the American Revolutionary War as they appeared in periodicals and as books. Thus Brock combined formal study with oral history.

When the 8th was inspected again the following year, its strength had risen to 337, with 142 new men enlisted since the previous inspection, 3 dead, 64 discharged and 15 deserted. 174 men were shown as having only one year's service, only 40 with between 2 and 8 years, 47 with between 10 and 20 years, and 96 with more than 20 years of service. The inspecting officer's comments were in the same vein as the previous year concerning the age of the NCOs. The men were "about half old soldiers who have been in the Back Settlements of Canada 11 years." He ordered that all the old soldiers were to be discharged: "twenty-four immediately and forty more approved of, almost all will be Recommended to Chelsea [i.e., the Royal Hospital]."

The firings and manoeuvres were performed "with great exactness of attention"; however "it may require two or three years to get rid of the old men and to form new NCOs."[45] DePeyster and his officers set about remaking the 8th with a will, and whether or not they agreed with Dundas's methods, they knew that they were required to master them. By the following year, 1788, when the regiment was inspected at Plymouth by Major-General Sir George Osborn,* its strength had actually declined to 308, but the percentage of young men had markedly increased. 219 had between one and 3 years' service and only 35 men now had over 20 years. 143 men had been enlisted since the last inspection, 6 had died and 152 had been discharged. Desertion continued to be low, with only 14 listed during the year. The officers were described as being of "Good appearance under arms – a remarkable fine corps." The NCOs, in contrast to the previous report, were now described as "good and soldier-like in appearance" and the men "at present low in stature … remarkably well set-up." The firing and manoeuvre exercises were well performed according to regulations;[46] DePeyster must have felt that he was making progress – but it would have meant long hours on the drill ground for officers and men alike. Young Isaac Brock, still an ensign, was learning his trade the hard way.

By 1789 the transformation of the 8th had been completed. While retaining the services of a cohesive body of experienced officers and bringing the best of the men into the cadre of NCOs, the rank and file had been completely refreshed. The regiment was still weak in numbers – only 341 all told – but 241 had between one and 3 years' service, while only 75 had more than 12 years. 252 men were described as English and 60 as Irish. In the inspection return the officers – Brock among them – were described in glowing terms as "expert at their duty," the NCOs "of good appearance and attentive to their duty." All in all this was "A good regiment … spirited warlike appearance" and, for the first time since its return from America, the 8th was graded as "fit for immediate service."[47]

After five years as an ensign in this highly professional regiment – a long time, reflecting both his own reticence because of his want of education, and his limited ability to obtain his next step – Brock was able, with the

---

* General Sir George Osborn, 4th Baronet (1742–1818) served in the 3rd Guards during the American Revolutionary War and was Member of Parliament for Horsham in Sussex.

help of his family, to purchase a lieutenant's commission when a vacancy occurred in the 8th, on 16 January 1790.[48] The ability of the family to assist him was largely a reflection of the success of his brother William, who had now embarked on his career as a banker in the City of London, the financial centre of Britain and, arguably, of the world. Richard Hocart of Guernsey has uncovered the details of how William became engaged in a City firm through the network of Channel Islanders engaged in finance and goldsmithing there. William joined the firm of Perchard and Carey – Peter Perchard having left Guernsey in 1746 – and after an apprenticeship as a goldsmith, joined his cousin, also Peter Perchard. When John Carey left the business, William joined and it became Perchard and Brock. In 1795 Benjamin Le Mesurier joined it and so it became Perchard, Brock and Le Mesurier of Warnford Court, Throgmorton Street, London. When Perchard retired in 1798, it duly became Brock and Le Mesurier.[49] William's success allowed him to help Isaac, and from here on Isaac Brock's career accelerated. This acceleration accompanied the destruction of the certainties of eighteenth-century life that fell out of the eruption of the French Revolution during the summer of 1789. Almost immediately the British government began to authorize increases in the strength of the Royal Navy and the army.[50] These increases in the army included a number of independent companies, in all 101 in mainland Britain plus more for Ireland and various overseas garrisons.[51] These companies were for the protection of areas that might be at risk: the Channel Islands were high on this list.

Usually there were six companies in each of Jersey and Guernsey with another at Alderney. A further four were added to the establishments of Jersey and Guernsey. According to his earlier biographers, Brock saw his opportunity: raising an independent company was the best way to make the next step up the military ladder to a captaincy when there were no other vacancies within his regiment. Accordingly, again with William's help, Brock was able to purchase a captaincy in January 1791.[52] His younger brother Irving is said to have received an ensign's commission in Brock's independent company. The difficulty with this account is that neither the inspection returns for the period nor the Army Lists show Brock as captain of an independent company; there is even a section in the returns for 1791 onwards that designates "officers who have raised men for rank." What is most likely is that Brock was in command for such a short time that the documentation simply did not catch up during a period of expansion and upheaval. It is also possible of course that the account is a mistake and that previous biographers have confused him with his brother John, who at a slightly later date, 1798, was a captain commanding an "Independent Company of Invalids," one of the eleven companies listed in Jersey.[53]

If Isaac did serve a spell with them, the fact that the independent companies were kept as garrison troops had a disadvantage: they had little hope of more active employment. Irving seems to have become disillusioned very quickly, sold out and joined his brother William's banking business as an apprentice. Isaac, however, was determined to stay with the Colours and to advance. But the 8th Foot was packed with long-serving officers: it was literally dead men's shoes. There would be no chance for Isaac of a captain's vacancy commanding a company in his own regiment.[54] The only way to obtain a regular company would be to transfer or exchange into another regiment where there was a vacancy and pay the difference. William again advanced Isaac the necessary funds as a charge against the bank rather than as a personal gift or loan. On 15 June 1791, aged twenty-one years and nine months, Isaac Brock exchanged into the 49th (Hertfordshire) Regiment of Foot, changing the blue facings of a Royal Regiment on his scarlet regimentals for the green of the 49th.

CHAPTER TWO

"Be Sober, Be Ready"

REVOLUTION, REVOLT AND DISCORD,
1791–1799

The 49th Foot was of much more recent origin than the 8th. It originated from two companies of the 22nd and six independent companies in Jamaica. In 1743 these eight companies became the 63rd Foot. With the removal of the Marine regiments from the Army List in 1748, the 63rd was redesignated as the 49th and in 1783 it was allocated to Hertfordshire – although county affiliations were loose at this time and regiments tended to recruit wherever they could. In the case of the 49th, this was Ireland, for it formed part of the Irish Establishment. In 1791 the colonel of the 49th was the undistinguished Lieutenant-General Alexander Maitland* and its commanding officer was the experienced Lieutenant-Colonel James Grant, who had served with the regiment since the American Revolutionary War.[1]

Like the 8th, the 49th had served in the Revolutionary War but had been initially more closely involved in the main theatre of operations. The regiment occupied Philadelphia in 1777 and played a prominent part in the battle of Brandywine Creek on 11 September 1777, where, having been wrongly accused by the rebels of killing the wounded and prisoners, the light company had dyed its cockades red so that should their enemies wish to try to take vengeance, there would be no question of mistaken identity. However the regiment had left mainland America to take part in the expedition against St Lucia in 1778 and there it remained for the next three years, removed from the war. In 1780 the Inspection Return reported that the regiment was so reduced by sickness that it had become ineffective and the remnants were to be drafted to other regiments.[2] In January 1781, for the first time in its history, the regiment arrived in the British Isles and was quartered at Cork, in the southwest of Ireland.

* The Hon Sir Alexander Maitland, 1st Baronet (1728–1848).

During the American War, a number of officers of the 49th had distinguished themselves: the then commanding officer, Sir Henry Calder,* who remained with the regiment until 1790;[3] James Grant himself at the battle of White Plains on 26 October 1776;[4] Captain Nicolas Wade of the light company and Lieutenant William Gore also at White Plains; and Lieutenant Joseph Bunbury of the grenadier company at the battle of Monmouth on 28 June 1778.[5] One of the most important accounts of the war by a non-commissioned rank came from Private Thomas Sullivan of the 49th.[6] However, by 1787 the regiment had only five officers still serving who had experience of war: Calder and Grant, Edward Phineas Maxwell, Richard O'Meara and Henry Benson. By the time of Brock's arrival this was down to two: Grant and O'Meara. The only other long-service veteran was Charles Leigh, who had served with the 49th since 1781.[7]

The losses of the West Indies station and the need to recruit the regiment are very visible in the Inspection Returns. In 1784 the 49th was inspected by Major-General Edward Stopford.† It mustered 363 men, of whom 249 were Irish; 239 men are shown as having three years' service or less and only sixty-nine had more than ten years with the Colours. The return also describes the height of the men, the majority of whom were short even by the standards of the time: 106 were below 5 feet 6 inches and another 195 below 5 feet 8½ inches. However, according to Stopford, the regiment "made a good appearance, properly armed. The men are young and in general well-made. The manual exercise was performed exactly to His Majesty's Regulations."[8] The officers and NCOs clearly knew their job and did their duty; however, there are some disturbing pointers elsewhere in the report. Since the previous inspection 280 men had been enlisted, but four had died, 137 had been discharged and the enormous figure of 119 had deserted. Clearly all was not well with discipline, and the degree of turnover, allied with a similarly high turnover among the officers, can have done little to produce a cohesive military body

The returns for the next three years tell a similar story: a predominantly Irish soldiery with high turnover, but capable of producing a good performance. In 1787 the strength of the regiment was given as 386, of whom 245

---

* Major-General Sir Henry Calder, 4th Baronet (c.1740–92).

†Later Lieutenant-General the Hon Edward Stopford (1766–1837). He served as a brigade commander under Wellington in the Peninsular War.

The West Indies, detail from map by Thomas Jefferys, c.1760. (Library of Congress)

were Irish; 102 new enlistments were recorded along with 37 deserters. The inspecting officer noted that "The private men of this Regiment are not equal as to size or countenance to some others in this Establishment."[9] In other words, although they were capable of performing the exercises laid down in the Regulations, the men were sullen and unwilling.

In early 1791 the 49th went back once more to the West Indies and it was in Barbados, or as it was then known, the Barbadoes, that Isaac Brock joined it. The island lies off the northeast coast of what is now Venezuela, at only 13 degrees north of the equator. Its climate is therefore tropical, with a steady temperature of about 27 degrees Centigrade all year with over 70 per cent humidity. Its wet season is from June to October. Its climate was tolerable for Europeans, but malaria and yellow fever were prevalent there as elsewhere in the Caribbean, the result of humidity, warmth, bad drainage and abysmal sanitation. The Barbadoes were an early British colony dating from the middle years of the seventeenth century; by the close of the English Civil Wars their importance as Britain's first experimental agricultural colony in the tropics led to the former Parliamentarian officer Sir Tobias Bridge being commissioned by Charles II to raise a regiment to garrison it in 1665.[10] Its chief product and source of wealth was sugar, and the labour needed brought a large influx of white English men in the 1680s and 1690s – some of them on penal servitude. The result was the largest white population of the Caribbean and its role as a springboard for colonisation in the Carolinas. Rising labour costs and the incidence of tropical diseases – although less marked than elsewhere – brought a large increase of black slave labour during the eighteenth century. By the time that the 49th arrived in the island, the population numbered 16,000 whites and 62,000 blacks.[11] From 1787 onwards, the influence of the abolitionist William Wilberforce and his followers began to be felt, and despite its reliance on slave labour, it was the only colony that supported the act to outlaw the slave trade.

The Inspection Return for the 49th in 1791 tells a similar story to that of previous years, although there is no record of the regiment being put through any manoeuvres, possibly because it was spread around the island in detachments. Its strength had increased markedly from the previous period, rising to 433 men, of whom 237 were Irish, and the rate of discharge and desertion was much reduced, to 59 and 21 respectively.[12] This may partly have been because there was less opportunity for either means of escape once the regiment was abroad; it may also indicate a different disciplinary regime with the change of commanding officer from Lieutenant-Colonel William Browne to James Grant.

Tupper, and various later biographers, have all reported the story of Brock and his duel soon after he arrived in Bridgetown, of how the peace of the regiment was being disturbed by an habitual duellist who was also a bully, and how, in consequence of a challenge being issued and accepted, the two met. Various theories have been advanced as to the cause of the quarrel, personal insult and the honour of an unnamed lady among them. None has been proved and we will never know the real reason for the duel. At the meeting, Brock, on the grounds that he was the bigger man and therefore at a disadvantage should pistols be discharged at the usual range of twelve paces, insisted on the duel being fought across the width of a handkerchief. The bully refused to fight on these terms and subsequently left the 49th in disgrace.[13]

The 1762 *Rules and Articles* forbade the issuing of challenges, duelling or even assisting at duels;[14] however in practice, so long as things were done discreetly, duels were winked at by the authorities. And in any case, the strict and unforgiving code of honour among gentlemen would not permit an insult to go unanswered. Dr Johnson's dictionary, published in 1755, speaks of honour in the context of reputation, adherence to what was right or to the required conventional standards of behaviour and the privileges of rank and station, as well as in terms of noble qualities. It was honour that placed a gentleman socially and determined his right to precedence: in other words it was not so much about moral or ethical excellence, rather the consequence of power or position. Thus a gentleman's honour and that of his family were all-important, transcending even the law of the land.

It is also a fact that it was much more common for gentlemen to "step out," as it was known, in Ireland than in England: Celtic tempers were touchier and readier to take offence, it seemed. But rarely did duels in Ireland end fatally. For the most part an exchange of shots or a few passes with the sword – enough perhaps to disarm an opponent or draw blood – would be enough to settle the matter. Indeed as recently as 1777, a code of practice intended to govern duelling throughout Ireland had been agreed. In a regiment with a high incidence of Irishmen, this could easily account for the frequency of duelling and for the shock of the other party at being offered

Jamaica, detail from map of the West Indies by Thomas Jefferys, c.1760. (Library of Congress)

terms that would certainly prove fatal. Brock had, therefore, accurately analyzed the psychology of his opponent – especially when the second unanswered question after the cause of the duel is answered.

This was, of course, who *was* the other party? No previous biographer has attempted to solve this question. He was described as a captain and indeed it would have been inappropriate for officers of different rank to step out, so this makes sense. Brock's fellow captains when he joined the 49th were Thomas Gibson, Charles Leigh, Charles Mitchell, Thomas Fownes Luttrell, William Burton, Robert Brownrigg and Edward Corry. An examination of the Army Lists and Inspection Returns shows all these officers still there two years later, with one exception: Edward Corry. Corry had been with the regiment since at least 1782 but had only advanced to captain in 1790; he was, according to the Inspection Returns, an Irishman; and he disappears abruptly soon after Brock's arrival, reappearing on half pay.[15] If the duel did actually occur – and we have no independent corroboration for it – then Corry was probably the other party.*

Some months later the regiment moved to Jamaica, nearly 300 miles

---

* He was probably a member of the family from Newry in County Down; an Edward Corry, a wealthy merchant, was Member of Parliament for Newry at this time – he may have been Captain Corry's father.

further north. Jamaica is the third largest island in the Caribbean after Cuba and Hispaniola and became a British colony under the Protectorate of Oliver Cromwell in 1658. Like the Barbadoes it relied heavily on black slave labour and from the earliest days slaves had escaped and formed free colonies in the mountains. These people became known as the Maroons; attempts by the British to subjugate them by force during the early eighteenth century failed, and after the first Maroon War a far-sighted treaty was signed in 1740 giving the Maroons considerable autonomy. Disillusionment by some of the Maroons, however, led to a second war in 1798, which ended with their surrender, deportation first to Nova Scotia and eventual resettlement in Sierra Leone. Physically, the climate of Jamaica was cooler, especially in the highlands, and the rate of sickness reduced; however, the social climate was far tenser. But in Kingston, with its larger population, there was rather more in the way of society for both officers and men than had been the case in the Barbadoes.

The political climate was tense too. In 1789 France erupted in revolution. For many British officers and American Loyalists, there was a degree of satisfaction in seeing the hated French afflicted with the ideas they had helped to foster in the American War. Relations between France and Britain had been subject to wild mood swings: some in the Whig party in Britain welcomed the revolution but Edmund Burke, a supporter of the American Revolution, accurately predicted the course of events.[16] The Terror and the emergence of an aggressive regime willing to export revolution was capped by the execution of Louis XVI on 21 January 1793. Beginning with the Declaration of Pilnitz by the Prussian king in 1791, a coalition had been building against republican France, which was already being viewed as a rogue state. As tensions mounted, the French government declared war on Austria in April 1792; immediately after the execution of the king, Spain and Portugal joined the coalition. Seeing enemies at every turn, the French government declared war on England and the Netherlands on 1 February 1793. "The kings of Europe advance against us," thundered the French radical leader Danton in the Assembly. "We throw at their feet, as a gauge of battle, the head of a king."

The ideas of the French Revolution were quickly felt in France's colonies. The island of Hispaniola was divided into two colonies, one French, one Spanish – now Haiti and the Dominican Republic. In 1791 many of the

"Pacification with Maroon Negroes," drawn from life in Jamaica by Agostino Brunyas. (Engraving from the author's collection)

520,000 black slaves in the French colony raised the flag of revolt under the leadership of Toussaint L'Ouverture, a literate former slave.* The Spanish colonial government supported the rebellion as a means of attacking France; the French colonial government, royalist in orientation, petitioned Prime Minister William Pitt† through the intermediary of the governor of Jamaica, General Adam Williamson,‡ to take charge of the colony. England

---

* François-Dominique Toussaint L'Ouverture (1743–1803).
† William Pitt the Younger (1759–1806), Prime Minister of Great Britain 1784–1801 and 1804–06.
‡ Lieutenant-General Sir Adam Williamson 1736–1798), Acting Governor of Jamaica 1791–95.

and the new French Republic now being at war, an expedition was despatched on 9 September 1793. The flank companies of the 49th were among the first troops to be sent, followed on 11 October by the battalion companies.[17] Aided by the slave revolt and Spanish troops coming in from the east, the British force rapidly gained control of the colony. At the same time, expeditions to Martinique, Guadeloupe and other French colonies stripped France of most of her Caribbean possessions.[18]

Seizing control of Hispaniola was much easier than holding it, especially in view of the environment. Malaria and "yellow-jack" were even more of a scourge than in Jamaica and the Barbadoes: 13,000 out of the original 20,000 British soldiers sent to San Domingo between 1793 and 1798 are estimated to have died, chiefly from disease. A total of 45,000 British soldiers are believed to have died there between 1793 and 1803 – half those sent to the island. This figure rose to a total of 75,000 by 1815.[19] This was a staggering drain on the military manpower of Britain and must at least in part explain the difficulties in raising the strength of the Peninsular army above 50,000 until 1813, and of maintaining the garrisons elsewhere – such as in the Canadas. The fortunes of the 49th Foot were typical: as early as December 1793 there were only three captains fit for duty and its strength was down to 366; Grant was clearly fearful that, as before in its history, the regiment would

Hispaniola, detail from map of the West Indies by Thomas Jefferys, c.1760. The island is today divided into Haiti and the Dominican Republic. (Library of Congress)

be broken up and drafted to fill other regiments.[20] A year later, its strength was down to 189,[21] although two companies had been retained in Jamaica to fight in the Maroon War.

Brock was oblivious to all of this despite his proximity to the unfolding drama. On the eve of the despatch of the expedition he became a victim of, probably, yellow fever or *vomito negro* as it was also known. Probably, since once he had recovered, it did not recur; those who recover from yellow fever without major organ damage are immune thereafter. Had he contracted malaria, it would have troubled him for the rest of his life and there is no record of this being the case. There is still today no cure for yellow fever and doctors can only treat the symptoms. In the first stage of the disease, which lasts four days, these are high temperature, nausea and vomiting, headache and aching muscles. The second, sometimes fatal, stage comes on a day or so later and victims suffer a very high temperature, lethargy, jaundice, kidney failure and internal bleeding.[22]

As a result of developing the second stage of the disease, Brock missed the expedition – and it was just as well given the death rate. As it was, Brock's first cousin Henry, a lieutenant in the 13th (1st Somersetshire) Regiment of Foot, died of the fever in Jamaica. Brock himself was cared for by his devoted soldier-servant, Private James Dobson, who remained with him until Dobson's death. The illness left Brock so debilitated that he applied for furlough and, having been granted leave, he went home to Guernsey to recover.

Back at home Brock again busied himself with the recruiting service and with improving the efficiency of the volunteer companies, or fencibles, raised for home defence.* Among these was the 1st Glengarry Fencibles, a corps of mostly Catholic Scottish Highlanders, many of whom had been

---

* The name fencible is derived from "defensible" and refers to volunteer units raised for the defence of the British Isles and territories. The units were placed under regular officers and were under the authority of the Commander-in-Chief. They could be deployed anywhere in Britain, but not overseas, and were designed to provide garrison troops in order to relieve regulars for active service abroad. They were distinct from the militia, which was under the authority of the Lords Lieutenants of Counties and whose soldiers were enlisted by compulsory ballot. Militia regiments were listed in the Army List and their officers, although amateurs, dressed like regular officers and had the same social and military status. Militia regiments did not generally serve outside Britain but after 1812 they could volunteer for foreign service.

John Vincent (1764–1848) as a major-general. The Irish-born soldier was already a veteran at the outbreak of the War of 1812, having seen action in Haiti, Holland and Denmark, and having been in Canada since 1802, like Brock. He commanded the British and Canadian troops on the Niagara frontier in 1813 and fought the battles of Fort George, Burlington Heights and Stoney Creek (By permission of the trustees of Muckross House, Killarney)

forced to quit their land during the Highland clearances. Their chaplain, Father Alexander Macdonell,* became a firm and lifelong friend of Brock. The organization of the local militia was also of great importance and the growing influence of Methodism did not help, for Methodists in the militia refused to attend the compulsory Sunday drills. After a long struggle, Methodists were granted the right to attend special drills on weekdays.[23]

In June 1795, again with help of William, Brock was able to purchase a major's commission for the sum of £2,000,[24] an outlay of £500 once he had sold his captaincy. Generally an infantry regiment would have two majors on its strength but there being none in the 49th, Brock immediately became the senior major. The second major, appointed on 1 September 1795, was John Vincent, who would later, like Brock himself, rise to general officer rank and achieve distinction in North America. At about the same time, Brock's mother, Elizabeth, died. His eldest sister, Elizabeth, and her husband, John Tupper, whose son was Brock's first biographer, moved into the family house in St Peter Port. At least Brock would have had the consolation of being close to his mother before her death – and she the comfort of his presence – along with his brothers and sisters, rather than, as is often the lot of the British soldier, hearing the news in some far-off theatre of war.

The 49th Foot returned from the West Indies in the summer of 1796 and

---

* Alexander Macdonell (1762–1840) later Bishop of Regiopolis, the first Catholic diocese of Upper Canada.

Brock rejoined the regiment when it assembled at Watford on 1 September. Sickness in the Caribbean had thinned the ranks dramatically and there was a need to fill them, and also to promote experienced men to fill the gaps among the non-commissioned officers. The two companies from Jamaica mustered 118 men but the rest of the 49th amounted to only 13 sergeants, 13 drummers and 16 men.[25] The uniforms and equipment were likewise worn out by the rigour of the sub-tropical climate and needed drastic overhaul. In December 1796 the regiment moved to Chelmsford and by the end of the year it had recruited up to a strength of 344.[26]

In October 1797, shortly after his twenty-eighth birthday, Brock was able to purchase a lieutenant-colonelcy in the 49th, again with his brother William's help.[27] There was no other way in which he could have secured the difference of £1,500 between the sale of his majority and his new rank. After a slow start – Isaac Brock had been an ensign for five years – he had risen to lieutenant-colonel in twelve years; today it would take at least twenty. His rise had been meteoric, especially in view of the fact that he had no combat experience; indeed it was only possible given the conditions of the day. He was, however, not yet in command of the regiment, for its incumbent commanding officer, Lieutenant-Colonel Frederick Keppel, was still in post. Keppel, a relative newcomer to the 49th, did not last much longer. The state of the regiment was not good, owing, as one authority said, to his "gross mismanagement and peculation."[28] The monthly returns and inspection reports show nothing of this,[29] but they do reveal the under-manning of the 49th Foot after the ravages of the West Indies, with at least two recruiting parties in Ireland and others spread far afield: Hertford, Chester, Bath, Chatham, Winchester, Farringdon, Dundee, Sheffield, Andover, Northampton, Hampstead and London. By the end of March 1798 the strength of the regiment had reached 481 rank and file out of an establishment of 760. The returns also reveal that Keppel was an absentee commanding officer: he is only shown as being present and on duty in one month, December 1796, between July of that year and March 1797. At the same time, the majority of the officers are also listed as being absent on leave with the exception of those conducting recruiting parties. This meant that the regiment was being supervised by the NCOs and a very small number of the company officers and staff; in such a situation, interior economy was bound to deteriorate.

Sir Roger Hale Sheaffe (1763–1851) as a major-general. Sheaffe came from an American Loyalist family and had been commissioned into the 5th Foot in 1778. He served in Ireland and in the Canadas until 1789 and transferred into the 49th in 1797. He knew much about soldiering but little about leadership. (Library and Archives Canada C-111307)

Keppel was advised to sell up and leave, which he duly did in April 1798, leaving Brock as the senior lieutenant-colonel and commanding officer of the 49th Regiment.[30]

At this point two men who would feature for good and ill in the remainder of Brock's life joined the 49th. The first was his younger brother, John Savery, who joined the regiment as its paymaster. Savery, it will be remembered, had entered the Royal Navy but he had found the disciplinary regime hard to swallow. The practice of mast-heading – sending midshipmen who were found wanting in their duty in the eyes of their officers to the very top of the masts and making them stay there for long periods – so infuriated him that he headed a campaign of disobedience. This could, of course, only end one way and Savery soon left the navy. The second was the incoming junior lieutenant-colonel: not Vincent, but a man six years older than Brock, who had also joined as a boy of fifteen, who also had no active service behind him, but who in character and temperament was as different from Brock as any man could be: Roger Hale Sheaffe.

When Brock took command, the 49th was at Yarmouth in East Anglia; it moved to Sandwich, Kent, in April 1798. This was a dangerous locality: in May 1797, mutinies had broken out in the fleet, in ships at Spithead off Portsmouth, and the Nore, which was close to Sandwich.[31] No sooner had these been put down than in May and June 1798 the revolt of the United Irishmen broke out in Ireland. This was suppressed with great ferocity but was followed by two attempted French invasions, a running insurgency for some months and ever more severe government repression.[32] The spirit of revolution spread from the fleet to a number of regiments quartered nearby, including the 49th, where discontent was fuelled by events in Ireland among the many Irishmen in the ranks. A seditious pamphlet that circulated among the regiments in and around Chatham in May 1797, for example, ends with the words: "The regiments which send you this, are willing to do their part. They will … make their demands as soon as they know you will not draw the trigger against them.… Be sober, be ready."[33]

No wonder the 49th was described as "sadly disorganized"; Brock could hardly have taken command at a more difficult time. He appears to have restored good order and discipline by patient, understated yet firm means, probably the methods with which he had grown up among the old campaigners of the 8th Foot, who would have seen little sense in savage discipline. Brock was clearly not a flogging man – he seems to have had a horror of it – and the disciplinary regime in the regiment was reduced to more humane levels. Corruption, including the plundering of the men's rations and pay by sergeants and corporals, was not tolerated either. On the other hand it was necessary for Brock and his officers, with trusted non-commissioned officers and men, to inspect barrack rooms and billets at all hours to make sure that no conspiracy was being hatched. It is said that he remained awake throughout the night with a brace of loaded pistols by him for many weeks. What is clear from the monthly returns is that the number of officers on leave or authorized absence dropped rapidly.* Once the warrant and non-commissioned officers of the regiment could be trusted to maintain good order without oppression, and the officers and men made to respond to strong leadership by example, things were turned around. It was said that the commander in chief, the Duke of York, remarked that "Colonel Brock, from one of the worst, had made the 49th one of the best regiments in the service."[34]

While these troubles were unfolding, the flank companies of the 49th were detached to join the expedition to Ostend. This was a raid aimed at destroying the lock gates on the Bruges–Ostend canal and so to impede

---

* The two majors at this point were John Vincent and William Hutchinson; and the captains commanding companies were Alexander Sharp, William Archer, Matthew, Lord Aylmer, Richard Newcombe, Thomas Smith, Samuel Milnes, Birkenhead Glegg, William Robbins and Adam Ormsby; the Captain-Lieutenant was Edward Cheshire (Army Lists).

the passage of boats being built for a planned French invasion of England. Although the lock gates were successfully demolished, the expeditionary force was subsequently surrounded and destroyed. The grenadier company of the 49th went into captivity; the light company escaped, having never been disembarked.[35]

Back at home, Brock and the 49th continued their itinerant life, moving to Broadstairs in Kent for a short spell and from there to St Helier in Jersey in July 1799. There they remained for six months until ordered back to Hilsea Barracks, Portsmouth. But the routine of military life was about to change: after another six months, the 49th marched first to Romsey and then to Barham, Kent, in July, where a great force was assembling for an expedition to the Low Countries.

CHAPTER THREE

"Ever Glorious to the 49th"

THE HELDER CAMPAIGN,
1799–1800

The Dutch Republic had been a member of the First Coalition against the French Republic after 1792 but in 1795, at the end of their campaign in Flanders, the combined forces of *Stadtholder* William V and his British and Austrian allies were defeated by the invading French army. The Dutch Republic was overthrown, William fled to London and the Batavian Republic, a French client state, was established. This gave France access to the considerable naval resources of the Netherlands, which it badly needed. Despite some early setbacks, a building programme brought the Batavian navy up to a strength that caused the major maritime power, Great Britain, concern – especially in terms of its potential contribution to a threatened French invasion of England or Ireland.

The First Coalition broke up in 1797, but Britain found a new ally in Czar Paul I of Russia. The new allies scored some successes in the land war against France in northern Italy and Switzerland. The British, especially Prime Minister William Pitt and Foreign Secretary Lord Grenville,* were anxious to maintain the initiative and stretch French forces out. The Low Countries seemed an excellent target for such an operation, with the Prince of Orange lobbying hard for a full military effort to reinstate him and insisting that a determined move by the British on Amsterdam would lead to a popular uprising against the French. Moreover, a combined campaign in the Low Countries had been a condition of the treaty of 28 December 1798 with the Russians. Under the terms of this treaty, further refined in June 1799, the Russians agreed to provide 17,500 men for the expedition to Holland, broken down into seventeen infantry battalions, two battalions of artillery

---

* William Wyndham Grenville, Baron Grenville (1759–1834): Pitt's first cousin; Foreign Secretary of Great Britain 1791–1801.

and a small number of support troops. In return, Britain would pay a subsidy of £88,000, plus another £44,000 a month so long as the troops were in the field. Britain herself would field a force of 35,000 troops and supply the transports and naval escorts; this would be the largest force sent from Britain since the end of the American Revolutionary War in 1783.

The British expeditionary force concentrated around Canterbury in Kent under the command of the Duke of York and was formed into three divisions under Lieutenant-General Sir Ralph Abercromby,* Lieutenant-General Sir James Pulteney† and Lieutenant-General David Dundas. Brock and the 49th Foot joined Abercromby's division, in Major-General Sir John Moore's brigade.‡ With them were the 2nd Battalion of the 1st Foot (the Royal Scots), and the 25th (Sussex),§ 79th (Cameronian Volunteers) and 92nd (Highland) regiments – a strongly Scottish brigade. The regiments assembling for the expedition were for the most part under-strength and were brought up to something like their establishment by drafts from the militia:[1] Brock received 130 men from various units, which brought the 49th up to 507 all ranks.[2] Many of the volunteers were drafted straight into the grenadier company to replace the losses of Ostend, but these men were at a low standard of training and physical fitness and there was little time to put this right. Even worse from the manpower point of view, the flank companies were all detached to form a composite advanced guard force.

A British fleet under Admiral Popham¶ had sailed to the Baltic to embark the Russians. It was decided not to wait until the Russian force arrived but in the meantime to despatch Abercromby's division to establish a bridgehead, into which the Russians and the rest of the British force, under the overall commander, the Duke of York, could disembark. However, a suitable landing site for an amphibious operation had to be identified, bearing in mind that there were no landing craft as such, only barges and ships' boats to land

---

* Lieutenant-General Sir Ralph Abercromby (1734–1801).
† General Sir James Murray Pulteney, 7th Baronet (1755–1811).
‡ Later Lieutenant-General Sir John Moore, K.B. (1761–1809), who commanded the British expedition to Portugal in 1808. He was killed at the battle of Corunna on 16 January 1809 while overseeing the evacuation of his force.
§ The 25th was allocated to Sussex until 1805; it later became the King's Own Scottish Borderers.
¶ Rear Admiral Sir Home Riggs Popham (1762–1820).

the troops. Eventually the northern end of the peninsula of North Holland, south of the Helder, was selected for several reasons. A landing here could be easily supported by British sea-power; the area was not heavily fortified; a large part of the Dutch fleet was based nearby and might be at least dislocated, if not actually captured, if the landing was successful; and finally, the terrain offered the possibility of an easy advance on the important objective of Amsterdam.[3]

British preparations were quickly discovered both by French agents and the British press, for lack of security bedevilled the British throughout the whole period of the Revolutionary and Napoleonic wars. However, the intended landing location was not known and the French and Dutch

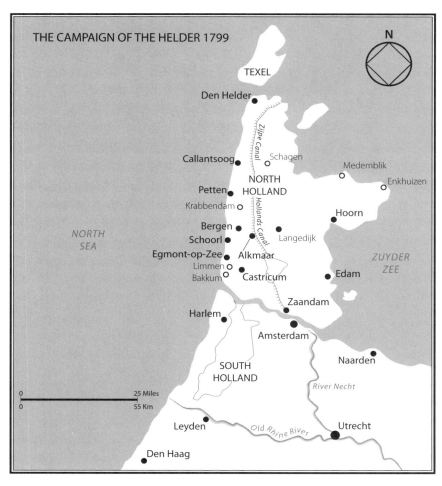

THE CAMPAIGN OF THE HELDER 1799

"Landing of the English Troops at Callantsoog" by Dirk Langendyck, 1799.
Langendyck watched the landing and sketched it; his picture bears out the accounts
of its being only lightly opposed. The sand dunes referred to later in the chapter can
be clearly seen to the right of the picture. (By permission of the National Maritime
Museum, Greenwich)

were therefore obliged to spread their forces thinly along the coastline. The
Batavian army consisted of two divisions, each of about 10,000 men. One
of these, commanded by Lieutenant-General Hermann Daendels,[*] was
deployed in the landing area with is headquarters at Schagen. The 15,000
French troops in Batavia were divided between Zeeland and the centre of the
country between Nijmegen and the coast. The entire Franco-Batavian force
was placed under the command of the French General Guillaume Brune.[†]

---

[*] Lieutenant-General Herman Willem Daendels (1762–1818)
[†] Général de Division (later Marshal) Guillaume-Marie-Anne Brune, 1st Count Brune (1763–
1815)

The invasion met with initial success. The Dutch fleet declined an action, leaving the disembarkation of the first British troops near Callantsoog on 27 August 1799 uncontested. Daendels collected his forces and tried to interrupt the landing during the afternoon, and it was not until late in the day that Brock and the 49th disembarked and joined the action. Sergeant James Fitzgibbon* of the 49th recalled that:

> The flat boats in which we were sent from the transports moved off for the shore.... Our mortar ships had been throwing bombs to the shore for a short time before.... The low line of sand-hills opposite our landing place was lined with troops. A volley was fired upon us as we jumped ashore. The regiments already landed charged up the hill and drove the enemy back at the point of the bayonet, while we landed without further molestation.... Had the enemy ... opposed our landing in earnest, the boats must have been destroyed or captured.[4]

* Later Colonel James Fitzgibbon (1780–1863).

Moore's skirmishers were active but there were no casualties, so that it can be guessed that there was little real fighting that day. Indeed Fitzgibbon says that Moore's brigade moved to the left of the British line while all the fighting was to the right.[5] Daendels had failed to build up his forces more rapidly than the landing force – a lesson upon which Brock must have reflected while on the Detroit and Niagara frontiers in later life – and, having failed to stop the landing, he concluded that the Helder fortresses were untenable. He therefore spiked their guns and evacuated their garrisons, leaving the invaders a fortified base. Abercromby was able to take up a position across the Helder from the North Sea to the Zuyder Zee, covered by the formidable obstacle of the great Zijpe Canal. Brock summarized matters thus in a letter to his brothers:

> ... the enemy most unaccountably offered no resistance to our landing; and that, after a well-contested fight of ten hours, he retreated, leaving us in possession of the Heights, extending the whole length of the peninsula ... to our utter astonishment, the enemy gave us no annoyance; on the contrary ... he evacuated the town [of Helder], which we took quiet possession of the following morning....[6]

This proved disastrous for Dutch morale. The sight of the flag of the *Stadtholder*, who immediately joined the expedition, further undermined the shaky loyalty of the Dutch fleet, which mutinied and then surrendered without firing a shot on 30 August.

The Batavian government, civilian population and army were, however, less willing to welcome their Prince back, and in the meanwhile the Franco-Batavian forces on the North Holland front were reinforced. Brune brought up a French division under General Dominique Vandamme[*] and ordered General Jean-Baptiste Dumonceau[†] to bring up the main part of his 2nd Batavian Division in forced marches from Friesland – they arrived at nearby Alkmaar on 9 September. The Franco-Batavian army now numbered about 25,000 men against about 20,000 British. Since British reinforcements were expected daily, Brune decided to attack Abercromby's

---

[*] Général Dominique-Joseph-René Vandamme, Count (1770–1830).
[†] Général Jean-Baptiste Dumonceau de Bergendal (1760–1821).

position at once. This was the battle of Krabbendam on 10 September, in which the Batavians and French were routed. Brock wrote of this that:

> ... the enemy made a most desperate attack in three columns, two on the right and one on the centre of the line: he could not avoid being beaten, as it was the most injudicious step imaginable, and his loss was in proportion very great.... The 49th was here again out of the way, with the exception indeed of Savery, whom nothing could keep from going to see what was doing on the right.... [7]

Once again, Brock and the 49th were not heavily engaged and no casualties were reported. With the French and Batavians in retreat, and naval superiority established, British reinforcements under the Duke of York and Russian troops under Lieutenant-General Ivan von Fersen* could be landed at Den Helder.

The Duke of York himself landed on 15 September and assumed command of the British army, which now amounted to about 30,000 men, including 1,200 light cavalry, as against some 23,000 French. Since the allies possessed superior forces and expected another 10,000 reinforcements, the Duke decided to strike a decisive blow as early as possible. The Dutch, who numbered about 12,000, were in a strong position around Langedijk; the French, by drawing in all detachments, had raised their field strength to 10,000 and they held Alkmaar, Bergen, Schoorl and Egmont-op-Zee. On 19 September the allied forces, formed in four columns, moved forward from Schagerbrug. The right column, commanded by von Fersen, was composed chiefly of Russian troops; the left-centre column, commanded by Pulteney, included two British brigades; the right-centre column, under Dundas, included the Guards brigade and two other brigades. The left column, commanded by Sir Ralph Abercromby, consisted of two squadrons of the 18th Light Dragoons; Major-General the Earl of Chatham's† brigade – the 4th and 31st Regiments; Major-General Sir John Moore's brigade; and Major-General the Earl of Cavan's‡ brigade – the 1st and 2nd Battalions of the 20th and the 63rd Regiments.

---

* General Ivan Ivanovitch Hermann von Fersen (d. 1801), a Saxon in the Russian service since 1790.

† Major-General John Pitt, 2nd Earl of Chatham, K.G., P.C. (1756–1835) was the Prime Minister's elder brother, later Master-General of the Ordnance.

‡ Richard Ford William Lambert, 7th Earl of Cavan (1763–1837).

Frederick Augustus, Duke of York and Albany, K.G., K.B., P.C. (1763–1827), was the second son of George III. He commanded the force in the Helder campaign. Although an indifferent field commander, he was a fine commander-in-chief from 1795 to 1809 and again from 1811 to 1827. He oversaw much needed reforms to the army that rendered it a very professional service in the last decade of the war with France.

The enemy's left was anchored on the high sand dunes that extended inland from the sea in front of the village of Petten to the town of Bergen. The ground over which the centre columns had to move was deeply intersected every three or four hundred yards by broad, deep ditches and canals. The bridges across the few roads leading to the points of attack had been destroyed and obstacles had been carefully arranged.

As things turned out, Abercromby's column took little part in this action. The troops began their march late on 18 September, but progress was very slow because of the appalling state of the roads. Abercromby arrived at Hoorn around 2.00 a.m. on 19 September and quickly rounded up the Dutch garrison. Brock remarked that "the 4th Brigade [i.e., Moore's] ... got possession of the city of Horn the following morning without a shot being fired: 200 prisoners were taken. Horn is a very populous, handsome city, and evidently in the interest of the Prince of Orange."[8]

The men were exhausted and Abercromby decided to wait until he had news of what was happening to his right, lest he become separated from the main force. It was not until noon that he received a message saying that Dundas had made good progress, but nothing was known of Pulteney. Abercromby belatedly put out a reconnaissance and found a mass of dikes and obstacles in front of him. The next message, at 4.00 p.m., told Abercromby that the Russians had been beaten and that he should retire to his starting position. The division turned round and began to march once more through a wet and foul night. Brock wrote that:

Nothing could exceed the joy of the inhabitants [of Hoorn] at our arrival, and in proportion as they rejoiced they mourned our departure, which took place before sun-set, in consequence of a fatal disaster that had befallen the Russians on the right … but whether the British were sufficiently brisk in coming to their assistance, is doubted.[9]

Morale was low not only among the townspeople but among the British troops; unsurprisingly, the militia men were physically not up to the hardship of the march, and the division rapidly degenerated into a mob.

Had the Russians overcome the opposition and had Abercromby been more active, the battle could have been won and the campaign effectively brought to an early and victorious end. The reality was that the battle ended inconclusively. The Dutch and French reoccupied all the positions from which they had been driven and their general line of defence was now covered on the right by flooded areas, the only roads across which were covered by field defences. The area between Alkmaar and the Zuyder Zee was thus made defensible by small numbers, while Amsterdam was secured on the landward side.

After the surrender of the Batavian squadron on August 30, the British fleet had become master not just of the North Sea but also of the Zuyder Zee. Remarkably, the British had not made use of this advantage: for a few days, for example, Amsterdam lay quite defenceless against attack. After the battle of Bergen, the British belatedly occupied the undefended ports on the Dutch coast and a number of islands in the Zuyder Zee, but the opportunity to capture Amsterdam had been lost.

On land, new Russian reinforcements arrived after 19 September. The Duke of York did not press his advantage for about two weeks, however, because of bad weather, and this allowed the defenders to complete the flooding of the low-lying areas and other defences. The weather improved in early October and the Duke of York then made his plan for what was to become known as the battle of Alkmaar, on 2 October 1799. It is also referred to as the second battle of Bergen.

The Anglo-Russian forces were once again deployed in columns, four of whose composition was little changed from Bergen and a fifth made up of the new Russian reinforcements. Abercromby's column was to advance on the allied right along the beach and sea dike. Brock reported that "the Brigade assembled before daylight at Petten, and formed the advanced guard of a column, consisting of 10,000 men, which was to proceed along the beach to Egmont op Zee."

In the centre were placed two columns of Russian infantry with 600 cavalry commanded by General Ivan Essen,* who had succeeded Fersen. Dundas's column would attack to the left of the Russians. Major-General Sir Eyre Coote's† brigade, detached from Pulteney's division, and Chatham's column were to support the Russians in their attack on Bergen and to maintain contact with Abercromby. Finally, on the extreme left, a column of about 7,000 British and Russian troops under Sir James Pulteney was to screen the exposed left flank of the army from an attack by Daendels's depleted division, support the other columns and exploit any opportunity to turn the enemy's flank. The main effort would be the capture of Bergen. Unlike the first battle of Bergen, this attack would be concentrated on a narrow front between Schoorl and the North Sea, with Abercromby's advance along the beach to a point beyond the left flank of the French effecting a single envelopment of the enemy position.

The first stages of the battle went according to the Duke's plan. To allow all columns to advance simultaneously, the start time had to be delayed until low tide at 6.30 a.m. Only then could Abercromby's column make use of the beach. Coote and Chatham drove in the French and cleared the dunes, and Essen's central column then advanced cautiously. Meanwhile, the French left fell back on Bergen. This was a strong position and York realized they had to be evicted from it. He therefore ordered a combined Anglo-Russian attack, but Essen held back and, as the two British brigades lacked the strength to storm the position alone, the allied attack stalled. The French, seeing the Russian hesitation, launched a fierce counter-attack from Bergen in two columns. These attacks were successfully held by the British reserve and the French were driven from the dunes after fierce fighting – but they still held Bergen.

While this was going on, Abercromby's column had been advancing steadily. The dunes rose steeply from the beach and from a few hundred yards in width to nearly four miles wide and 150 feet high around Bergen itself. There were patches of thick scrub in which the enemy's sharpshooters could hide, and which also made contact between companies and regiments hard to maintain. This was very difficult country for an advance, and even more so for troops trying to keep in formation. It was the sort of terrain

---

* Lieutenant-General Ivan Nikolayevich Essen (1759–1813).
† Lieutenant-General Sir Eyre Coote, G.C.B. (1759–1823); he was stripped of the G.C.B. in 1816 on account of a scandal.

where looser American-style tactical formations scored heavily over the more rigid Prussian ones. The incoming tide made the beach narrower all the time and forced the infantry to march through the loose sand and hard going of the dunes, while the cavalry on the right flank had to wade through the surf. After some time, the French became aware of the advance; James Fitzgibbon recalled that "About 8 o'clock the advance commenced skirmishing, and the column was halted" and the French brought up sharpshooters, who started to exact a toll, especially among the British officers:

> The enemy then appeared in small force, and the 25th was ordered up the sand hills, but, he having increased, the 79th followed, and it was not long before the 49th was also ordered to form on the left of that regiment. It is impossible to give you an adequate idea of the nature of the ground, which I can only compare to the sea in a storm.[10]

Fitzgibbon also recorded that:

> The first man I saw killed was a fine handsome young ensign, a lieutenant of grenadiers, who had volunteered from the South Middlesex Militia to the line, still wearing the uniform of his late regiment. He carried one of the Regimental Colours, and was one of the finest-looking men I had ever seen.[11]

The French too had brought up reinforcements that blocked the advance from a strong position on the dunes overlooking the beach. Brock had divided the 49th into two battalions: one of six companies under his own command; and the other of four under Sheaffe, which was echeloned to protect the exposed left flank. Brock went forward on horseback to reconnoitre the ground on the left of the 79th Foot and found that the French had already turned its left. "My determination," he wrote, "was instantly shaken," for there was no cover at all to be had. He turned his horse around and went to rejoin the regiment, which he met in the process of moving forward. The troops under Sheaffe had already made contact with the enemy, who were trying to get round behind the left flank and turn the whole position. Leaving Sheaffe with his four companies to block this attempt, Brock led his battalion forward:

> The instant I came up to the 79th, I ordered a charge, which I assure you was executed with the greatest gallantry, though not in the greatest order,

as the nature of the ground admitted of none. The enemy, however, gave way on every side, and our loss would have been trifling had the 79th charged straightforward.[12]

The 79th Foot fell in behind the 49th, exposing the right flank of Brock's battalion. Brock sent his grenadier company, under Captain the Lord Aylmer,* to clear the enemy from this area. As he wrote:

> For my part, I had every reason to be satisfied with the conduct of both officers and men, and no commanding officer could be more handsomely supported than I was on that day, ever glorious to the 49th. Poor [William] Archer brought his company to the attack in a most soldierlike manner; and even after he had received his mortal wound, he animated his men, calling them to go on to victory.[13]

There is an apocryphal story that Savery Brock, although a paymaster, rode forward to join in the fighting. His horse was shot from under him and as he picked himself up, Isaac called to him, "By the Lord Harry, Master Savery, did I not order you, unless you remained with the General, to stay with your iron chest? Go back to it immediately!" Savery is said to have retorted, "Mind your regiment, Master Isaac; you would not have me quit the field now?" This exchange is said to have caused great mirth among the troops – as well it might, to see their all-powerful lieutenant-colonel put down.

The engagement continued for several hours and was fought by both sides with great tenacity; Abercromby had two horses killed under him and Moore was again wounded and stunned. Brock too was wounded, but only slightly. He appears to have been struck in the throat by a spent musket ball which did not penetrate his neck, as he was wearing a thick cotton kerchief, wound over a black silk cravat, against the cold. The force of the blow was enough to knock him off his horse and stun him – but not for long, for he "never quitted the field."[14] James Fitzgibbon was captured along with men from several other regiments, "five officers and one hundred and seventeen men,"[15] marched first into Alkmaar and later by stages to Valenciennes, where they remained until exchanged some weeks later.

By noon Abercromby's force was within a mile of Egmont-op-Zee and

---

* Matthew Whitworth-Aylmer, 5th Baron Aylmer (1775–1850), C-in-C British forces in Canada, Lieutenant-Governor of Lower Canada, and Governor-General of British North America from 1830 until his recall in 1835.

56

Moore's brigade shook out into line once more, with the 49th on the left between the grenadier companies and the 1st Foot. Fierce fighting went on for another hour; companies broke up into small groups and there was genuine hand-to-hand combat at close quarters. Finally, the French gave way and the British troops managed to push forward to the road between Bergen and Egmont-op-Zee, cutting off the French extreme left from the main body. Brune, still at Bergen, ordered Vandamme to take personal charge at this dangerous point, while Daendels was ordered to send Batavian cavalry and infantry from his position on the extreme right wing, by way of Alkmaar, to reinforce the French on the left. When Vandamme got to Egmont, he saw that Abercromby's horse artillery had advanced too far along the beach and become isolated. He believed he saw a chance to turn the battle by leading a cavalry charge on these guns, but he had not seen the British cavalry, which managed to ambush him and rout him. The French cavalry turned tail and retreated all the way to Egmont.

Darkness was now falling and, as usual at this time, the coming of night and real exhaustion signalled the end of battle. Abercromby, aware that he had advanced beyond the position in Bergen, decided to spend the night at the beach. His men and their horses suffered greatly from thirst, since there was no fresh water in the dunes. Thirst was a constant problem to men who had to load their muskets by biting off the tops of their cartridges and holding the ball in the mouth while they poured the charge down the barrel, for they would inevitably ingest quantities of powder and this had a dehydrating effect. Late in the night rain fell, which slaked the men's thirst but added to the discomfort and lack of shelter. As Brock said, "You cannot conceive our wretched state, as it blew and rained nearly the whole time. Our men bore all this without grumbling, although they had nothing to eat but the biscuits they carried with them, which by this time were completely wet."[16]

The troops slept on their arms, under occasional fire from the French guns. The 49th had lost two officers killed – Captain William Archer and Ensign Ginn[*] – along with a sergeant and thirty men; Major William

---

[*] No officer of that name appears under the 49th in the Army Lists. Either he served for such a short time that his details were never recorded, or else he was one of the attached officers of militia. One officer of that name does appear in the 1800 Army List in the South Hants Militia. He could be the officer described by Fitzgibbon, who mistook the South Middlesex for the South Hants.

Hutchinson, Captains Alexander Sharpe and William Robins, Lieutenant James Urquhart and Ensign Henry Wall* were wounded along with a sergeant and fifty men; and Lieutenant Robert Johnson, a sergeant and twenty-two men were missing.[17] This made a total of eight officers, three sergeants and 102 men out of action – about 20 per cent of the regiment's strength. By historical norms, this would be enough to reduce its combat effectiveness severely, which may account for why it was not heavily engaged in the later fighting. The loss of officers was particularly serious and evidence of either their prominence in the battle or the accuracy of the French sharpshooters, or both.

In the French camp, Brune, though not directly threatened by Abercromby, felt that the advance along the beach had effectively turned his left and cut communication between Bergen and Egmont. He therefore decided to give up the position in Bergen and withdraw early next day, 3 October, to a line from Wijk-aan-Zee to Castricum and Uitgeest. Abercromby followed up steadily but there are no further reports of casualties in the 49th. Therefore, although the tactical battle had ended with only a slight advantage for the British, the consequences were great. Alkmaar, abandoned by the French and Batavian troops, opened its gates to the British and prudently hoisted the orange flag of the former regime. Brock wrote of entering Alkmaar on 5 October, "where we enjoyed ourselves amazingly. Alkmaar is a delightful city; but the inhabitants are rank patriots, and none of the higher class remained to welcome our arrival."[18]

With the retreat of the Franco-Batavian army, the greater part of the North Holland peninsula was now in Anglo-Russian hands. However, large parts of the country had been flooded, depriving the British of supplies they might have obtained from the farmland. As a result, supplies had to be landed at Den Helder and brought forward along near-impassable roads; food, fodder for animals and ammunition began to run short and sickness began to take its toll in the sodden climate.† The Duke of York, now

---

* In some accounts, the officer's name is given as Hill. Since there is no-one of that name in the 49th, according to the Army List, it seems likely that this is a misreading of the clerk's hand in the manuscript return.

† Malaria and typhus were both common in the wetlands of the Low Countries at this time. British troops who picked up these diseases during the campaign and during the later Walcheren campaign and survived would continue to be dogged by recurrences throughout

headquartered in Alkmaar, wasted as little time as possible in pressing the offensive, for he knew that Brune had been reinforced with six French battalions from Belgium. In contrast, his own force was already reduced to no more than 27,000 effective soldiers.

On the morning of October 6, the Duke launched an attack in three columns against the French: Abercromby along the beach, Essen in the middle and Dundas on the left. The Duke seemed to have had no more than a probing attack in mind, but early success tempted the Russians to attack the village of Castricum in force. The fighting there went on all day and drew in troops from both armies; Abercromby personally brought up his reserve brigade to attack Castricum late in the afternoon. A final French effort nearly succeeded, but the British cavalry restored the situation and drove the French back in disorder. Victory seemed close, but the advance of the British was broken by a further counter-attack, this time by Batavian cavalry. The Anglo-Russian troops in their turn retreated in disorder to the villages of Bakkum and Limmen, pursued by the Franco-Batavian cavalry. Only darkness prevented disaster.

All this time the French division of General Louis Gouvion* and the British column of Abercromby had been fighting a separate battle near the beach and in the dunes. Apart from an artillery duel, in which Gouvion's Batavian artillery inflicted heavy losses on the British, neither side pushed to gain the initiative, especially after Abercromby left with the British reserve to join Essen. The fight intensified during the evening when Abercromby returned and tried to attack. The French held their ground. The battalion companies of the 49th seem to have been out of the worst of it throughout the day for no casualties were reported; as Brock tartly remarked "during this severe contest we were snugly in church."[†19] The light companies were more closely engaged but their losses cannot be distinguished from the return of the composite battalions to which they were attached – but no officers appear among the dead or wounded.

On the night of 6 October, both armies were back roughly where they

---

the rest of their lives. Dealing with Walcheren fever, as it was known, was a constant source of problems to Wellington's medical establishment throughout the Peninsular War.

* Général Louis Jean-Baptiste Gouvion, Count Gouvion (1752–1823).

† "Church work" or "in church" meant anything that went on slowly, or was dragged out and delayed.

The evacuation of the English and Russians from Den Helder. This is clearly an administrative embarkation, out of contact with the enemy, and was witnessed by the artist. Several women can be seen, almost certainly regimental wives who were permitted to follow the drum on a scale of ten per company. (Engraving after J.A Langendijk)

had been that morning. Anglo-Russian losses had been heavy – about double those of the Franco-Batavians – but not dangerously so. However, the Duke of York convened a council of war with his lieutenants-general and they took counsel of their fears; the outcome was that the Anglo-Russian army withdrew to the original bridgehead, giving up all that had been gained since 19 September. The cities of Hoorn, Enkhuizen and Medemblik were evacuated and the following Batavian troops were even able to prevent the burning of the warehouses full of naval stores. The retreat was executed in such haste that two field hospitals full of British wounded were left in Alkmaar, along with 400 women and children who had followed the drum from England with their soldier husbands.

The withdrawal was completed on 8 October, and from the French and Batavian point of view, the situation existing before September 19 had been restored. The weather had taken a turn for the worse, with gales making supply from the sea more difficult; on 13 October, only eleven days' of supply were available.[20] The Duke of York, facing the prospect of a winter siege in which his troops might well starve, decided to approach Brune with a proposal for an "honourable capitulation" and this was transmitted by General Knox* on 14 October.

The negotiations were brief. Brune at first demanded the return of the captured Batavian ships, but the Duke of York threatened to breach the sea-dike near Petten, which would flood the reclaimed land of the Zijpe polder. The Dutch generals were not much impressed by this threat since they had themselves spent the previous weeks flooding most of the peninsula to prevent the allied advance and knew that the process could be reversed without much difficulty, and they advised Brune to this effect. But Brune was not reassured and quickly agreed to a convention very favourable to the Anglo-Russians (later, credible rumours circulated of a number of "magnificent horses" given by the Duke of York to Brune as an incentive). In this, the Convention of Alkmaar, signed on 18 October, there is no mention of the return of any ships. The Anglo-Russian troops were permitted to embark without interference before 1 December. There would be an exchange of 8,000 prisoners of war, including captured Batavian seamen. The British agreed to return the fortresses at Den Helder with their guns in good order, and an armistice went into force immediately. The 49th Foot embarked with the 79th at Den Helder on 28 October and landed at Yarmouth, whence they marched to quarters in Norwich.[21]

Because the evacuation was carried out under terms favourable to the British and Russians, and the troops were extracted cleanly, public and parliamentary opinion was at first well pleased. Only later was the expedition counted as a failure. It had not been exactly triumphant for the Batavian Republic either, which had lost twenty-five of its fifty-five ships; nor for the *Directoire* in Paris, which soon afterwards fell to Napoleon Bonaparte's coup of 18 *Brumaire*. This coup ended the chaos of the revolutionary government and instituted a regime on the Roman model, headed by three consuls, who effectively shared dictatorial powers. Napoleon installed himself as First Consul, the final step towards his subsequent assumption of complete personal power as Emperor and the dissolution of the ideals of liberty, equality and fraternity that had inspired the revolution.

---

* Brigadier-General the Hon John Henry Knox (dates not verifiable).

CHAPTER FOUR

"An Immediate and Vigorous Attack"

COPENHAGEN, 1800–1801

After its return from the Helder, the 49th Regiment marched to Yarmouth on 1 January 1800 and from there to Bungay, where it remained until April, when it was ordered to Colchester. In June, the regiment marched to Hilsea Barracks near Portsmouth, where it embarked for Jersey in July 1800. It must have been a pleasant interlude in Brock's life, close to home and among people he knew. The regiment obviously made great efforts to recruit men, for by the time it was ordered back to Portsmouth in February 1801, its strength had reached 795.[1] There was time for relaxation as well, the officers receiving "many attentions" from the islanders, among whom "the fine person and manly bearing of Lieut-Colonel Brock are still favourably remembered."[2] Not so favourably though that Brock could find a wife. He was now thirty, still young for a lieutenant-colonel, but of an age to marry and with an income and a position in society able to support a wife and family. Perhaps Brock felt that, with war still looming, it would not be fair to marry and then depart for God only knew how long on campaign – perhaps never to return. He also knew from his own experience that service in, say, the West Indies would be a death sentence for a wife and small children.

From this time in Jersey a clue emerges as to the character of Brock's subordinate, Roger Hale Sheaffe, which was to come to the fore subsequently. James Fitzgibbon spoke highly of Sheaffe's abilities but had a low opinion of his ability to command respect, which was in sharp contrast to his view of Brock. While Brock was on leave in the summer of 1800, Sheaffe assumed command:

He was the best teacher I ever knew, but he was also a martinet and a great scold. His offensive language often marred his best efforts.... To such a state of feeling was the regiment worked up by this man's scolding, that upon the return of the senior officer, his first appearance on the parade was greeted by three hearty cheers from the men. This outbreak of welcome was promptly rebuked by the returned colonel and the men confined to barracks for a week.[3]

Fort Regent, atop a granite cliff overlooking St Helier, Jersey, where the 49th Foot was stationed after the Helder expedition, as it appeared in the early nineteenth century. (Author's collection)

The 49th was not the only military presence from the Helder expedition in the Channel Islands. The Russian troops could not be transported home immediately as the Baltic was freezing up. Under the Bill of Rights in 1689 that followed the Dutch invasion and the seizure of the English throne by William of Orange, the introduction of foreign troops into England had been prohibited. The Russians were therefore taken to the Channel Islands, where they remained until the following June. The graves of many, killed by malaria contracted in the Low Countries, still lie below Vale Castle in Guernsey. At first they were well behaved, but as usual with troops, too much hard liquor led to trouble of various kinds. One soldier was shot by a Guernsey farmer while stealing vegetables and this almost led to a revenge attack by a large body of Russians, which was averted by the personal intervention of Sir Hew Dalrymple, the lieutenant-governor.* When the Russian troops boarded their transports, the guns of Castle Cornet at St Peter Port were kept loaded with canister to prevent them disembarking again.[4]

The 49th had been ordered home as a prelude to active service, this time in the Baltic. The troops did not know the latter detail, for the regiment immediately marched to Horsham and began to settle in. James Fitzgibbon, who was there, said that:

> An express however, arrived the following morning from the Horse Guards, ordering our immediate return to Portsmouth. At Chichester an order met us to be on the south sea-beach at nine o'clock the following morning ... conjectures were rife as to our ultimate destination.[5]

In the aftermath of the Helder expedition, the eccentric Russian Czar Paul arranged a League of Armed Neutrality, joined by Russia, Sweden and Denmark, to enable free trade with republican France in opposition to the British blockade. The British viewed the League as very much in the French interest and a serious menace because it threatened the supply of timber and naval stores from Scandinavia that were vital to the British fleet. In early 1801 the British government assembled a fleet at Yarmouth with the intention of breaking the League. The British needed to act before the Baltic ice thawed and released the Russian fleet to join forces with the Swedish and Danish

---

* Sir Hew Whiteford Dalrymple, 1st Baronet (1750–1830).

fleets, which would produce a combined fleet of more than 120 ships. The British fleet was under the command of Admiral Sir Hyde Parker,* with Vice-Admiral Horatio, Lord Nelson,† as second-in-command. After much prodding the hesitant Parker sailed on 12 March 1801 with orders to close on Copenhagen and detach Denmark from the League by "amicable arrangement or by actual hostilities," followed by "an immediate and vigorous attack" on the Russians at Reval and then Kronstadt. The British fleet reached the Kattegat on 19 March, where Parker learned that the Danes had rejected British demands.

Attacking the Danish fleet would be difficult as Parker's slow pace had allowed the Danes to prepare their positions well. Most of the Danish ships were not fit for sea but were moored close to the shore along with powerfully armed hulks to act as a line of floating batteries off the eastern coast of the island of Amager in front of the city in the King's Channel. The northern end of the line terminated at the Trekroner (Three Crowns) forts, which were armed with sixty-eight heavy guns – firepower equal to that of a large ship-of-the-line. North of the forts, in the entrance to Copenhagen harbour, were two ships-of-the-line, a large frigate and two brigs, all rigged for sea, and two more hulks. Batteries covered the water between the Danish line and the shore, and further out to sea a large shoal, the Middle Ground, constricted the channel. The British had no reliable charts or pilots, so soundings had to be taken in the channel right up to the Danish line.

Parker had given Nelson the twelve ships-of-the-line with the shallowest drafts and all the smaller ships in the fleet, while he himself stayed with the remainder of the fleet to the northeast of the battle, screening Nelson from external interference. Nelson's plan was for the British ships to approach the weaker, southern end of the Danish defences in a line parallel to the Danes. As the leading British man o'war drew alongside a Danish ship, it would anchor and engage the enemy. The following line would pass outside until the next ship drew alongside the next Dane, and so on. Troops would assault the Trekroner fortress once the fleet had subdued the Danish fleet. Bomb vessels would sit outside the British line and bombard the Danes by firing over it; should the British be unable to subdue the strong northern defences,

---

* Admiral Sir Hyde Parker, 6th Baronet, (1739–1807).
† Vice-Admiral Horatio Nelson, 1st Viscount Nelson, 1st Duke of Bronté, K.B. (1758–1805).

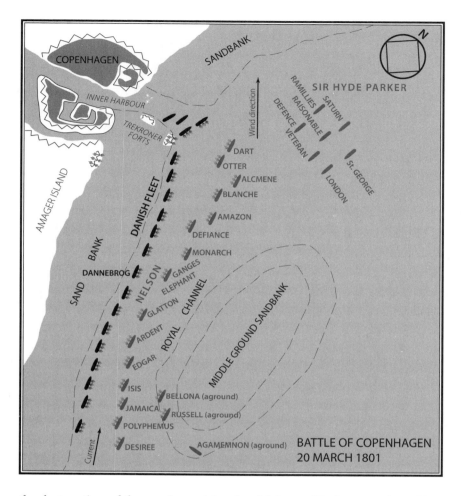

BATTLE OF COPENHAGEN
20 MARCH 1801

the destruction of the southern ships should, it was felt, be enough to allow the bomb vessels to approach within range of Copenhagen and force negotiations by threatening it with bombardment.[6]

As there were no marines available for the expedition, the army was called on to provide troops for the storming of the Trekroner forts. Detailed for this task were a company of the 60th Royal Americans under Lieutenant-Colonel William Stewart[*] and the whole of Brock's regiment, along with 500 seamen from the fleet. Although Stewart brought only a company, he was the senior man and had command of all the embarked forces – but it would

---

[*] Later Lieutenant-General Sir William Stewart, G.C.B. (1774–1827) commanded the 2nd Division under Wellington and was later a Scottish Member of Parliament.

Nelson's squadron passing the Kronborg fort, which controlled the entrance to Øresund and thus the passage to Copenhagen, 30 April 1801, in a painting by Robert Dodd. The ships are, from front to rear, *Ganges, Elephant, Glatton, Ardent, Edgar* and *Isis*. Brock was on board the *Ganges*; other contingents of the 49th were on *Ardent, Edgar* and *Isis*. (By permission of the National Maritime Museum, Greenwich)

be Brock who would lead the assault. Stewart's company was embarked on Nelson's flagship, the *Elephant* (74 guns); Brock himself was on the *Ganges* (74) under the command of Captain Thomas Fremantle,* with the rest of the regiment distributed on the *Defiance* (74), *Agamemnon* (64), *Russell* (74), *Polyphemus* (64), *Edgar* (74), *Bellona* (74) and *Monarch* (74).

The battle raged from 10 in the morning until 3.30 in the afternoon and it was here that Nelson made his famous reply to his signal lieutenant, that he had a right to be blind sometimes and he really did not see Hyde Parker's signal to break off the action. After more than five hours of heavy bombardment, a truce was agreed and negotiations began that later ended in the submission of the Danes. The intense resistance of the Danes had made any

---

* Later Vice-Admiral Sir Thomas Francis Fremantle, G.C.B., G.C.H. (1765–1819). The Australian city of Fremantle is named after him.

landing impossible and the 49th played a passive role. Even so, there were thirteen men killed and two officers and thirty-nine men wounded during the action, most of them on the *Monarch*. The detachment on the *Monarch* consisted of the inexperienced grenadier company of the 49th Foot, which may explain why they did not have the sense to take cover during the action. Brock's brother Savery was aboard the *Ganges*, putting his naval training to good use by helping to serve the quarter-deck guns. While pointing one of the guns, a grape shot tore off his hat and blew him over. A naval officer reported Brock's reaction, certain as he was that the shot had killed his brother: "I now hear Sir Isaac exclaim, 'Ah! Poor Savery is dead!' But Savery was not an instant on his back; in the same moment he rubbed his head, assured his brother he was not injured, and fired the gun with as much coolness as if nothing had happened."[7] Savery was a tall and powerfully built young man, over six feet tall, but even so it was a very lucky escape.

As the truce came into force, Brock went with Fremantle to the *Elephant* and watched Nelson write his celebrated letter to the Danish Crown Prince which opened the negotiations. There are undocumented stories that Brock and Nelson engaged in conversation when Nelson learned of Brock's connection to the then Captain Saumarez, which is certainly possible but any such account would be guesswork. The next day, Nelson landed in Copenhagen for talks. Lieutenant-Colonel Stewart reported that "the population showed an admixture of admiration, curiosity and displeasure." In a two-hour meeting with the Crown Prince, Nelson was able to secure an indefinite armistice. Negotiations continued by letter and on 8 April Nelson returned in person with a formal agreement. The armistice was reduced to fourteen weeks, but during it Armed Neutrality would be suspended and the British allowed free access to Copenhagen. In the final hour of negotiations the Danes learned that Czar Paul had been assassinated. This made the end of the League very likely and freed the Danes from the fear of Russian reprisals, allowing them to agree to terms. The final peace agreement was signed on 23 October 1801, but the Danes' resentment against Britain never abated and they remained strongly aligned to the French cause to the very end of hostilities in 1814 even when other allies and clients had dropped away.

On 12 April Parker sailed to Karlskrona, but the Swedish fleet declined battle. On 5 May Parker was recalled, his reluctance to push the matter having exhausted the patience of the government in London. Nelson assumed command and, leaving six ships-of-the-line at Karlskrona, he sailed east-wards, arriving at Reval on 14 May to find that the ice had melted and the Russian fleet had departed for Kronstadt. He also found out that negotia-tions to end the Armed Neutrality had started. With the situation changed, one officer of the 49th reported that they were treated "with the greatest attention" by the Russians;[8] on 17 May the British withdrew.

Most of the 49th Foot remained on board the fleet as it charted the great belt of Baltic sandbanks and bars before re-passing the straits and returning home. On 1 September the regiment was at Colchester, where its strength was reported as 796 and continued to rise as drafts were received. Mean-while, the Peace of Amiens, which brought an end to hostilities, was signed on 25 March 1802. Under this treaty, the British government recognized the French Republic and almost immediately began to reduce the strength of the fleet and the army. On 6 June the 49th marched to Tilbury and there embarked for Quebec, far from the seat of war with France and far, so it must have seemed to Isaac Brock, from the possibility of advancement and distinction.

CHAPTER FIVE

"Nothing Should be Impossible for a Soldier"

BRITISH NORTH AMERICA, 1802–1807

I n the late eighteenth century, Americans for the most part regarded France with affection for her support of their cause in the Revolutionary War. The beginning of the revolution in France therefore brought satisfaction in many quarters of the United States, but the Terror showed such an unacceptable face that, after the declaration of war by France against Britain in 1793, the U.S.A. continued to trade with both belligerents. Indeed on 19 November 1794 the U.S.A. and Britain went so far as to sign a treaty of friendship, commerce and navigation. This caused so much friction between the U.S.A. and France that in July 1798 Congress passed an act declaring the U.S. government free of all treaty obligations towards France[1] and even began preparations for war. In France, the Directory rapidly realized that matters had got out control and resolved to regain American goodwill, inviting the U.S. to send commissioners to France to negotiate a new treaty. By the time the commissioners actually arrived in Paris, the coup of *Brumaire* had made Napoleon Bonaparte First Consul and virtual dictator; Napoleon at once demonstrated his personal interest in the treaty negotiations by appointing his brother Joseph as one of the French commissioners, and the result was a significant diplomatic success. The Convention of Paris, concluded in September 1800, declared friendship and peace between the French and American republics.

The real significance of this convention lay in its provision for free trade and a lowering of tariff barriers, for even in 1800 Britain was piling up a large war debt which could only be serviced by exports of manufactured goods. Since nearly one-third of this export trade was to the U.S.A.,[2] any diminution of it must assist France. At the same time, Bonaparte was engaged in the negotiations with London which led to the Peace of Amiens in 1802 and in concluding the second, secret, Treaty of San Ildefonso with Spain. By this latter treaty, France agreed to obtain Tuscany for the Duke of Parma – brother-in-law to King Charles IV of Spain – in return for which the Spanish government agreed to cede the territory of Louisiana to France, an arrangement which was subsequently confirmed in the Treaty of Lunéville in February 1801.

The vast wilderness of Louisiana had been part of the eighteenth-century French territories in North America until forty years earlier and it seems likely that Napoleon dreamed of replacing the lost Canadian *Nouvelle France* with another, linking the islands of the Caribbean – Martinique, St Lucia,

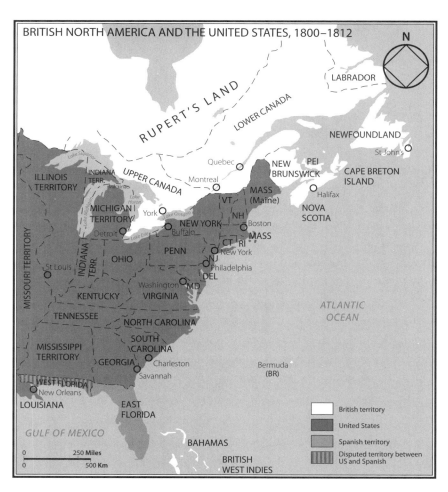

Guadeloupe and Hispaniola – to the Mississippi valley and thence into the centre of the continent to create a French-speaking new world which would overshadow Spain, Britain and the U.S. But France could hardly take possession of the territory while still at war with Britain, for to do so would only invite the British to seize it, and thus the Peace of Amiens provided the opportunity for Napoleon to secure the territory. However, the Spanish government insisted that Napoleon promise never to cede the territory to a third power.

The news of the deal seemed to President Thomas Jefferson* to renew the prospect of confrontation with France and pushed him to seek the purchase of what would be called the Louisiana Territory.[3] In January 1803 he sent James Monroe† as Minister Extraordinary and Plenipotentiary to Paris, and the matter was soon arranged. A treaty of cession was signed on 30 April 1803 which transferred Louisiana to the U.S.A. for 60 million francs ($15 million). On 20 December 1803 New Orleans became an American city and the size of the United States was almost doubled. To the British, the old Franco-American alliance seemed as much a threat as ever and its obvious target would be the Canadas.

Nearly 1,100 miles of frontier fixed by the Treaty of Paris in 1783 separated the United States and the two provinces of British North America generally referred to as the Canadas. The Constitutional Act of 10 June 1791 had created Upper and Lower Canada and given them the same sort of representative government enjoyed by Nova Scotia, New Brunswick and Prince Edward Island. The creation of two provinces meant that the Loyalists, who had fled the United States after the Revolutionary War, would now form the majority of settlers in Upper Canada and permit the introduction of British common law in both provinces. A series of acts were shortly introduced, which abolished the use of the French Civil Code in Upper Canada and provided for the use of the common law for criminal matters and the Civil Code for non-criminal matters in Lower Canada. In terms of religion, Crown lands were allotted to the Church of England in both provinces to

---

* Thomas Jefferson, third President of the United States (1743–1826), was the principal author of the Declaration of Independence from Britain that began the Revolutionary War.
† James Monroe (1758–1831), fifth President of the United States.

counter the influence of the Roman Catholic Church as well as of Protestant faiths based in the United States.

Each province received an elected Legislative Assembly and appointed Legislative and Executive Councils. Upper Canada was to be administered by a lieutenant-governor appointed by the governor-general of British North America, while Lower Canada was administered directly by the governor-general. The Legislative Council of Upper Canada was to have a minimum of seven members while that of Lower Canada was to have fifteen members, all of whom would hold their appointments for life. The Legislative Assembly of the upper province was to have at least sixteen members while that of the lower province was to have fifty. In both provinces the governor-general or lieutenant-governor had the power to appoint a Speaker and call elections but in neither did the elected assemblies control revenues nor were the appointed councils accountable to these assemblies. Although it solved immediate problems related to the settlement of the Loyalists, the Constitution Act of 1791 brought about a whole new set of political problems, some of which were common to both provinces, while others were unique to one or the other.

The province of Upper Canada, with its capital at York (today's Toronto), consisted of the territory west of the Ottawa River and by 1812 supported a population of 80,000. Most of the people of European origin lived in scattered settlements seldom far from the American border; the initial wave of pro-Crown Loyalists had been followed by Americans who came for cheap land and whose sympathies were generally republican. Lower Canada, by contrast, was more densely populated, with around 330,000 people, of whom over 250,000 were of French origin. The growing commercial city of Montreal lay 330 miles east of York and the fortified city of Quebec,* seat of British administration, was further east still. What connected the settlements was the waterway of the St Lawrence River and the Great Lakes, on whose navigation the government of this part of British North America depended. Another 400 miles eastwards, separate from the Canadas but closely associated with them, were the provinces of Cape Breton, New Brunswick, Prince Edward Island and Nova Scotia. Here the population was made up largely of English and Scottish immigrants and Loyalists, who all supported

---

* Unless otherwise noted, Quebec means the city often known today as Quebec City.

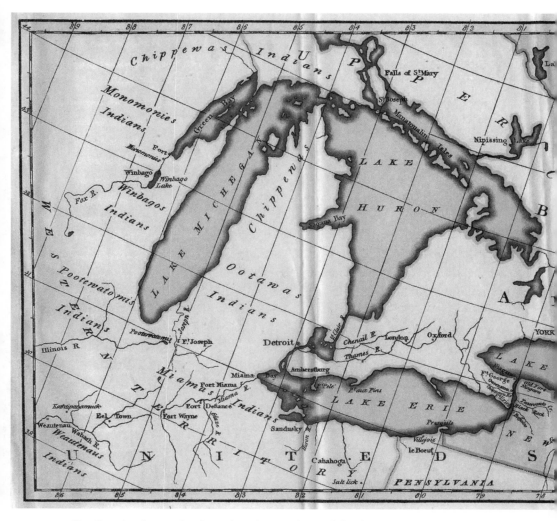

The Canadas, from a sketch attributed to Brock. (Cruikshank, *Documentary History*)

the Crown to the hilt: the Loyalists in these provinces later provided six battalions to the army before the end of the War of 1812, as well as maintaining
links to the anti-war states in New England, from where the British army
continued to be supplied in both peace and war.

There was little doubt about the loyalty of the people in the Maritime
Provinces or those of British and colonial descent in the Canadas, but what
of the French in Lower Canada? The coming of the French Revolutionary
War had brought great fear among the American Loyalist and British set-

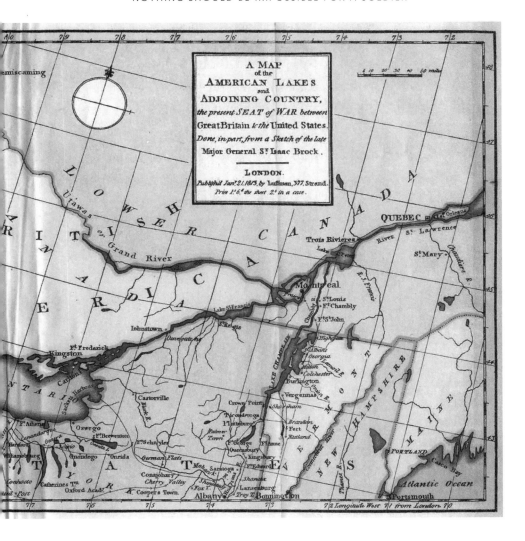

A MAP
of the
AMERICAN LAKES
and
ADJOINING COUNTRY,
the present SEAT of WAR between
GreatBritain & the United States.
Done, in part, from a Sketch of the late
Major General S.ʳ Isaac Brock.

LONDON.
Published Jan.ʳ 21.1813, by Luffman, 377, Strand.
Price 1ˢ 6.ᵈ the sheet 2ˢ in a case.

tlers in Canada, especially the former. Had they not lost everything in the American Revolution and did not the same fate perhaps await them once more at the hands of the French? The ethnic tensions which this fear had created were if anything heightened by the introduction of the Constitution of 1791, which created a representative form of government for the first time in the Canadas, since it tended to over-represent the non-French element of the population. Scare stories of invasion by French fleets, or from across the border in Vermont, only made things worse. But the beginnings of a rapprochement were created as early as 1793 by the lay, but more especially by the clerical, leaders of French Canada, who had quickly seen the revolution in France for what it was. In November of that year Bishop Hubert of Quebec* issued an unequivocal circular letter which stated that the "bonds which attached them to France had been entirely broken, and that all the loyalty and obedience which they formerly owed to the King of France, they now owed to His Britannic Majesty."[4]

A petition to the governor in 1805 from the new Bishop of Quebec, Michel Denaut, asking for full civil recognition, made the allegiance of French Canadians very plain, saying that: "Catholics have continued to have Bishops who, after taking the oath of allegiance have always exercised their functions with the permission of His Majesty and under the protection of the different Governors, the petitioner being the fourth since Canada happily passed under the crown of Great Britain."[5]

There were also loyal manifestos in Quebec and Montreal and votes of money from the provincial legislative assembly for the prosecution of the French war. Thus it was the French Revolution which first broke the emotional link with France, even though the distinctive French culture and language survived. Overcoming their own suspicions and then transforming this fear of revolution into an active ingredient of coalition would be a major challenge for Brock and his superiors in the coming years.

For Lieutenant-Colonel Isaac Brock and the 49th Foot, the voyage across the Atlantic and up the St Lawrence was long and tedious. It was not until 23 August 1802 that the first companies of the regiment, under Major John Vincent, disembarked at Quebec and transferred to *bateaux*, flat-bottomed boats 30 to 40 feet long, with a beam of six feet in the centre and with a removable mast for rigging a sail when the winds were favourable. Such a craft would carry up to 9,000 lb of passengers and freight but would draw only 20 inches of water. Bateaux were open, leaving their crews and passengers exposed to the elements. At the time the 49th arrived, fifty private bateaux were employed on the route from Montreal to Kingston. Up to thirty more, in government ownership, were used to move troops, engineer department stores and trade goods for the native people, employing a total of 350 men, who were mostly French Canadians.

---

* Jean-François Hubert (1739–97).

A journey lasting ten weeks to cross the Atlantic Ocean as far as Halifax, Nova Scotia, and then on another 1,000 miles to Quebec was not unusual. Quebec was the highest point on the great seaway of the St Lawrence that could routinely be reached by ships sailing directly from Britain – and that only during the summer months, for the extreme temperatures of the continental winter froze the water and closed the channel to navigation from late October to April. From Quebec, traffic would trans-ship into smaller craft to travel nearly 200 miles up-river to Montreal. Upstream from Montreal there was a series of rapids as far as Prescott, requiring every passenger and scrap of cargo to be repeatedly unloaded and moved by portages on the rough tracks that bypassed each rapids; but from Prescott to Fort George, by river and lake, was clear sailing, though often in the teeth of westerly winds. Montreal to Kingston was 180 miles, Kingston to Fort George another 160 and Fort George to Amherstburg almost 250 miles, including the portage around the great falls at Niagara.

With a length of 1,635 nautical miles, the St Lawrence River system is one of two great waterways draining the North American continent, the other being the Mississippi River, and before the development of modern road and rail networks, it was the principal means of communication from the Atlantic to the heart of the continent. The St Lawrence was the route followed by Europeans exploring and exploiting the interior of the northern part of the continent from the sixteenth century on. Relatively short portages allowed explorers using small boats to reach the other great river systems – the vast watersheds of the Mackenzie and Hudson Bay that provided access to three-quarters of what is now Canada, and to the south, the Mississippi system that allowed access to the Gulf of Mexico.[6]

Since 1802, the river has changed considerably: the construction of locks, the digging of new channels and dredging have drowned many islands, changed shorelines and inundated land where communities once thrived. Rapids that were once feared have been calmed and movements along the river simplified.[7] The average width of the upper St Lawrence in the nineteenth century was 1.3 miles, while the depth varied considerably. The many islands in the upper river created channels, only some of which were navigable, forcing all craft to travel by fixed routes both up and down the river and across it. As a result, traffic passed through several choke points so that from a military standpoint it was relatively easy to disrupt.

Fort George, as seen from Fort Niagara, about 1800. Fort George was a protected depot and administrative headquarters. Fort Niagara, on the American side of the Niagara River, was far better fortified. (Watercolour by Edward Walsh. Library and Archives Canada C-000026)

Along this long and vulnerable route came every immigrant, every traveller, every soldier and government official, every ounce of materiel, every letter from home. The entire burden of defence, communication and administration depended on controlling this waterway and by the time news from one end of the route had reached the other, any situation could have changed fundamentally. Orders could be irrelevant or downright wrong and therefore any official or military officer marooned at the far end of this thread would have to rely on his own resources, judgment and intuition.

Brock followed Vincent's detachment with the rest of the 49th Foot on 25 August; both wings were united at Montreal in October, where the regiment remained until the following summer. At this point, Brock shifted his headquarters to the small town of York with a wing of at least four companies detached under the command of Lieutenant-Colonel Roger Sheaffe to garrison Fort George at the northern end of the Niagara River, with detachments at Chippawa above Niagara Falls, Fort Erie at the eastern end of

Lake Erie, Amherstburg at the western end of Lake Erie, Sandwich at the northern end of the Detroit River and Fort St Joseph, a distant outpost at the northern end of Lake Huron, near the river from Lake Superior. At York, the grenadier company was quartered in a blockhouse at the east end of the town. The rest of the wing was quartered in the Garrison, where there was another blockhouse and a number of log huts beside Garrison Creek not far from the present site of Fort York. The eastern blockhouse was close to the Don River marshes and in July Brock noted that a number of the grenadiers

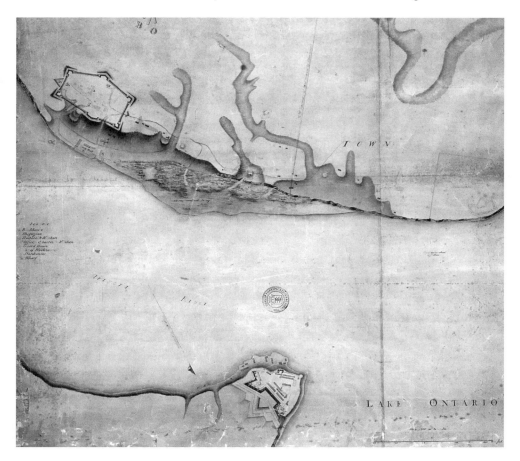

"Plan of Fort George, Upper Canada, shewing the Works of Defence ordered to be constructed in 1799" (detail). This plan, bearing the stamp of the Inspector General of Fortifications, shows the position of Fort George (upper left) and Newark ("town") in relation to the American Fort Niagara, across the river. (Ordnance Drawing Office, Royal Armouries Collection, H.M. Tower of London)

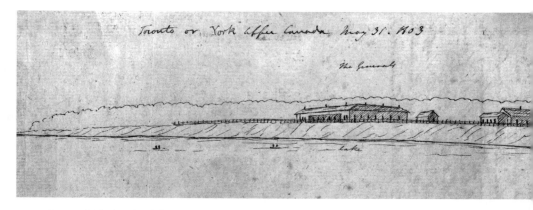

Pen and ink sketch of the Garrison at York in May 1803 by Lieutenant Sempronius Stretton. At left, on the west side of Garrison Creek, is "The Generals" or Government House. On the right, on the east side of the creek, are the blockhouse and huts, protected by a stockade on the land side. (Library and Archives Canada C-014822)

were "falling ill of the Ague and Fever," while men located at the Garrison "continued in perfect health." Brock therefore moved all the men into the Garrison, "although I am perfectly aware that they will find but sorry accommodations."[8]

The forts in British North America were low, square constructions intended primarily for meeting the native people, protecting the fur trade and giving reassurance to settlers; the main buildings were of logs constructed around a central square and strong enough to serve as blockhouses if an enemy should penetrate the outer defences. These outer defences usually consisted of a strong earth rampart with log palisade and firing platforms for infantry and the few artillery pieces that were the main armament. The main effort of Sheaffe's small force was on the Niagara River, which formed the border with the U.S.A., and which ran from south to north rather than east-west, from Lake Erie to its outflow in Lake Ontario.[9] This fluke of geography meant that British North America lay to the west of the river and the U.S.A. to the east.

In May 1803 the Peace of Amiens with France collapsed and Europe returned to war; Napoleon Bonaparte soon began gathering troops and barges on the French coast for a projected invasion of England. At home, the militia was embodied, units of volunteers formed and regular troops stood to arms. But out here in the Canadas, the duties of the garrison were hardly

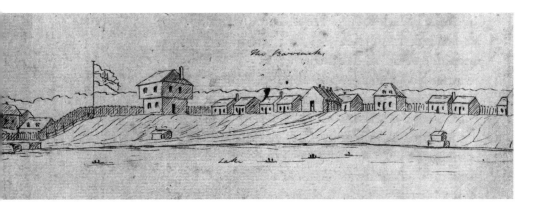

onerous; apart from the usual long hours spent on the drill ground there were only routine fatigues, patrols and guards. Neither was there much in the way of leisure activities, social life or recreation to engage the off-duty soldier – except drink. On the other hand, there was the lure of the U.S.A., from which constant efforts were made to encourage desertion from the British army. Once on United States territory, a man was free and stood every chance of making a new life where land was to be had for the taking. This was particularly attractive to the many Irishmen in the ranks of the 49th Foot; indeed when war did finally break out, there were documented occasions, such as during the British attack on Fort Erie in 1814, when the attackers were jeered at by the Irishmen fighting for the other side.

On 7 August 1803 Brock was woken by his sergeant-major, James Fitz-gibbon, who has been mentioned several times already. He was an Irishman from County Limerick, although a Protestant, and a man in whom Brock had taken a particular interest. Fitzgibbon was only twenty-two but had already been a sergeant at the time of Copenhagen, been reduced to the ranks after an altercation with Major William Hutchinson but later reinstated. He had then, while acting as pay sergeant to the grenadier company, undertaken an extraordinary journey from Chelmsford to the Duke of York's headquarters in London to sort out an apparent loss of money, later found to be an accounting error.[10] Fitzgibbon was dedicated to Brock, describing him as "the father of the regiment."[11] Fitzgibbon informed Brock that three men of the 49th had deserted while on sentry duty along with two others of the 49th and two men and a corporal of the 41st Regiment. They were later identified as Corporal James Carroll and Privates James Campbell, James Coughlin,

Matthew Cullin, Thomas Kennedy, Timothy Byrne, James Fitzpatrick and James Willis.[12] The men had stolen a boat and set out across the lake, probably heading for the U.S. garrison in Fort Niagara. Brock himself personally took charge of the pursuit, setting out from York soon after midnight. It was daybreak by the time he reached Fort George. Sending a party to search the American shore of the Niagara, a risky business as it involved a deliberate breach of U.S. territorial integrity, he himself scoured the Canadian shore. The party from the fort under Lieutenant Edward Chesshire, with a native scout, rounded up the fugitives and brought them back.[13] Although successful, the episode earned Brock a rebuke from Alexander Grant,* the lieutenant-governor of the upper province, for his having trespassed on U.S. soil without permission from above.

The austerity of military life in Upper Canada was not helped by the attitude of Lieutenant-Colonel Roger Sheaffe, who commanded the wing of the regiment stationed at Fort George. By all accounts Sheaffe was an old-fashioned disciplinarian, much given to flogging and confinement, and intent on curbing the opportunities for desertion by rigorous controls: limited walking-out privileges and no walking-out at all, even to go fishing, unless in full undress uniform. He tolerated no use of service weapons for hunting even when the men paid for their own powder and shot, hunting and fishing being about the only recreations available apart from drink. There had been frequent desertions from the garrisons along the border and the near-success of the desertions from York obviously encouraged some men of the 49th who had had enough of Sheaffe's torments. A plot was formed in the immediate aftermath of the desertion incident to murder Sheaffe and possibly others – or at least to confine all the officers – and to spike the fort's guns, plunder the ammunition and then to cross over to the U.S. Two deserters from the 49th who had previously made it to Buffalo, along with several Americans, were to meet the plotters at a house on the far bank of the Niagara.

By some mischance, the plot leaked out; it is said because of a conversation overheard during or after a meeting of the plotters in Knox's Tavern in Newark, for it was afterwards reported that the men were "cautious of opening their minds in the canteen." A frequent complaint among the Irish

---

* Alexander Grant (1734–1813).

at this time was the scourge of the informer, and an informer was certainly found – his anonymous testimony is preserved[14] – who gave away the gist of the plot. The informer was almost certainly Private John Daly, who had been approached to persuade him to desert, and the source of the leak may well have been Private John Fitzpatrick. Sheaffe, greatly alarmed, consulted his officers, who told him frankly that the mood of the men was ugly. Sheaffe, despite his failings as a leader of men, seems to have recognized his own shortcomings and, to his credit, also recognized that Brock could defuse the situation better than he could. Hastily, he wrote a letter to Brock and, so it is said, sent it by the hand of an NCO who may well have been involved with the plot, in the government sailing packet that afternoon.

The message reached Brock that same evening just as he returned from a shooting party. Reading it, and knowing the messenger, Brock formed the view immediately that he was in the conspiracy. One account says that Brock took up his gun and told the NCO that unless he gave the names of the conspirators then and there, he was a dead man; the NCO, taken by surprise, blurted out some names. However, since Sheaffe already had this information, it was probably in the note. It is also hardly likely that a known conspirator would have been entrusted with a letter sealing his own doom. It is far more likely that the captain of the packet carried the note, and since the packet was a government vessel, the captain was probably an officer of the Provincial Marine. Brock boarded the packet with Fitzgibbon and ordered it to turn round immediately and head for Fort George. The winds were contrary and it was noon the next day before they arrived, by which time the men were at dinner.

Various accounts are given of how Brock encountered the ringleaders. In one, the chief offenders were actually the sergeant and corporal of the guard, Sergeant Thomas Clarke and Corporal William O'Brien, which would indicate that the plot was to be hatched that day;[15] in another, he placed the officers at the doors of the barracks and went around with handcuffs to detain the plotters.[16] There were twelve all told, including a Private John Rock, who had been a sergeant until the previous year but had been reduced to the ranks. However he did it, Brock's moral authority was clearly strong enough to subdue any resistance. The plotters were all immediately shipped off to Quebec, where they were tried by court-martial along with the eight deserters from York. The charges were brought by Sheaffe and the trial conducted

Execution by firing-squad. This would have been the fate of those men of the 49th Foot convicted of desertion and mutiny at Fort George and elsewhere. The expressions of the victim kneeling on his coffin in front of his freshly-dug grave, and of those waiting their turn with their hair standing on end, are extraordinarily vivid; the closeness of the firing party to the target may also come as a surprise although it is an accurate depiction. (Library and Archives Canada)

by Brock's friend Colonel John Vesey.* Seven men from the 49th (Privates William Murdoch, Richard Company, Isaac Pope, Francis Quinn, Michael Lynch, Michael Morland and Timothy Byrne) and two from the 41st (Matthew Cullin and James Willis) were transported for life – either to the West Indies or more likely to New South Wales or the Cape of Good Hope. Six men from the 49th (O'Brien, Rock and Clarke, Privates William Clarke, Thomas Shughrue and John Fitzpatrick) as well as Private Thomas Kennedy of the 6th and Corporal James Carroll of the 41st Regiment received the death penalty and were shot at Quebec on 2 March 1804.[17] "The unfortunate sufferers declared publicly that, had they continued under the command of Colonel Brock, they would have escaped their melancholy end...."[18]

---

* John Agmondisham Vesey purchased a commission in the 11th foot in 1778; in 1804 he was a lieutenant-colonel with the Newfoundland Fencibles. He was clearly a friend of Brock, who helped him with the purchase of land in Upper Canada. He was promoted to major-general at the same time as Brock and sent to Sicily.

Brock hated the thought that men with whom he had served in combat in the Low Countries and at Copenhagen should have been brought to this:

> I cannot reflect on the dismal, but undoubtedly highly necessary, example, lately inflicted, on men who I have so long known, and in some instances had cause to praise, without feeling considerably.... This day being the anniversary of the victory of Copenhagen I wish to keep it with some degree of splendour but I feel my spirits are not equal to it....[19]

Brock was almost immediately ordered to take command at Fort George himself. Although insisting on good order and military discipline, it is clear that he at once eased the more vexing, petty rules and made the men's lives more bearable by providing facilities for sports, games and recreation and allowing them to go shooting or fishing. The men rapidly cheered up, as soldiers will, and desertions ceased. As to the cause of the mutiny, Brock wrote that:

> Whenever the command of the Regiment devolved by my absence on Colonel Sheaffe, he unquestionably required more from the Non Commissioned Officers, than I knew was useless [sic] to expect from them. He did not sufficiently study the character of the men and his ardent zeal made him sick with eagerness after perfection where it was not to be found. Sergeants, for trifling errors, were too often reduced … [he] has, I regret exceedingly to be obliged to observe, many enemies, who have been in the habit of propagating reports highly injurious to his character … he possesses little knowledge of mankind – I am willing to admit, however reluctantly, that his conduct has had some influence in producing the disgraceful transactions that occurred here … he has greatly fallen in the estimation of the men.[20]

Even by the standards of the day, when discipline was far more rigid than now, this is a damning indictment of a regimental officer which, had the 49th seen active service, would probably have resulted in Sheaffe's early death from friendly fire. Brock had not only a far better grasp of how to command a battalion and what regime of discipline to impose in a remote station than Sheaffe, but this penetrating insight shows that he also had a marked ability to judge character. However, in spite of all that had passed, Brock stood up for Sheaffe, whose career might have been brought to an end by this affair. Writing to the assistant to the governor, he stressed that despite Sheaffe's mismanagement of the men,

> Colonel Sheaffe's imperfections proceed immediately from an error in judgement. No man understands the duties of his profession better than Colonel Sheaffe, and to his abilities I own myself greatly indebted … the source of the mischief did not flow from him. It is to be found in the situation of the place and in the temptations which are perpetually offered to the unwary soldier.[21]

Brock went on the say that he believed that the lesson Sheaffe had received "cannot fail of opening his eyes to the necessity of regulating his conduct to the times and place" and that "the usual confidence" should be placed in Sheaffe, without which his position would be fatally undermined: "he must inevitably fall to the ground, and become the scoff and ridicule of the whole Regiment – on the other hand if he is judged undeserving of support, no scruple should prevent his being told that the good of the service calls for his removal."[22] The acting governor, Dunn, decided, it seems, to give Sheaffe the benefit of the doubt.

Winter comes early to Canada, and as the weather closed down normal activities in the autumn of 1803 Brock returned to his books both for his own amusement and to continue the education of Fitzgibbon, which had begun in Quebec. According to Fitzgibbon's own account, "At that time my ignorance of my real deficiencies was very great, and I thought myself master of the language. But … I went into Town the same day and bought a Grammar and Dictionary, Books which I had never seen before…."[23] After the thwarted mutiny, Brock told Fitzgibbon that "I not only desire to procure for you a commission but I also wish to have you qualify yourself to take your place among gentlemen. Here are my books, make good use of them."[24] Through patronage, Brock secured a commission as ensign for Fitzgibbon in February 1806, although the purchase of uniform and kit threw Fitzgibbon into debt to the tune of £150. Brock then appointed him as adjutant of the 49th[25] and three years later he secured Fitzgibbon a lieutenancy free of purchase. Fitzgibbon distinguished himself throughout the later War of 1812 and then settled in Canada, becoming a colonel of militia. He ended his days as a Military Knight of Windsor, thus repaying Brock's trust and patronage. It should not be thought, however, that Brock was an easy taskmaster. His

Irish-born James Fitzgibbon (1780–1863) fought throughout the War of 1812, including a remarkable victory at Beaver Dams against a much larger force, and went on to a long career in public service in Upper Canada. (McGill University Library)

much-repeated rebuke of Fitzgibbon at about this time speaks volumes. When Fitzgibbon failed to accomplish an order on the grounds that it was impossible, Brock snapped impatiently, "By the Lord Harry, sir, do not tell me it is impossible. Nothing should be impossible for a soldier. The word impossible should not be found in a soldier's dictionary."[26]

At some point in 1804 Brock met and then cultivated the acquaintance of Robert Nichol,* a Scotsman living at Port Dover who had considerable business interests in milling, brewing and distilling. To some, including James Fitzgibbon, it was a surprising relationship. Nichol, he recalled many years later, was a "mean looking little Scotchman, who squinted very much" and kept a "Retail Store of Small Consideration" at Fort Erie.[27] To be sure, a tradesman would normally have been considered unfit for the society of an officers' mess, even in so remote a location as Fort George, but the commanding officer is a god in the little world of his own regiment and Nichol's presence gradually became accepted. It seems, as later events bear out, that Brock recognized talents for gathering information and intelligence in Nichol which might be extremely useful. Nichol was, for example, an ardent and early champion of the development of canals in the Canadas. Brock asked Nichol to prepare a report, which was presented to the Assembly of the upper province as a "Sketch of Upper Canada, showing its resources in men, provisions, Horses &c." Fitzgibbon saw this document

---

* Robert Nichol (c.1774–1824) had emigrated from Scotland, held a militia commission as early as 1803 and was active throughout the War of 1812 though his businesses suffered severely. He was prominent in public life after the war until the end of his life (*Dictionary of Canadian Biography*).

in 1813 "and by that time every statement was proved to be most accurate and Valuable."

Late in 1805 Brock was selected for promotion to colonel,[28] and thus having passed beyond the power of purchase and patronage to the higher ranks of the staff – the highest rank held in a regiment of foot was lieutenant-colonel – he had to bid farewell to the 49th. Handing over command to Sheaffe, he took long furlough and in October 1805 went home to Guernsey. While there, he visited as many of his brothers and sisters as he could. His eldest brother, John, was dead, killed in a duel at the Cape, but William was doing well at his bank and Savery was still serving under Sir John Moore. Elizabeth and Mary were in London and Berkshire respectively, with their husbands and families. While Brock was at home, the newspapers reported Nelson's victory over the French and Spanish fleets at Trafalgar in October 1805, which established British sea control and ended the threat of invasion, and Napoleon's Grande Armée abandoned its camp at Boulogne, just across the English Channel, and marched east to Austria.

CHAPTER SIX

"The Most Volatile
and Easily Led Astray"

ACTING COMMANDER-IN-CHIEF, 1805–1807

Napoleon was not finished with Britain, and one of his weapons was economic warfare through his Continental System. This system had begun as early as 1793; that it developed as it did, however, was the result of Napoleon's inability to carry through the invasion and conquest of Britain. After this, the system was really the only way he could attack the British directly. In the aftermath of the collapse of the Peace of Amiens, French client states and allies were obliged to adopt the embryo system, closing their ports to British goods, but it was not until after Napoleon's crushing defeat of Prussia in 1806 that the Continental System was codified in the Berlin Decrees.[1] The important articles of the Berlin Decrees were, first, that the British Isles were placed in a state of blockade; secondly, that all commerce and all correspondence were interdicted; and third, in the fifth article, that all merchandise belonging to Britain, or coming from its factories and its colonies, was forbidden. The Milan Decrees in 1807 further extended the system by increasing the pressure on neutral nations like the U.S.A., but incidentally doing little harm to Britain.[2] Given that only one-third of Britain's trade was with Europe, while two-thirds was with the rest of the world,[3] it was the indirect effect of the system which most nearly brought disaster to Britain and which was to bring her into armed conflict with the United States.

In response to the Continental System, the British government tried to do two things: first, to keep open the seas so that any neutral nation, especially the United States, could trade with Britain. This the Royal Navy generally succeeded in doing, in spite of the best efforts of French privateers;[4]

British trade remained sufficiently lucrative to fund subsidies to her allies until the crisis of 1811. Secondly, the British government aimed to penalise any neutral state which adhered to Napoleon's system. The mechanism for achieving this was the Orders-in-Council, issued from January 1807 in response to the Berlin Decrees.[5] The first order stated that "No vessel shall be permitted to trade from one port to another, both of which ports shall belong to or be in the possession of France or her allies, or shall be so far under their control, as that British vessels may not freely trade threat."

Subsequent orders and a system of licences increased the pressure on both neutrals and states within the Continental System to defy Napoleon, and thus British goods continued to reach Europe in neutral ships, which were further encouraged by relaxation of the British Navigation Acts. After 1808 the licence system became a vital measure for keeping Wellington's Peninsular army fed, chiefly on American grain from 1808 to 1813, after which, following the destruction of Napoleon's army in Russia, more grain began to be available from that country.

In the United States, controls imposed by both France and Britain were bitterly resented, although it is doubtful if either President Thomas Jefferson or his successor, James Madison,* realized that the Berlin Decrees would bring on a total war. In 1807 Jefferson introduced an Embargo Act, which prohibited U.S. trade with all foreign nations. This act did far more harm than good to the U.S. economy, was widely ignored and was replaced in 1809 by the Non-Intercourse Act, which prohibited trade with either France or Britain until each dropped their blockade decrees. This act was intended to force both belligerents to abandon their controls, but again it did more harm to the U.S. than to France or Britain.

While Brock was on leave, therefore, relations between Britain and the U.S. were deteriorating badly. In the spring of 1806, things were judged so serious that the Canadian militia was briefly embodied for full-time service. Although the scare died down after a short time, Brock could not know this and he abandoned leave in June 1806. Without waiting for the regular packet, he left London on 26 June for Milford Haven, from where he sailed to Cork and there intercepted a Guernsey privateer, the appropriately named *Lady Saumarez*, in which he returned to Quebec.[6]

---

* James Madison (1751–1836), fourth President of the United States.

On reaching Quebec on 27 September 1806, Brock found himself temporarily commanding all troops in the Canadas,[7] following the resignation and departure of Colonel Barnard Foord Bowes* – who was later killed in June 1812 at Salamanca in Spain – and pending the arrival of a more senior officer from England. It was probably just as well that Bowes had left, for he and Brock would have been sure to disagree. Bowes was clearly a devotee of old-fashioned standards of discipline and turnout: not for him the comfortable, round, low-crowned felt hat worn in place of the cocked hat or the shako, or the loose trousers in place of breeches and gaiters. Inspecting the 49th Foot at Quebec in May 1806, he pointedly remarked that "The Regiment has been commanded by Lieutenant Colonel Sheaffe since 1st November 1805; great care and attention has been paid by that officer to his corps, which is much improved in appearance ... dressed conformably to His Majesty's regulations."[8]

This was a very big step for a young colonel, not long out of command of 600 men, and at an early stage Brock would have been exposed to the strategic debate on the defence of British North America. The British controlled the seas and had the largest navy in the world, but given their global commitments and the need to maintain a blockade on the coast of Europe, it was uncertain whether they could defend Upper Canada against the Americans. Several questions were always in the air. First, would Lower Canada be the centre of their efforts, or would that lie in Upper Canada? Secondly, was it desirable to keep all or part of the Upper St Lawrence? With the experience of having conquered Canada and now having to defend it, the British understood where the weaknesses were. These questions had been debated for twenty years and were not fully resolved before war eventually broke out.

Two defensive concepts emerged after 1784. The first can be described as a defence in depth, whose origins went back to 1793, when Lord Dorchester,† the governor-general in Quebec, wrote to John Graves Simcoe,‡ his subor-

---

* Later Major-General Barnard Foord Bowes (?–1812). He was married to the daughter of Sir John Johnson, the chief of the Indian Department.
† Sir Guy Carleton, K.B., 1st Baron Dorchester (1724–1808).
‡ Lieutenant-General John Graves Simcoe (1752–1806) commanded the Queen's Rangers and served with distinction during the Revolutionary War. He was the first lieutenant-governor of Upper Canada, 1791–1796, and is remembered for having ended slavery there. He later served as commander-in-chief in San Domingo (Haiti).

The city of Quebec in the late eighteenth century. In the centre is the Château St Louis, official residence of the governor-general. (Watercolour by Elizabeth Hale. Library and Archives Canada C-013096)

dinate in Upper Canada, saying that "should hostilities commence, the War cannot be confined to Upper Canada, and the greatest part of the Forces may eventually be drawn from thence, whatever may be the inconvenience of that Province."[9] There were simply too few troops to defend all of the Canadas against attack by the Americans; the British might, with what they had in North America, retain Quebec until the Royal Navy delivered reinforcements, which would allow Upper Canada to be regained at some future date.

The alternative view was that Upper Canada could be defended and Simcoe outlined a concept of forward defence in response to Dorchester's suggestion that Upper Canada would have to be abandoned. By improving the militia, relocating the garrisons, building up fortifications, developing better relations with the native people and maintaining "command of the water," the forces at hand could "act with an efficacy more than adequate to their insufficient numbers."[10] Simcoe held that if Upper Canada were not properly defended, the Americans would be inclined to sever communications with Lower Canada or send an army down the St Lawrence. The fall of Upper Canada would then be inevitable. If the St Lawrence was fortified, or at least its access from Lake Ontario at Kingston, this would "prevent the Subjects of the United States bordering upon the Lakes from entertaining the most distant hopes of carrying into execution their claim to pass down the River St Lawrence." Simcoe concluded that concentrating regular troops and resources in Montreal and Quebec would invite the Americans to try to do exactly what the British feared most.

At the time Brock assumed command, the British regular army in the Americas numbered some 35,000, although the majority, 23,000, were permanently stationed in the valuable colonies of the West Indies. Of the remaining 11,000 men, the largest contingent, 9,000, formed the garrison of the Maritime Provinces and of Quebec, with little left to send to the upper province or even Montreal. Of the troops in the Canadas, half were in five British regular regiments of foot and eight companies of artillery. These were the 6th, shortly afterwards replaced by the 1st Battalion of Brock's old regiment, the 8th; and the 41st, 49th and 100th Regiments, plus the 10th Royal Veteran Battalion after its arrival in 1807. The 100th was a very new and inexperienced regiment, as its high number showed, composed largely of Irish soldiers, who "are of all others the most volatile and easily led astray."[11] The majority of the men in the 100th were, however, Protestants of Scottish stock from the north of Ireland. The regiment began to arrive in May 1806, when the inspection return shows 232 of its 506 men (from an established strength of 950) in the Canadas.[12] Brock developed a high regard for the capabilities of this regiment and its commanding officer, Major John Taylor: "The good effects of his exertions and intelligence are strikingly visible in every department of the corps.... He has succeeded in establishing an interior discipline and economy, which I have never before witnessed in so young a corps...."[13]

Despite his good opinion, the 100th was too weak in numbers, especially as a shipwreck drowned one of the detachments of the regiment on its way to the Canadas, and too inexperienced to be dispersed guarding the outposts along the frontier of the upper province. This duty continued to fall on the 41st Regiment under Lieutenant-Colonel Henry Procter.[*]

---

[*] Later Major-General Henry Procter (1763–1822). He served throughout the War of 1812

Brock's 1807 inspection report on that regiment summed things up very clearly:

> The very great distance of the quarters the 41st now occupy ... its dispersed state and the many evils by which it is surrounded will, however great the zeal and intelligence of Lieut-Colonel Procter and the other officers, so far affect the discipline and morale of the men, as to justify my saying that both the zeal of the one and the other must, without the possibility of a remedy, progressively suffer in proportion as the regiment remains stationed in the Upper Province. The 41st Regiment, having a considerable number of old soldiers, is better calculated for that service than either the 49th or 100th....

The other half of the available troops were in four North American fencible regiments, raised by authority of the Duke of York in 1803. These were the Royal Newfoundland Regiment, the Royal Nova Scotia Regiment, the King's New Brunswick Regiment and the Canadian Fencibles. Although they were part of the British regular army, men enlisted into these regiments were bound to serve only in British North America.

The 1,200 British troops in Upper Canada were to be reinforced in time of war by the militia. This was some 4,000 strong in Upper Canada, compared with 6,000 in Nova Scotia and potentially 60,000 in Lower Canada. Since eastern North America had been first settled in the seventeenth century, militia service had been a part of life for all males aged sixteen to sixty. Their duties when called out included not only warfare, for which every man was supposed to provide his own musket, powder and shot (although few did so), but also physical labour. For the most part these men were unarmed and untrained and affiliated to sedentary locally based units of similar capability to their counterparts in the U.S., although some units of trained militia did exist.

By now Brock strongly believed that war with America was inevitable at some point and he set out to put the frontier in as good a state of defence as he could, given the limited resources left over after the demands of war with Napoleon and the security of the home islands and the most valuable colonies had been satisfied. While at home, Brock had put before

---

but after his defeat by the Americans at the Battle of the Thames in 1813 he was officially reprimanded and retired from active service.

Isaac Brock in the uniform of a colonel. This picture was the basis of a number of studies after Brock's death, but it is the only authenticated likeness of him during his life in the Canadas. It was authenticated by Ludwig Kosche in 1985. (Pastel, probably by William Berczy. © 2010 The States of Guernsey. By permission of Guernsey Museums and Galleries)

the Duke of York a scheme to increase the available forces in the Canadas without drawing on the field army at home, by raising a battalion of veterans. This was a bold attempt to deal with the problem of desertion across the frontier by unattached, dissatisfied young soldiers in isolated outposts, who were easy prey for seduction by the Americans, of which he wrote that:

... the artifices employed to wean the soldier from his duty, conspire to render almost ineffectual every effort of the officers to maintain the usual degree of order and discipline, and the facility with which it can be accomplished, exacting a more than ordinary precaution on the part of the officers, insensibly produce mistrust between them and the men.... Experience has taught me that no regular regiment, however high its claim to discipline, can occupy the frontier posts of Lower and Upper Canada without suffering materially in its numbers.[14]

The way to deal with this was to concentrate the regular regiments as a striking force under proper discipline in the larger cantonments while using the veterans and Canadian militia to garrison the remote outposts. Veteran soldiers, who had completed their Colour service with the regular army, and their families, would be given grants of land that would tie them in to the country, provide an incentive to defend the territory and remove incentives for desertion. Brock had presented his request for a regiment of veterans to the commander-in-chief at the Horse Guards, after which the adjutant-general, Lieutenant-Colonel James Willoughby Gordon,* who had been present at the meeting, wrote to Brock on 17 January 1806 to convey the commander-in-chief's "thanks for the communication of his very sensible observations ... which his royal highness will not fail to take into consideration at a seasonable opportunity."[15] The 10th Royal Veterans Battalion was formed for service on 25 December 1806[16] and arrived in Quebec under Major Donald Macpherson in 1807.[17] That it was accompanied by wives and families – initially at the rate of twelve per company – is borne out in its standing orders:

Soldiers (that are married to women that can earn as much as their husband's pay) and can eat well, are excused from messing with their companies; but if, on the contrary, their wives are idle, and trust to them for support, such men must be appointed to a mess, to prevent their being starved, and that the women may be induced to be industrious, on no other account will their husbands be permitted to live with them.[18]

Brock also renewed his acquaintance with the men of Glengarry, whom he had known in the Channel Islands in 1793. His old friend Father Alex-

---

* Later General Sir James Willoughby Gordon, G.C.B., G.C.H., Quartermaster-General of the British army (1772–1851).

ander Macdonell had emigrated to Upper Canada with a large number of Catholic Highlanders, dispossessed by enclosure and the Highland clearances. Macdonell introduced him to another of his clan, Lieutenant-Colonel John Macdonell, late of the Royal Canadian Volunteers, who proposed raising a regiment of fencibles from among the men who had established Glengarry County in Upper Canada, which when embodied would be stationed at Montreal.[19] Recommending this move in a letter dated 12 February 1807 – and the appointment of Alexander as its chaplain – to the Secretary of State for War and Colonies and well-known proponent of Catholic emancipation William Windham,* Brock pointed out that given the small number of troops available:

> This corps ... would be always immediately and essentially useful in checking any seditious disposition, which the wavering sentiments of a large population in the Montreal district might at any time manifest. In the event of invasion, or other emergency, this force could be easily and expeditiously transported to Quebec.[20]

Moves were made to raise the corps, but in 1808 Governor-General Sir James Craig wrote to Lord Castlereagh that their zeal exceeded their abilities and that he had found it impossible to raise the required numbers in a reasonable time and had therefore withdrawn his letter of authorization to the corps.[21] In the end, the corps was embodied in 1811 as the Glengarry Light Infantry.

One way to make the most of a small force is to increase its mobility and agility. In the Canadas, roads were few and badly made, all but impassable in bad weather. The obvious alternative was to use the inland waterways of the Great Lakes, control of which was the cornerstone of the defence of British North America. While many explorers, traders and soldiers had negotiated the Upper St Lawrence during the 150 years up to the end of the Revolutionary War, there were hardly any European settlers along its shores until the arrival of a significant influx of Loyalists in 1784. A total of thirteen new townships were established across what became Upper Canada. Within a short period, the population of the north shore of the St Lawrence between

---

* William Windham (1750–1810) was Chief Secretary for Ireland in 1783 and Secretary of State for War and the Colonies from 1793 to 1801 and again from 1806. His espousal of the Treaty of Amiens brought his temporary departure from political life.

Cornwall and Elizabethtown (later Brockville) rose by nearly 2,000, with more than 1,100 added to the Cataraqui area (later Kingston). By 1785 this rose to more than 6,000 people.[22] Their arrival brought a dramatic increase in the requirements for transport up and down the river to support the growth of settlements: food supplies had to be imported until agricultural production increased; manufactured and most finished goods also had to be brought in.

When the Loyalists arrived, there were no roads into Upper Canada. With the assistance of the garrison a highway of sorts was constructed from Montreal to Kingston, but even as late as 1812 only two sections were complete, from Montreal to Lake St Francis and from Cornwall to Prescott, and these were rough roads, which deteriorated rapidly if heavily used during wet weather.[23] Paradoxically, the best time to travel by land was in the winter when the ground was frozen, but a better alternative was to use sleighs on the frozen river. However, these did not have the carrying capacity to meet the needs of the increased population. There was neither a public nor a private commercial ground transport service until the winter of 1808, when a stagecoach began to run regularly between Montreal and Kingston using the frozen river. A regular fortnightly courier service between the same two towns was then established in 1810. Thus the St Lawrence River remained the natural transportation corridor on which boats could carry much more cargo than was possible by road during the open season. Water travel could be expensive, as every journey incurred added costs for tolls, towing, portage around rapids and wages, but for freight it was still a far cheaper alternative to road haulage. For example, to transport a 24-pdr gun from Montreal to Kingston cost approximately £200 (about £7,000 in 2010),[24] a fraction of what it would have cost to move by land.

Compared to the American side, the Canadian side of the St Lawrence became more heavily populated, its infrastructure more developed, and it was thus better able to defend itself. As the lifeline for Upper Canada, the St Lawrence was exposed to the United States but it was also the main route to move British troops into Upper Canada and a garrison was necessary for the security of the province. With the advantage of mobility on the waterway, the British could respond more quickly and in greater force to any American threat. The larger population also supported a larger militia, which could augment or support British forces. Thus the second-order effect of this in-

The town of York in 1804. In this view, looking eastward along the waterfront toward the mouth of the Don River, the insalubrious blockhouse, where men fell "ill of the Ague and Fever," can be seen in the distance. (Watercolour by Elizabeth Hale. Library and Archives Canada C-040137)

crease in population was to alter the strategic and operational concepts for the defence of what remained of British North America.

The lesson of maritime power at Copenhagen had not been lost on Brock, and here he can be seen applying the same principles of operational mobility and force projection through maritime power. His first priority was the consolidation of command and control. The Provincial Marine and the dockyards belonged to the commissariat, a civilian department under the Treasury in London. The Provincial Marine consisted of a motley collection of armed vessels, some of which dated from the time of the French and Indian Wars, which carried official dispatches, passengers and freight for the fur trade, but its main function was to be the transport service for the army, for which the militia could be called out to assist.[25] On 18 November 1806 all Provincial Marine and dockyard responsibilities were transferred from the commissariat to the quartermaster-general's department. This included the bateaux service: "The Batteaux Masters or others having Batteaux committed to their charge … will respond to and receive orders from the Quartermaster General's Department."[26]

From this time on the Provincial Marine was increasingly developed as a force capable of naval action in case of war. Under the assistant quartermasters-general at Kingston and Amherstburg, forty-one boats were to be kept in constant readiness and repair in the harbours of Quebec, Montreal, Three Rivers, St John's, Kingston, Fort George, York and Amherstburg. Its fighting vessels on the upper lakes consisted of the 16-gun sloop *Queen Charlotte* and the 6-gun schooner *General Hunter*. These were more than a match for the few small American craft in the area. On Lake Ontario the Marine had the 22-gun corvette *Royal George,* which easily overmatched the American 16-gun sloop *Oneida.* There were also three armed schooners on Lake Ontario and another on Lake Champlain, but none were fully armed, manned nor even properly maintained in peacetime. Much remained to be done before the force was ready for war, but with these administrative arrangements in place, it was at least more effectively run. This was a wise precaution and one that paid dividends when war came and the Provincial Marine was fully activated; it is fair to say that Brock's action in 1806 was largely responsible for the existence of the force that six years later provided naval superiority and command of the Great Lakes, thus making a successful defence of Upper Canada feasible.

As well as looking for ways to increase the dependable manpower and mobility of the army, Brock also put in hand a series of measures to improve the physical defences, especially of Quebec. British strategy in the event of a large-scale American attack depended on holding the fortress as a bastion and refuge, to which the army could withdraw and there await reinforcement from home along the vital line of the St Lawrence. In essence there was nothing wrong with this strategy given the need to apply strict priorities on resources; America remained an afterthought for the British government, which is hardly surprising. But the question which clearly vexed the British government throughout the decade was, despite the continued need to confront and destroy Napoleon, how could the naval and military power of England be exerted to end an American war as soon as possible? In 1807 Lord Castlereagh[*] re-stated the basic elements of British strategy in North America:

---

[*] Robert Stewart, 2nd Marquis of Londonderry, 1st Viscount Castlereagh, K.G., G.C.H., P.C., (1769–1822) was Secretary of State for War and the Colonies 1804–06 and 1807–09 and Foreign Secretary of Great Britain 1812–22.

There are only two capital objects which could fully repay the expense and danger of an [American] expedition. One, the seizure of the town and harbour of Halifax in Nova Scotia … the most important naval station in the North American continent, the other the capture of the fortress of Quebec, which would place them in the sovereignty of His Majesty's Canadian Possessions.

… your first object will be to preserve Quebec, to which all other Considerations must be subordinate.[27]

On land, a strategic and operational defensive was to be maintained, for establishing economy of effort here was the only way to support the main effort in Europe; once Bonaparte was defeated, attention would turn to "Brother Jonathan,"* but not before. As late as the middle of 1813, an exchange of letters between Sir George Prevost and Lord Bathurst† confirmed this; Bathurst told Prevost that "The correct view which you expressed on the two points most essential to the defence of the Canadas, the maintenance of naval superiority on the Lakes and the uninterrupted communication with our Indian allies."[28] Brock had already come to the same conclusion about communications from the work he had commissioned from Robert Nichol, but the plan still required the citadel of Quebec to be strongly held.

The net result of British strategy to date had been the neglect of all fortifications except Halifax. Brock found the defences elsewhere in poor shape, especially at Quebec, where the west wall of the citadel was in urgent need of repair and improvement, the artillery was old and insufficient to keep a besieging force at a distance, and trees and bushes had grown up, obscuring the fields of fire. Regular reports of the weakness of the defences had been submitted by the chief engineer and the senior artillery officer in the province in the half-yearly reports to the Master-General of the Ordnance in London,‡ and some proposals had been made, but these were mired in

---

* Brother Jonathan, or sometimes Cousin Jonathan, was the Americans' early personification of their nation from 1783 to 1815; he was displaced during the War of 1812 initially by the female figure of Columbia, but more and more by Uncle Sam.

† Henry Bathurst, 3rd Earl, K.G., P.C. (1762–1834) was Secretary of State for War and the Colonies from 1812.

‡ The Master of the Ordnance had, in 1671, absorbed the duties of the Master of the Armouries and become the Master-General, with a seat in the Cabinet. This officer was responsible

argument between the administration on one side and the Committee of Engineers on the other.[29] Of particular note had been the work of the military engineer Ralph Henry Bruyères[*] in 1802. His "Report of the state of the public works and buildings at the several military posts in Upper Canada" addressed to Colonel Gother Mann,[†] commanding engineer in the Canadas, and Mann's subsequent plans which, although he departed from Quebec in 1804, formed the basis of Brock's subsequent works. From his post in London, Mann did much to assist in engaging the Board of Ordnance and its resources to support the works.[30] Bruyères' document presented a dismal picture of neglect and decay throughout the Canadas. Urgency seemed in order after the episode of the USS *Chesapeake* and HMS *Leopard* on 22 June 1807, which resulted from the British government's instructions that HM Ships should seek to recover deserters and impress British subjects from American ships, even if they had American citizenship papers. Seeking to recover deserters, the *Leopard* had opened fire on the unprepared *Chesapeake* and in the course of this action several Americans were killed. Although a formal expression of regret was issued by the British government, President Thomas Jefferson issued a fiery proclamation on 27 October 1807 against "the many injuries and depredations committed on our commerce and navigation."

Brock estimated that the work in Quebec would require between 600 and 1,000 men every day for six weeks. There were not sufficient men in the garrison to meet the bill and cover all the other guards and duties. Brock turned to the civil administrator of Lower Canada and President of the Executive Council, Thomas Dunn,[‡] at Montreal – who had assumed the authority vacated by the outgoing lieutenant-governor, Sir Robert Milnes[§] – suggesting in a letter of 17 July 1807 that either civil labour or embod-

---

for providing the sinews of war and remained so until the Crimean War exposed the failings of the Board of Ordnance. His post was wound up in 1856, although both he and the Master of the Armouries re-emerged around the turn of the nineteenth century. At the time of this account, the office was held by John Pitt, 2nd Earl of Chatham, K.G., P.C. (1756–1835).

[*] Ralph Henry Bruyères (1765–1814).

[†] Later Major-General Gother Mann (1747–1830), an experienced engineer who drew up most of the plans that Brock put into effect.

[‡] Thomas Dunn (1729–1818).

[§] Sir Robert Shore Milnes, 1st Baronet Milnes (1754–1837) was Lieutenant-Governor from 1799 to 1805.

Detail of a map of Quebec by Thomas Jefferys, 1760. (Library of Congress)

ied militia be used.[31] The council replied that the only way of finding men would be to embody the militia.[32] This had been tried before but had met with disobedience. Did Brock have the means to compel men to their duty? And how were they to be paid and fed when they were entitled to the same rates as regular soldiers? This would cost around £30,000 from the civil exchequer.[33] Brock replied, expressing surprise and disappointment at such a defeatist attitude:

> Colonel Brock is therefore obliged to observe, that … coercively collecting a body of men, which, under such circumstances, would be of more detriment than service to the regular army. Colonel Brock cannot, therefore, look for any assistance from that quarter, but, should an emergency arise,

he is confident that voluntary offers of service will be made by a considerable number of brave and loyal subjects … even now several gentlemen
are ready to come forward and enrol into companies men on whose fidel-
ity they can safely rely.[34]

Brock received a similar lack of support over measures to establish a drill
ground on the old garden of the Jesuit College in Quebec,[35] over the cost of
maintaining the Indian Department[36] and over civilian encroachments on
military land. Undeterred, Brock pressed on anyway with whatever labour
could be spared, relying on his own study of fortifications to guide him. He
received more encouragement from home than from his own superiors, an
indication that his stock stood high in London. In July Secretary of State
Windham wrote back to him on various matters and, while telling Brock to
mind his manners when dealing with the King's representative, nevertheless
told him that a new governor-general would soon be appointed to resolve
matters. In the meantime Windham gave him authority to use the Jesuits'
garden and to pay the expenses of the Indian Department through the civil
government and not through the military chest.[37] A similar instruction was
sent by Castlereagh to Dunn, which despite its soothing tone of support
cannot but have left Dunn smarting.[38]

Over the course of the next year, the work went on; a hospital was built
and the ramparts were restored with the support of the Master-General and
the Board of Ordnance in London and under the direction of the Inspec-
tor-General of Fortifications and Works, Major-General Robert Morse. But
the most notable improvement was a grand battery of eight huge 36-pdr
guns, each weighing nearly six tons and capable of throwing heavy shot
to a range of one-and-a-half miles. These guns could dominate the whole
navigable channel and the heights opposite the citadel. The citizens dubbed
this "Brock's Battery"; however when the new governor-general, Sir James
Craig, arrived he named it the King's Battery, of which Brock in a letter to
his brothers in July 1808 said tactfully that this was "the greatest compli-
ment, I conceive, that he could pay to my judgement."[39]

Tensions with the Americans remained high for some time after the episode of the *Leopard* and the *Chesapeake*. In May 1808 Robert Nichol reported
to Brock that the American forts of Detroit and Mackinac had been strongly
reinforced and worse, that boats belonging to the North West Company

had been fired on and then seized by the garrison of Fort Niagara, opposite Fort George. Procrastination over repairing the defences of Quebec and of raising proper militia showed a want of resolution by the civil authorities in the face of such aggressive moves and brought the failings of the sedentary militia into sharp relief. Brock could do little about the former, but he could do something at least about the latter. On 25 July 1807, immediately after his rebuff by the Executive Council, he wrote to Castlereagh enclosing the correspondence and asking for instructions. His argument was that, first, the existing militia law was simply inadequate. Secondly, while an indiscriminate distribution of arms to the population would be "highly imprudent and dangerous," there were enough men of spirit who might be selectively engaged in an active militia. Last, that the argument about pay and rations was specious, for generally "in all British Colonies, of which I had any knowledge, they on all occasions defrayed their own expenses."[40] Brock followed this up on 6 September, shortly before the coming of winter could be expected to end direct communication by sea with England, with a letter to James Willoughby Gordon, the adjutant-general, advising that although relations with the U.S. were increasingly tense,

> The president [i.e., Dunn] has not judged it proper to adopt any other step, than merely to order one-fifth of the militia, which amounts to about 10,000 men, to hold itself in readiness.... The men thus selected for service being scattered along an extensive line of four or five hundred miles, unarmed and totally unacquainted with every thing military, without officers capable of giving them instruction, considerable time would naturally be required before the necessary degree of order and discipline could be introduced among them. I therefore very much doubt whether, in the event of actual war, this force could assemble in time, and become useful.[41]

On the other hand, the regular army needed militiamen to take over static duties so that the regulars could be formed and ready to meet an invasion. Many French Canadians had offered to form companies of infantry, batteries of artillery and troops of horse if only they could be supplied with arms – but Dunn had refused to do so.[42] The only effective militia in Quebec was the English battalion, described a year earlier by Milnes:

… most of whom have clothed themselves and by constant attention to drill are equal in appearance to regulars; of these there are 275 privates, independent of the Canadian (i.e. French) companies, who came forward on the same principle, except that few of the privates are equal to clothing themselves.[43]

As things stood, Brock felt unable to send any regular force out for more active duties as to do so would mean that the vital bastion of Quebec would be unprotected. This would be a lost opportunity, for the terrain and roads were so rough and the obstacles so many that a relatively small force should be able to cause great disruption to the invader.

… the Americans are busily employed in drilling and forming their militia, and openly declare their intention of entering this province the instant war is determined upon; they will be encouraged to adopt this step from the defenceless state of our frontiers; the means at my disposal are too limited to oppose them with effect in the open field, and I shall be constrained, unless his honour the president make exertions, which I do not think him at this moment disposed to do, to confine myself to the defence of Quebec.[44]

Finally, Brock told Gordon that Lieutenant-Governor Francis Gore* had arrived to take over command in Upper Canada and had asked for a detachment of regular troops. Brock had refused to weaken Quebec but had prevailed on Dunn to let him release 4,000 muskets and other stores – powder, shot and so on – from the arsenal in Quebec, leaving Brock with only 7,000 muskets for any militia force raised in the lower province. He duly issued 5,000 of these in September to the militia embodied by Dunn.[45]

To be fair to Dunn, he had called out the militia for a general review; he had ordered one-fifth to be embodied[46] – and they had obeyed. The *Quebec Mercury* newspaper described the event with great enthusiasm:

… never, on any similar occasion, could there be manifested more cheerful alacrity and zeal, than were shown on these occasions, as well by the Canadians as by the British. Numbers volunteered their services. The Artillery company, the two flank companies, and Captain Burn's battalion

---

* Francis Gore (1769–1852) was Lieutenant-Governor of Upper Canada from 1806 until 1815 (*Dictionary of Canadian Biography*).

company, who are the strongest and best disciplined of the British have, to a man, formally tendered their services....[47]

Moreover, Dunn had summoned the Council to find the best means to pay for their equipment and training; and he did urge Castlereagh to appoint a governor-general with combined powers over both the civil and military administrations as the best method of putting a militia law into full effect in the face of growing hostility and sabre-rattling in Washington.[48] Nor does Brock appear to have disliked Dunn: in his first despatch after assuming the post of governor-general, Sir James Craig reported that Dunn was generally held in high esteem, particularly by Brock, that they were on excellent terms and their disagreements were a matter of regret to both.[49]

From his point of view, Brock was facing the timeless struggle between the primacy of the civil authority and the requirements of sound military preparations. As a military officer he had analyzed the problem and worked out a plan to solve it in so far as resources would permit. He obviously made his feelings felt in plain words, for in May 1807 Dunn wrote at length to Windham in London complaining of Brock's tone.[50] Across the gap of years, one can sense Brock almost dancing with frustration as the civil authorities, probably afraid of provoking American wrath that they felt they could not in the long term resist, wrung their hands. "Ah," we can hear them say, "Dear Colonel Brock, you simply do not understand the bigger picture...." And in any case, administrations are seldom prepared to spend resources for pre-emptive measures until a problem has become a crisis and the crisis is staring them in the face.

A month later, on 16 October 1807, a letter from HMS *Horatio* in the St Lawrence announced to Dunn and to Brock the arrival of a new governor-general, Sir James Craig. Amid the smoke of a salute of seventeen guns, Craig disembarked and drove into the city of Quebec.[51]

CHAPTER SEVEN

"Craig's Reign of Terror"

THE CANADAS,
1807–1811

Sir James Craig was no stranger to North America, having served in the Revolutionary War. He had then gained further experience of colonial fighting and administration at the Cape of Good Hope, in India and in the Mediterranean. He found the people and the government of Lower Canada far from united against the coming threat from the south; most of the population, and therefore also the majority of the Legislative Assembly, were French, while the majority of the appointed Legislative Council were British. Although, as we have seen, French Canadians had no wish to welcome the Americans or Napoleon and had tried hard to make this plain, there was considerable and open suspicion by the British; and Sir James Craig's advisers were of course British to a man. The general feeling was that it only wanted the appearance of an American force to make the French Canadians rise in revolt and join the republic. American agents were undoubtedly active among the French, and American propaganda did much to increase division between the two nationalities of the Canadas. It is a fact that the French Canadians proved for the most part unshakeable in their loyalty when war did come, but at the same time the people retained a firmly French cultural identity and a belief that the Assembly, as representing the people, should govern them. The British, on the other hand, believed just as firmly that the King's representative should govern them.

It is not hard to understand British suspicion, given that Britain was engaged in a life-or-death struggle with Napoleonic France. Brock was not immune to this view – far from it – and as a Channel Islander his feelings should, again, not surprise us. Writing to James Gordon in September 1807, he felt that while the French Canadians might resist the Americans, "how far the same sentiments would actuate them were a French force to join [the

Sir James Craig, K.C.B. (1748–1812), Captain-General and Governor-in-Chief of British North America, 1807–1811. He began his career aged fifteen as an ensign, served throughout the American Revolutionary War and was badly wounded at the battle of Bunker Hill. (Engraving after painting by Gerrit Schipper. Library and Archives Canada C-024888)

United States], I will not undertake to say...."[1] Writing in December 1809 to his brother William, he said that "A small French force, four or five thousand men, with plenty of muskets, would most assuredly conquer this Province. The Canadians [i.e., the French-speaking inhabitants] would join them almost to a man...." This was one of the milder views that Craig would have heard from the moment of his arrival and his assumption of the offices of both civil administrator and military commander-in-chief.

What would the new governor-general have made of Isaac Brock? There was no question about his competence, despite his disagreements with Dunn; in a very early despatch, Craig wrote to Castlereagh underlining the creditable way that Brock had exercised the command[2] – which should have been discharged by a major-general: Brock had carried out the task as a very young colonel. He would have found, perhaps, no great intellect, but a fund of good sense and an agreeable companion very much at ease in good society, a firm upholder of military standards and discipline, but one who knew how and when to temper justice with kindness. Brock undoubtedly commanded respect and liking among his peers and his subordinates. William Hamilton Merritt,* for example, described him as "active, brave,

---

* Later Lieutenant-Colonel William Hamilton Merritt (1793–1862) was captured at Lundy's Lane in 1814. After the War of 1812 he was a member of the Legislative Assembly of Upper Canada.

vigilant and determined. He had a peculiar faculty of attaching all parties and people to his person."[3]

Brock was, although in rank only a colonel, already a considerable figure in both the administration and the social life of Quebec. The latter city was second only to the great naval base of Halifax in Nova Scotia. Smart society in Quebec, at least during the summer when many ships put in carrying visitors, was very active and the officers of the garrison, Brock among them, were kept busy. Brock wrote to his brother Irving in July 1810 that "Upwards of three hundred vessels have already arrived – a prodigious number." To his sister-in-law the following day he wrote that:

> The May fleet, which sailed from Portsmouth the 24th, reached us in thirty days.... We have been uncommonly gay the last fortnight: two frigates at anchor, and the arrival of Governor Gore from the upper province, have given a zest to society. Races, country and water parties, have occupied our time with a continued round of festivity. Such stimulus is needed to keep our spirits afloat. I contributed my share to the general mirth in a grand dinner given by Mrs Gore at which Sir J. Craig was present, and a ball to a vast assemblage of all descriptions.[4]

Only a month after he arrived, Craig issued a general order in which he spoke favourably of the militia and exhorted the soldiers to be particularly vigilant against American agents, an order that raised fears of imminent war. In fact an American invasion was unlikely in the depth of winter and Craig probably felt reasonably secure. His military strength had increased with the arrival of the 10th Royal Veterans and he had received the 98th Regiment from Halifax before the St Lawrence froze. He wasted no time in putting the militia on a sounder footing, issuing a Militia General Order to the inhabitants of Lower Canada on 24 November 1807 telling them to maintain readiness.[5] He requested more arms from the Board of Ordnance in November 1807 for both the upper and lower provinces.[6] Lieutenant-Governor Gore mustered the militia of the upper province in December 1807, issued arms, drafted every fourth man for short notice call-out and ordered drills twice a week under regular NCOs from the garrisons.[7] Opening the Legislative Assembly on 29 January 1808, Craig again spoke warmly of the militia and referred to the menace of Napoleonic France: "... an implacable enemy is exerting every resource of his power, hitherto unexampled in the world,

A garden party given by Sir James Craig at Spencer Wood (today Bois-de-Coulonge park). This picture gives an excellent impression of civil and military dress and manners of the day; the band of the 100th Foot can be seen playing in the foreground. (Print after a watercolour by George Heriot in 1809, courtesy of Dianne Graves)

and which is controlled by no justice or humanity in attempting our ruin."[8]

Behind Craig's preparations lay a hard look at the strategic possibilities for the defence of British North America and he clearly came to the same view as Lord Dorchester: that is, that Upper Canada might have to be abandoned. In December 1807 Craig outlined the orders he had received for defending Canada to Lieutenant-Governor Gore:

> ... the preservation of Quebec as the object of my first and principal consideration, and that to which all others must be subordinate. It is the only post, defective as it is in many respects, that can be considered tenable for a moment ... [it affords] the only door for future entry of that force which it might be found expedient, and which the King's Government might be then able to send for the recovery of both [Upper and Lower Canada] or either ... for if the Americans are really determined to attack these provinces ... I fear it would be in vain for us to flatter ourselves with hopes of making any effectual defence of the open country, unless powerfully assisted from home.[9]

Craig thus underlined the primacy of maintaining Quebec but said later in the same letter that in the event of war he would not try to hold any other part of Lower Canada; rather, he would send all available regulars and trained militia to the upper province to harass the rear of an invading force. Gore not surprisingly agreed with this policy, but pointed out that with the likely force ratios (or relative strengths), only a partial defence would be possible, although this should be concealed from the population generally and thus from American spies and agitators.[10]

Craig's view of the nearness of the enemy found an echo in London, in spite of the demands of the war in Spain, which was just beginning, and the drain on manpower for the maintenance of colonies in the West Indies, the Cape and the Mediterranean. Spain, a once powerful country that for centuries had been France's rival, had been transformed by Napoleon's treachery through the secret treaty of San Ildefonso into a vassal: the country was invaded and occupied, King Ferdinand imprisoned and replaced by the Emperor's brother Joseph. In dishonouring Spain, Napoleon triggered first a popular revolt and then a British intervention in both Spain and Portugal. Napoleon himself defeated the British expedition in Spain under Sir John Moore, who was killed during the evacuation of the force from Corunna on 16 January 1809. The British main effort then switched to Portugal, where Sir Arthur Wellesley, escaping the censure accorded two more senior generals for concluding the Convention of Cintra and allowing a beaten French army to escape, was placed in command of the British, Hannoverian and Portuguese armies. The Peninsular War demanded a force that rose to 55,000 men, formed into nine divisions, augmented by Portuguese and German troops, not counting those employed in Catalonia. It would continue for the next five years, a constant drain on French resources that became known as "the Spanish ulcer." Napoleon had made a fatal strategic miscalculation which, when later combined with the Russian campaign and the adverse effects of the Continental System, brought him down.

By 1813 the strength of the British regular army would increase to 255,000 men, of which the largest proportion was deployed for the defence and internal security of the British Isles – especially Ireland. But in early 1808 this was all far in the future. For now, the British government was sufficiently alarmed by the evidence of American (and possibly French) aggressive tendencies following the *Leopard* affair that a considerable re-inforcement of 3,000 men, including two companies of artillery and the 1st Battalions of the 7th, 8th and 23rd Regiments of Foot, under Sir George Prevost,* was despatched to Halifax; further reinforcement was not ruled out. There was also a direct warning that "although measures will be taken to support with regular troops His Majesty's American subjects, yet much of the exertion must be made by the people themselves."[11] To enable the militia to be properly trained and equipped, 16,000 muskets and uniforms and camp stores for 10,000 men would also be sent, along with a supply of money in gold, quantified in later despatches as £100,000,[12] although equip-ment would only be issued in case of actual mobilisation. In addition, six regular lieutenant-colonels were despatched to the Canadas as inspecting field officers, to oversee the training of the militia. The control of this force clearly remained in the hands of Prevost, who would make two companies ready to move to Quebec at short notice, but otherwise there was "no time to be lost in establishing communication with Sir G. Prevost, so that in case of attack the forces may be moved to the proper quarter." Gore agreed with the policy;[13] in March 1808 the Consolidated Militia Act was approved by the legislature of Upper Canada, providing the necessary authority.

By the end of the spring session of the Legislative Assembly of Lower Canada in 1809, the threat from France and the subversion of the French population of the Canadas by French and American agents had clearly be-come inseparable in Craig's mind. On 15 May he summoned the Assembly to the house of the Legislative Council and announced his intention of dis-solving the Assembly, saying:

> When I met you at the commencement of the present session, I ... expect-ed from you a manly sacrifice of all personal animosities and individual dissatisfaction, a watchful solicitude for the concerns of your country, and a steady perseverance in the executing of your public duty with zeal and despatch. I looked for earnest endeavour to promote the general harmony of the Province, and a cheerful abstinence from whatsoever might have a tendency to disturb it, for due and therefore indispensible attention to the other branches of the Legislature, and for prompt and cheerful co-operation and assistance in whatever might conduce to the happiness and

---

* Major-General (later Lieutenant-General Sir) George Prevost, Bt (1767–1816).

welfare of the colony.... I am sorry to add that I have been disappointed in all these expectations.[14]

This speech inaugurated what became known among the French Canadians as "Craig's reign of terror." The governor-general seemed capable of seeing only the possibility of treason and latent Bonapartism in the French community;[15] he suppressed the radical newspaper *Le Canadien* and locked up its editors without trial; he went so far as to propose the revocation of the Constitutional Act of 1791 and the reorganization of the Canadas in order to nullify French influence – even at the cost of favouring recent American settlers, who were much disliked by the French and whose loyalty was highly dubious. The French in the Canadas disliked these settlers partly because they stood for the same breakdown of established authority as the revolutionaries in France, and partly because they feared being swamped by a hostile population.[16]

Brock, with Craig's arrival, had been relieved of his responsibilities as commander-in-chief of all forces in both provinces and he now held the command of the forces in Lower Canada only, with his headquarters in Montreal. There is no doubt that at this point Brock agreed with Craig's assessments. Writing to his brother William in late 1809, he remarked that:

> It may appear surprising that men, petted as they have been and indulged in every thing that they could desire, should wish for a change [i.e., from British to American rule]. But so it is.... How essentially different are the feelings of the people from when I first knew them. The idea prevails among them that Napoleon must succeed, and ultimately get possession of these provinces. The bold and violent are becoming every day more audacious.... The governor will, it is foreseen, have a difficult card to play next month with the assembly, which is really getting too daring and arrogant.

Later Brock wrote that Craig had completely mastered the French interest in Lower Canada and showed real contempt for the French:

> By their conduct they have fully exemplified the character of their ancestors. The moment they found they could not intimidate by threats, they became as obsequious as they had been violent. The house of assembly passed every bill required of them....[17]

When in March 1808 Craig moved Brock to Montreal and gave him the style of brigadier-general, then an appointment rather than a rank (in that it conferred on a colonel the authority to command a formation of brigade size), it was an obvious sign of approval of all that he had done in the face of opposition from the civil government.[18] Here he was close to his old regiment, the 49th Foot, in whom he retained great interest and affection. He wrote to his brothers in July that:

> I get on pretty well here, but this place loses at this season the undoubted advantage it possesses over Quebec in winter ... the weather has been exceedingly hot the last week, the thermometer fluctuating from 94 degrees to 100 degrees in the shade.[19]

In September Brock returned to command the troops in Quebec, having been superseded by the arrival of Major-General Gordon Drummond* as commander of the forces in Lower Canada. "I do not approve much of the change," he wrote to his brothers on 5 September,

> as being separated from the 49th is a great annoyance to me.... My nominal appointment has been confirmed at home, so that I really am a brigadier. Were the 49th ordered hence, the rank would not be a sufficient inducement to keep me in this country. In such a case, I would throw it up willingly.

Brock kept up a lively correspondence with his brothers and sisters, allowing for the lapse of at least twelve weeks for a return trip to bring mail, even longer in winter. Writing to Irving in July 1810 to thank him for making purchases on his promotion to brigadier, he said: "The different articles arrived in the very best order, with the exception of the cocked hat which has not been received – a most distressing circumstance, as, from the enormity of my head, I find the utmost difficulty in getting a substitute in this country."[20] There were also frequent references to his nephews and nieces, especially Maria and Zelia Potenger and Henrietta Tupper, and thanks for letters from them.

Much of Brock's routine work focused on the inspection of British and Canadian units; what he found often left much to be desired. In his inspection report to the Horse Guards on the Canadian Fencible Regiment

---

* Later General Sir Gordon Drummond, K.C.B. (1772–1854).

in June 1810, for example, he remarked on "the incapacity of the greater part of the captains, [which has] … presented difficulties not easily surmounted." He went on: "From the advanced age of several of the captains … no great assistance can reasonably be expected from them in the field."[21] This situation was created by the presence of a number of captains holding temporary rank in the Canadian Fencibles, as in other regiments. As a measure of economy when the regiment was formed in 1803, the Horse Guards had laid down that five of the captains would come from British regular regiments and have permanent rank, while the remaining five vacancies would be filled from other fencible or even militia regiments and would have temporary rank. When Brock made his inspection, there were six captains with temporary rank and only four with permanent rank. The average age of the temporary captains was fifty, while that of the permanent captains was thirty-seven. Nor had the temporary captains any experience of training troops.[22]

In the Iberian Peninsula, in the late summer of 1810, Sir Arthur Wellesley's army had just completed its withdrawal back behind the lines of Torres Vedras, having scorched the earth in its wake, and settled in for the winter, while the French armies suffered from lack of food, fuel, shelter – and from the unwelcome attentions of the guerrillas along their lines of communication. There, reputations were being made on active service whereas Brock was faced with mundane tasks while others were fighting. No wonder that his desire to return to England and thence to Portugal was undiminished, as his reference to leaving with the 49th if they were ordered home demonstrated. Craig's opinion of Brock was, however, too high to allow him to go. Writing to his sister-in-law, Mrs William Brock, in June 1810, Brock said that:

> The spirit of insubordination lately manifested by the French-Canadian population of this colony naturally called for precautionary measures, and our worthy chief is induced, in consequence, to retain in this country those on whom he can best confide. I am highly flattered in being reckoned among that number…. Some unpleasant events have likewise happened in the upper country, which have occasioned my receiving intimation to proceed thither…. Should, however, a senior brigadier to myself come out in the course of the summer, I shall certainly be fixed in the upper province, and there is every probability of such an addition very soon.

Since all my efforts to get more actively employed have failed, since fate decrees that the best portion of my life is to be wasted in inaction in the Canadas, I am rather pleased with the prospect of removing upwards.[23]

In July 1810 Quebec witnessed the arrival of Brigadier-General Francis, Baron de Rottenburg,* a former general of the French Royal Army, who had fought for the freedom of Poland against Russia. Rottenburg had joined one of the foreign corps raised by the British from 1795 onwards. In 1798 he raised the 5th Battalion of the 60th Royal Americans and wrote a standard text on the training and employment of light troops, the *Regulations for the Exercise of Riflemen and Light Infantry*. In 1809 he commanded a brigade in the Walcheren campaign and now he was to take command in Quebec, while Brock was sent to command the military forces in the upper province. This was purely a matter of precedence for Rottenburg was some years Brock's senior, but Rottenburg also possessed the patronage of the Duke of York, who had ordered his manual to be brought to the attention of all British officers. He had the added advantage of a young, beautiful and popular wife. "It is vanity in the extreme," wrote Lieutenant-Colonel William Thornton,† the Military Secretary,

> To attempt to describe the general admiration and estimation of his cara et dolce sposa; she is young (twenty-three,) fair, beautiful, – lively, discreet, witty, affable, – in short, so engaging, or rather so fascinating, that neither the courier nor my paper will admit to doing her justice.[24]

Brock's move had been in the wind for some time, as has already been noted. Writing to his sister-in-law on 10 July, he said that:

> I return this moment from waiting upon Sir James, who sent for me, to say he regretted he must part with me, as he found it absolutely necessary that I should proceed upwards without delay. I am placed in a very awkward predicament, as my stay in that country depends wholly upon contingencies. Should a brigadier arrive I am to be stationary, but otherwise return to Quebec.... Unless I take up every thing with me, I shall

---

* Later Major-General Francis de Rottenburg (1757–1832).

† Later Lieutenant-General Sir William Thornton, K.C.B. (c.1779–1840), Colonel of the 85th Regiment.

be miserably off, for nothing beyond eatables is to be had there; and in case I provide the requisites to make my abode in the winter in any way comfortable, and then be ordered back, the expense will be ruinous.[25]

He had grown to like Quebec and had made himself thoroughly at home. If he moved lock, stock and barrel to York he might just as quickly be summoned back by Craig. "But I must submit to all this without repining, and since I cannot get to Europe I care little where I am placed ... I have the most beautiful garden imaginable [in Quebec] with an abundance of melons and other good things, all of which I must now desert!"

To describe Brock's new command as dispersed would be akin to describing the Sahara as being somewhat on the dry side. The population of Upper Canada was small by comparison with the lower province but it was growing – not least through immigration from the U.S.A. One contemporary estimate put it at 77,000 of whom only one in six could be accounted a Loyalist.[26] This contrasted unfavourably with the total of 677,000 Americans spread throughout the states of New York, Kentucky, Ohio and northwestern Pennsylvania and the territories of Illinois, Indiana and Michigan – although, as has been noted, close to the border along the waterway the local population was sparser on the American side. Brock wrote soon after his arrival that the country was "getting very populous and rich ... Quakers especially come in great numbers, and bring with them large sums."[27]

At the furthest extremity of his command was Fort St Joseph, 1,500 miles from Quebec, on the island of that name at the head of Lake Huron and close to the connecting waterway with Lake Superior. It was a small post consisting of a stockade enclosing a blockhouse garrisoned, in June 1812,* by a detachment of the Royal Artillery and one company of the 10th Royal Veterans. Its original purpose, like that of the old British, now American, Fort Michilimackinac (or Mackinac as it was more properly called) which lay about forty miles to the southwest on an island close to the entrance to Lake Michigan, was to provide an assembly point for trading and parley with the native people and some reassurance to the fur trappers and traders.

From St Joseph, the frontier ran for 200 miles down the centre of Lake

* The figures that follow for the strength of the various garrisons is that up to June 1812, immediately before the declaration of war by the United States.

Huron, whose shores were remote, forested and largely uninhabited, until it met the St Clair River and the small lake of that name, and then south again down the twenty miles of the Detroit River to Lake Erie, an area which was already more heavily settled and farmed along the banks of the river. A couple of miles down the Detroit River was the former British Fort Lernoult, now the American Fort Detroit, and farther down, at the southern end of the river on the Canadian side, was Amherstburg, a village of about 100 houses. Amherstburg was the arsenal and dockyard of the Provincial Marine on the upper lakes as well as another rallying point for the native people. Its fort, Malden, was in poor shape and Brock made sure it was put into better order by the end of 1811. Its regular garrison consisted of a detachment of the Royal Artillery, a detachment of the 100th Regiment commanded by Major John Taylor, which Brock increased to 120 men – two companies – of the 41st Regiment under the command of one of the inspecting officers of militia on his staff, Lieutenant-Colonel Thomas Bligh St George. In addition, there were in theory about 500 militia available.

From Amherstburg the frontier turned slightly north of east, through Lake Erie. On the southern side of Erie were three more American outposts: Sandusky on the lake shore; and Forts Meigs and Miami on the Maumee River near today's ciry of Toledo. On the Canadian side, the settlement pattern began to thicken along the 220 miles or so of the lake shore, through Moraviantown on the Thames River, Port Talbot and its surrounding settlements and Port Dover. At the eastern end of Lake Erie was the fort of the same name, which was held by one company of the 41st Foot, opposite the village of Buffalo in the United States.

From Fort Erie, the frontier turned northwards along the thirty-six miles of the Niagara River to its outflow into Lake Ontario. The next outpost on this section of the border was Chippawa with a small regular garrison of about thirty men from the 41st Regiment and opposite it, the American Fort Schlosser. Just downstream from Chippawa, divided in two by Goat Island, were the huge falls, where the untrammelled mass of waters thundered out of the upper lakes. The site of the falls was marked constantly by a cloud of vapour visible for miles. In modern times, although still an awe-inspiring sight, the diversion of water through tunnels to generate hydroelectric power has reduced the flow over the falls to around half of what it would have been in 1811. Over the last 15,000 years the falls have eroded their way upstream at the rate of about three feet every year from their original location at present-day Queenston, with the result that north of the falls the Niagara River flows through a deep gorge almost ten miles long. This gorge was a considerable obstacle to lateral movement, for as well as the difficulty of actually crossing the fast-flowing water in oared boats or sailing craft, there were few places where it was possible to bring horses, guns and wheeled vehicles down to the river and then up the opposite side. Because of the difficulty of navigation, this was one of the few stretches of the frontier to have a good all-weather portage road running parallel to the river on both the American and the Canadian sides, on which freight was moved by land around the falls and the gorge, and it was thus a prime site for an American attack.

Another three miles north was Queenston and opposite this village, the American village of Lewiston. At the northern end of the Niagara frontier lay Fort George, the military headquarters and principal depot of the upper province, and the small town of Newark (today's Niagara-on-the-Lake). The troops in Fort George consisted of a company of artillerymen and 400 men, or three companies, of the 41st Foot, all under the command of Colonel Henry Procter. About a mile away on the American side where the Niagara River opened into Lake Ontario was Fort Niagara, a formidable fortification that had first been established by the French as early as 1671, had been captured and heavily fortified by the British and then handed over to the United States in 1796.

From the outflow of the Niagara River the border followed the middle of Lake Ontario, the lowest of the Great Lakes system, for about 140 miles to where its outflow marked the beginning of the St Lawrence River, at Kingston, the easternmost permanent garrison in Brock's jurisdiction. Kingston, being at the head of navigation of the St Lawrence, was a key point in maintaining communication between Quebec and the whole of Upper Canada, making it an attractive target for an attack from Sackets Harbor, about thirty-five miles away on the American side of Lake Ontario. It was garrisoned as strongly as could be afforded within the limits of available resources by four companies of the 10th Royal Veterans under Major Donald Macpherson, supported by 1,500 militia.

Between Kingston and Fort George, on the northern shore of the lake opposite Fort George and about twenty-five miles distant by water, was the provincial capital of York. The little town had a good harbour and dockyard and contained the major arsenals and magazine of the province. The garrison of its fort – more of a depot than a fortified position – consisted of three companies of the 41st, supported by about 1,500 militia.[28] The vulnerable points were therefore Amherstburg, Niagara and Kingston, which were where the strongest garrisons were located, with the spaces between covered by the Provincial Marine, small outposts, the militia and those native warriors prepared to support the British.

In September 1810 Brock was at his new headquarters in Fort George, where he had dealt with the attempted desertions some years before. The town and its taverns he had described rather unflatteringly as "the nest of all wickedness." From there he wrote of having been "on the move" for some time, probably getting to know his dispersed garrisons. His command was, as he knew well from his previous experience as acting commander-in-chief, disunited, for command of the artillery and engineers actually lay with Major-General George Glasgow in Quebec and ultimately the Board of Ordnance in London in the case of the artillery and Lieutenant-Colonel Ralph Bruyères commanding the Engineer Department. Brock had also, it seems, travelled in the United States, having "been as far as Detroit, a delightful country...."[29] Detroit was a name familiar to him from his early years in the 8th Foot under Arendt DePeyster, so one cannot but assume that curiosity got the better of him – even if he went no closer than the Canadian side of the Detroit River. It would be attractive to make a case that Brock saw the war that was coming and fixed on Detroit as an early target. This may indeed be so but it cannot be shown conclusively from the available evidence. In the same letter he wrote of sending more letters "via New York," which was an accepted route for mail during the months from late October to April when the St Lawrence was closed.

At least in Fort George Brock had the company for a while of Major John Vincent and Captains John Glegg* and John Williams of the 49th, all of whom he knew, who were there for duty at a general court-martial. The 49th Regiment was garrisoned at Montreal and was therefore the nearest avail-

---

* Later Lieutenant-Colonel John Bachevoyle Glegg (1773–1861), who served on Brock's staff as aide-de-camp after his promotion to major-general.

able reinforcement for his command; but Montreal was outside Brock's area of responsibility and, much as he would have liked more frequent contact with his old regiment, visits like this one were a comparative rarity. Otherwise, compared with Quebec and even Montreal, society was to say the least, provincial. There was some social life in the capital of Upper Canada, York. Brock did his best, giving "a splendid ball to the beau monde of Niagara and its vicinity."[30] He clearly got along well with Lieutenant-Governor Gore, describing him as "as generous and honest a being as ever existed. His lady is perfectly well bred and very agreeable. I found an ample recompense in their society (i.e., in York) for the inconvenience of travelling over the worst roads I ever met with."[31]

Brock's personal quarters at York were inside the Garrison but he seems to have been a regular guest of Judge William Dummer Powell* and the adjutant-general of the militia, Æneas Shaw,† at his wooden house, Oak Hill, near York. There are persistent stories, especially that published in 1908,[32] that here he met and fell in love with Æneas's daughter, Sophia Shaw, and that they would have married but for the war. This is a nice Edwardian fable, but there is little or no evidence to show that Brock felt other than an affectionate regard for Miss Shaw, who was more than twenty years his junior; most respectable authorities regard the story as apocryphal.[33] Brock's aide, John Glegg, who was, in the way that aides-de-camp and military assistants uniquely are, "intimately acquainted" with his master's "sentiments on most private subjects," does not mention any arrangement with Miss Shaw.[34] Even allowing for the fact that at that time young ladies often did marry older gentlemen, as in the case of de Rottenburg, the gap in age is startling, for Sophia was of an age with Brock's nieces. Brock's friends clearly wished him to marry. His friend Colonel John Vesey wrote on his departure from England for service in Sicily under Lord William Bentinck that "I wish I had a daughter old enough for you, as I would give her to you with pleasure. You should be married, particularly as fate seems to detain you so long in Canada – but pray do not marry there."[35]

At Fort George, Brock lodged with his friend Lieutenant-Colonel John

---

* William Dummer Powell (1755–1834) was a lawyer, judge and Assembly member. Originally Loyalists from Boston, the family arrived in Quebec, via Britain, in 1779.

† Later Major-General the Hon Æneas Shaw (c.1755–1814).

Inside Fort George. This is an excellent contemporary view of troops drilling – probably the 41st Foot – in front of the distinctive wooden buildings of the fort. (Painting by Edward Walsh. William L. Clements Library, University of Michigan)

Murray* and his wife, mutual friends of Colonel John Vesey and his family, until he had engaged a housekeeper and made arrangements to move into Government House.† Here in Newark, Brock worshipped at St Mark's Church; the American officers of Fort Niagara would regularly cross the river to join the congregation and Brock would have had many an opportunity to assess their worth. In the churchyard there was for many years a stone known as Brock's seat (now removed to the inside of the church), on which local tradition says that he would sit in fine weather, contemplating the far shore. At some point in his early service, as we know, Brock had become a Freemason. The only two meeting houses in Upper Canada were

---

* Later Lieutenant-General John Murray of the 100th Regiment (?–1832). He was Inspecting Field Officer in 1811, took an active part in the campaigns in the Niagara area in 1813 and 1814 where he was wounded. Not to be confused with Lieutenant-General Sir John Murray, 8th Bt, who commanded a division in the Peninsular War.

† The house was burned down during the American occupation in 1813. The court-house now stands on the site.

in York, where Brock would have been welcome when he presided over the civil government, and in Newark, close to Fort George,[36] the first lodge of Upper Canada and one that had been founded by members of Brock's first regiment, the 8th.

A more austere life did have some compensation, for Brock wrote to his brother Irving in February 1811 saying that his health was quite restored – from what is not apparent. There is no evidence of a recurrence of his illness in the West Indies and he speaks of having considered travelling to Ballstown, near Albany, in the United States to take the waters there,* indicating perhaps a gastric condition or maybe even gout, as a later reference to him at Detroit by an American officer describes him as walking with a cane.

One sees continuing evidence of the benevolent humanity of Brock's nature during his time in Upper Canada. Among many well-documented examples is that of a former barrack master of Kingston who died leaving his widow and eight children in distress; this appears to have been Robert Clark, who had been a sergeant major in his first regiment, the 8th Foot, then clerk and storekeeper on Carleton Island. Brock obtained a commission for John, the eldest of the orphaned boys, in the Lincoln Militia, employed him on permanent duty in the recruiting service under Lieutenant-Colonel David Shank† and arranged for lodging and rations for the rest of the family. Brock also answered the petition of another unnamed old soldier of the 8th who had fallen on hard times and for whom he arranged free rations.‡ It appears unlikely that Brock knew the man personally for he appears to have been in the Canadas since the time that the 8th left in 1783. It seems most likely that the man had served under Isaac's elder brother John and had realized the family connection; since he was in the 8th there is also the possibility of a Freemasonry connection as the organization was well known for looking after its own. On this occasion Brock received a mild rebuke from Craig, whose military secretary, Colonel Thornton, wrote telling him that:

---

* This was a spa where people of society would take the mineral waters just as they would at Bath. It was known as Ballston Spa.

† Later Major-General David Shank (1756–?), a veteran of the Revolutionary War and first Lieutenant-Colonel of the Canadian Fencibles from 1803.

‡ The ration allowed to a pensioner was generally two-thirds that of an enlisted man. See N.K. Crowder, *British Army Pensioners Abroad 1772–1899* (Baltimore, 1995).

Colonel Edward Baynes (1768–1829), the adjutant-general in Quebec. He was a veteran with service that included the West Indies, South Africa and the East Indies. (From Richardson, *War of 1812*)

I have not failed to communicate to Sir James your account of and your charity towards the poor old fellow. He has in consequence directed the allowance of the ration to be authorized and continued to him; but I am to remind you of the danger of establishing precedent of this nature, and to request, in the general's name, that you will refrain as much as possible from indulging the natural benevolence of your disposition in this way, as he has hitherto resisted all applications of this sort.[37]

Thornton asked Brock to advise him of the old soldier's name, but the answering letter has long since disappeared from the files and no previous biographer has attempted to find further details. An examination of pension rolls for the colonies provides a potential identification of the old soldier: Sergeant Hugh McClieve, who had been discharged from the 8th Foot with thirty-one years' service.* A later note in the record indicates that Brock may have exercised further patronage on his behalf, for McClieve is described as having been appointed a barrack master at Fort George in 1811.[38]

Brock's move to the remote regions of Upper Canada seems to have strengthened further his resolve to leave for Europe if an appointment could be procured. He had clearly written again in October 1810 to the adjutant-general in Quebec, Colonel Edward Baynes, who wrote back to say that:

---

* A Hugh McClive appears in the Register of Births, Marriages and Deaths for Chippawa, living in the village of Stamford, where he died in 1822.

I gave Sir James your letter to read … I know that he is strongly impressed with the necessity of having a person like yourself for some time in the Upper Province, that a scrutinizing eye may correct the errors and neglect that have crept in and put all in order again.[39]

This was followed a few days later by another letter from Baynes, saying that Craig sympathized with Brock's wishes, but losing him would be awkward, for:

He had written in such strong terms, urging the necessity of a third general officer being kept constantly on the staff of the Canadas [the other two being Glasgow and De Rottenburg], and assigned as a principal reason the advantage of an officer of that rank being stationed in the Upper province, that he does not conceive himself at liberty to overset an arrangement which he has been two years soliciting the means to carry into effect … that you regretted the inactive prospect before you, and looked with envy on those employed in Spain and Portugal, he said 'I make no doubt of it, but I can in no shape aid his plans in that respect; I would not, however, be the means of preventing them … I would not oppose it if he could obtain an appointment to the staff on service….' I tell you this, my dear general, without reserve, and give you, as far as I can recollect, Sir James' words. If he liked you less, he might perhaps be more readily induced to let you go.… [40]

After Christmas, the recently arrived quartermaster-general in Quebec, Colonel James Kempt,* gave Brock a strong hint that a further promotion to major-general was likely to be his and that his stock was very high in London:

… you have no reason to, believe me, to dread being unemployed in any rank while you wish to serve, – this opinion, my dear general, is not given rashly or upon slight grounds, – before I came to this country I had, you must know, several opportunities of hearing your name mentioned at head quarters, both by General Calvert and Colonel Gordon, who unquestionably spoke the sentiments of the then commander-in-chief, and in such a way as to impress me with a thorough conviction that few officers of your rank stood higher in their estimation.[41]

---

* Later General Sir James Kempt, G.C.B. (1765–1823), commanded a brigade in Spain under Wellington and was present at Waterloo. He became Governor-General of British North America 1828–30 and Master-General of the Ordnance in Lord Grey's administration.

Kempt went on to say that as soon as circumstances allowed, Craig was willing to grant Brock six months' leave to return home and secure an appointment in Spain or Portugal. Brock was obviously also well thought of by the Duke of Kent and the Duke of York.[42]

Almost immediately on arrival in Upper Canada Brock found himself thrust into aboriginal affairs. In the aftermath of the Louisiana Purchase in 1803, both Craig and Gore had revived the policy of alliance with the western nations. In April 1808 Gore had held a private meeting with the chiefs of the Shawnee people at York through the agency of the Indian Department and its superintendent, Matthew Elliott,* a lieutenant-colonel in the Essex Militia to whom the native chiefs were much attached. It is clear that as a result of this the native warriors would respond to a call to arms from Craig, and in the meantime they would be supplied with arms, ammunition and trade goods as an earnest of friendship.[43] This was bound to be a source of friction with the United States. American movement westwards into aboriginal territories had already brought a great deal of violence with atrocities on both sides, but there was far less pressure on the Canadian side of the border as the impetus for westward expansion was simply not there. Fur traders were active and there were persistent U.S. claims that Craig's policy towards the native people manifested itself in supplies of arms, ammunition and liquor – in other words, the British were paying the aboriginal people to do their work for them.

Craig had in fact given orders that the native warriors were to be discouraged as far as possible from attacking Americans and Brock did his best in Upper Canada to enforce this.[44] However, his sympathies clearly lay with the aboriginal peoples. Writing to Sir James Craig on 27 February 1811, he commented that giving out presents on the one hand, and urging restraint on the other, was sending a message that the native people, and probably the Americans too, were bound to misinterpret:

> Our cold attempt to dissuade that much-injured people from engaging in such a rash enterprise [i.e., war against the Americans] could scarcely be

---

* Matthew Elliott (1739–1814) was born in Donegal and emigrated to Pennsylvania in 1761. He identified with the Loyalists during the Revolutionary War and settled in Amherstburg around 1783. He was superintendent of the Indian Department from 1808. He was killed at Burlington Heights in 1814.

expected to prevail, particularly after giving such manifest indications of a contrary sentiment by the liberal quantity of military stores with which they were dismissed.[45]

Every spring, the native people gathered in their hundreds at places like Amherstburg, to trade furs and receive blankets, muskets, powder and shot and ironware as a form of subsidy from the British government, represented by the Indian Department. Although Elliott, the superintendent, was a military officer, his department, it will be remembered, came under civil control in Quebec; Craig's instructions on this were explicit,[46] but Brock complained that he had no control over Elliott's activities.

> Elliott … is an exceedingly good man, and highly respected by the Indians; but, having in his youth lived a great deal with them, he naturally imbibed their feelings and prejudices … this sympathy made him neglect the considerations of prudence, which ought to have regulated his conduct.[47]

Craig's instructions did however stipulate that where military officers were present at councils with the native peoples, they were to report what they observed. Following Craig's instructions, Brock wrote to Major John Taylor at Amherstburg on 4 March explaining the policy in detail and reproving Taylor for not keeping him better informed of talks between Elliott and the warriors there.[48]

In Lower Canada, friction continued between Craig and the Legislative Council on one hand and the Legislative Assembly on the other. He obviously feared that the French population was rife with disaffection at the hands of either Bonapartist or American agents. On 12 December 1810 Craig opened the Assembly and in his speech outlined a temporary act which had previously been passed, aimed at "establishing regulations respecting aliens or certain subjects of His Majesty who have resided in France." Craig enjoined the Assembly to put this act into force along with the regulation of trade with the U.S.; however, the assembly members clearly feared that it would be used to arrest and imprison any French Canadian suspected of disloyalty. Well they might, for almost immediately after his speech Craig arrested a Monsieur Bedard on a charge of high treason. An exchange followed in which the Assembly affirmed its loyalty and protested against Craig's methods in the strongest terms its members dared. Craig replied, agreeing to deal with the Assembly's concerns, but in sarcastic terms that left no-one in any doubt about his real opinion of them. Craig's determination to maintain the rule of the British Crown against what he saw as the dangers of foreign subversion was unshaken. A further disagreement followed about the position of judges in the Assembly.

Tension with the United States over maritime affairs surfaced again in May 1811 with the affairs of the *Guerriere* and the *Little Belt*.* On 1 May HMS *Guerriere* had stopped the brig USS *Spitfire* and impressed a U.S. citizen. The heavy frigate USS *President* was ordered to pursue and recover the man but on 16 May, the day of the battle of Albuera in Spain, mistook the small, old-fashioned frigate HMS *Little Belt* for her quarry. After an exchange of gunfire, the much heavier *President* mauled the British ship, although both ships returned safely to port. The continuing disputes over impressments and trade convinced Craig that war was coming sooner rather than later. This, along with continuous warfare with the Assembly, told on Craig's health, which had never been strong. In the spring of 1811 his health broke down and he resigned the governorship, leaving Dunn in charge of the civil administration and Lieutenant-General Gordon Drummond in command of all military forces in both provinces. Craig departed on 19 June 1811 but before he left, Baynes wrote to Brock on Craig's behalf, apologizing again for having been unable to agree to his requests for leave to return to England – Brock simply could not be spared.[49]

To underline his evident esteem for him, Craig asked Brock to accept his horse, Alfred, as his charger. Alfred was a big grey, ten years old and with an even temperament. When the horse arrived at York that summer, Brock was immediately delighted with him. At about the same time, Kempt's prediction that promotion was likely came true. On 4 June 1811, by order of the Prince Regent,[50] but almost certainly at the instigation of the Duke of York, who had replaced Dundas as commander-in-chief, Brock was promoted to major-general on the staff of British North America.

---

* *Little Belt* is an anglicisation of the original Danish name, *Lillebælt*. The ship was captured by the Royal Navy at Copenhagen.

CHAPTER EIGHT

"The Fittest Person"

UPPER CANADA,
1811–1812

I t was not until three months after Craig had left that the new governor, Sir George Prevost, arrived in September 1811. Prevost, then aged forty-six, was a British lieutenant-general, from a family with Swiss origins, born in Paramus in British New Jersey in 1767. Although he spoke French fluently, he should not be considered a foreigner in British service as he was born on British territory and was brought up and educated in Britain. His uncle James had played a key role in the formation of the 60th Royal Americans and the entire Prevost family, including George's father and half-brother, served in it. Sir George too had served in the 60th and had made a name for himself during successful operations in the West Indies, commanding troops at every level from battalion to division. He successfully defended San Domingo from a French attack in 1805 and led a divisional-sized force in the reduction and capture of Martinique in 1809. He had been governor of St Lucia and San Domingo and had successfully conciliated the French population there. In 1809 he had been transferred to Nova Scotia to prepare the colony for war and, if necessary, assume the command and government of British North America at short notice. In Nova Scotia he had again been a popular governor and it was widely predicted that he would take a different tack with the French Canadians than Craig had done; these predictions proved correct.

Prevost was faced not with the possibility of war with the United States but rather the near certainty of it, although he himself placed great faith in the hope of reconciliation, especially if the Orders-in-Council were revoked. This explains why he tended to tread carefully where U.S. opinion was concerned and why he restrained Brock's tendencies towards pre-emptive offensive action. The U.S. Congress had met earlier than usual, on 6 Novem-

Sir George Prevost (1767–1816), Governor-General and Commander-in-Chief of British North America, 1811–1814. His position thus required him to be soldier, politician, administrator and diplomat. (Library and Archives Canada C-143042)

ber 1811, and the Republican "War Hawks" had gained influence in the lower house out of proportion to their numbers. Demands for the revocation of the British Orders-in-Council grew louder; there was a clear message in President James Madison's address to the Congress:

> With this evidence of hostile inflexibility, in trampling on rights which no independent nation can relinquish – congress will feel the duty of putting the United Sates into an armour, and an attitude demanded by the crisis, and corresponding with the national spirit and expectations.[1]

To achieve this "armour and attitude," Madison asked for increases in the regular army, a corps of volunteers, additions to the navy and increases in stocks of arms and ammunition. Prevost, by contrast, knew that he could look for little help from home while Britain was engaged in her life-and-death struggle with Napoleon right at a time, moreover, when the Continental System was at or near its most effective.

Prevost clearly held a high opinion of Brock, as when Gore was granted furlough in England[2] Brock was appointed President of the Council, or Administrator, of Upper Canada, effectively combining the civil and military government in his hands.[3] He was, in Prevost's words, "the fittest person" for this task.[4] Brock moved to York on 23 September and was sworn in on 9 October 1811.[5] This avoided the problems that had vexed him when trying to gain the support of the civil authorities in Quebec, where he could direct military units but could not compel civilians without recourse to martial law. Although in principle, when facing an emergency, a concentration of authority in one senior figure is sound and followed the precedent of Craig and Prevost's position in Lower Canada, in practice Brock did not find it an easy ride. He had to face the problem of many military officers entrusted with the coordination of military and civil authority: he could give orders to his military subordinates and demand that these orders be put into effect, and indeed the military had the structures and resources in place to ensure that orders would be carried out; but he could not issue orders to the civilians, no matter how necessary it might be that they should step forward and take their share of the effort in preparing for war. Instead of being able to command he had to consult; rather than control, he must co-ordinate; instead of issuing communications he had to listen to them; and rather than demand intelligence he had to provide information.

On promotion to the rank of major-general, Brock was entitled to a small personal staff and had asked for Captain John Glegg from the 49th Foot as his aide-de-camp.[6] In addition he had a brigade major, Captain Thomas Evans* of the 8th Foot, and later Lieutenant-Colonel John Macdonell as his provincial aide.[†] The other members of the staff were the senior surgeon, James Macauley; the fort major, Lieutenant Donald Campbell; and the provincial barrack master, Thomas Newman.[7] He also had to spend at least £300 in buying the correct uniforms and hats – which, it seems, reached him in early 1812.[8] Despite the satisfaction of his promotion, Brock had to endure the spectacle of a number of his acquaintances and friends heading off for active service in Europe while he remained in the wilderness. John Vesey had already gone. In October 1811 Kempt left to command a brigade in Spain and Thornton to command a regiment of foot; these last two subsequently achieved distinction in the Peninsula. Thornton was well connected to the military secretary to the commander-in-chief, Sir Henry

---

* Later Lieutenant-General Thomas Evans, C.B. (1776–1863). Evans came from humble origins and later married Harriet Ogden, daughter of a prominent Loyalist family in the Canadas.

† Lieutenant-Colonel John Macdonell (1785–1812) was appointed to the post on 15 April 1812. He served as member of the Legislative Council for Glengarry and was Attorney-General of Upper Canada.

Torrens,* which partly at least explains his appointment. Thornton wrote to Baynes, sending a message to Brock, on 2 August 1811: "Pray give a hint in private to Generals Brock and Sheaffe, that if the former were to ask for a brigade at home, or on European service, and the latter to be put on the staff in Canada, I am almost certain they would succeed."[9]

Clearly Brock took this hint, for on 17 October he received a letter from Torrens saying that he had recommended Brock to the Duke of York for a command in Europe and that the Duke was willing to grant it, but only if another officer could be found to replace Brock. This could be overcome, however, "as Major-General Sheaffe is on the spot, and has strong claims to employment on the staff, his royal highness will have no objection to furnish Sir George Prevost with an authority to employ that officer in your room...."[10]

Sheaffe in fact was not quite on the spot but on furlough in England. He had been promoted to colonel in 1808 and then in 1811 to major-general,[11] but he was junior in seniority to Brock and he was unassigned to any command and therefore was on the half-pay of a colonel. That this hurt him financially would have been well known to Torrens and Prevost, who were clearly anxious to assist him.

Faced with the disparity in population between the United States and the Canadas and the odds on land that would over time be brought to bear on his small contingent of British regulars, Prevost had no choice but to improve the force ratios by the traditional British tactic of coalition building. The available partners were strange bedfellows indeed and at first sight, not comfortable ones: British and British immigrants; Indians, as the native people were then called; and French Canadians. The successful assembly of such a coalition, and through it the survival of what would become an independent Canada, must be counted as one of the more remarkable achievements of British colonial rule in North America.

On moving to Quebec in 1811, Prevost embarked on a policy not merely of conciliation but of recognition of the French Canadians as the dominant ethnic group in Lower Canada, who had no desire to be submerged either

---

* Major-General Sir Henry Torrens, K.C.B. (1779–1823), later Adjutant-General of the Army. His son was killed at Fort Erie in 1814 and is buried in the cemetery at Lundy's Lane.

by English or American influences. It was just as well that Brock, given his strong views, was kept away from this process. Prevost had no particularly rosy view of the leadership of French Canada. They were politicians out for whatever they could get, in his view, but their fears could be harnessed. He established excellent relations with the Legislative Assembly of Lower Canada, which by the outbreak of war had become so co-operative (in contrast to that of the upper province), that it voted almost £100,000 for the war. He also raised the status of the Roman Catholic Bishop of Quebec, although at the cost of the enmity of the Anglican Bishop, to whom he paid neither more nor less heed than his predecessors had done. His efforts to gain recognition for and engage the support of the Catholic Church were certainly supported by the Prince Regent, who, aside from his morganatic marriage to a Catholic lady, had supported the Catholic Emancipation bill for Ireland in 1797 and had also supported the covert return to Britain of exiled Catholic schools and religious communities fleeing from persecution on the continent during the French Revolution.

The Legislative Assembly of Lower Canada was equally supportive in the matter of the militia. Both Brock in Upper Canada and Prevost in Lower Canada pushed hard to raise the capability of the militia, and in French Canada such was the strength of support for Prevost that the assembly agreed to embody 2,000 militiamen for ninety days of training, extended to a year's service on the outbreak of war, provided the men were not enlisted into British regular regiments. Finally, when Lieutenant-Colonel Charles de Salaberry* raised the *Voltigeurs Canadiens* in April 1812, the ranks were filled within a matter of days. Thus under Prevost's enlightened leadership any proposed alliance between Napoleonic France and the United States gained no traction in French Canada. The newspaper *Le Canadien*, for example, which it will be remembered had been closed down by Craig, led the way in opposing adventures by any outside power and went so far as to refer to Napoleon Bonaparte as "the lawless leader of France."[12] So strong had dislike of both the French emperor and the United States become by 1812 that any inter-ethnic quarrels were effectively submerged in the face of the common threat.

---

* Lieutenant-Colonel Charles de Salaberry (1778–1829) of the 60th Royal Americans came from a prominent French-speaking family in Lower Canada and was serving as aide to de Rottenburg when given the task of forming the *Voltigeurs*.

Although Brock played no part in bringing French Canada into an effective anti-republican coalition, he had a major part to play with the other available partners, the native peoples; having dealt with the aboriginal nations from the very beginning of his service in the 8th Foot, this would not have struck him as anything other than normal business. Rapprochement with the French in the Canadas was not enough of itself to alleviate the short-term difficulties of the military situation. It also required the active engagement of Britain's native allies. The use of local irregulars to make good shortages of regular troops was already established British practice not only in North America but also in India; it would later spread to the West Indies, Africa and South-East Asia as the Empire grew. Recent examples have been in Sierra Leone from 2000, where hunting brotherhoods were harnessed to provide an irregular corps, the Civil Defence Force, to support British and Sierra Leone regular troops, and in Iraq from 2006, when Kurdish and Arab tribes were brought to the Iraqi government's side by negotiations brokered by Jordan. That the American-led coalition in Afghanistan took so long to adopt this practice may say something about its lack of success there.

Left to themselves, armed local irregulars could quickly run out of control and it was always necessary to establish a spine of government authority, through embedded officers, who would supervise activities using money, food, arms and ammunition, and be the means of bringing help from regular forces should the irregulars be outmatched by heavy opposition. This was the job of the Indian Department, using men like Joseph Brant,[*] his son John Brant, Matthew Elliott, William Claus[†] and John Norton, who frequently were of mixed ancestry, giving them ties of kinship to a traditional society. Relations between the Indian Department and the British army were touchy, for the army saw the Mohawk war-chief John Norton as the only effective officer of the Indian Department, viewing the rest as self-seeking and idle. As with the French Canadians, the alliance with the aboriginal people was brought about through the subordination of national interest in the face of a unifying threat; and like the French Canadian alli-

---

[*] Joseph Brant, or Thayendanegea (1743–1807) was a Mohawk chief and prominent supporter of Great Britain, who was perhaps the best known native North American of his generation.

[†] William Claus (1765–1826) served in the Revolutionary War in the 60th Royal Americans and thereafter served in the Indian Department. He was a member of the Executive Council from 1818 to 1826.

John Brant, or Ahyonwaeghs
(1794–1856) was the son of Joseph
Brant and led his Mohawk people
north to settle in Upper Canada after
the Revolutionary War.

ance it was also the product of patient diplomacy over many years. During the eighteenth century, both the British and French had sought alliances with the native people, who were after all experienced warriors well used to local conditions.

For their part, the aboriginal peoples, and especially the most influential group in the Northwest,* the Iroquois Confederacy – a league of aboriginal nations sharing the Iroquoian language and embracing the Seneca, Cayuga, Oneida, Onondaga, Mohawk, Delaware and Tuscarora nations† – had been nominally allied to the British by the Treaty of Utrecht in 1713, but had used alliances with both the British and French to serve their own interests. The Iroquois had a strong tradition of communal ownership of property and a well-developed political structure based on matrilinear families, both of which would come to the fore in 1812. The eventual triumph of the British over the French in North America brought one highly significant political development, the Royal Proclamation of 1763, which was aimed at the avoidance of conflict. This important measure was to be a profound influence on subsequent history, for it laid down that aboriginal land could not

---

* The Northwest (or Old Northwest) encompassed the state of Ohio and the future states of Indiana, Illinois, Michigan and Wisconsin.

† The Iroquoian language group also included the Huron and other nations and most were settled in permanent or semi-permanent defended villages, unlike the Algonkian language group, who were largely nomadic.

John Norton, or Teyoninhokarawen (c.1760–1825) was born in Scotland of a Scots mother and a Cherokee father. He arrived in the Canadas as a private soldier in the 65th Foot in 1784 and later went into the fur trade, through which he knew Joseph Brant and became involved in Indian affairs. Among his many achievements was a translation of St John's Gospel into Mohawk. He was to play an active role throughout the War of 1812. (Portrait by Mary Ann Knight. Library and Archives Canada C-123481)

be sold except to the Crown, and that the hinterland was closed to agricultural expansion. Explicitly, the proclamation stated that it was essential to the interests of the Crown

> … and the security of our colonies, that the several Nations or Tribes of Indians with whom we are connected, and who live under our Protection, should not be molested or disturbed in the Possession of Such Parts of Our Dominions. Territories as … are reserved to them … any lands whatever, which, not having been ceded to or purchased by Us as aforesaid, are reserved to the said Indians.… And we do hereby strictly forbid … any Purchases or settlements whatever, or Taking Possession of any of the lands above reserved, without our especial leave and licence.[13]

In later years, this proclamation was to be used as part of the Indian argument for recognizing aboriginal title to non-ceded lands.[14] Not unnaturally, it was heartily loathed by the American colonists and became one of the acts used to justify the American Revolutionary War. That war shattered the Six Nations as most Oneidas and Tuscaroras fought for the rebels, while most of the remainder fought on the side of the British – but all fought in pursuit of their own interest.

With the end of the Revolutionary War, the Treaty of Paris in 1783 brought the surrender of all British and native claims south of the Great Lakes and a large-scale resettlement of Britain's aboriginal allies in the Can-

adas – a large group of Iroquois, for example, led by Joseph Brant, settled
on the Grand River, on the north shore of Lake Erie, and after Jay's Treaty
in 1794 3,000 more were settled in Upper Canada. In 1788 the U.S. Congress
passed the North-West Ordinance, which opened up the land west of the
Ohio River to settlement by white-owned land companies, speculators and
farmers. The large population of aboriginal peoples resident in the area was
not consulted about this measure. At first few people made the trip and Indian tribal disunity prevented any serious opposition to the newcomers. But
once white settlement began to gather momentum, aboriginal raiding soon
developed into all-out war, and the aboriginal peoples inflicted some serious defeats on poorly-trained American troops until resistance was finally
crushed in 1794. Thus from early days, the United States was identified in
the minds of the native peoples with oppression: the Iroquois term for the
American president was – and remains – the same as "town destroyer."[15] But
the Canadas, where the great king – the "White Father" as the native people
called George III – offered sanctuary, protection and trade with the North
West Company and the British Indian Department, were identified with the
traditional way of life, although the Department officers sometimes used
rather heavy-handed methods.

By 1809 a forty-year-old aboriginal leader had begun his rise to prominence in the American Northwest. This was Tecumseh, who was perhaps as
great a statesman as any in North America at that time. The son of a Creek
mother and a Shawnee father, he had been brought up in what would later
be Ohio. As a result of his experiences there as white settlement developed,
he became convinced that there had to be a better strategy for the aboriginal nations than random raiding. This led him eventually to the concept of
territorial security through unity. Joined by his brother, who was generally
known simply as the Prophet (Tenskwatawa), they established the settlement of Prophetstown on the Tippecanoe River. Here in 1809 Tecumseh
first propounded the idea of a pan-tribal or aboriginal national confederacy. This idea gained ground so rapidly that the governor of the territory,
William H. Harrison* (later known as "Old Tippecanoe") decided that a
salutary lesson was needed. This lesson, the destruction of Prophetstown,
was duly delivered on 8 November 1811 soon after Brock's arrival in Upper

* William Henry Harrison (1773–1841), 9th President of the United States.

The Shawnee leader Tecumseh (c.1768–1813) sought to unite North American native peoples in a grand alliance to protect their lands. Respected as the "Wellington of the Indians" by Brock, he allied his force with the British, but his efforts were cut short by his death at the Battle of the Thames in 1813. (Lossing, *Pictorial Field-Book of the War of 1812*)

Canada.[16] In its aftermath, Tecumseh and his followers sought help from the British in Amherstburg and offered their fighting strength in return. Brock realized that the uncompromising attitude across the border had driven the already pro-British natives, athirst for revenge, into his arms.

This was not so of the entirety of the native nations. The Grand River people, who were Six Nations or former Iroquois Confederacy members, of whom the largest group were the Mohawks, and who were worn out by war with the Americans, disgruntled by lack of attention to their land claims and unconvinced by the weak stand of the British Indian Department led by Matthew Elliott and William Claus, elected to stay neutral. Brock made a determined effort to bring the Grand River people to his cause in the spring of 1812. In mid-May he attended a council meeting at which he suggested that the Grand River people should form three companies of warriors,[17] each of which would take a turn of duty of one month on the Niagara frontier, but the suggestion was rebuffed until such time as their land claims were settled. This apparent intransigence masked not only divisions among the Grand River people about whether or not to sell land to white settlers but also the shady dealing of Claus in the matter of sales. Brock was clearly sympathetic to the native peoples' claims – both from the point of view of right as well as necessity – and made a serious attempt to resolve the issues. In this he largely failed, although he did secure delivery of interest payments on money managed by the British government on behalf of the Grand River people.[18]

Chief Raweanarase of the Onondaga asked Brock if the British would help the western tribes if the Americans made war on them but did not invade the Canadas. Brock was thus placed in a thoroughly awkward position, being obliged to repeat the line from Prevost and the Indian Department, which he believed to be wrong, saying that he had no authority to give help while Britain and the United States were at peace.[19] For the Grand River people, given their fear of the Americans and their anger about land ownership issues, this was simply not enough and so he was politely rebuffed – although the door was not completely closed. Not long afterwards, in June 1812, a delegation of Senecas from New York arrived to lobby for continued neutrality on the part of the native peoples. Mohawk chief John Norton was among those who argued against the visitors – with some effect for, although the Grand River people remained divided, the visitors failed to achieve their aim.[20] It was fear of the United States, however, more than

"Costume of Domiciliated Indians of North America," 1807. This scene at a hunting camp shows how native life had incorporated useful European technologies, such as cloth and guns. (Aquatint by Joseph Stadler from watercolour by George Heriot. Library and Archives Canada C-012781)

support for Britain, that informed the Grand River people's stance and their allegiance to the British at this point was fragile in the extreme.

It is probably fair to say that the aboriginal peoples were, by this time, more of a moral force than a physical one. Their support had been a key factor in the wars with the French in the middle of the eighteenth century, and the perception of their uncivilized way of war, of massacres and atrocities, was strongly ingrained in many Americans. However by 1810, although both sides still courted the native people, their numbers had declined, largely as a result of the importation of European diseases such as syphilis, smallpox, tuberculosis, diphtheria, measles, rubella and the like. From the Mississippi River eastwards through the American Northwest and the Canadas, there were probably no more than 50,000 men, women and children. This population produced a theoretical maximum of 10,000 warriors; theoretical, because the nature of authority in this still-primitive society meant that each individual followed his own wishes and came and went as he chose,[21] just as the tribesmen of Afghanistan and the Federally Administered Tribal Areas of Pakistan do today. On only one occasion was Tecumseh able to muster more than 500 warriors (in Michigan in 1813). The native warriors were superb scouts and skirmishers; they could draw off disproportionate numbers of troops from a battle; they could deceive, divert and distract. They could also interdict supply lines, attack rear areas and ambush marching troops – again all requiring an adversary to use valuable forces for security rather than on the battlefield. Like the Spanish guerrillas fighting with Wellington, they were likely to come off badly in formal battles but, used properly, could present a conventional opposition force commander with a dilemma that could not be solved with the troop numbers available to American commanders in 1812.[22] As well as the psychological effect that the perception of savage warriors has on inexperienced troops or militias, the interaction of regular and irregular forces creates circumstances in which an enemy army has to deal with the irregular force by dispersing in garrisons, guarding routes and convoys – all to the detriment of concentrating its force on the opposing regular army. But should that same army try to concentrate against the opposing regular army, and ignore anti-irregular operations, it finds its communications raided, its depots looted and its isolated outposts made untenable.[23]

It was to be some months before Brock and Tecumseh met in person but the relationship, at least with the Six Nations and those Algonquin who adhered to Tecumseh, if not with the Grand River people, was in place. Because of this, throughout the War of 1812, the British were able to maintain a tenuous superiority on the lakes and thus their lines of communication over the 1,100 miles of frontier, with the active support of the aboriginal people – perhaps as many as 6,000 – who declared for the allied cause, while the Americans were always looking over their shoulders. In the face of what the Americans believed to be a determined British policy of encouraging native depredations against white settlers, there was an additional serious influence on U.S. strategy through the perceived need to protect the Northwest. The territorial governors demanded troops and action and the result was that, throughout the war, American planning was deflected toward this area and away from the most important and vulnerable objective – the St Lawrence, the lifeline of the Canadas. This was a highly important, perhaps decisive, effect of aboriginal engagement on the course of the war. Of all his many achievements, this was perhaps Brock's most significant.

Prevost had achieved a great deal with the Legislative Assembly of Lower Canada and had raised two units of provincial troops, one each for Lower and Upper Canada, and five battalions of select embodied militia for the defence of the lower province. Brock had a far harder time with the Assembly in Upper Canada. Despite his partial success in harnessing the combat power of the native people, he needed the white population of the province, from whom the militia was drawn, to take an active part in preparations for its defence.

Brock's troubles came from three sources. First was the general view among the inhabitants of Upper Canada that any war with the United States was lost before it began, and therefore why make a bad situation worse by fighting? Second were the large numbers of settlers from the republic and their anti-British views; and third, he faced the possibly well-meaning but ultimately dangerous "anti-establishment" views of a proto-Whig faction that included the Irish immigrant and Assembly member Joseph Willcocks,[*]

---

[*] Joseph Willcocks, or Willcox, (1773–1814) diarist, politician, printer, publisher, journalist, army officer and traitor. He turned out as a volunteer at Queenston. This was probably the result of Brock's force of personality as much as Willcocks's ideas of patriotism. But by the following June Willcocks was leading a unit of Canadian renegades in the U.S. Army and

Justice Robert Thorpe* and Surveyor-General Charles Burton Wyatt.† Loy-alist backbone could be stiffened by evidence of commitment from the government in Quebec and the clear message that the province could be defended: what we would now call an information operation. Pro-American subversion could be dealt with by a firm hand and the right regulations.

The last source of trouble was the least easy to address and the most like-ly to give trouble with required emergency legislation. The general view of the Whig faction may be summarized as being that any increase in authority by the Crown or government meant a corresponding reduction in liberty elsewhere. In the assembly, this faction argued that the colonial government, being so far from the mother parliament in London and not always subject to its acts, was by its nature prone to abuse of power. Their opposition to the government of Grant, and later Gore, had been focused on the issue of land reform. Gore had responded to the challenge by having the appoint-ments of Thorpe and Wyatt withdrawn in 1807[24]. Willcocks had then moved to Newark and started a radical newspaper, the *Upper Canada Guardian; or, Freeman's Journal.* He also continued to serve in the Legislative Assembly and by 1812 the group he led controlled around half the votes in the twenty-three-member chamber.

During the fourth session of the Fifth Provincial Parliament in February and March 1812, Brock put forward a number of measures in the Assembly aimed at putting the province on a war footing. His view was that, at a time of national emergency, personal liberty had to take second place to the needs of national security; he was able to pass supplementary clauses to the Militia Act, but only after the required length of service was reduced from

---

was appointed to police the occupied area of the Niagara. In July 1814 the attorney-general managed to bring two dozen traitors, including Willcocks and his closest henchmen in absentia, before a court. After a full hearing before a civilian jury, twelve were found guilty of high treason and eight were hanged— the so-called "Ancaster Bloody Assize." Willcocks himself was killed fighting for the Americans at Fort Erie in September 1814 (*Dictionary of Canadian Biography Online*).

* Justice Robert Thorpe (1764–1836) was, like Willcocks, an Irishman. He was appointed to the King's Bench in Upper Canada in 1805 until his dismissal; despite his reputation as a troublemaker he received an appointment in Sierra Leone in 1808 but was also removed from there.

† Charles Burton Wyatt (1778–1840) was appointed surveyor-general in 1804. He appealed unsuccessfully against his later dismissal from the post but did succeed in a libel action against Gore.

Major-General Æneas Shaw
(c.1755–1818), Brock's adjutant-
general of militia. A Scottish-born
veteran of the Revolutionary War,
he moved to New Brunswick after
the war and came to Upper Canada
in 1792, becoming a leading
citizen of the province.(Archives of
Ontario, 605017)

eighteen months to one year.[25] He was not able to pass a clause requiring recruits to abjure any former or alternative allegiance; this was to prevent the
enlistment of American settlers who might then abscond with their weapons. This measure was defeated by the casting vote of the chairman.[26] On
the credit side, the act authorized the formation of flank companies for each
battalion, which were to train for six days every month.[27] These companies
were in effect cadres of relatively well-trained men around which larger
bodies of militia could be formed rapidly:

> The chief object of the Flank Companies is to have constantly in readi-
> ness, a force composed of Loyal, Brave, and Respectable Young Men, so
> far instructed as to enable the Government, on any emergency, to engraft
> such portions of the Militia as may be necessary, on a stock capable of
> giving aid in forming them for Military service.[28]

Brock's adjutant-general of militia, Major-General Æneas Shaw, sent
out a suggested clothing schedule for each militiaman, advising the officers
not to appear different from the men,[29] lest they attract the unwelcome attentions of American sharp-shooters. But while the men came forward in
many cases, the necessary arms and equipment took several more weeks to
be delivered to the communities along the upper St Lawrence. Despite these
shortages, training appears to have commenced shortly after the passage
of the bill. Brock emphasized that every man "capable of bearing a musket
along the whole of that line [Kingston to Glengarry] ought to be prepared

to act." He also directed a reconnaissance of the ground near Johnstown, opposite Oswegatchie, to locate a suitable site to construct a work to serve as a rallying point, protect stores and "to preserve a free communication between the two provinces."[30]

However Brock's attempt to have *habeas corpus* partially suspended was defeated, as was a bill to restrict the movements of foreigners and a bill to pay a reward of £5 for every deserter from the British army who was apprehended, for the Whigs were having none of this.[31] Brock, disgusted, dissolved the Assembly on 6 March, telling both houses that "Any attempts to disseminate disaffection among us will be repelled with indignation, and you will not fail in your respective stations to point out and bring to justice all such persons who by their conduct may endanger the public tranquillity."[32]

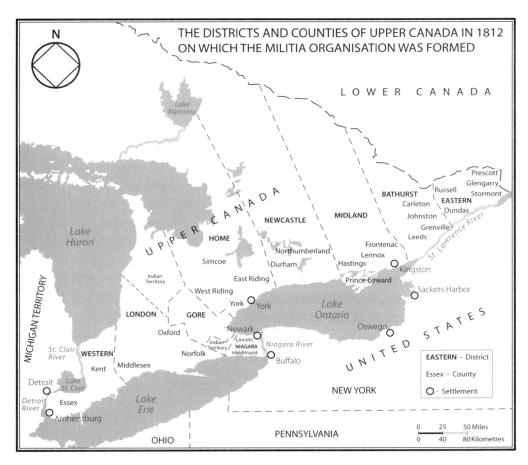

Brock called an election on 5 May 1812. During the weeks leading up to it, Willcocks and his associates did their best to spread misinformation about the Militia Act. Well aware of the influence of "Mr Willcocks and his vile coadjudicators"[33] on public opinion, Brock made a determined effort to win Willcocks over. He was, like Brock, a Freemason and a member of the Newark Lodge, which would have helped greatly. Willcocks was asked to dinner at Government House and from then on it became common knowledge that he had thrown in his lot with Brock – perhaps one might cynically take the view that having lost the patronage of Wyatt and Thorpe, he found Brock a useful substitute. On the other hand it is possible that close acquaintance with Brock convinced him that the president was neither a tyrant nor an enemy of liberty after all, and was merely doing what was necessary for the security of the province. At all events, in June 1812 Willcocks ceased publication of the *Guardian* and, although much abused by his former associates, became a supporter of the government.

CHAPTER NINE

"A System Strictly Defensive"

UPPER CANADA,
OCTOBER 1811–JUNE 1812

The 6th of October 1811 was Brock's forty-second birthday and he clearly expected mail from home on the fortnightly government packet from Montreal to York due that day. All that came, however, were newspapers – and they contained evil news. During 1811 Napoleon's Continental System had all but succeeded. Throughout Britain, factories were shutting for the want of markets for their goods, and mills and mines were closing their doors amid great social unrest; more businesses failed in 1811 than at any other time in British history up to that point. The income to the Treasury slumped, credit dried up and there was a sustained run on the pound. For Britain, engaged in a battle for its very existence, this potentially spelled ruin. Because of its worldwide empire, economic base and strategic reach – through naval power – Britain was arguably the only major power able to conduct strategy through means other than military power. Without a large army on the continent, she relied on naval blockade and financial subsidies to her major allies, who had large armies, and those subsidies came from trade revenues. In one year, Britain was able to subsidize the coalition against Napoleon to the tune of almost £7.5 million– a huge sum in those days when a gentleman could live very well on £600 a year and a private soldier was paid less than £20 – and equating to £5.8 billion at today's value when calculated against average earnings.[1]

The financial climate alone brought many banking houses and commercial companies to ruin and, looking over the newspapers, which dated from the summer of 1811, Brock noted a long list of bankruptcies. What brought him up short was that among them was Brock and Le Mesurier, the firm of his brother William, which had been declared insolvent on 12 July.[2] William had lost between £12,000 and £13,000 – the equivalent of £1.3

million today if calculated using the retail price index. Brock immediately wrote to Savery:

> … really my poor head will not allow me to say more, that tomorrow I enter into the official duties of president of this province. The salary attached to the situation is £1,000 [per annum, the equivalent of £75,000 today], the whole of which, I trust, I shall be able to save, and after a year or two even more.… Yesterday was the first truly gloomy birthday I have ever passed.[3]

Brock's immediate reaction was to help his family, as they had helped him. However, when mail did arrive on 30 October, the true extent of the disaster became apparent.[4] Because the purchase price of Brock's commissions up to the rank of lieutenant-colonel had been entered as a charge against William's business rather than as a personal gift or loan, these sums were now due to William's creditors. The amount involved came to £3,000: three years' salary for Brock, provided he kept the civil administration as well as his military rank, or else he would have no choice but to sell out. He would have to pay the debt somehow – it was a matter of honour. Writing to his brother after the event, William summarized the problem:

> You will have received … a letter from our assignees, desiring to be informed in what manner the debt, which appears in our books as owing to you, is to be liquidated. Too well do I know, my dear Isaac, your inability to pay it off yourself. It now amounts to something above three thousand pounds. The assignees will not, I believe, take any unpleasant steps to enforce the payment, yet it will be natural that they shall expect some sort of security from you.[5]

The news had soon leaked out in the Canadas and William followed his remarks with a remarkable testimony of how his brother was regarded among people in Upper Canada:

> It was reported that legal proceedings were commenced against you; and upon this report a young man lately from Canada, a Mr. Ellice, called on Charles Bell to enquire if it were so, and told Bell that rather than that anything unpleasant should happen to you, he would contrive to pay the debt himself. Besides his attachment to you, he told Bell that you were so beloved in Canada that you would not want [for] friends who would feel pleasure in assisting you to any amount, if necessary.

There was still more bad news arising from the cause of the bankruptcy. It appears that William had invested heavily in Baltic blockade-running to beat the Continental System. For those that succeeded, returns were excellent as British goods were always in demand and fetched high prices in times of shortage. However there were hazards: weather, privateers and confiscations in port. In William's case, a large convoy that he had backed had been all but destroyed so that the investment was lost; the Lloyd's Names, that is, the individual members of Lloyd's – which was a society not a company – who had underwritten the insurance from their personal wealth, were similarly ruined. Clearly Irving, who was a partner in the business, had disagreed with the amount of risk involved but William had gone ahead anyway, and now there was bitter acrimony in what had always been a close family. Brock wrote back to Irving:

> To what a state of misery we are fallen – poverty I was prepared to bear – but, oh! Irving, if you love me, do not by any action or word add to the sorrows of poor, unfortunate William. Remember his kindness to me – what pleasure he always found in doing me service. Hang the world, it is not worth a thought – be generous and find silent comfort in being so, Oh! My dear boy, forget the past, and let us all unite in soothing the griefs of one of the best hearts that Heaven ever formed. I can well conceive that the causes of his ruin were excited by too ardent a wish to place us all in affluence – his wealth we were sure to divide – why refuse him consolation? – it is all, alas! I can offer.… I sleep little, but am constrained to assume a smiling face during the day: my thoughts are fixed upon you all.… You know the position to which I am lately raised. It will enable me to give up the whole of my salary, £1,000 yearly, and I shall enclose a power of attorney to enable you to receive it – do with it what justice demands – pay as fast as you receive, unless indeed want among any of you calls for aid.…[6]

With war close, the last thing that Brock needed, as a front-line commander, was personal preoccupation and distraction. But there was no escaping this, which had the potential to end his career; it would also have put paid to any plans to marry – even supposing that such plans existed – unless he could land a wealthy heiress. In Upper Canada in 1811 this was indeed a rare species. It was as well that he could submerge himself in the task at hand. Surveyor-General Thomas Ridout* wrote from York on 18 December 1811 that "General Brock intends making this his headquarters, and to bring the navy, engineers, and all departments here in the spring. He told me a day or two ago that he will build an arsenal...."[7] Ridout reported correctly, for in January 1812 Brock sent the acting deputy quartermaster-general, Captain Andrew Gray, to examine the Provincial Marine and over-all situation. Gray found the officers in the Lake Ontario division "extremely inefficient, and ... totally unfit for the situation."[8] Of the two senior officers of the service, one was recommended for transfer and the other for replacement. There was great "need of a man of energy and one who can be trusted at Kingston."[9] Since protecting the squadron in the exposed location of Kingston required a disproportionate part of the forces in Upper Canada, Gray recommended moving the naval base to York. Brock, implementing these recommendations with Prevost's support, ordered the enlistment of 100 seamen, replaced the two senior officers on Lake Ontario and launched plans to move the squadron from Kingston to York by the end of 1812.

Shortly before the turn of the year 1811, Brock sent a despatch to Prevost summarizing his view of the situation in the upper province.[10] He began by saying that the small and dispersed garrison had given rise to a general view among the population that resistance to the Americans in the event of an invasion would be fruitless. However opinions were shifting. His appointment to the unified authority, an increase in the supply of stores and ammunition and "the substitution of a strong regiment" – that is, the 41st Foot in place of the 100th in August 1811 – had created optimism. Brock himself had recently toured the Niagara frontier and found far more confidence and a belief that they could look for help to Quebec. He also stated that he believed the militia would turn out for duty.

He went on to recommend that, in the event of hostilities, he should be allowed to go on the offensive at once to seize the initiative in the area of Amherstburg and the western border which:

> ... if supplied with the means of commencing active operations, must deter any offensive attempt on this province, from Niagara westward. The

---

* Thomas Ridout (1754–1829), born in Britain, moved to Upper Canada from Kentucky after the Revolutionary War. He was a member of the Legislative Assembly and the Legislative Council of Upper Canada.

American government will be compelled to secure their western frontier from the inroads of the Indians, and this cannot be effected without a very considerable force. Before we can expect an active co-operation on the part of the Indians, the reduction of Detroit and Michilimackinac must convince that people, who conceive themselves to have been sacrificed, in 1794, to our policy, that we are earnestly engaged in the war.

Brock then said that as things stood, these two forts were weakly held but easily reinforced and that the militia of Ohio, composed as it was of hardy, warlike men, would be better diverted to their own defence than allowed to take part in an invasion of Upper Canada. To carry out such a scheme, Brock intended to reinforce the 700 regular troops at Amherstburg with another 200 from York and Fort George. Given the bad state of the roads at this time of year, a move would not be possible for at least a month, which would allow time for Prevost to comment on the proposal.

Turning to the situation on the upper lakes, Brock highlighted his dependence on the small naval force there. Maritime agility would be essential for freedom of manoeuvre during future offensive operations and Brock recommended the construction or hire of enough shallow-draft gunboats to cover Lake Erie and Lake Huron.

Brock then considered the Niagara frontier, indicating that this was the most likely place for the American main effort; any other offensive moves by them would be in support of this, or diversionary. Brock could assemble up to 3,000 militia and 500 Indians in that area, which would mean the Americans must attack in strength. However, this force would have to be stiffened by a strong force of regular troops. Brock remarked that a troop of cavalry would be useful here and that enough volunteers had come forward to form one, provided that arms could be supplied to them. He also remarked on the need for gunners, drivers and horses for his artillery. The question of arms for the cavalry was addressed by Prevost in January 1812 with satisfactory results, but the want of gunners remained unanswered.[11]

Next, Brock outlined the situation at the key town of Kingston. He had here the best body of militia in the province, as well as the Glengarry Light Infantry nearby, led by a number of regular officers. Besides garrisoning Kingston, the militia would have to watch the American fort at Ogdensburg, from which a strong American attack could be expected. Brock had

GREAT ADVANTAGES,
to those who enlift for
Capt. LIDDELL's Company of the
GLENGARY
LIGHT INFANTRY FENCIBLES.

EVERY Young Man who afpires to ferve His Majefty in this fine Regiment now raifing, will do well to confider without delay, the very advantageous terms on which he enlifts. He is to receive FIVE GUINEAS BOUNTY, and is only required to ferve in the *Canadas* for *Three Years*, or *during the War*, which probably may not laft fo long, when he will, beyond a doubt, receive the Reward of his Services, by obtaining an allotment of the rich and fertile Lands of Upper Canada, or Lower Canada, if more convenient. This important Grant will make every Soldier of the Corps an Independant Man, at the expiration of his Service; enabled thereby to fettle comfortably on his own Farm, in a fhort time he will have every Luxury of Life about him: he will be able to take his Wife and Family to Church or Market in his own Cariole, and if he has not a Wife, it will be the fure means of getting him a good one, for Fortune always favors the Brave, and flinty muft be the heart of that Damfel, and vain her pretenfions to tafte, who could refift a *Light Bob of the Glengary's* when equipped in his new *Green Uniform*, which will unqueftionably be the *neateft in the Service.*

Look around you! See how many rich and refpectable Inhabitants of Canada, who were formerly Soldiers, that are now enjoying the reward of their Services, and who date their Profperity from the time when they received their Grants of Land on being difcharged. The fame advantages will be yours. Such of you, on the réduction of the Corps, as are not then Officers, and who prefer the tranquil Pleafures of a Rural Life, may, by induftry and good management, hope to reach the higheft honours which the Province can beftow. In this happy Country, Merit and Ability muft ever lead to Preferment, and the Man poffeffed of thefe qualities, may have it in his power to chufe whether he will be a Colonel of Militia, a Juftice of the Peace, or a Member of the Houfe of Affembly. Brave Countrymen! you muft be quick in your acceptance of fuch Offers as thefe, or you will certainly mifs the Golden Opportunity; terms fo evidently advantageous muft foon complete the Regiment, and thofe who are too late, will have caufe all their lives to reproach themfelves for being fo blind to their own interest. No deception is intended; for the affurance of General SIR GEORGE PREVOST, as certified by *Colonel Baynes*, Adjutant General, muft convince the moft incredulous, that His Royal Highnefs the PRINCE REGENT will gracioufly attend to His Excellency's Recommendation, by beftowing a Grant of Lands upon every Soldier who has faithfully ferved for the stipulated period.

N. B. A few Taylors, Shoemakers, Carpenters and Black Smiths, will meet with great encouragement in the Corps; a Serjeant Armourer Quarter Mafter Serjeant, Serjeant Major, Bugle Major, Paymafter's Clerk and Ten Pay Serjeants will be wanted, and fuch men as are qualified for these Offices, will fee the neceffity of an early application.

A recruiting notice for the Glengarry Light Infantry Fencibles, listing the advantages available to those who volunteered. (Author's collection)

Lieutenant-Colonel John Macdonell (1785–1812), Brock's provincial aide-de-camp. He was killed soon after Brock at Queenston Heights, 13 October 1812. (Toronto Reference Library T-17053)

proposed the raising of the Glengarries some years before, it will be re-membered, but it was not until now that the regiment was given official sanction[12] under the command of a Catholic officer of the 8th Foot, Major "Red George" Macdonell.* Prevost, who had already established the Cana-dian Fencibles in Lower Canada, now undertook to provide more regular officers, including Lieutenant John Shaw of the 49th as a captain command-ing a company, whom Brock almost certainly recommended.[13] Every regular officer selected to command a company had to enlist thirty men and every lieutenant, fifteen. The only non-regular officer appointed to a company was Alexander Roxburgh of Kingston. By May 1812 the strength of the Glen-garries had reached 600, assisted no doubt by £4 of bounty money per man and the promise of 100 acres of land at the end of the war. This size of corps allowed the appointment of a colonel and Prevost exercised his power of patronage by appointing the adjutant-general, Edward Baynes. The lieuten-ant-colonelcy and executive command was given to Francis Battersby of the 8th Foot, leaving Macdonell as major.

Finally, Brock sent Prevost a copy of his Militia Act, which provided the enabling authority for mobilization of the militia. He asked for a regular of-ficer to command the militia, and a commissariat-general. A few days later he acknowledged Prevost's instructions to establish arms depots around the province, but pointed out that many weapons previously issued over the years to the militia had been lost and that this loss reduced his ability to comply. He also pointed out the lack of secure stores for both weapons and

---

* In theory the penal laws were still in force and forbade Catholics from holding commissions in the army. However the needs of the war with France had caused these laws to be slowly relaxed, especially in Scottish and Irish regiments.

ammunition.[14] This attention to detail rather belies a comment made by Brigade Major Thomas Evans after Brock's death: "Poor General Brock's high spirit would never descend to particulars, trifles I may say in the abstract, but ultimately essentials."[15] Evans was wrong: it was not Brock's task as commanding general to attend to every trifle himself – that was the job of the staff. What Brock did was to identify tactical problems that might have operational or strategic consequences and rectify them.

Brock's assessment of the situation from the point of view of a military commander at his level is essentially sound and borne out by later events. Given the need to harness the white civilian population and maintain the alliance with the native peoples, his suggested course of action makes sense. His proposal was bold and demonstrated that Brock had a firm understanding of what we would now call the operational level of war – or as it was then thought of, grand tactics. He recognized several key principles of war: the primacy of the offensive, speed, seizure and maintenance of the initiative, and good intelligence to lead operations; however, he was wanting in some other respects, especially the requirement to secure one's own force and for a solid logistic supply. Moreover, he missed the vital and over-riding principle of political primacy, for Brock was at variance with the view at the strategic level – from London, and from Sir James Craig – which he must have heard repeatedly during his years in Quebec.

For his part, Prevost had recently received a set of instructions and guidance, in the name of the Prince Regent, that placed limits on his actions before the commencement of war. These were the exact opposite of what Brock proposed: given the constraints on resources and the need to hold Quebec and the St Lawrence, Prevost was not to undertake any offensive action "except it be for the purpose of preventing or repelling Hostilities or unavoidable Emergencies."[16] Prevost therefore replied to Brock's proposals in a short letter on Christmas Eve, 1811. He approved Brock's measures regarding the militia but urged caution in encouraging aggression by the native people. He also acknowledged the growing hostility of the U.S. government towards Britain and therefore:

> ... I feel justified in recommending such precaution as may place you in
> a state of preparation for that event; and with this view you must endeav-

our to trace an outline of co-operation, compensating for our deficiency in strength. I agree with you as to the advantages which may result from giving, rather than receiving, the first blow; but it is not my opinion war will commence by a declaration … we must expect repeated petty aggressions from our neighbours, before we are permitted to retaliate by open hostilities.[17]

Prevost's response to his instructions from London was to develop a report on options for the defence of British North America in 1812 for Lord Liverpool, the Secretary of State for War and Colonies. The report provided an overview and assessment of the provinces in British North America with comments on specific stations, and in tone it follows closely the previous analysis of Lord Dorchester and Sir James Craig. This report is central to an understanding of the intentions of the commander-in-chief in British North America and the state of the defences in the spring of 1812.[18] It also highlighted other factors that influenced strategy, like the protection of the northwest fur trade and the command of the navigation of the lakes. Upper Canada was described as "the most contiguous to the Territory of the United States" and in the "event of war, more liable to immediate attack." The posts in Upper Canada were poorly fortified, lightly garrisoned and exposed. The most critical point was Kingston, as it was "open to sudden attack, which if successful, would cut off the communication between the Upper and Lower Province and deprive us of our naval resources." The proximity of American posts "with good Harbours" posed an immediate threat to Kingston. To preserve communications between Upper and Lower Canada, a strong contingent of regulars supported by militia would be needed at Kingston. At the western end of the province, Fort St Joseph was a poor fortification but occupied an important position along the communication line between Lake Huron and Lake Superior. In doing so, it provided some protection to the northwestern fur trade. Like Amherstburg, it was a point of assemblage for friendly natives, a factor of considerable importance to the British. Amherstburg was also home to a dockyard and naval station. On the north shore of Lake Ontario, York was poorly fortified but had a good harbour. Its "retired situation from the American frontier makes it a position particularly desirable.…" Along the Niagara River, Fort George, Chippawa and Fort Erie were contiguous to American territory. In the event of

Montreal, seen here from across the river, was the highest navigable point on the St Lawrence before encountering rapids. It was an important and growing commercial centre and entrepôt for the fur trade and for goods being sent further inland. (Library of Congress)

war, the capture of Fort Niagara, across the Niagara from Fort George, was important to securing communication along the Niagara River.

As for Lower Canada, the outline defensive plan was clear. Quebec, with "the only permanent fortification in the Canadas," and Montreal, as "the principal commercial city in the Canadas," were the vital ground. The security of both depended on an "impenetrable line on the South Shore ... with a sufficient flotilla to command the Rivers St Lawrence and the Richelieu." The factor underscoring Prevost's thinking was the importance of maritime power. British control of the lakes in 1812 provided security for Brock's flanks and patrolled the large open spaces between the garrisons. It also aided rapid movement, allowing Prevost the ability quickly to shift his meagre resources of men and munitions from front to front.

Montreal would, Prevost felt, be the first object of any American attack, while Quebec was "the key to the whole and must be maintained." The fortifications needed improvement to withstand a "vigorous and well conducted siege" and await reinforcement from the empire. Prevost stressed that "it would be in vain ... with the hopes of making an effectual defence of the open country [i.e., Upper Canada], unless powerfully assisted from Home." For Prevost, control of the city of Montreal was without doubt a decisive point on the road to success in any campaign in the Canadas, far more so than control of York or Kingston. It dominated the St Lawrence and controlled access both to the Great Lakes and to Quebec and the Maritime Provinces. Through the city passed large quantities of supplies for the allied army in the Canadas, supplies not just from Europe but in large measure from New England as well. No wonder that the town had been a priority target in the campaigns of 1760 and 1775. Prevost clearly understood Montreal's importance, as his defensive plan showed by the placing of the military main effort in Lower Canada – if necessary at the cost of abandoning Upper Canada. From there, de Rottenburg kept a close watch on military developments south of the frontier; he also did all he could to encourage the continuing trade from New England along the Lake Champlain route. As Prevost pointed out, much later in the war, "two thirds of the army in Canada are at this very moment eating beef provided by American contractors, drawn principally from the states of Vermont and New York … it is expected that Congress will take steps to deprive us of these resources."[19]

Despite the importance of Montreal, with the limited resources that might be added to his already paltry forces in wartime, Prevost concluded "the preservation of Quebec as the first object, and to which all others must be subordinate." There could be no question of weakening it:

> Defective as Quebec is, it is the only post that can be considered tenable for a moment, the preservation of it being of the utmost consequence to the Canadas, as the door of Entry for that Force the King's Government might find it expedient to send for the recovery of both, or either of these provinces … it would be in vain the General should flatter himself with the hopes of making an effectual defence of the open Country, unless powerfully assisted from Home:– All predatory or ill concerted attacks undertaken presumptuously without sufficient means can be resisted and repulsed:– Still this must be done with caution, that the resources, for a future exertion, the defence of Quebec, may be unexhausted.[20]

Prevost had encouraged the highly important fur trade, already mentioned, run by the Hudson's Bay Company, the North West Company and smaller enterprises like the Michilimackinac Company. This mattered both from the point of view of revenue and from that of maintaining relations with the native people. As a result of Prevost's encouragement and protection of their trade, the companies agreed to "enter with zeal into any measure of Defence, *or even offence,* that may be proposed to them."[21] The companies felt certain of being able to control Lake Superior, where they maintained two vessels, one of 120 tons and one of 60 tons, both of which were capable of carrying guns, but were less certain of being able to maintain a line of communication across Lake Huron. Another two vessels of around 100 tons, each mounting four guns, were based at Sandwich and a large number of heavy canoes. The companies clearly supported Brock's view that the American fort at Mackinac should be reduced as soon as possible. Accordingly, the companies were prepared to lend their ships to the service of the British government and to form a corps of *voyageurs* for military service.[22]

The diplomatic situation was clearly delicate and Prevost was well aware of both his instructions from London and the considerable body of antiwar feeling in many of the United States – a feeling that could easily be turned by precipitate action. He also knew that any casualties suffered early in the war would not be easily replaced, certainly not before the onset of winter. It might take three months for a request for reinforcements to reach England and another three months to transport them to the Upper Province. If winter intervened this might add another four months – the losses from one campaigning season might not therefore be met until well into the next. Given that according to generally accepted historical norms, a unit becomes combat ineffective after about 30 per cent casualties, especially among the leadership, unnecessary fighting would reduce Prevost's forces to incapacity faster than he could rebuild them – and faster too than the Americans could bring up their replacements.

In March 1812, John Macdonell made a covert reconnaissance of Detroit and Brock sent his report on to Prevost as evidence that a pre-emptive blow could be struck. Prevost replied sternly:

> Whatever temptations may offer to induce you to depart from a system strictly defensive, I must pointedly request that, under the existing circumstances of our relations with the Government of the United States, you will not allow them to lead you into any measure having the character of offence, even should a declaration of war be laid on the table of the Congress.... there prevails throughout the United States a great unwill-

ingness to enter upon Hostilities and also because the apparent neglect at Detroit might be but a bait to tempt us to an act of aggression, in its effect uniting parties.… You are nevertheless to persevere in your preparations for defence and in such arrangements as may upon a change in the state of affairs enable you to carry any disposable part of your force offensively against the commun [*sic*] enemy.[23]

This is not as reactive a stance as it might at first appear. Prevost had first-hand knowledge of American affairs from his time in Nova Scotia, whence he had twice sent a spy into the United States to gain detailed information on the intentions of the government and the state of the armed forces; Brock did not have this information. Prevost continued to believe that the anti-war party in the U.S. could prevail, that British efforts to maintain friendly relations could prove successful, but that pre-emptive action on the part of the native people could give the war party the ammunition it needed to achieve a declaration of war. Prevost's plans for the defence of the Canadas also differed significantly from those of his predecessors, who had stressed the defence only of Quebec: Prevost did believe that the whole of the Canadas could be defended. But this was a secondary theatre in the wider British war effort and his instructions were not to defeat the Americans but to prevent the loss of the Canadas. He was therefore operationally on the defensive but could allow tactical offensives – which he later did – to restore the situation or in response to aggression.

But Prevost's concept for the defence of the Canadas was not shared by Brock, although he had earlier in his career agreed with the views of Craig and Prevost. The reasons for his change of mind and heart are unclear and may only be inferred from a study of Brock's character. His temperament and experience made him reject any notion of remaining on the defensive or surrendering the initiative to the Americans. However, one man claimed responsibility for Brock's conversion. Writing after the war, Lieutenant-Colonel "Red George" Macdonell claimed he convinced Brock of the idea during dinner.[24] The real explanation is probably a combination of personal factors, advice from his subordinates and perhaps from observations made while touring the upper province. Whatever the reasons, Brock genuinely believed an active defence could succeed. If the western natives were armed and encouraged to fight and Mackinac and Detroit taken immediately upon declaration of war, the American forces directed at Upper Canada would be diverted westward. If the British maintained naval superiority on Lake Ontario and Lake Erie, the only other place left for an American attack would be the Niagara region, which should be strongly reinforced.[25] Prevost agreed with these ideas on military grounds but could not approve of them, as his instructions from London did not authorize the conduct of pre-emptive offensive operations.

It may be that Brock did not understand Prevost's position, but this is unlikely given his time as acting commander-in-chief. It did not help at all that he and Prevost never met face to face, which from the point of view of developing mutual trust and understanding between commanders – a fundamental requirement for any general and his subordinates – was highly unhelpful. Prevost was certainly remiss in not visiting Upper Canada to gain some understanding of the situation there and to demonstrate the commitment of the British government. Correspondence between the men contains several cases of Brock asking when he might expect Prevost at York, and Prevost claiming pressure of work in Lower Canada.[26] To be fair to Prevost, his diary was probably just too full. He had arrived in September 1811, commenced a review of strategy and a full programme of legislative reform based on sixty pages of instructions from London, made changes to the executive and legislative councils, and reviewed the structure of the militia – all this in the teeth of opposition from officials who supported Sir James Craig's views rather than his. It was therefore necessary for him to be at the seat of government rather than spending at least thirty days travelling and inspecting posts in the upper province.

Prevost and Brock thus communicated by letter only and one has the feeling that Brock, like many officers before and since deployed in remote commands, could not help feeling that local conditions were being misread by those without detailed knowledge. We are left with the possibility that Brock was working directly against his higher commander to thwart what he believed would be a betrayal of the upper province and its people: a matter of honour, therefore. John Norton seems to support this view, writing in his journal of the war that Brock's appointment to the upper province was well received:

> … the decisive manner in which General Brock always spoke and acted was a very favourable feature in his military Character, and filled with confidence every true Loyalist, who was determined to defend the Country to the last, – whilst his discernment, candour and rectitude entirely confounded the spirit of Party, and exposed the Mystery of Calumny.[27]

If true, this was potentially a dangerous course for Brock personally and one that would have been viewed professionally with grave disfavour had it been pursued openly, for the first loyalty of a subordinate must be to his superiors. It was potentially a dangerous course, too, for British North America if Prevost's overall strategic concept is considered valid. Brock was, moreover, committing Britain to a strategy that no-one was calling for either in London or in North America: the expansion of Crown authority into the territory of the United States. In the end Brock's early death, coupled with the lack of preparation of the U.S. Army and the ineptitude of American generalship, allowed him to get away with this course of action. Had he lived and faced the revived U.S. Army that took the field in 1813 and 1814, we can only speculate whether he would have been up to the challenge.

In January 1812 Brock's prayers appeared to have been answered. Word arrived from England that if he wished he could leave Canada by permission of the Prince Regent and return to England, where he would be found a command in Spain:[28] the good opinion of him at the Horse Guards and the lobbying of his family and friends had at last paid off. But now that the chance had come, Brock could not take it. For one thing, war was close and Brock's personal pride, sense of duty and sense of what honour demanded would allow him neither to walk away from a fight nor to leave a job undone. Then there was the personal factor. With a debt of £3,000 hanging over him, Brock could simply not afford to give up the £1,000 a year salary as president of the council and risk losing at least half his pay as a major-general if he could not be found a post on the active list. He therefore wrote to Prevost to say that "The state of public affairs with the American government indicating a strong presumption of an approaching rupture between the two countries, I beg leave to be allowed to remain in my present command."[29] This decision, one received with relief by Prevost, sealed Brock's fate.

Over the winter Brock continued the administration of the province, doing his best to stiffen the will of the people to resist a probable invasion. He visited troops and ordered work to strengthen defences, especially at Amherstburg, York, Chippawa, Fort George and Fort Erie. He saw to the raising, training and equipping of militia units, and persuaded Prevost to lobby London so that any soldier wounded during fighting with the Americans, or the family of any soldier killed, would be placed on the United Empire List and given a grant of land in the same way that Loyalists after the Revolutionary War had been rewarded.[30] He continued to parley with the Grand River people to bring them actively into the coalition;[31] and he advised Prevost again that urging peace on the aboriginal nations would only diminish their trust in the British "until at length they lose it altogether."[32] He made large purchases of foodstuffs in the United States. In February 1812, for example, he purchased salted pork, 2,000 bushels of Indian corn, flour and live oxen;[33] the corn was almost certainly intended for the native people, to allow existing stocks of wheat and wheat flour to be husbanded for the troops. The general shortage of gold, which had to be used to buy food in the U.S.A. and to pay subsidies to the native people, made the use of hated paper money necessary for paying local suppliers and troops.[34]

From the native people, the fur traders and his outposts, Brock had good knowledge of American movements. In May 1812, for example, he warned of reinforcements of regulars and companies of the Ohio militia into Detroit.[35] He again lobbied Prevost on the subject of Detroit and Mackinac, writing that "unless Detroit and Michilimackinac be both in our possession immediately at the commencement of hostilities, not only the district of Amherstburg but most probably the whole country as far as Kingston, must be evacuated."[36]

Prevost's view continued to be one of caution, even on the edge of ruin. Writing to Lord Liverpool in early April 1812 Prevost said that:

> I have reason to expect the next measure of hostility which Mr Madison will practice will be ... a declaration of War against Great Britain; I have therefore deemed it expedient to address myself on the occasion to the General Officers ... recommending the utmost caution and prudence in their intercourse with the United States. ... my letter on this subject to Major Gen. Brock, that to Sir John Sherbrooke contains the same restrictions except as respects the Fort of Detroit.[37]

Brock's position in response to this was one of outward obedience to his superior, while at the same time preparing for what he saw as the inevitable collapse of the policy. As late as 16 May he assured Prevost that "It will be my study to guard against every event that can give them any cause for complaint...."[38]

B rock was in a position that many officers of his rank at that time would have understood when despatched to colonies or theatres of war far from the seat of government. Sir George Prevost, his superior, was similarly placed. Brock had to concentrate on the command of fighting troops, of combined arms, soon to be engaged in war, but as the senior officer in Upper Canada he also had to plan and execute a campaign in an extended theatre of operations. Then, as civil administrator, he was responsible for

A contemporary picture of the uniform of the British infantry in 1812, as well as a look at English civilian attire and the process of recruiting the raw material of the army. (From R. & D. Havell, *The Costume of Yorkshire* (1814). By permission of Science, Industry & Business Library, New York Public Library, Astor, Lenox and Tilden Foundations)

managing both the civil and military aspects of his country's policy and strategy, and the spending of its blood and treasure. The exercise of command by a general like Brock was not therefore just leadership. His command encompassed three essential functions: leadership, the management of men and resources on campaign, and decision-making.

Leadership at Brock's level was and is bound up with the spirit and motivation of the troops, their trust in the skill of their commander, their own courage and experience. In the British army the essential qualities of a leader are still held to include courage, willpower, the ability to communicate ideas and beliefs, the human touch, professional expertise, loyalty – including the development of subordinates – and the willingness to accept responsibility. There is little doubt that Brock possessed all these qualities in good measure and had demonstrated them repeatedly; he was by any standards a true leader and his officers and men reacted instinctively to his qualities. He was also possessed of what is arguably the first quality of a military leader, courage, both physical and moral, which was especially true in the late eighteenth and early nineteenth centuries, as has been discussed in the opening chapter. Brock knew very well that if the officers – and especially the general – were brave and seen to be brave, their courage would inspire the troops; they would trust his decisions even if it meant hardship. Shared experience, especially where it involves privations, danger, the loss of comrades, can be a powerful bond that will engender deep feelings of mutual trust and affection. It is easy for anyone to be brave for a short time, but for a commander like Brock what was most wearing was that he had to be brave all the time. And he needed great reserves of moral courage to take hard decisions that would result in death and mutilation.

Turning to campaign management and decision-making, it must be acknowledged that in Brock's day there was an inescapable connection between the campaign and the battle: the campaign was constructed to achieve strategic objectives and was designed to bring the enemy to battle, a battle that would be the decisive act of the war – the concept of the campaign will be examined in more detail in chapter 10. This was Brock's real problem, since the strategic objectives as seen from London focused on the need to avoid battle except on very favourable terms, while seen from Washington they required early closure and success. Since the enemy had a vote, London's wishes were unlikely to be long maintained.

Thus Brock the general had to consider first the enemy, the object of his problem. Superior intelligence and the generation of superior tempo would have been foremost in his mind when formulating his probable course of action, and this can clearly be seen in his proposals to Prevost. Once he had formulated one or more courses of action, he would have had to test them against the factors that could create decisive conditions: the available time and space, the limited resources and the environment. Under resources were such things as the relative strength and capability of the forces, the morale and discipline of the troops, the quality of subordinate leadership or staff work and the availability of logistic support. The environment included climate and weather and its effects, the prevalence of diseases, the density and attitude of the civilian population and, in particular, the terrain – which was not important in itself but only in the way it could confer advantage, as with the possession of naval supremacy on the lakes. In theory these factors weighed as heavily on the Americans as on him; in practice it was not so simple. Environmental factors probably did bear equally, but time and space were different equations. While Brock had to deal with an extended line of communications along the waterway and so across the Atlantic to England, Hull and Dearborn also faced enormous challenges in running an extended line of communications through often hostile territory. These factors of time and space, therefore, governed the flow of resources *to* the front as well as what could be maintained *at* the front. This will be examined in more detail in chapter 11.

Brock would also have had to satisfy himself on a number of key questions at the outset of his planning, and these have not changed much since, despite the alteration in circumstances: Which military conditions must be attained to achieve strategic and operational objectives? What sequence of actions was most likely to produce these conditions? How should military resources best be applied to accomplish that sequence of actions? Were the associated risks acceptable? Risk is all about the likelihood of a course of action going well or badly and the impact, for good or ill, of that. The adverse consequences of risk are threats, and the benign consequences are opportunities; usually one is presented with both. Brock, like any general, therefore would accept risks on campaign when he felt obliged to do so to fulfil his mission, and if he could accept the consequences of failure. If he felt that he must accept them but could not stand failure, he would be

Lieutenant Daniel Claus was the son of Colonel William Claus of the British Indian Department. This is one of a very few examples of the uniform of the 49th at this time as they moved to join Brock's command. Daniel Claus was killed at Crysler's Farm in 1813. (Library and Archives Canada C-095817)

forced to find ways to mitigate those risks. If the risks themselves could not be mitigated, he would have to mitigate the effects of failure. In weighing these, he had to distinguish between strategic risks and operational risks. Strategic risks may, if they go wrong, bring ruin because they will affect the national standing and ability to influence events at home or abroad: for the British government, the key strategic risk was the security of the city of Quebec and the line of communication – and one must question whether Brock understood this over-riding imperative. Operational risks may incur threats to the campaign – through bad planning or execution – or they may present an unforeseen opportunity that can be exploited. But even the best general cannot exclude the possibility that risks may arise during a campaign because of events outside his control, such as a change of government, or else through the performance of his force, which might be better or worse than expected. For Brock, the coming months were nothing unless a series of risks to be calculated and played out.[39]

Even before war broke out it is possible to determine that Brock was an intuitive decision-maker on campaign – no tortuous councils of war for him – but he had the duty of fostering mutual trust and understanding among his subordinate commanders, while reserving the right to make decisions himself. Like many with well developed intuition, his timing was usually excellent, as was his ability to recognize a change in the tactical situation and to be in the right place at the right time. To make decisions in changing circumstances, on the basis of the best available information, posed for Brock the age-old question of where to place himself to do the essential three things that a general had to do properly to exercise command: that is, to find out what was going on, to communicate his intentions to his subordinates (and his superiors), and to keep in contact with his staff so that they could solve problems and shift resources. He faced the choice of whether to command in Fort George to oversee the most vulnerable part of the frontier; or well forward in Amherstburg, the point of greatest danger; or to stay back in York, where he could also control the civil administration; for command and control in a war is a question of communications in relation to time, so that decisions can be made that will control the course of events. There was no one simple answer for Brock and thus over the coming months he faced frequent, difficult journeys to be in the right place at the right time, to receive the best available information, review the situation, make fresh estimates in the light of events and amend his plan as required – since as any soldier knows, no plan survives contact with the enemy.

CHAPTER TEN

"Mr Madison's War"

THE UNITED STATES, BRITAIN AND THE CANADAS, JUNE–JULY 1812

Negotiations over the grievances of the U.S. government with the British minister in Washington, Sir Augustus Foster,* seemed to President James Madison to be going nowhere. His address to Congress on 1 June 1812, which preceded the declaration of war on Britain, set out the grievances for which the United States felt obliged to fight: the impressment of American seamen from U.S. ships; the violation of American territorial waters by the Royal Navy and a succession of incidents between ships, like the *Chesapeake* and the *Leopard*; the inadequate notice given before the imposition of "mock blockades"; and the regulation of trade with Europe by a neutral nation through the Orders in Council.[1] The tone of the address was hostile to Britain, but not especially friendly towards France, for Madison had a vague feeling that somehow Napoleon had manoeuvred the British and U.S. governments into conflict. The stated purpose of this conflict was to put an end to the interference with U.S. trade and shipping; but its hidden purpose and method was to be the largely unrelated business of a land war to seize the British colonies in North America. A consequence of this would be to extend further the already stretched naval and military resources and funds of France's most implacable enemy.

On 4 June the House of Representatives voted 79 to 49 in favour of war and on 17 June the Senate followed with a majority of 19 to 13; war was declared the next day.[2] Foster asked for a suspension of hostilities until word could be sent to London, but this was denied. He wrote to the Foreign Secretary before his departure that "This extraordinary measure seems to have been unexpected by nearly the whole Nation; & to have been carried in op-

---

* Sir Augustus John Foster, 1st Baronet (1780–1848).

President James Madison (1751–1836). Though he declared war, his administration offered uncertain leadership in the early stages of the conflict, both in choice of military commanders and in strengthening the American army. (Library of Congress)

position to the declared sentiments of many of those who voted for it...."[3]

To Henry Clay and the War Hawks in Congress,* the timing for such a war seemed right. Bonaparte was at the height of his power and was preparing to attack Russia: only Sicily, Sardinia, Sweden, Portugal and parts of Spain were outside his influence, and it could be only a matter of time before the British and their few clients were forced to treat, as they had been in 1783. The natural consequence would be that, just as the American colonies had moved to a republican form of government then, so would the Canadas now, under the guidance and tutelage of Washington. Though the term had yet to be coined, it was the "manifest destiny" of the United States to rule the whole of the continent of North America. Somehow, against the evidence and probably on the strength of the activities of Joseph Willcocks and his like, Madison's government convinced itself that the greater part of both the English- and French-speaking population of the Canadas would welcome an American invasion. The odds at first glance appeared favourable: the American population in 1810 numbered just over seven million people,[4] compared with 500,000 people living in British North America.[5] But a war would also be fought by the 12,500,000 people of Great Britain, not just those in the Canadas and the Maritime Provinces.

---

* Modern scholarship indicates that the War Hawks, although vociferous and influential, were a much smaller faction than has been thought – perhaps only a core membership of eleven men.

A major factor that Madison overlooked was the nature of Bonaparte's government. It was no longer, and had probably never been, the sort of enlightened republicanism envisaged by the American revolutionaries of 1775 and the French revolutionaries of 1789; it was a despotism as absolute as anything seen before or since. Had Britain been defeated, the Napoleonic policy of continual expansion might soon have repudiated the Louisiana Purchase and sought to subvert both French Canadians and French and Spanish colonists in the Floridas and Louisiana, thus bringing about an open confrontation with the U.S.A. For these reasons, along with the very real dislike of Madison and his policies, as well as of Bonaparte, there were many people in the United States who had no enthusiasm for Mr Madison's war. This was particularly the case in Vermont and New York, which in addition fared very well commercially from those contracts which accounted for two-thirds of the supplies bought by the British army in the Canadas, the Maritime Provinces, Spain and Portugal. With the coming of war, this valuable trade could easily be lost. Nor had Madison understood the fears of the French in Canada, preferring to take comfort in their dislike of Sir James Craig.

But for others, especially in the south and the new west of the U.S., there was no doubt about the identity of the enemy. To establish the republic in a position of advantage, from which its grievances could be righted, there seemed only one correct course of action. Since any naval war would, given the sheer strength and size of the Royal Navy, only ever be an inconvenience to Britain, it was proposed to conquer the Canadas using naval forces to control the Great Lakes and the U.S. Army to conquer territory. Thomas Jefferson had declared his belief that an advance on Quebec would be "a mere matter of marching." At the same time, the vociferous Kentuckian Henry Clay had declared that "I trust I shall not be presumptuous when I state that I verily believe that the militia of Kentucky are on their own competent to place Montreal and Upper Canada at your [Madison's] feet."[6]

But on the very day that the British minister left Washington for Britain, 23 June 1812, a new British government led by Lord Liverpool snatched the rug from under the Americans' feet by ending the major cause of grievance: the Orders in Council were repealed.

The entire establishment of the U.S. Army which was to accomplish this mere matter of marching was, in 1812, only 10,000 regulars, unsupported by either a staff system or logistic infrastructure. From 1783 onward, the U.S. had built up a small professional army, but the regular service was undermined by the "nation in arms" concept – that the main shield of the republic was the citizen soldier mobilized only in times of war for limited periods. The regular force was neglected, particularly after the Republican Party came to power in 1803, and although it had been marginally increased in 1808–09, it was still very small. In June 1812 the army consisted of seven infantry regiments, one artillery regiment, one light horse-artillery regiment and one regiment of dragoons. Five of the seven infantry regiments were in the newly-acquired Louisiana Territory, as far from the Canadas as it was possible to be while still being on U.S. soil; one was guarding the Mississippi and only one, the 4th Infantry, was deployed in the field in the Northwest. The artillery regiment was dispersed at small posts along the seaboard and frontiers, the light artillery regiment had no horses and the dragoon regiment was dismounted. No less than eighteen new regiments of infantry and one of light dragoons had been authorized in the spring of 1812, but they would not be ready for service until the autumn at least. On paper, therefore, the odds were even between the Americans and the regular British army garrisons in North America.

The U.S. Army's establishment was further increased by Congress to 36,000, or thirty-one regiments, during the course of 1812, following Madison's request, plus 50,000 volunteers – an enormous force far exceeding the small British garrison, but almost totally lacking in competent officers and NCOs. Most of the former were either raw young men or elderly veterans of the Revolutionary War. To make things worse, because of the dislike of military professionals, the government refused to appoint military or naval commanders-in-chief. Major-General Henry Dearborn,* a Revolutionary War veteran and former Secretary of War, was pulled out of retirement and made "senior general" but he had no control over troop movements outside his immediate area, which was Lake Champlain, nor did he want the respon-

---

* Major-General Henry Dearborn (1751–1829) had served in the Revolutionary War and had been captured by the British during the abortive attack on Quebec. He was nominated by James Madison as Secretary of War but the Senate rejected the nomination.

sibility – at best he was an advisor to the government and an indifferent one at that. There was no naval officer higher than the rank of commodore and that rank was a temporary one. There were two other major-generals in the army in 1812, James Wilkinson* and Wade E. Hampton,† who hated the sight of each other, causing a division in the officer corps. In the spring of 1812 the government appointed about a dozen other general officers, mostly aged veterans of the Revolutionary War or from the state militias, none of whom was capable of exercising operational command. Most of these elderly generals had to be replaced within a year: the average age of an American general officer in 1812 was fifty-five; two years later it had fallen to thirty-three.[7]

The army was equally deficient in training and in practical experience, and although it tried to adopt a new, flexible system of tactical manoeuvre,[8] it never succeeded in implementing this during the war. Equipment too was in short supply, for a good deal of the army's clothing and equipment usually came from Britain. The national defences, especially the frontier posts at Plattsburgh, Ogdensburg, Sackets Harbor, Oswego, Niagara, Schlosser, Detroit, Presqu'isle and Mackinac, the port fortifications and the arsenals were all neglected.

Part of the problem was that the powers of the federal government were much weaker in 1812 than now – people spoke of *these* United States, not *the* United States – and the federal government had limited means of raising money; customs and excise duties were its major sources of income, and these had been much diminished by the Embargo Acts. Throughout the War of 1812, the U.S. federal government was in serious financial straits and it was fundamentally bankrupt by 1814. There was, therefore, a greater reliance on the military forces provided by each of the states – the militia, which at a theoretical strength of 100,000, was the traditional bulwark of the American people against oppression. It was this citizen army which, according to popular mythology, had wrested victory from the redcoats and Hessians (the massive French and Spanish military assistance of the later years of

---

* General James Wilkinson (1757–1825) had served in the Revolutionary War and was governor of the Louisiana Territory in 1805. He served in the army again during the War of 1812; after his death he was discovered to have been a Spanish agent.

† General Wade E Hampton (1752–1835) came from an influential South Carolina family. He had also served in the Revolutionary War and made a disastrous return to duty in the War of 1812.

the Revolutionary War was conveniently forgotten). Post-revolutionary America had no love for a regular army, but every man between the ages of eighteen and fifty was theoretically liable for service in the militia. Almost twenty years of peace, a generation in effect, had eroded the capability of the militia. Its discipline and training were lamentable, leading to much friction with regular units; its officers were elected; and men with farms to run were unwilling to tramp off to the Canadas. But not all was gloomy: there remained a strong core of hardy men well skilled in shooting and field-craft, although in general terms the ability of the militia to conduct even limited operations was greatly in doubt.[9] An additional problem was that state laws invariably prohibited men from being called out for periods longer than six months; this was compounded by the federal constitution, which made it clear that no militiaman could be forced to serve outside the boundaries of the republic, so the militia could not be used as an offensive force. To get around this problem, the federal government tried to raise units of "volunteers in federal service" who could serve on foreign territory for up to a year, but as the state militias offered higher pay, shorter periods of service and less chance of getting killed, thus attracting the best officers and men to the service of the state rather than the federal government, the federal volunteer units were never very effective.

Strategy is the achievement of national objectives using such ways and means as are available, appropriate and legal. Tactics is the business of fighting battles and engagements. Between the two lies the operational level of war, which modern doctrine describes as the vital link, or gearing, between military strategic objectives and the tactical employment of forces in battles and engagements. It is the level at which campaigns and major operations are planned, sustained, sequenced and directed. "It is," says the British army's doctrine publication *Operations*, "the responsibility of the operational level commander to determine the campaign plan required to achieve the desired military strategic end-state within the designated theatre of operations." In this, it draws heavily on the writings of Brock's contemporary theorists, Baron Antoine Jomini and General Karl-Maria von Clausewitz. Explicit in the design of a campaign is the defeat of an enemy, which is defined by the British army as so diminishing the effectiveness of the enemy that he is either unable to participate in combat or at least cannot fulfil his intentions. This is a notion that Brock and his contemporaries understood completely. It encapsulates both the physical destruction of an enemy's ability to prosecute war and the destruction of his will to fight. The latter is often more efficient, if more indirect, for as Napoleon himself remarked, "More battles are decided by loss of hope, than by loss of blood." Its ways are pre-emption, dislocation and disruption; its means include firepower, superior force ratios, superior tempo, simultaneous action and surprise.

The business of the operational level and its commander is campaigning. A campaign can be defined very simply as a set of military operations planned and conducted to achieve a strategic objective, within a given time and geographical area. Thus a campaign is set within the context of operational art: it is not just grand tactics, or strategy writ small. Clausewitz points out two key concepts for the operational general. First, the principle of culmination – that is, the point at which one side starts winning and the other starts losing, either offensively or defensively. Secondly, the notion of the decisive act, or the decisive operation, that which causes an enemy to culminate – that is, to be unable further to develop offensive operations and thus to surrender the initiative. War is seldom so straightforward as to permit of one single decisive act; usually what is decisive is a combination of several actions. But herein lies the very essence of generalship at the operational level: determining those things that are going to be decisive, and then bringing those circumstances to pass. Therefore sequencing events through a series of decisive points is a key part of planning, as is deciding on simultaneous actions and effects to overwhelm an enemy. Invariably, what is going to be decisive will have a direct relationship to the centre of gravity of an opponent, which must be attacked, and to one's own, which must be protected from attack. By centre of gravity we mean those characteristics, capabilities or localities from which a nation, an alliance, a military force or even a loose confederation like today's Al-Qua'eda derives its freedom of action, its moral and physical strength, or its will to fight. Its neutralization will therefore inevitably bring about defeat. In nineteenth-century terms this was usually something physical, such as the enemy's army or his capital city. However it can be a group of people or a person; a resource, natural or industrial; or even something intangible like the will to resist.

Although none of the major protagonists in the Canadas in 1812 – Prevost, Brock, Dearborn, Hull – would have expressed themselves in those terms, they would certainly have understood this notion of the operational level. Although military theory at the time spoke only of strategy and tactics, the campaign was a well understood idea, as was the concept of operational manoeuvre, usually referred to as grand tactics. As to the problem of what was likely to be decisive, this was a question that clearly vexed the British government throughout the period. Despite the continued need to confront and destroy Napoleon, how could the naval and military power of England be exerted to end an American war as soon as possible? To find the answer, Lord Bathurst asked the advice of the Duke of Wellington. Despite a lack of detailed knowledge, books or maps, Wellington wrote one of the most telling appreciations of the situation in the Canadas that has ever appeared: "Any offensive operation founded upon Canada must be preceded by the establishment of a naval superiority on the Lakes … the defence of Canada and the co-operation of the Indians depends on the navigation of the Lakes.…" Then in direct answer to the question, he wrote:

> In such countries as Canada, very extensive, thinly peopled, and producing but little food in proportion to their extent, military operations are impracticable without river or land transport. Coastal amphibious operations are liable to the same objections, though to a greater degree, than an operation founded in Canada. I do not know where you could carry on such an operation which would be so injurious to the Americans as to force them to sue for peace.[10]

So perhaps, with the benefit of hindsight, we may conclude that with no identifiable centre of gravity, the American war was unwinnable by either side. At the time, however, there was a strong view on the U.S. side to the contrary.

In 1812 U.S. operational plans were based on the suggestion by Dearborn that the Northern Department of the Army should launch simultaneous attacks against Montreal, Kingston and Niagara. This was a reasonable concept provided there were enough troops available, since it would play exactly to British fears and their weakness in numbers, preventing them from moving or concentrating their scarce resources of men. Whether the real intention was to conquer the Canadas or simply apply enough force to oblige the British government to address the issue of maritime rights by sucking resources away from the war with Napoleon, remains a matter of debate. If it was a land-grab, it was a singularly ill-timed one, for in the same week that Madison declared war, Napoleon invaded Russia and in so doing not only wrecked his own Continental System but also enabled the British to assemble the coalition that would eventually finish him. Even if the U.S. had succeeded in seizing territory, the experienced, battle-hardened British army and the Royal Navy's huge fleet would eventually descend and seize enough of the vulnerable parts of the U.S.A. – New Orleans, Savannah, Charleston, even perhaps New York – to make an exchange necessary as the basis of a peace, a peace that would simply restore the *status quo ante bellum*. To go to war in order to end up where one already is makes little sense.

The final plan saw the main effort in the Northwest, where Brigadier-General William Hull,* the governor of the Michigan Territory, would lead an army built around the 4th Infantry Regiment and a large contingent of militia from Ohio and Michigan to reinforce Detroit and then invade Upper Canada within weeks of war being declared. Supporting attacks to spread the British out, fix them and cut communication with Quebec would be made across the Niagara River and against Montreal by troops under Dearborn's command, although the resources required and the timing of this attack remained in the air.[11] Had simultaneous attacks been made, Brock's forces would indeed have been fixed; the failures of American political leadership and of generalship here were the major factors contributing to the failure of the campaign of 1812. Brock's successes must therefore be seen against this background of unpreparedness.

Hull was an intelligent man and he had made a careful analysis of his situation; albeit he tended to take counsel of his fears. At about the same time that Brock was analyzing his position in relation to American military power, Hull was doing the same. While the overall ratios of population and resources favoured the U.S., in the border areas those ratios were reversed and the relative perceptions are fascinating. The same factors that bore on Brock's planning also bore on Hull's and in the case of resources, his situation, without control of the waterways, was even more precarious than that of his opponent. The Canadian side of the frontier in Upper Canada was more heavily populated and better developed than the American side and

---

* Brigadier-General William Hull (1753–1825) had served in the Revolutionary War and was appointed first governor of the Michigan territory in 1805. Much of his correspondence was quoted in his court-martial after the surrender of Detroit in 1812.

Brigadier-General William Hull (1753–1825), veteran of the Revolutionary War, was past his prime and proved no match for Brock at Detroit. (Lossing, *Pictorial Field-Book of the War of 1812*)

the British controlled the line of communications that really mattered – that along the waterway. In early June 1811 Hull had begun to set out these issues in his despatches to Washington:

> In the event of war with England, this part of the United States will be peculiarly situated. The British land forces at Amherstburg and St. Joseph's, are about equal to those of the United States, at this place [i.e., Detroit] and Michilimackinac. The population of Upper Canada is more than twenty to one as compared to this territory.… A wilderness of near two hundred miles separates this settlement from any of the states … the British have a regular force, equal to ours. The province of Upper Canada has on its rolls, a militia of twenty to one against us.… What then will be the situation of this part of the country? Separated from the states by an extensive wilderness, which will be filled with savages, to prevent any succour, our water communications entirely obstructed by the British armed vessels on Lake Erie, we shall have no other resource for defence, but the small garrisons, and feeble population of the territory.… if there is a prospect of war with England, what measures are most expedient? In my mind, there can be little doubt. *Prepare a naval force on Lake Erie superior to the British, and sufficient to preserve your communication.*[12]

Further correspondence in March 1812 shows that as time went on he had become less hopeful of success, not more:

POLICE.

WHEREAS, authentic intelligence has been received that the Government of the United States of America did, on the 18th instant, declare War against the United Kingdom of Great Britain and Ireland and its dependencies, Notice is hereby given, that all Subjects or Citizens of the said United States, and all persons claiming American Citizenship, are ordered to quit the City of Quebec, on or before TWELVE o'clock at Noon, on WEDNESDAY next, and the District of Quebec on or before 12 o'clock at noon on FRIDAY next, on pain of arrest. ROSS CUTHBERT,
C. Q. S. & Inspector of Police.

The Constables of the City of Quebec are ordered to assemble in the Police Office at 10 o'clock to-morrow morning, to receive instructions.

Quebec, 29th June, 1812.

A notice to American citizens to quit the city of Quebec following the declaration of war in June 1812. (Author's collection)

... the British force which can be brought to operate against us in the territory, is more than ten to one, including the Indians. It requires no difficult reasoning to determine what must be the consequence – that part of the United States *must* fall into the hands of the British government, with all the inhabitants – the forts at Chicago, Michilimackinac and Detroit, and all the public stores.... [13]

Hull then set out his reasoning, which was remarkably similar to that of Prevost in terms of what control of Montreal would mean; his analysis of the logistical situation was gloomy, but professionally accurate:

The Army which marches into the country must open roads through the wilderness, and the supplies and provisions of whatever else may be necessary, must pass by land through the state of Ohio. If the conquest of the Canadas is the object of the government, they will then have an army in a proper situation to commence operations, and at the same time protect the defenceless inhabitants.... The answer may probably be, to leave the Michigan territory to its fate, and direct the force to Montreal.[14]

Early correspondence also reveals Hull's psychological state in relation to the native people. Plainly, the man was terrified; indeed, it is arguable that he was beaten (in his own mind) before ever war was declared. In the same appreciation as his pessimistic assessment of British power, he showed his hand in relation to the native nations:

The policy of the British government is to consider them [i.e., the aboriginal people] as allies, and in the event of war, to invite them to join their standard. The policy of the American government has been to advise them, in the event of war, to remain quiet in their villages.... Unless strong measures are taken to prevent it, we may consider beyond all doubt, they will be influenced to follow the advice of their British Father ... a large proportion of the savages will join them.... It would be easy for them, aided by the councils of the British agents, to commit depredations on the scattered frontier settlements of Ohio, Kentucky, Indiana....[15]

Hull repeatedly urged the Secretary of War to avoid a large-scale war with the aboriginal nations and to recognize the interdependence of the British and their native allies: numbers mattered for the British, while the native people, he said, "cannot conduct a war without the assistance of a civilised nation."[16] That being so, an adequate American force in the Detroit area was essential as was the converse: the removal of the British base of operations at Amherstburg, from which so much influence was exercised. The development of this train of logic explains Hull's course of action during the opening weeks of the war but also shows the extent of his fears. On the Canadian side of the frontier, the civilian authorities and much of the population were in a similar state. If ever there has been an example of how what Clausewitz called "the strong will of a proud spirit"[17] could dominate events, this is it.

CHAPTER ELEVEN

"A Force Which Will Look Down All Opposition"

HULL AND THE INVASION OF THE NORTHWEST, JULY–AUGUST 1812

Lieutenant-General Sir George Prevost had been warned by the British consul-general in New York at the end of May 1812 that a declaration of war was imminent;[1] official notification reached him from the U.S.A, via public announcements.[2] It took five weeks for this notice to be passed on to Brock, a delay which might have had unfortunate consequences – as it did for a number of American outposts. However, private mail sent by express from Washington to Thomas Clark of Queenston, the local agent of the John Jacob Astor fur trading company, reached Brock at York on 25 June, seven days after the declaration of war. Prevost had already put several important precautionary measures in hand. The 41st and 49th Regiments of Foot had been due to leave North America at the end of their long tour of duty, to be replaced by the 1st Battalion of the 1st Foot, or Royal Scots, and the 103rd; the latter was only 750 strong and composed for the most part of very young soldiers and boys.[3] Prevost had already been given permission, in the event of war, to retain all four regiments,[4] so the 41st and 49th stayed where they were, in Upper Canada and at Montreal respectively, as did the 100th, which had been due to move to Halifax. The 103rd Foot disembarked at Quebec on 15 July and the 1st was ordered to follow unless the onset of winter made it necessary for the regiment to be held at Halifax. At the same time, the authorized strength of the Glengarry Light Infantry was raised to 600 men and the Voltigeurs Canadiens to 300.[5]

At the outbreak of war Brock had just over 1,000 men of the 41st Foot, 250 of the 10th Royal Veterans, 90 Royal Artillery gunners and 50 Provincial Marine seamen – a total regular force of 1,400 men.[6] During June five companies of the Royal Newfoundland Fencibles arrived in the province under the command of Major Rowland Heathcote, adding about 400 more to this total. Most of these men were employed with the Provincial Marine or to escort the bateaux service; they were followed a short time later by the two flank companies, which were employed as fighting troops on land. Both the 41st and 49th Foot were short of officers, but this was not because there were none on the strength; according to the Army List, the 41st had 2 majors, 11 captains, 24 lieutenants and 22 ensigns; the 49th was not so well off with 2 majors, 11 captains, 14 lieutenants and 9 ensigns[7] – but this was still ample to exercise command of the regiment. However, many officers appear to have been on long leave in England. This is particularly apparent among the captains commanding the companies of the 41st, where only four of the eleven can be identified as being in the Canadas.* This may appear surprising on the eve of war, but it should be remembered that both regiments expected to leave the Canadas imminently, probably for Spain, and it is hardly surprising that the officers took their due leave to arrange their affairs.

Brock issued orders on 2 July 1812 to form the troops on the vulnerable Niagara frontier into four divisions – really no more than small battalions – composed of regulars and militia. The First, or right, division was located at Fort Erie and commanded by Captain William Derenzy of the 41st. It consisted of 200 men of the 41st, about two companies therefore, and the same number of men from the 3rd Lincoln Regiment of Militia, with two 3-pdr guns. The Second, or right centre, division was located at Chippawa and commanded by Lieutenant Richard Bullock of the 41st,† with 100 of his own men of the grenadier company and 200 men of the 2nd Lincoln Regiment of Militia, with two 6-pdr guns. The Third, or left centre, division was located on Queenston Heights and commanded by Captain Peter Chambers‡ of the 41st with 100 of his own men and 200 militiamen from the flank companies of the 5th and 6th Lincolns under Captain Samuel Hatt, along with two 3-pdr guns. The Fourth, or left, division was to be located at Fort George and commanded by Colonel Henry Procter, assisted by Lieutenant-Colonel Johnson Butler of the Lincoln Militia. It consisted of 200 men of the 41st and 300 militiamen from the flank companies of the 1st and 4th

* William Derenzy, Adam Muir, Joseph Tallon and Peter Chambers.
† Not to be confused with his father, Captain Richard Bullock of the same regiment.
‡ Later Lieutenant-Colonel Peter Latouche Chambers, C.B. (1788–1828).

Lincoln Regiments of Militia.[8] Procter would have overall charge of that section of the frontier from Newark to Fort Erie, assisted by Claus of the Indian Department, who would command the militia between Newark and Queenston, and Lieutenant-Colonel Isaac Clarke, who would do the same from Queenston to Fort Erie.

Brock had already prepared a memorandum listing the measures he required in the event of war, although it is not certain how and when this was submitted to Prevost. Since most if not all the measures were approved and many had already been implemented, it is probable that Prevost had received it early in 1812. In this memorandum,[9] Brock asked for a large draft of recruits for the 41st that had arrived in Quebec with the opening of the St Lawrence to be sent to Upper Canada so that he could concentrate the bulk of the regiment at Amherstburg ready for operations against Hull, and to supplement the 41st with fifty gunners (gunners were still in short supply) and up to six 8-inch mortars for siege operations. He would also need the 49th or "some other effective regiment" with supporting artillery to reinforce the Niagara frontier along with "an officer of rank" to take charge there. Brock went on to reiterate the requirement to form flank companies in each militia regiment, which in most cases had already been done, and to form a volunteer corps of up to 1,200 men.[10] In addition to manpower and ordnance he went on to describe the enhancements needed for the Provincial Marine: removing the naval yard from Kingston to York, building bateaux and gunboats and fortifying the harbour at Amherstburg.

Brock had been to Amherstburg on 14 June, taking with him a reinforcement of 100 men of the 41st, and then went on to visit the other garrisons on the Niagara frontier at Chippawa and Fort Erie, returning to York on 20 June. Once he had the news from Washington, the flank companies of the militia were called out immediately, producing about 800 additional trained troops, followed by the remainder of the units for garrison duties, or about 4,000 men if all turned in for duty.[11] All these men would draw the same pay and rations as their regular counterparts,[12] producing a severe strain on the available money supply as well as on the rationing system. Two additional volunteer units formed up just before the declaration: first, a troop of volunteer cavalry; and secondly, a "car," or wagon, brigade formed by a number of farmers' sons with their draft horses, who undertook to move ammunitions and stores for the army under the direction of Captain

William Holcroft, who commanded the artillery company distributed across the upper province. With these measures in hand, Brock returned immediately by bateau to Fort George, thirty miles away.

There were still, however, shortages of arms, ammunition and clothing of all kinds. Brock had appointed his old friend Robert Nichol as quarter-master-general of militia;[13] once mobilisation was under way, Brock reported to Prevost that "Nearly the whole of the arms at my disposal have been issued. They are barely sufficient to arm the militia immediately required to guard the frontier.... The Militia assembled in a wretched state in regard to clothing; many were without shoes, an article which can scarcely be provided in this country."[14]

The same news of war reached Brigadier-General William Hull at the Miami Rapids on 2 July.[15] Hull's army, plodding slowly towards Detroit, consisted of the 4th U.S. Infantry Regiment, the unit that had conducted the action at Tippecanoe, under Lieutenant-Colonel James Miller,[*] and 2,075 Ohio Militia[16] under Lieutenant-Colonels Lewis Cass,[†] Duncan McArthur[‡] and James Findlay.[§] Progress was slow, for the terrain was swampy, and where it was not swampy it was heavily forested. The path was narrow and had to be cleared and levelled to allow the passage of wheeled vehicles and guns. There had been heavy rain, which added to the problems of the toiling men, already assailed by heat and clouds of predatory insects. The 4th Infantry reached Dayton, Ohio, on 7 July, and on 10 July the regiment joined part of Hull's force near Urbana. Here a council was held with the Wyandots, part of the Shawnee and other neutral tribes to negotiate the building of a road with blockhouses through aboriginal territory.[17] As the column advanced it was tracked by other warriors sympathetic to the British; Tecumseh was all in favour of an ambush but Lieutenant-Colonel Thomas Bligh St George needed every man he had to finish work strengthening the defences of Fort Malden. The advanced guard of Hull's force had arrived in Detroit on 5 July,

---

[*] Later Brigadier-General James Miller (1776–1850). He redeemed himself for his failures in 1812 during his service at Lundy's Lane in 1814 with the 21st Infantry. He was later the first governor of the Arkansas Territory.

[†] Later Brigadier-General Lewis Cass (1782–1866). He was subsequently governor of the Michigan territory 1813–31, Secretary of War 1831–36 and minister in Paris 1836–41.

[‡] Duncan McArthur (1772–1839) was later the 11th governor of Ohio.

[§] James Findlay (1770–1835) was later mayor of Cincinnati.

followed a few days later by the main body less the garrisons left at various blockhouses to secure the line of communication, raising the force there to more than 2,000 men and fulfilling Brock's prediction. As well as the threat of invasion over the Niagara River, Brock now had to contend with a large force on his right flank, well able to subdue Amherstburg and roll up his defence from the rear, but already keeping his forces and the native warriors there, fixed.

The arrival of Brock himself at Fort George and mobilization of the flank companies of the militia were enough, it seemed, to dissuade Hull from making an immediate move on that place. Brock had clearly considered an early move against Detroit and Mackinac but his own resources of

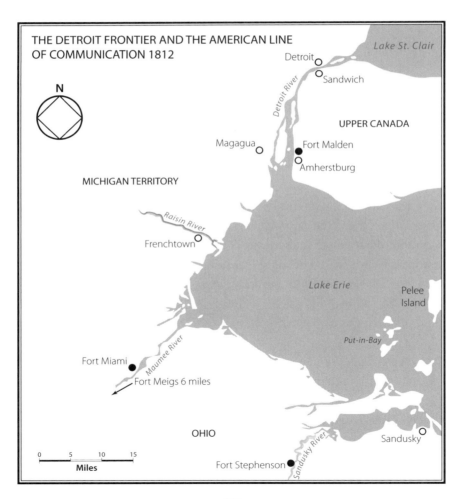

THE DETROIT FRONTIER AND THE AMERICAN LINE
OF COMMUNICATION 1812

Lake St. Clair

Detroit

Sandwich

Detroit River

UPPER CANADA

Magagua

Fort Malden

Amherstburg

MICHIGAN TERRITORY

Raisin River

Frenchtown

Lake Erie

Pelee Island

Put-in-Bay

Fort Miami

Moumee River

Fort Meigs 6 miles

OHIO

Sandusky

0 5 10 15
Miles

Fort Stephenson

Sandusky River

N

men, arms or munitions were still few and the enemy appeared unlikely to do much harm; he also considered moving against Fort Niagara, but this fort could be attended to at any time. Until the Americans made the first move, pressure from Prevost and want of means decided Brock to confine himself, for the time being, to defensive operations.[18] Prevost underlined his point in a letter on 10 July, saying: "Our numbers would not justify offensive operations being undertaken, unless they were solely calculated to strengthen a defensive attitude. I consider it prudent and politic to avoid any measure which can in its effect have a tendency to unite the people of the United States."[19]

The defences of both Fort George and Fort Malden had been considerably improved over the preceding months and both were strongly garrisoned; additional guns arrived around 12 July and were soon mounted. One officer wrote from Amherstburg that "our Force here consists of 300 Regulars, 850 Militia and about 400 Indians, so that I think we have no reason to be afraid of our Yanky Friends...."[20] Moreover on the day after the garrison had received news of the declaration of war, a cutting-out expedition from the *General Hunter* and the garrison of Fort Malden seized an American schooner, the *Cayahoga*, which was clearly unaware of the news, containing forty officers and men of Hull's army, all the officers' baggage, the entire stock of medical stores – and all of Hull's official correspondence.[21] Another American sloop, the *Commencement*, was also seized by the *Queen Charlotte* off Fort Erie. From the captured correspondence Brock had a complete insight into the state of Hull's mind. This explains why his reaction to Hull's immediate encroachments onto Canadian soil was limited. He must have seen that Hull was cautious, afraid of exposing his force to superior odds and as likely to withdraw as to advance. All he had to do was contain Hull until the time was right to strike.

To the civilian population of Upper Canada, their worst fears seemed to be realized. In the election of 5 May, Joseph Willcocks had been returned for the 1st Lincoln and Haldimand riding with a resounding majority, although several of his supporters were not. Brock had high hopes of this Assembly with its many new members, which included his attorney-general, John Macdonell.[22] He summoned an emergency session, which was planned to run from 27 July to 5 August, but he found the members fearful, unwilling

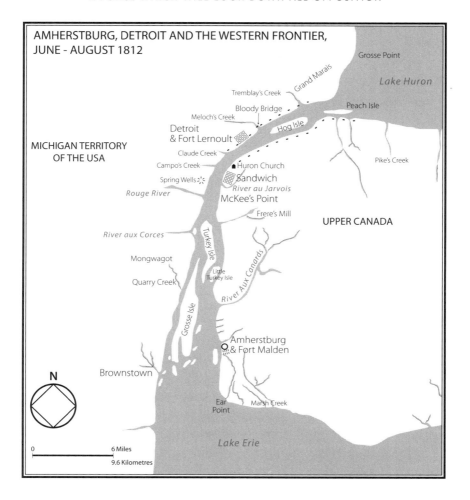

AMHERSTBURG, DETROIT AND THE WESTERN FRONTIER, JUNE - AUGUST 1812

to offend the Americans and more concerned for their own property than for the collective security of the province. "A more decent House has not been elected since the formation of the Province – but I perceive at once I shall get no good of them…,"[23] he wrote to Prevost. To the Assembly he made his position plain:

> From the history and experience of our Mother Country, we learn, that in times of actual invasion or internal Commotion, the Ordinary Course of Criminal Law has been found inadequate to secure His Majesty's Government from private Treachery as well as from Open disaffection, and that at such times its Legislature has found it expedient to enact Laws

restraining for a limited period, the liberty of Individuals in many cases where it would be dangerous to expose the particulars of the Charge; and altho' the actual invasion of the Province might justify me in the exercise of the full powers reposed in me on such an emergency, yet it will be more agreeable to me to receive the sanction of the two Houses.[24]

Despite the language of his address, his attempts to pass restrictive legislation were defeated through the influence of radicals[25] like the Ancaster mill owner and businessman Abraham Markle;* Willcocks too, despite having decided to support the government, would only go so far, claiming that he was an enemy "of the measures of the King's Servants in this colony" but at the same time a "constant adherent to the interests of the Country."[26] Brock, seeing no benefit in keeping the Assembly in session, prorogued it on 5 August.[27] The Assembly did not meet again until the end of the war. Writing to Baynes, Brock said that:

> A full belief possesses them all that this province must inevitably succumb. This prepossession is fatal to every exertion. Legislators, magistrates, militia officers, all have imbibed the idea, and are so sluggish and indifferent in their respective offices.... Most of the people have lost all confidence. I, however; speak loud and look big.[28]

The defeatist beliefs of many in Upper Canada gained more strength on 12 July. During the night of the 11th, American troops from Hull's army were ferried across the Detroit River and occupied the village of Sandwich (today part of Windsor, Ontario), which consisted of perhaps twenty houses.[29] Most of the inhabitants fled and the small garrison of regulars and militia withdrew towards Amherstburg without a fight. Indeed Colonel St George had been warned by local sources that a landing in force was imminent and that the Canadian militia would probably not stand and so had withdrawn the bulk of his force with its guns and baggage from Sandwich, leaving only a small detachment.[30] Hull set up his headquarters in the house of François Baby,† a member of the Provincial Assembly and colonel of the

---

* Abraham Markle (1770–1826) was of Dutch ancestry, from New York. He settled in the Niagara area after the Revolutionary War.
† François Baby (1763–1856) was a member of the Legislative Assembly of Upper Canada and a member of one of the leading families of the province.

1st Kent Militia. Here he hoisted Old Glory on Canadian soil and issued a stern proclamation to the inhabitants:

INHABITANTS OF CANADA! After thirty years of Peace and prosperity, the United States have been driven to Arms, The injuries and aggressions, the insults and indignities of Great Britain have *once more* left them no alternative but manly resistance or unconditional submission.…

Separated by an immense ocean and an extensive Wilderness from Great Britain you have no participation in her counsels no interest in her conduct. You have felt her Tyranny, you have seen her injustice.… The United States are sufficiently powerful to afford you every security.…

I come prepared for every contingency. I have a force which will look down all opposition and that force is but the vanguard of a much greater. If contrary to your own interest & the just expectation of my country, you should take part in the approaching contest, you will be treated as enemies, and the horrors, and calamities of war will Stalk before you.

If the barbarous and Savage policy of Great Britain be pursued, and the savages are let loose to murder our Citizens and butcher our women and children, this war, will be a war of extermination.

The first stroke with the Tomahawk the first attempt with the Scalping Knife will be the Signal for one indiscriminate scene of desolation, *No white man found fighting by the Side of an Indian will be taken prisoner.* Instant destruction will be his lot.[31]

Although he was ridiculed at the time and afterwards for this proclamation, Hull had done exactly what Brock feared most and had done so with firmness and determination. Hundreds of Canadians, including some whole settlements, applied to Hull for protection; many even offered collaboration. The militia began to desert – St George in his despatch had given details[32] – or at best to refuse to turn out, and even the native nations seemed to be losing heart. The Ojibwas of Lake St Clair and some other native peoples joined the white population in applying to Hull for protection in return for their neutrality.[33] The air of defeat was palpable and it spread: Brock had to issue a stern warning to troops on the Niagara frontier, for example, against allowing American citizens to wander the streets of Newark and openly examine the defences.[34] Worse still, the flank companies of the Norfolk Militia refused to march to Amherstburg when ordered to do so, and even Brock expected the early loss of that place:

I do not imagine General Hull will be able to detach more than one thousand Men, but even with that trifling force I much fear he will succeed in getting to my rear. The Militia will not act without a strong Regular force to set them the example, and as I must now expect to be seriously threatened from [Niagara] I cannot, in prudence, make strong detachments....[35]

The extent of Brock's fears at this time did not become apparent until later, when writing to Lord Bathurst, the Secretary for War and the Colonies, he admitted that:

I considered my situation at that time extremely perilous; not only among the Militia was evinced a disposition to submit tamely, five hundred in the Western district having deserted their Ranks, but likewise the Indians of the Six nations, who are placed in the heart of the Country, on the Grand River, positively refused, with the exception of a few individuals taking up arms – they audaciously announced their intention ... to remain neutral, as if they wished to impose on the Government the belief that it was possible to sit quietly in the midst of War – This unexpected conduct of the Indians deterred many good men from leaving their families and joining the Militia – they became more apprehensive of the internal than the external enemy, and would willingly have compromised with the one to secure themselves from the other.[36]

Amherstburg had to be Hull's target, for it was a directive from the Secretary of War himself that had sent him over the river for that very purpose: "... consistent with the safety of your own post you will take possession of Malden and extend your conquests as circumstances may justify."[37] Sandwich might help the Americans to control river traffic, collect support from American settlers and disaffected Canadians, provide training for his inexperienced troops and secure supplies, but it was the dockyard and resources of the Provincial Marine at Amherstburg that would assure control over the whole of the upper lakes. Hull was not so sure, writing that "The British command the water and the savages. I do not think the force here equal to the reduction of Amherstburg."[38] He was not, however, about to disobey the direct order of his chief. Instead he summoned a council of war – a recipe for compromise and indecision – on 14 July, which voted to delay any assault on Malden until heavy guns could be got across the river and into position.

One group of aboriginal people certainly held firm to the British cause:

Amherstburg in 1804. The picture, although not contemporary, has been researched in considerable detail and gives an excellent impression of the small town on the Detroit River and its wharf, protected by a blockhouse. Fort Malden lies off to the left, outside the picture. (Painting by Peter Rindlisbacher, by permission of the artist)

Tecumseh and his 400 warriors, many of whom were from the nations of the Northwest, remained at Amherstburg. As Matthew Elliott wrote, Tecumseh had "showed himself to be a determined character and a great friend to our government."[39] The garrison at Malden hourly expected the Americans to appear and these fears grew stronger when on 16 July around 300 Ohio Militia and a few regulars under Lewis Cass appeared about five miles northeast of Amherstburg on the Aux Canards creek. The Aux Canards was the only remaining obstacle between Amherstburg and the Americans; it was a deep, muddy stream, not easy to ford, and the one bridge, which through negligence had not been thrown down, was held by a sergeant's guard of the 41st with two small field pieces.

This time the redcoats did not immediately retire and so, leaving a few riflemen to keep the British pinned down, Cass took the rest of his men upstream, forded the watercourse and came on, intending to take the position

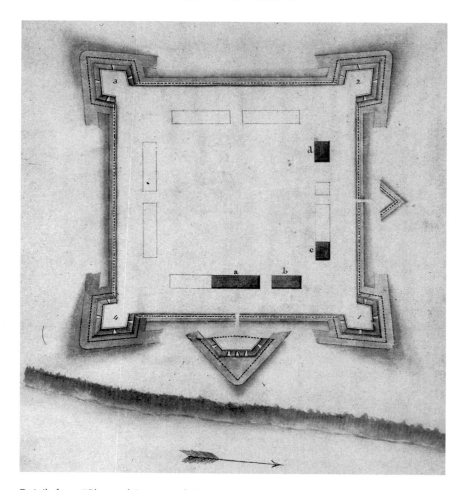

Details from "Plan and Sections of the Works of Defence proposed to be constructed at Amherstburg...." The fort at Amherstburg changed little from this 1799 plan by Gother Mann. The structures within the fort are: (a) blockhouse; (b) storehouse for Indian Dept.; (c) house for Indian Dept. storekeeper; (d) magazine. (Library and Archives Canada NMC-22930)

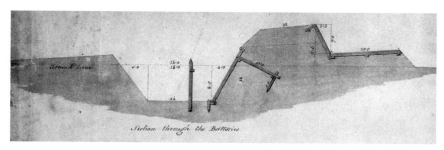

in the flank. By the time Cass and his men appeared at the bridge, the small garrison had been strengthened by a platoon or so of militia from Malden and about fifty native warriors, probably led by Tecumseh himself. This was not enough of a force to face down the Americans but it was enough to save the guns. The British and Tecumseh's warriors drew off, leaving Cass in possession of the obstacle, along with two British prisoners – Privates John Dean and James Hancock, who was wounded – and the initiative.[40] The British and their native allies expected a major battle the next day, but it was not to be. To their considerable surprise and relief, the Americans had retired back to the north side of the Aux Canards. The British reclaimed the position and threw down the bridge, leaving only a couple of beams in place.

Cass, it appeared, had been ordered back by Hull, whose determination, initially strong, had been sapped by the reports of large numbers of native warriors massing in support of the British. The reports from the Aux Canards made him hesitate – and then pull back. Instead of pushing on, he preferred to wait for more reinforcements, put his artillery into better condition for an assault on Fort Malden and hope for more desertions from the Canadian militia. The effect on the morale of his own force was highly damaging; and conversely it restored the hopes of the British and Canadians. That more battles *are* decided by loss of hope than by loss of blood, Hull would soon discover for himself.

The Americans made another, half-hearted, attempt on the Aux Canards on 19 July but a reinvigorated defence by the British and their allies pushed them back, Tecumseh's warriors snapping at the heels of the withdrawing American force almost to the outskirts of Sandwich. Brock himself was still detained between his headquarters at Fort George, where the threat was as yet unidentified, and the provincial capital at York by the meeting of the Legislative Assembly. He decided at the very least to issue a rejoinder to Hull's proclamation:

> … where is the Canadian Subject who can truly affirm to himself that he has been injured by the Government in his person, his liberty, or his property? Where is to be found in any part of the world, a growth so rapid in wealth and prosperity as this Colony exhibits.… The unavoidable and immediate consequence of a separation from Great Britain, must be the loss of this inestimable advantage, and what is offered you in exchange? To become a territory of the United States and share with them that ex-

clusion from the Ocean, which the policy of their present Government enforces. ... cooperate cordially with the King's regular Forces to repel the invader, and do not give cause to your children when groaning under the oppression of a foreign Master to reproach you with having too easily parted with the richest inheritance on Earth.[41]

Poor stuff perhaps, but Brock was concerned about the effect of Hull's proclamation on both the Canadians and the native people. To add substance to his own words, he despatched Captain Peter Chambers of the 41st Foot to Moraviantown with Lieutenant Charles Lenn and a detachment of fifty regulars and 200 men from the 1st Norfolk, 2nd Norfolk, Oxford and Middlesex militias under Major George Salmon[42] to prevent American raids from Sandwich, and Colonel Henry Procter – his most capable subordinate – with a reinforcement of the 41st to take charge at Amherstburg. Brock was clearly annoyed at Lieutenant-Colonel Thomas Bligh St George's having permitted the American troops to cross the river unopposed, then abandoning Sandwich without a fight, and had in consequence lost confidence in him. "By the Lord Harry," Brock is reputed to have exclaimed, "he has allowed the enemy to cross the river in open day without firing a shot!" Worse, St George had waited three days before telling Brock what had occurred.

Brock clearly considered an operation across the Detroit River, perhaps aiming at Fort Detroit itself, at this time, but the lack of enthusiasm among the militia and the aboriginal warriors caused him to abandon this idea.[43] Henry Procter arrived at Amherstburg on 26 July to find that there had been a more serious action the previous day when a strong American force under Major James Denny, making another attempt on the Aux Canards position, was ambushed by a large party of native warriors. The action rapidly turned into a rout and the fleeing Americans lost five killed, two wounded and one prisoner – only their speed of flight saved them from worse.[44] These skirmishes on the Aux Canards were small beer, but their moral effect was considerable: the Ohio militiamen could, it seemed, rapidly be reduced to a shambles. Hull's imagination magnified the native warriors' numbers and in his mind's eye he saw thousands of them descending on him, his men and their families. Unwittingly perhaps, Tecumseh played to Hull's fears by taking his warriors across to the American shore and raiding on the American supply line.

On the day following the first action on the Aux Canards, an event took place that was again small in scale but great in its moral effect. Far to the north, Captain Charles Roberts, commanding the little British garrison at St Joseph's, captured the small American fort at Mackinac without a shot being fired. Mackinac had long been a centre for the fur trade with the native people, having been founded as a Jesuit Mission in 1671, and its situation was therefore very well known. Brock had issued orders to Roberts on 26 June to take the place, but these had been immediately cancelled[45] until Brock was sure that war had been declared and the United States should be the aggressor. Meanwhile, Roberts had not been idle and had assembled fifty of his own men from the 10th Royal Veterans. These, however, were scarcely crack troops, for Roberts wrote of them that they were "always ready to obey my orders" but they were so much "worn down by unconquerable drunkenness, that neither the fear of punishment, the love of fame or the honour of their country can animate them to extraordinary exertions."[46] Happily, they were joined by 160 volunteers, formed into three companies, from the *Voyageurs* of the North West Company under the colonelcy of Lewis Crawford, along with the company's brig, *Caledonia.*[47] About 300 native warriors from Algonkian nations under Tecumseh's influence – some enthusiastic Sioux, Winnebagos and Menominees and some more wary Ojibwas – brought to the fight by the fur trader Robert Dickson,[*] completed the force.[48] On 28 June Brock again wrote to Roberts with definite orders to take the fort, but Roberts received a further message from Brock on 15 July "with orders to adopt the most prudent measures either of offence or defence which circumstances might point out...."[49] Roberts was somewhat confused by this sequence of instructions for greatcoats-on-greatcoats-off and, moreover, he believed that Mackinac would shortly be reinforced; he also knew that he could not keep his aboriginal contingent together indefinitely and he therefore decided that he had been given latitude to do as he saw fit.

On the morning of 16 July, four days after Hull's landing at Sandwich (of which he had no knowledge), Roberts set out with his force in a flotilla of canoes and bateaux, convoyed by the *Caledonia.* After he had left, a des-

---

[*] Robert Dickson (1768–1823) had been a fur trader among the western Indians from his youth. He was one of the first white men to travel up the Missouri River to its source and had great influence among the aboriginal people.

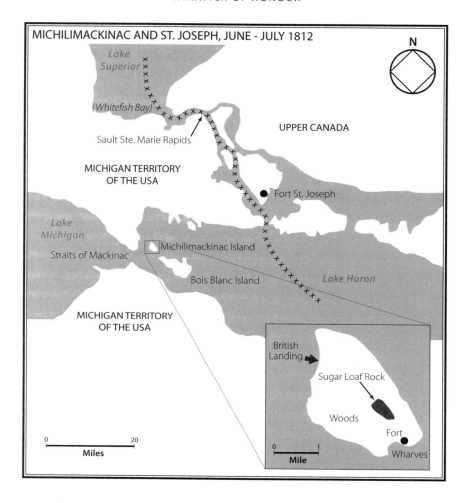

MICHILIMACKINAC AND ST. JOSEPH, JUNE - JULY 1812

N

Lake Superior

(Whitefish Bay)

Sault Ste. Marie Rapids

UPPER CANADA

MICHIGAN TERRITORY OF THE USA

Lake Michigan

Fort St. Joseph

Straits of Mackinac

Michilimackinac Island

Bois Blanc Island

Lake Huron

MICHIGAN TERRITORY OF THE USA

British Landing

Sugar Loaf Rock

Woods

Fort

Wharves

0   20
Miles

0   1
Mile

patch from Prevost arrived, telling him to secure his post, which would only have increased his uncertainty, but as things turned out Roberts did not see this despatch until after he had completed his operation. The force landed at Mackinac at 3.00 a.m. the following morning and spent the remaining hours of darkness dragging two iron 6-pdr guns into a position from which to bombard the fort. At dawn Roberts summoned the garrison to surrender. Its commander, Lieutenant Porter Hanks of the U.S. Artillery, knew nothing of the declaration of war;[50] his force of sixty-one men was no match for the opposition and at midday he surrendered.[51] Apart from the military stores seized, of which a complete inventory was made, 700 packs of furs were found in the fort and the whole lot was valued at £10,000, or $50,000

– around £750,000 at today's prices.[52] The American regulars were released on parole until exchanged using one of the schooners captured at the fort as a cartel. Among the prisoners were three British deserters, including Hugh Kelly of the 49th Foot, Redmond McGrath of the 5th and Alexander Parks of the Royal Artillery, who were held pending Brock's decision on their fate. They could expect no mercy.

Brock received the news on 29 July and immediately sent word on to Prevost. He was clearly delighted and he pointed out to Prevost that Roberts' conduct "has been distinguished by much zeal and judgement, and his recent eminent display of those qualities, Your Excellency will find, has been attended with a most happy effect."[53] Brock lost no time in issuing a General Order praising Roberts and the troops who had repulsed American moves on the Aux Canards, in a move designed to strengthen morale.[54] Prevost received the news in early August and he expressed the view that "great credit" was due to Roberts; however, he was clearly relieved to hear that the attack had been made in response to Hull's invasion.[55] It is possible that Prevost resented being shown as timid by this bold stroke and vented his anger on Roberts, who received no reward for his success – ordinarily he could have expected at least a brevet promotion.

Brock's pleasure at the fall of Mackinac was reduced by personal loss. After more than twenty years' service with him, his servant James Dobson* had died after a long illness. Brock, it is reported, visited him daily, ensured he had the best of care and was sitting by him at his death. Private Thomas Porter† of the 49th was sent to look after Brock but must have been conscious that he would never fill the void left by Dobson's death. The relationship between a general and a long-serving personal aide, no matter

---

* It is not possible to ascertain Dobson's age. He first appears in the roll of the 49th Foot in the Inspection Return of 1791 in WO 27/71 – the first occasion on which non-commissioned ranks are listed by name – where he is a Private; it is possible that even then he was an old soldier with no prospect of promotion, raised out of the hardships of barrack life by Brock as his servant.

† Thomas Porter returned to England after Brock's death with his effects. He received an honourable discharge and pension from the Duke of York "as a small tribute to the memory of a most gallant and valuable officer." (*Correspondence*, p. 236) His brother William was also serving with the 49th at his time; the two brothers had followed their father, William Porter, into the regiment; he had served under Brock in the Helder and at Copenhagen, where he was killed while on board the *Monarch*.

Fort Mackinac. The high ground on to which Captain Roberts and his men hauled the gun that compelled the garrison to surrender can be seen to the right rear of the fort. (Lossing *Pictorial Field-Book of the War of 1812*)

how great the gap in rank, is uniquely close and founded on personal trust and respect; it can provide a general officer with a valuable sounding-board or sanity check on his command style and the effect of his orders. For a commander surrounded by deference, such an aide will be one of the few people who will have the confidence to tell the general that he is wrong. We cannot be certain that this relationship existed between Brock and Dobson, especially as they lived in an age of far greater deference than ours, but James Fitzgibbon seems to have performed something of this function when he was Brock's sergeant-major and from all we know of Brock's humanity, it is reasonable to assume that his friendship with both Dobson and Fitzgibbon was genuine.

The happy effect of Mackinac was chiefly noticeable among the aboriginal people, who came in from all quarters, convinced at last that the British meant business. Immediately before the news arrived, Brock had again tried to persuade the Grand River people to join the allies and had received "loud and apparently warm professions"; however when it came to action, they decided on neutrality, encouraged by American promises that their lands and rights would be respected if they did so. Only a handful answered Brock's call to assemble at Fort George in July.[56] Once the Assembly had been prorogued on 3 August, Brock therefore turned to Joseph Willcocks, who was known to have influence with the aboriginal people, although the nature of this influence remains obscure.[57] Willcocks was asked to undertake a special mission to persuade the chiefs of the Grand River people to support the British. Although delayed by illness, Willcocks duly carried out the mission and, after much discussion by the Grand River peoples, by September had turned neutrality into active support.[58]

The fall of Mackinac, of which Hull learned on 4 August, did nothing for his lack of confidence. He wrote to the Secretary of War that as many as a thousand native warriors had taken part in the operation, which was a vast exaggeration. To make matters worse, on 2 and 3 August Tecumseh and his followers had again crossed to the American side of the frontier and descended on two aboriginal settlements at Magagua and Brownstown, which lay on Hull's line of communication. About seventy men from these villages joined Tecumseh – under pressure, they claimed, but no American believed this.[59] As the British controlled the waterways, Hull had no choice but to use this road for supply and now, it appeared, it was cut. Word had already been sent to the governor of Ohio and a convoy of seventy packhorses carrying flour, along with 300 cattle, was being driven north, escorted by a detachment of 165 troops under Captain Henry Brush;* a further fifty men of the Michigan militia held a small fortification at the River Raisin ford. Moving faster was another party of twenty-five French-Canadian volunteers, escorting mail for Hull. Coming from the other direction was a third American detachment of 200 militiamen under Major

---

* Henry Brush (1778–1855) was a lawyer who later served in the 16th Congress of the United States.

Thomas Van Horne,* escorting the south-bound mail and aiming to link up with the incoming supply column.

On 5 August a small band of native warriors, perhaps only twenty-five strong, accompanied by one or two British officers of the Indian Department, left Amherstburg for Brownstown on the orders of Colonel Henry Procter. It appears that the dates of the incoming and outgoing mail deliveries were known.[60] Just south of the village, they met the French volunteers, killed or wounded all but five, and seized the mail. The sound of battle was heard by Van Horne, whose column was well organized with a screen of scouts, advance and rear guards, which included some mounted dragoons, and his main body in two columns with the mail in the centre. The aboriginal warriors were well aware of the American dispositions and, although heavily outnumbered, sprang a successful ambush near the River Raisin ford, killing around twenty Americans, capturing the mail and scattering the rest of Van Horne's command. The survivors straggled back into Detroit over the next two days, telling fearful tales of scalp and slaughter,[61] although Hull's later despatch to the Secretary of War made it sound like an American triumph. This double victory by so small a force of warriors ranks as one of the most remarkable in the history of North American irregular warfare, and those aboriginal people who had held back now flocked to Tecumseh, emboldened by his victory and the news from Mackinac. By the time Brush's supply column closed on the River Raisin, he found the road blocked by the native warriors. There was no question of pushing on without a relief force from Hull, but Hull's ability to maintain even his own supply line was fast diminishing as he went on the defensive, and in doing so surrendered the initiative to Brock.

---

* Thomas B. Van Horne served as a major in the Ohio Volunteers in 1812 and later as lieutenant-colonel with the regular 26th Infantry and 19th Infantry. He was active throughout the war.

CHAPTER TWELVE

"A More Sagacious Warrior"

SEIZING THE INITIATIVE IN THE NORTHWEST, AUGUST 1812

The two consignments of Brigadier-General William Hull's mail and despatches captured by the British on 5 August were taken to Brock, along with those captured from the *Cayahoga* on 2 August. Brock himself set out from Fort George on 6 August with sixty regulars of the 41st Foot, 300 picked volunteers from the militia and a 6-pdr gun from the car brigade under Captain Isaac Swayze.[*] He meant to call first on the Grand River people to encourage them to join forces with him and then to reinforce Amherstburg as soon as possible.[1] Having read the despatches carefully, Brock passed them on to Prevost, who also found them extremely interesting – so much so that his earlier caution was to an extent eased.[2] Prevost had already done what he could further to reinforce Brock from the slender resources available: on 1 August one company of the 49th Regiment had arrived at Kingston from Montreal, escorting stores and munitions for the upper province, as well as hard cash to pay the militia. On the following day three more companies under Major Alexander Ormsby were also ordered to Kingston, and clothing for 2,000 men had been despatched along with four 6-pdr guns. Prevost also detached Lieutenant-Colonel Christopher Myers of the 70th Regiment to take charge under Brock on the Niagara frontier,[3] and Colonel Robert Lethbridge as Inspecting Field Officer of Militia.[†]

---

[*] Isaac Swayze was born in New York in 1751 and died aged seventy-seven near Niagara in 1828.

[†] As noted in chapter 5, there were six of these officers: apart from Lethbridge, a colonel, the others were all lieutenant-colonels, but given the local rank of colonel to place them, without dispute, above the militia commanding officers. By mid-1812 they are named in the Army List as Thomas Bligh St George, late 41st Foot, John Murray, Angus Warburton late 91st, Cecil Bisshopp late 1st Guards and Thomas Pearson late 23rd Fusiliers. Of these, Pearson was by far the most experienced and distinguished, having commanded the 23rd Foot, been wounded three times, and ended up commanding the elite Fusilier Brigade at

On 31 July Prevost had also despatched Major-General Roger Hale Sheaffe to assist Brock, recognizing that Brock had to undertake the civil government as well as the military command over a wide geographical area.[4] Brock probably viewed this appointment with a degree of scepticism but could not refuse; it may even have been that he felt sorry for Sheaffe, who had languished without employment. Writing to his brothers after the fall of Detroit, he said that "There never was an individual so miserably off for the necessary assistance. Sir George Prevost has kindly hearkened to my remonstrances, and in some measure supplied the deficiency."[5] Sheaffe assumed command on the Niagara frontier, taking authority over Lieutenant-Colonel Myers, on 19 August.[6]

On 13 August, the day after Prevost received Hull's captured despatches, a detached company of the 49th at Lachine, which had been there since 1 July on internal security duties following an armed uprising by men resisting being called up into the militia, was ordered forward to Kingston, and the remainder of the regiment was ordered from Montreal to Kingston.[7] With them came also reinforcements for the Royal Newfoundland Regiment, the 10th Royal Veterans and an additional gunboat. These additions raised the total of regular troops under Brock's command to around 2,500.[8] Once the 49th had been concentrated at Kingston on 22 August it was embarked on bateaux for Fort George, reuniting Brock with his old command for the first time since he had left Montreal. Brock kept six companies, including the flank companies, at Fort George, commanded by Lieutenant-Colonel John Vincent, and returned four companies under Alexander Ormsby to Kingston, because of the threat to that place and its importance.[9]

As well as what was now a reasonable striking force on land, Brock had command of the lakes and a force of ships capable of transporting his force rapidly, thus making up in mobility what he lacked in absolute numbers. At Fort Erie were the schooners *Lady Prevost* and the captured *Nancy;* the force on Lake Ontario came under the command of Captain Hugh Earle and consisted of the 22-gun corvette *Royal George,* a small ship but mounting

---

the end of the bloody battle of Albuera in May 1811. He served with distinction throughout the rest of the war in North America, fighting at Crysler's Farm, Oswego, Chippawa, Lundy's Lane and Fort Erie, during which time he received two further wounds. He ended his career as a major-general. See his biography by Donald E. Graves, *Fix Bayonets! A Royal Welch Fusilier at War, 1792–1815* (Toronto, 2005).

24-pdr guns; the smaller brig *Earl of Moira* with sixteen 24-pdrs; the armed schooners *Prince Regent, Duke of Gloucester, Simcoe* and *Seneca;* and twelve gunboats. At Amherstburg under Captain George Hall* were the brig *Queen Charlotte* and the armed schooner *General Hunter.* Across the water from Kingston at Sackets Harbor the Americans were building fast, working on the 24-pdr brig *Oneida* and the armed schooner *Julia.* Two U.S. schooners had been captured and burned by a party of militia soon after the declaration of war and an inconclusive fight between the two flotillas followed some days later; for now, however, the British retained control of the supply line up the waterway.

With these reinforcements, Brock's force, although barely enough to do what he wanted of it, was close to the limit of what he could support logistically. Upper Canada, although better developed than the U.S. territories across the border, could not support a large force and feed the civilian population. It produced seasonal crops of wheat, fruit and vegetables, and pork, supplemented by fish and wild game, as well as forage for horses. Both Upper and Lower Canada were exporters of such agricultural produce as wheat, flour and biscuit. In 1801 and 1802 exports of wheat increased from 660,000 to 1,000,000 bushels. Between 1808 and 1811 exports declined to 399,168 bushels and then to 97,553.[10] Canadian meat supplies were generally inadequate, and their availability was affected by the supply of corn and peas required to fatten cattle and pigs. The surpluses could be bought by the military commissariat, which was the interface between the army and the public, responsible for buying supplies in the Canadas and in the United States. During war, the typical method of obtaining supplies was through local purchase, contract, requisition or seizure. Supplies were then warehoused and distributed to where they were needed. However a static military force, as opposed to an army moving through the territory, would rapidly consume local surpluses. Any extra food required would have to be brought in along the tenuous line of communication across the lakes, using valuable shipping.

Thus while it was relatively easy for Brock to work out where and when his

---

* George Benson Hall (?–1821) served throughout the war and was later elected a member of the Provincial Assembly.

combat forces should be positioned, it was quite another matter to get them there and then sustain them. The risks involved in his logistic calculations were huge, and supply had, therefore, to be a major factor in his operational planning and execution, just as it was for his opponents. In Hull's case things were further complicated by expeditionary warfare on hostile territory. What supplies were available or could be expected; the available transport by land and water; the length, security and nature of the line of communication; the available manpower and the time needed to bring up replacements; the medical arrangements for dealing with wounds, non-combat injuries and diseases; the organization of the force and its general administration: all these things mattered as much then as now.

Logistic responsibilities in the British army were divided between several departments. Munitions were supplied by the Board of Ordnance and issued when demanded by the quartermaster-general. Medical and hospital stores were handled by the Medical Department. Camp and field equipment came from the Quartermaster-General's Department, and each regiment supplied personal equipment ("necessaries") and clothing. All these natures were held, moved, obtained or issued by the stores branch of the commissariat, which was also responsible for the procurement, forwarding, issue and accounting for rations and for all land and inland water transport for the army. The accounts branch of the commissariat was responsible for the raising and disbursement of funds, the maintenance of records and acted as a comptroller of the army. Until 1809 the commissariat lacked a proper establishment and it was employed only in times of war or active operations.[11] However, as a result of experience in the Iberian peninsula, the rank structure had developed and included commissary-general, deputy commissary-general and assistant commissary-general. A commissary official for Upper Canada was appointed shortly after the creation of the province and he was given an assistant commissary at Niagara and a deputy at Detroit. Simcoe had lobbied to have the senior official, along with shipping responsibilities, placed under his government, but his request was not supported, for the Treasury felt no need to change its position. Despite the division of the former Quebec into Upper and Lower Canada, the authority of the commissary-general at the city of Quebec extended over both provinces, making the commissary of military stores and provisions in Upper Canada subordinate to him.[12] The commissary-general held a commission from the

War Office as well as the Treasury, making him fully responsible to the com-mander-in-chief in London while being accountable to the Treasury at the same time. The support of the commissary-general and his staff was vital to the successful conduct of any military operation and it was important that they understood the field commanders' intentions and general scheme of manoeuvre.

The commissary-general for British North America, William Robinson, had been appointed in August 1810 but did not assume his duties until Sep-tember 1811. Once in Montreal, he had set about invigorating his new com-mand, as he found it rife with irregularities and badly organized, as much because of neglect as of problems to do with time and space, personnel and working conditions. Robinson had only sixteen officers to maintain provision depots along a 1,700-mile line of communication and to manage the supply system.[13] The increased demand in the field was partially met by transferring officers and staff from Robinson's headquarters and from Nova Scotia, but this in turn weakened his ability to deal with the larger problems of the entire theatre of war.[14] Deputy Commissary-General Edward Couche was assigned to Upper Canada just before the war. He was responsible for depots in the four posts of Kingston, York, Fort George and Amherstburg and for a small store at Fort St Joseph.[15]

Before he could launch any operation, Brock and his quartermaster-gener-al had to determine how this structure would be employed to see that the army was fed, clothed, armed, ammunitioned, resupplied, reinforced and cared for. If they did not do this, the force would rapidly cease to be effective. Modern doctrine summarizes the factors governing the development of any logistic plans and systems as demand, distance, duration and destination. While nei-ther Brock nor Hull would have thought of things in these terms, they were clearly aware of the principles involved, as their respective correspondence with Prevost and the Secretary of War shows. Above all, by planning carefully according to these factors, operations had to be kept within reach of adequate sustainment. Beyond this reach, their troops would receive inadequate supply and operations would culminate rapidly.

Both armies needed a system of depots and units to transport logistic stocks – hence the raising of the car brigade – and distribute them to the point of use. Inseparable from this was the need to understand the environment in which any campaign would take place. This included, for example, route

A Mohawk warrior drawn by Lieutenant Sempronius Stretton, 1804. A somewhat different image from that commonly held of the native warriors of northeastern North America. (Library and Archives Canada C-014827)

selection, security and maintenance; the effects of terrain, obstacles, climate, weather and altitude. In North America at that date this was a huge challenge. Not only were roads of poor quality and few in number, but for the U.S. forces they were subject to frequent attack. The native warriors who interdicted the American supply routes would no doubt have appreciated and understood the tactics used by the Taliban in Afghanistan or Iranian-backed insurgents in southern Iraq in 2006.

Relying solely on supplies carried along the bad roads of early nineteenth-century North America made the army vulnerable. Requisition remained, therefore, an important method of securing food for men and horses. This was an orderly process in which units were allocated an area. Random plundering caused not only indiscipline and problems with the population but was inefficient. Requisition and seizure were much disliked and employed only as a last resort as they created animosity from the local populace, making it more difficult to obtain supplies later on from farmers unless the promise of payment was meticulously made good. The problem of feeding the army has probably undergone the biggest change in the years since 1812, for with the technology to can, dry, condense and freeze food, the field ration requirements for the combat elements of a modern infantry brigade of around 3,000 men for one day will be a mere ten pallets, and thus can be carried on a single

8-tonne supply vehicle. This was far from the case in 1812 when only drying of meat or fish, pickling and salting were feasible. Therefore, even with a system of depots, living off the land was an absolute necessity. A force of even 5,000 men in the North American woods of 1812 could not possibly carry all its food for men and horses without ceasing to do everything else. Secondly, for an army in the field, standing crops (other than grass) and livestock were not the same thing as food: the army had to spend time gathering raw materials, grinding corn, baking bread, slaughtering animals, salting meat and so on.

Finally there was the problem of medical support, the task of which was to maintain the fighting strength of armies both by preventing and curing sickness and by returning the wounded to duty. Good medical services thus contributed not only to the physical strength of the army but also to its moral strength, by reassuring the soldiers that they would be well cared for in the event of sickness or wounds. This is one area in which modern practice has changed the face of war: in Brock's day, a badly wounded man would expect to die – of blood loss, shock, thirst or subsequent infection. Nowadays, these factors only apply to irregular combatants in remote parts of the world, such as the Taliban in Afghanistan or the Revolutionary United Front in Sierra Leone, as I can testify from personal experience in these theatres of war. A soldier in a regular army can expect treatment at every stage from the point of wounding to a fully equipped hospital, with systems in place for rapid evacuation. Provided he is identified and put into the medical system, the odds are that the wounded soldier will live. In 1812 a soldier who entered the medical system would generally die slightly later than he would otherwise have done, unless his wounds were relatively light.

Even before he learned of Brock's arrival at Fort George, Hull had already had enough. Now being openly referred to as "Old Lady" by his own officers, he saw himself in a precarious position: his supply line was cut, he was surrounded by hostile natives, the planned attack across the Niagara had been delayed on account of inadequate resources, and in consequence Brock was moving troops to Malden. As one commentator wrote later, "though a soldier on occasion, he probably never had the opportunity to form correct soldierly standards."[16] His own men were close to mutiny, not because they were fearful but because they despised the timidity of their general. Major James Denny of the Ohio Volunteers wrote that "Our General is losing all the confidence he had in the army. He holds a council of war every day, and nothing can be done – and councils again. The result is still the same."[17] One council of war summoned by Hull on 6 August had voted for an immediate attack on Fort Malden.

What Hull did not know – and had he done so it might well have caused him to act differently and thus save his career – was that Prevost's adjutant-general, Baynes, had been sent under a flag of truce to meet General Dearborn at his headquarters in Greenbush, New York, carrying proposals from Prevost for a cessation of hostilities. Prevost had been prompted to make this approach by the departing British minister in Washington, Sir Augustus Foster. Foster had learned of the revocation of the Orders-in-Council on arrival in Halifax and had immediately sent a fast boat with the news to Washington as well as approaching Prevost. Dearborn sent Prevost's letter straight on to the Secretary of War,[18] having assured Baynes that with the exception of Hull's army, U.S. forces would "act merely on the defensive" while these proposals were being considered. In Dearborn's view, there was nothing to be lost:

> We shall lose no time, or advantage, by the agreement, but rather gain time without any risk. It is mutually understood, that all preparatory measures may proceed, and that no obstructions are to be attempted, on either side, to the passage of stores, to the frontier posts.... all circumstances considered, it may be well to avail ourselves of the occasion, until we are better prepared for acting with effect....

Dearborn wrote informing Hull of the developments and his exemption from the provisions of the agreement on the same day, but too late. The day before, 8 August, Hull withdrew all but 250 men from Sandwich, back across the river into the fort at Detroit;[19] there would be no further offensive moves into Canada until his supply line was secure. To seize and maintain the initiative, a commander needs five circumstances to be present: the will to action, the means to take that action, the ability to mount offensive operations, the identification or seizure of an opportunity and the ability to sustain his actions logistically. Hull had the means and the ability to sustain action but he had surrendered the will, the offensive and the opportunity to Brock. The initiative passed in that moment from the U.S. Army to the British and their allies – in the person of Isaac Brock.

Brock's negotiations with the Grand River people had persuaded about sixty warriors to join him – the first indication of a change of heart among the native nations there. He then set off by land for Long Point on Lake Erie, where he had ordered the assembly of a force to reinforce Amherstburg against the threat from Hull's force; ten small, open boats had been gathered. According to John Macdonell there was "hardly one fit for service" and it took a great deal of work into the following afternoon to get them ready.[20] On 8 August he was at Port Dover and two days later at Port Talbot, where his flotilla had grown to twelve sailing craft and several smaller boats. In these various craft he brought the men of the 41st Foot, the various militia companies and the native warriors almost the full length of Lake Erie. With more boats Macdonell thought that at least another 100 men could have been taken. From Port Talbot on, to conceal his movements, Brock moved at night, hugging the lake shore.[21] The weather was changeable and the troops were frequently soaked by rain; Macdonell wrote at the time that "It has rained almost continuously since we encamped last night, and although the men have been completely drenched, they continue in excellent spirits and behave in the most orderly and obedient manner."[22]

At one point, it is said that Brock's own boat ran aground and that he himself plunged into the water to lead the men in pushing her free – all this, as well as the need to row the boats in periods of calm when they could not be towed by the sailing craft, meant that travel by bateau was no picnic. On 11 August the troops embarked at midnight, with the officers being ordered to ensure that the men's weapons were ready for use. A detachment of two officers and thirty men was detailed off to form a piquet immediately on landing.[23] In his subsequent General Orders, Brock made specific reference to the rigours of this journey, which was fully 200 miles across open water: "In no instance have I seen troops who would have endured the fatigue of a long journey in boats during extremely bad weather, with greater cheerfulness and constancy, and it is but justice to this little band to add that their conduct throughout excited my admiration."[24]

On 14 August Brock and his men arrived at Amherstburg, where he announced his arrival in General Orders. In these same orders he made a point of congratulating the troops at Fort Malden on "the spirit manifested by those who have remained doing duty, and the judicious measures adopted by Colonel Procter," which had compelled Hull to make "so disgraceful a retreat."[25] This was a pointed remark aimed at those of the militia who had failed to turn out for duty. Brock also praised the work of the Indian Department and then went on to address the subject of the militia's conduct. Rather than start a witch-hunt and punish vice, Brock decided that encouragement and a second chance stood a better hope of persuading the militia to virtue:

> The Major General cannot avoid expressing his surprise at the numerous desertions which have occurred from the ranks of the militia, to which the circumstance of the long stay of the enemy on this side of the river must in a great measure be ascribed. He is willing to believe that their conduct proceeded from an anxiety to get in their harvests and not from any prediliection [*sic*] for the principles or Government of the United States.

He was also clearly well aware that pay was in arrears due to the shortage of coin and asked for returns of all those who had remained on duty.

The troops available in the Western District around Amherstburg were to be formed into three so-called brigades. So-called, because a brigade would normally consist of at least three regular regiments, with attached artillery and light troops. Brock's brigades were scarcely more than battalion size. The first brigade was to be under Colonel Thomas Bligh St George's command – in spite of this man's previous failings Brock needed senior officers – and would consist of the two flank companies of the Royal Newfoundland Regiment under Major Robert Mockler, who had brought the reinforcements into Upper Canada, along with the Kent Militia and the 1st and 2nd Regiments of Essex Militia: a total of 313 officers and men. The second brigade was commanded by Captain Peter Chambers and comprised fifty men of the 41st Foot and all the detachments of volunteers from the 1st, 2nd and 3rd York Militia, 5th Lincoln, Oxford, 1st Middlesex and 2nd Norfolk militias that had accompanied him from Fort George: a total of 250 officers and men. The third brigade was the remaining 252 officers and men of the 41st Foot under Captain Joseph Tallon. Henry Procter was to command the whole of the field force under Brock's direction; Brock himself also retained command of his small personal staff – Robert Nichol, John Glegg, John Macdonell, with Lieutenant James Givins of the 5th Foot, who was appointed as a provincial aide on 14 August; the Provincial Marine; the artillery; a troop of cavalry from the Essex Militia; and the commissariat train. The whole force amounted to 117 officers, 131 NCOs and 1,112 men.[26]

Then there were the native warriors. On the day after Hull's withdrawal, 100 men of the light company of the 41st under Captain Adam Muir and a small number of volunteers from the militia had crossed the river to join the force of almost 300 warriors led by Tecumseh himself: their objective was to interdict Hull's supply route. A second detachment of the 41st under Lieutenant Richard Bullock followed Muir and arrived just in time to join the action. Down the route from Detroit came 600 regulars and Ohio militia led by Lieutenant-Colonel James Miller, with a 6-pdr gun and a howitzer, detached by Hull to open up the route and bring in supplies. The force was well disposed with mounted scouts to the front and a strong advanced guard. At about 4.00 p.m., the combined British and aboriginal force sprang an ambush on Miller's men near Magagua, expecting to repeat the devastation of earlier episodes. But this time the Americans fought back, picking particularly on the redcoats, prominent among the trees; the attackers lost eleven warriors and five regulars killed and fourteen regulars wounded, along with an indeterminate number of warriors, including Tecumseh, who was slightly wounded in the neck. The British and their allies had to break off the ambush to conduct a fighting withdrawal back to their boats; the Americans, despite winning the day, lost eighteen dead and sixty-four wounded. Discouraged, wet through from a heavy thunderstorm, hungry, uncertain and with an order from Hull to return to the fort, Miller turned round and went back to Detroit the next day.[27] He was followed on 12 August by the last detachment from Sandwich. The isolation of Detroit was still a fact.

At about the same time, Hull sent further orders to Captain Nathan Heald, commanding the American Fort Dearborn at what is now Chicago, to evacuate his small force and retire on Detroit. With Mackinac gone his position was, Hull felt, unsupportable. News of the evacuation quickly spread among the native people, whose hostility and confidence were rising in the wake of the fall of Mackinac and they began to gather around Fort Dearborn. Heald tried to buy them off with his stock of trade goods, but as the sixty-six men of the garrison with their twenty-seven women and children, baggage and animals moved off on 15 August, they were ambushed by several hundred Indians. Two-thirds of the Americans were killed, the rest taken prisoner.

Tecumseh and his men were back at Amherstburg on 13 August. Just before midnight, a ragged volley of musketry was fired in salute by the warriors from their camp on Blois Blanc Island, where they were still awake celebrating their adventures with the Americans. The firing was a salute to welcome the arrival of Brock and his small force. Matthew Elliott went out into the night to find Tecumseh and to bring him, at the general's request, straight to Brock. Soon afterwards, Tecumseh arrived in the headquarters with the other aboriginal leaders: Roundhead, Splitlog, Walk-on-the-Water and Warrow. Brock had just finished speaking to Henry Procter and the officers of the garrison; Tecumseh saw a big man, taller and stouter than any native American, but alert, keen-eyed and obviously ready for action.

The best information on Brock's appearance at this crucial early period of the war comes from some contemporary accounts, as well as from his biographer and nephew, Ferdinand Brock Tupper, and was pulled together in a scholarly analysis by Ludwig Kosche.[28] Two U.S. officers described Brock after they had seen him at Detroit in August 1812. The first, Colonel William Stanley Hatch, spoke of him as an "officer of distinction" and went on to say that "His personal appearance was commanding; he must have been six feet three or four inches in height; very massive and large boned, though not fleshy, and apparently of immense muscular power."[29] Lieutenant-Colonel, later General, George Sanderson said much the same although his dislike of Brock was evident and colours the description: "a heavily built man, about six feet three inches in height, broad shoulders, large hips and frame, walking with a cane. One of his eyes, the left one I think, was closed, and he was withal the ugliest officer I ever saw."[30] Tupper, who, although he had not known Brock, was more inclined to be complimentary, said of him that "In stature he was tall, erect, and well proportioned, although in his latter years his figure was perhaps too portly.... His fine and benevolent countenance was a perfect index of his mind, and his manners were courteous, frank and engaging."[31] William Hatch and John Richardson, who both saw him in life at this time, say that he was "tall, stout and inclining to corpulency."[32]

Brock seems to have borne a marked resemblance to his brother Daniel, which was remarked on both by Tupper and later by Sir James Kempt when he visited Guernsey and met Daniel in 1834.[33] He shared the family tendency to a large head, which is apparent in several family portraits and to which he referred in his letter to Irving just after his promotion to brigadier-general, mentioned in chapter 7.[34] What we do know is that the Museum of the Niagara Historical Society has a cocked hat ordered by Brock with an internal circumference of 24 inches and that, from the evidence of the coat he was wearing at the time of his death, he was indeed 6 feet 2 or 3 inches tall, with a waist measurement of 47 inches and a chest measurement of 53 inches,[35] not far off the dimensions of Henry VIII at the same age. We do not know the colour of his hair. The only authenticated picture of him as an adult is the pastel (see page 95) probably painted by William Berczy in Quebec sometime in 1808 or 1809,[36] which may have accompanied a petition from the artist asking to paint a more formal portrait of Brock.[37] As a likeness it is well in keeping with the descriptions given by Tupper and others, although when John Glegg wrote to William Brock in December 1812, he said that "I regret to say that I never possessed a good likeness of your Brother, nor did he ever sit for it being taken in this country."[38]

For his part, what Brock saw, at least according to John Glegg, was that:

> Tecumseh's appearance was very prepossessing; his figure light and finely proportioned; his age I imagined to be about five and thirty; in height, five feet nine or ten inches; his complexion, light copper; countenance, oval, with bright hazel eyes beaming cheerfulness, energy and decision. Three small silver crowns, or coronets, were suspended from the lower cartilage of his aquiline nose; and a large silver medallion of George the Third … was attached to a mixed coloured wampum string, and hung round his neck. His dress consisted of a plain, neat uniform, tanned deerskin jacket, with long trousers of the same material, the seams of both being covered with neatly cut fringe; and he had on his feet leather moccasins, much ornamented with work made from the dyed quills of the porcupine.[39]

Brock himself wrote of Tecumseh to Lord Liverpool: "A more sagacious or a more gallant warrior does not, I believe, exist. He was the envy of everyone who conversed with him."[40] The meeting was very short, for the hour was late. Brock expressed appreciation for the respect explicit in the salute, but asked that the warriors should conserve ammunition for use against their enemies rather than waste it on salutes. Tecumseh agreed and the party broke up, with an agreement to meet again in council after daybreak.

When they met again, Brock laid out his intentions. Having read Hull's despatches and seen his withdrawal back over the river – a withdrawal he

had publicly described as disgraceful – Brock had not only a full understanding of the enemy's physical strength, dispositions and supply situation, but also a good picture of his opponent's state of mind; in other words
from a military intelligence point of view, he had complete penetration of
the other side. He had faced down a bully in the West Indies years before by
accurately assessing the psychology of his opponent and he clearly meant
to do the same again now and force Hull to give up Detroit. He would cross
the river with as large a force as could be assembled and try to draw the
Americans out of the fort to fight a pitched battle. If he could not draw Hull
out, he would storm the fort. Brock later wrote that "I crossed the river with
an intention of waiting in a strong position the effect of our fire upon the
Enemy's Camp and in the hope of compelling him to meet us in the field."[41]
He knew that 350 militiamen under Lewis Cass and Duncan McArthur had
left the fort to link up with Brush's supply convoy at the River Raisin, thus
reducing the overall force ratios, so that the timing and the odds would
probably never be better. Although he did not know of the ceasefire agreed
between Dearborn and Prevost, this too played to his advantage by neutral-
ising the threat on the Niagara and allowing him to deal with the threats
sequentially.

Although the entire plan was never written down and this account is a
reconstruction, it seems clear that Brock believed, rightly, that by destroying Hull's army, he would neutralise the main threat against Upper Canada,
allowing him to concentrate his meagre forces for what he felt sure would
be a more dangerous attack on the Niagara frontier. Had his intelligence
in the Niagara area been as good as it was at Detroit, he might have felt
less pressure, for the American force there was far from ready to launch a
serious attack. However, Brock proceeded on the basis of the information
he had, rather than what we possess with the benefit of hindsight. On the
basis of that information, his was a plan founded on psychological factors
and on deception, for it was plain that the very idea of the native warriors
filled Hull with terror and Brock immediately set out to fuel these terrors.
The plan to attack was not popular with his subordinates: all save John
Macdonell were opposed to it, including both Henry Procter and Robert
Nichol. But Brock was having none of their fears. One account says that he
listened to their objections and then said firmly and in a friendly tone, "I
have decided on crossing. And now, gentlemen, instead of further advice,

I entreat you to give me your cordial and hearty support."[42] To the native leaders, by contrast, this was what they thirsted for. There is an apocryphal story told by James Fitzgibbon,[43] much quoted in Canadian accounts, that Tecumseh turned to his followers and said, "*Ho-yo-o-e!* This is a man!" Fitzgibbon was not present at the meeting but claimed to have heard it from first-hand accounts, so it may be true. John Glegg, who was present, did not report the remark but recorded Tecumseh as having said that he was glad that the King, their father, had awoken and had allowed his soldiers to fight alongside their Indian brothers.[44] The other chiefs present spoke in agreement and the general meeting broke up.

Brock then took Tecumseh, Procter, Matthew Elliott and other key subordinates to a further meeting in Elliott's farmhouse,[45] where the fine details of the attack were hammered out. When drinks were offered, Tecumseh refused, even promising to keep his followers sober until the Americans were humbled. Brock, knowing well the effects of hard liquor on aboriginal fighting abilities and their subsequent behaviour, said approvingly that "If this resolution be persevered in, you must conquer."

As well as playing on Hull's fear of atrocities, Brock also meant to play Hull's own words in his proclamation back at him. Later that day, Brock sent a letter to Hull with Macdonell and Glegg under a flag of truce, requiring the immediate surrender of Detroit: "It is far from my intention to join in a war of extermination, but you must be aware, that the numerous body of Indians who have attached themselves to my troops, will be beyond controul [*sic*] the moment the contest commences."[46] Hull indignantly rejected this demand and Brock issued his orders for the attack.

CHAPTER THIRTEEN

"Intimidated by the Confidence of Our Advance"

THE FALL OF DETROIT, AUGUST 1812

Matthew Elliott of the British Indian Department was over seventy years old, and with the benefit of his long experience he had assembled a plan of Detroit from his own observations and those of others. The fort had originally been built on the river in 1701 by the French explorer La Mothe Cadillac,* to give access to the headwaters of the Mississippi basin, and named Pontchartrain. It had been twice besieged by the indigenous people and once burned to the ground. After the end of the Seven Years' War in 1763, it passed into British hands. During the Revolutionary War, the site was deemed unsatisfactory, probably because it was too low-lying and open to bombardment from the river. It was accordingly demolished and a new fort, Lernoult, constructed to the north of the original site above a low escarpment, which shows up clearly on the Board of Ordnance survey of 1779. Its re-builder, after whom it was named, was Richard Beringer Lernoult of the 8th (The King's) Regiment, who was still with that regiment when Brock joined it as a young man. British accounts from 1812 continue to refer to the post as Fort Lernoult, although the Americans had officially renamed it Detroit in 1805. In a letter to Brock dated 11 January 1811, Matthew Elliott described the fort as being equipped with twenty 24-pdr guns, four 12-pdrs, one 10-inch, two 8-inch and four 4½-inch howitzers, six mortars of various calibres and four 6-pdr field pieces for the militia. There were also "field equipage complete" and forges for heating red-hot shot, to be fired at shipping on the river. The fort was manned by about fifty artillerymen and fifty infantry soldiers. In addition, the armed schooners *Adams*, *Amelia* and *Selina* and the sloop *Contractor* were all in the vicinity.[1]

---

* Antoine Laumet de la Mothe, Sieur de Cadillac (1658–1730).

216

As has been noted, Brock himself may have made a personal visit to Detroit before the war. Even if he had not done so, he had, in addition to a complete intelligence picture of his enemy's mental state and dispositions, a wealth of detail about the fort and the surrounding area. He had the report from Macdonell's covert reconnaissance; he had a similar report from Lieutenant-Colonel Thomas Bligh St George, from which a detailed plan, also describing the approaches to Detroit from the west, was drawn by Captain Matthew Dixon of the Royal Engineers.[2] He would also have had access to the plans drawn up by the Board of Ordnance for the construction of the fort, which was a square earthwork with ramparts more than twenty feet high, topped by a log palisade, enclosing between two and three acres, each side being about 100 yards long, with a blockhouse at each corner. There was a gate and gatehouse and a double row of sharpened pickets, one of which was at the base of a six-foot-deep, twelve-foot-wide ditch in front of the earthworks and one obliquely in the earth walls, whose excavation

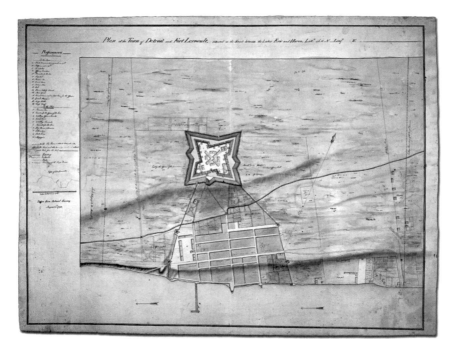

Detroit and Fort Lernoult from the plans of the Board of Ordnance, 1779. (Ordnance Drawing Office, Royal Armouries Collection, H.M. Tower of London)

had provided the ramparts. Firing platforms for the guns were cut into the top of the earthwork. In addition, he had a detailed and up-to-date plan of the fort, dated 26 January 1812, which the author annotated: "Not knowing the dimensions of the various parts of the walls, it was impossible to lay it down by any scale, it is however hoped it will be sufficient to give a general idea of its strength, and the range of its guns." The plan is signed "RR". This is almost certainly Robert Reynolds,* whose father, Thomas, had been the commissary to the garrison of Lernoult from about 1760 and had owned a property in the town, on St Louis Street, from 1780. When Lernoult was handed over to the Americans in 1796, the family had moved to Amherstburg, where Reynolds kept his appointment until his death in 1810. His son Robert immediately succeeded him as commissary.[3] Finally, it is said that when Brock and Tecumseh met at Amherstburg, Brock asked Tecumseh to give him his view of the ground. Tecumseh is said to have taken out his knife and drawn a sketch on a piece of birch-bark – as good as paper – which captured the detail of the area.[4] Brock therefore had about as much intelligence on the terrain as was available given the technology of the time.

The town of Detroit, lying outside the fort, was inhabited by about 1,000 souls, a mixture of French and English settlers occupying 150 houses, surrounded by a picket palisade and reinforced by four small bastions. Within the town and outside the walls of the fort were barracks and a magazine, which was probably intended either for the local militia or for trade goods for the native people, or both. The town had actually been built between the fort and the river, which meant that the fort's guns had to fire over the houses at long range to engage targets on the water. Hull had improved the defences by preparing floating batteries, and the earth ramparts and log palisades were strong enough to resist attack unless beaten down by the fire of heavy guns.

It seems possible that there was a weak spot in the defences that was known to Brock: the clue is in his despatch after the action in which he says that "the Enemy had taken little or no precaution towards the land side...."[5] This would mean that the heaviest guns were directed towards the river, and without constructing platforms to bear their weight they could not be

---

* Robert Reynolds (1782?–1864) later built an important property in Amherstburg, which still survives. His sister Catherine was a noted landscape painter.

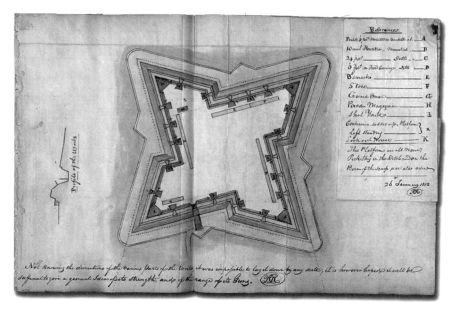

Fort Detroit in January 1812, by Robert Reynolds (detail) (Author's collection)

moved to the land side, and this seems to be borne out in the description of the pieces on Robert Reynolds's map. It may also have indicated that the defences were in a lesser state of repair or that undergrowth had been allowed to grow up, obscuring the line of attack from inland, or a combination of any of these factors.

Of course, Hull's arrival had greatly increased the garrison, which now numbered 582 regulars of the 4th U.S. Infantry and the regular gunners, who together garrisoned the fort itself. There were about 1,000 Ohio and Michigan militia, after the various detachments had been deducted, who were dispersed around the fort on the landward side – interesting, given the hint that the defences may have been weak or incomplete there – and in the small redoubts that protected the town, behind the picket fence and in the houses of the town of Detroit, ready to fight off any attack by native warriors. An advanced battery of two 24-pdrs and a 6-pdr had also been thrown up about a mile south of the fort, commanding the approach from the south along the portage road. British reconnaissance had not detected it, probably because it was screened from view across the river by the houses of Detroit.

With these dispositions and the detached bodies of militia, Hull had no forces left to hold the river bank and contest any landing. John Norton reported that the area was usually held by a piquet of about 100 militia men, but that this had been withdrawn.[6] Moreover when contesting an obstacle like a water feature, the defenders should hold both sides: to surrender the far side merely hands freedom of action to the attacker. By withdrawing from Sandwich, this was exactly what Hull had done.

Despite their numbers, American morale was not good. Exasperation with their general continued to grow in the ranks inside Fort Detroit; it is even said that there was a conspiracy to remove him from command. Certainly Lieutenant-Colonel Lewis Cass wrote to Governor Meigs of Ohio that:

> ... this army has been reduced to a critical and alarming situation. We have wholly left the Canadian shore and have abandoned the miserable inhabitants who depended on our will and power to protect them, to their fate.... That Malden might have been easily reduced I have no doubt,... But the precious opportunity has fled.... The British force is opposite and our situation has nearly reached its crisis.[7]

When looking in detail at the composition of the assaulting force, especially its want of heavy guns, one has to question whether Brock was serious about attacking a fortified position, held by a force more than twice his size, well supplied with artillery, ammunition and food. Certainly a prolonged siege was out of the question: Brock had no sappers to construct field works, no siege train and insufficient troops to invest the fort. Even if there was a weak spot in the defences, he had little chance of making a viable breach with the throw-weight of shot available and an insufficient number of troops to prevail in a close-quarter battle with heavy losses. One is forced to the conclusion that this was a gamble, a demonstration designed to tip Hull psychologically over the edge in order to fulfil the great Chinese military theorist Sun Tzu's maxim, that the acme of success in war is to win without fighting.

When crossing any obstacle, whether a watercourse, a minefield or a linear fortification, an assault force must first secure the home bank, then effect a lodgement or bridgehead on the enemy bank large enough to prevent the enemy from interfering with operations; then it must establish ferries or bridges with enough capacity to build up the assault force at a rate faster than the opposition can bring its forces to bear in order to achieve favourable force ratios and then break out of the bridgehead. There must also be sufficient direct and indirect fire support available to suppress enemy fire and give cover to the assaulting troops. Brock's orders required the troops to be ready for embarkation at McKee's Point, just south of Sandwich, at 3.00 a.m. on Sunday, 16 August – Alexander McKee being an officer of the Indian Department with a property in the area. This meant an approach to the embarkation site of fifteen miles, or up to five hours' march, from Amherstburg; Thomas Bligh St George was ordered to march his brigade that evening and "canton" the men close to the embarkation site. There is no specific mention of the other two brigades; however we know from the journal of Charles Askin[8] that at least one other brigade had continued from Amherstburg by boats of the Provincial Marine, in the craft that were to be used for the crossing.

The first to cross to the far side of the Detroit River, less than a mile of water, well before dawn, were around 500 warriors, accompanied by Matthew Elliott, who was ordered to scout the landing site two miles south of the fort, between a small tributary of the Detroit, the Rouge River, and Spring Wells; this was Brock's bridgehead force. Originally the warriors had been directed to land well to the south, below Grasse Island, to avoid detection, but when it was clear that the U.S. piquet had been withdrawn, they landed much closer to the fort. Once Elliott sent word back to Brock that the far bank was not held in any strength, the main force would cross and head for the objective, Fort Detroit.

The assault force formed by Brock's three brigades consisted of 330 regulars of the Royal Artillery, the 41st Foot and the flank companies of the Royal Newfoundland Regiment, the sixty or so warriors of the Grand River nations and 400 Canadian militia, a total of 730 British and Canadians out of an available force of 1,370; the rest remained to secure Amherstburg and man the battery at Sandwich. At the suggestion of the brigade major, Thomas Evans, many of the militia had been kitted out with discarded coats from the 41st: red with red facings. Brock later acknowledged Evans's quick thinking, writing that "Your thought of clothing the militia in the 41st cast off clothing proved a most happy one."[9] Although these were old and faded, they were enough to deceive an enemy from a distance. The men were ordered to stand-to at 4.00 a.m. and the crossing began as soon as it was light with Brock's three small brigades being ferried across in small craft, covered by the guns of the Provincial Marine ships. Askin was in the 2nd Brigade and reported that the 3rd Brigade, consisting entirely of regulars accompanied by Brock and his staff, crossed first, followed by the militia. There were enough boats to lift two brigades at once and, given the width of the river, the entire operation should have been completed in about one hour. John Norton, however, reported that "The Breadth of the River as well as the Scarcity of Boats – caused us some delay, ere we were in readiness to advance."[10] Askin said that the whole force was on the far bank between 6.00 and 7.00 a.m. By the time the landing was completed, unopposed, and the troops formed up, 16 August had turned into a warm, sunny day with a pleasant breeze off the lake.

Fire support was provided from three sources. First, as soon as Hull had withdrawn from the Canadian side of the river, Colonel Henry Procter had ordered the construction of a battery immediately opposite Detroit under the direction of Captain Matthew Dixon, who, it will be remembered, had drawn up the plan of the fort and therefore understood the target. This had been done secretly, at night, masked by a grove of mature oak trees, so that the work was not seen by the Americans until the guns were in position and the trees felled.[11] The battery mounted one 18-pdr gun, two 12-pdrs and two 5½-inch mortars, crewed by naval gunners under the command of Captain George Hall of the Provincial Marine; none of these were heavy enough for serious siege warfare, but they were capable of knocking down a wooden stockade, provided they were not suppressed by the larger number of heavy guns mounted in the fort. Secondly, there were the guns of the accompanying brig *Queen Charlotte* and the schooner *General Hunter*. The brig mounted 24-pdrs, and although ships were vulnerable to the heavy guns of fortified positions on land, the two craft would be well within range; they could throw a great deal of suppressive fire onto the shore, should the landing be opposed by U.S. infantry without entrenchments. Last, the assault force carried with it three 6-pdr and two 3-pdr guns crewed by regular artillerymen commanded by Lieutenant Felix Troughton. These were guns designed to give close supporting fire to infantry or cavalry during field operations and could have little effect on prepared positions; however, their moral effect on the troops was important.

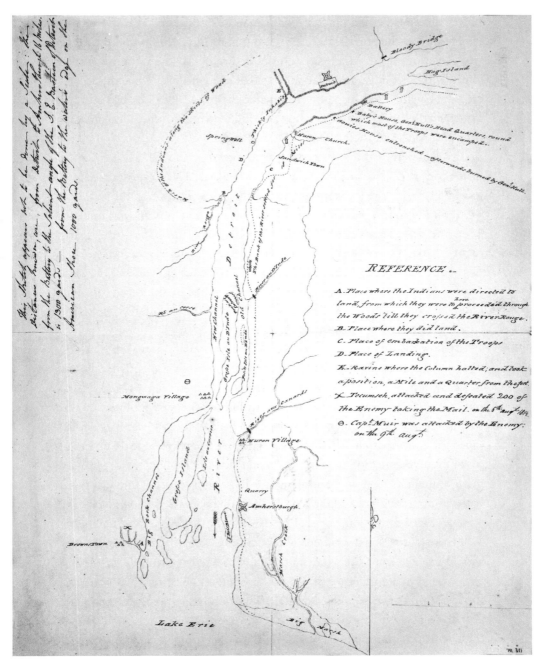

Brock's sketch of the attack on Detroit, 16 August 1812. (William L. Clements Library, University of Michigan)

It was the guns of Hall's battery that began the attack on Detroit. Fire had been opened the previous afternoon so that the guns could find the range and elevation; seven American 24-pdrs had returned the fire but without effect, and both sides' guns had fallen silent as night fell.[12] Once the assault crossing began, the British guns re-opened their fire. The guns and mortars now had the range, and according to Hull's own account, "almost every shot and shell had their effect."[13] Mortar shells were particularly effective against wooden forts for they could be lobbed over the defences and burst inside confined spaces, causing enormous damage. At least one documented round fell inside the fort's mess hall and then passed through the wall into an adjoining room, mangling during its passage three officers and injuring a fourth, "scattering their brains and blood against the walls of the apartment".[14] One of these was the unlucky Lieutenant Porter Hanks, the paroled American commander of Mackinac. Another round exploded near the gatehouse, killing two soldiers instantly; a third exploded on the parade ground, killing another man, and yet another exploded in the hospital, decapitating a patient and killing a surgeon.[15]

By now the fort was full of civilians, as the population of Detroit, terrified by the approach of the British and more especially the native warriors, had crowded in. Those who saw the warriors described them as "an extraordinary spectacle, some covered with vermillion, others with blue clay, and still others tattooed in black and white from head to foot." It was like "standing at the entrance to hell, with the gates thrown open to let the damned out for an hour's recreation on earth."[16] Then there were some service families, including Hull's own wife and daughters: "The fort at this time was filled with women, children, and the old and decrepit people of the town."[17] "... all was panic and confusion," according to one witness, "crying infants clinging to their half-distracted mothers, older children everywhere but where they should be."[18] Most of the women and children had been moved earlier into a root cellar in an orchard just outside the fort; as the British fire increased, the remaining women, mostly military wives who were preparing bandages and sewing charge bags, were taken to join them.

The British column marched straight up the portage road along the river, as Lieutenant John Richardson described it, "with the river close on our right flank and a chain of alternate houses and close fences on our left,"[19] and was preceded by a screen of warriors acting as scouts or skirmishers; the

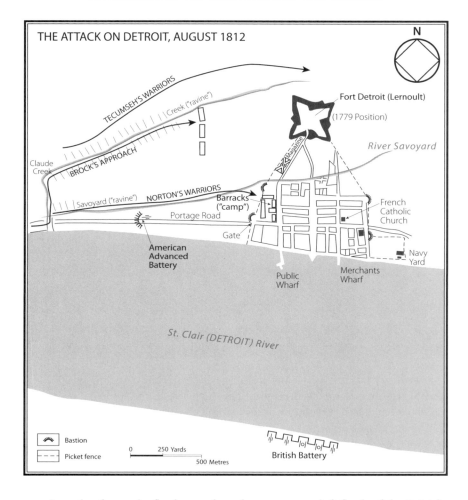

THE ATTACK ON DETROIT, AUGUST 1812

warriors also formed a flank guard on the western or left flank of the British, about one-and-a-half miles away.[20] Next came an advanced guard formed by the grenadier company of the 41st Regiment under Lieutenant Richard Bullock and then Brock's small train of artillery hauled by the car brigade. Behind them came the rest of the 41st Foot, the Newfoundlanders and the militia, all commanded by Procter. The usual distance between sections and companies had been doubled to increase the length of the column,[21] so that with all the red coats, it made for a formidable appearance – as John Norton recorded, "So as to give the whole Body the appearance of Regulars."[22] Lewis Cass said that, according to American witnesses, the British column totalled twenty-nine platoons.[23]

The wharf and town of Detroit. This is the view that Brock and his troops would have seen as they approached from the south up the river road. One of the small blockhouses protecting the settlement can be seen, as can the French church. When compared to the Board of Ordnance map, this sketch appears remarkably accurate. (William L. Clements Library, University of Michigan)

Brock himself rode with the advanced guard – probably not on Alfred, for despite popular myth there is no record of the horse having been shipped from York, nor would the boats used for the voyage have permitted the embarkation of a spirited horse for any length of time. As the column marched north towards Detroit, crossing Campe's Creek on the way, Brock was intercepted by Matthew Elliott and Tecumseh, who reported that Cass and McArthur's detachment had been seen about three miles to the south. They were showing no sign of urgency in returning, however, despite hearing the cannonade, for they had made camp and were roasting an ox. Even so, this was too close for comfort and Brock had no desire to be taken in the flank or rear by this force. Accordingly he decided to press on with an attack rather than wait Hull out.

As the column closed on the fort, John Norton suggested that he should scout to the left, where there were some enclosures, a few deserted houses and a "ravine" which might conceal an ambush. This ravine has long since disappeared under the urban sprawl of modern Detroit and it is not possible to say how wide, deep or long it was, but in all likelihood it was an incised watercourse, probably dry at that time of the year, at least deep enough to conceal a standing man. From the general lie of the land, this ravine ran from the outskirts of Detroit down to Claude Creek and was likely the course of the little River Savoyard; the escarpment noted on the 1779 survey probably also provided some additional dead ground from the fort's guns. Brock agreed, telling Norton in a friendly way to be careful. In the ravine Norton found the families of a number of French Canadians, descendants perhaps of the original settlers, who had taken shelter there. Ignoring them, Norton's group pushed on up the ravine until they closed to 150 yards from the edge of the village, where they could observe the American militia behind their picket fence. On seeing the warriors, the militia, according to Norton, fled, joined by some horsemen – the American force included two troops of cavalry.[24] The warriors tried to intercept them but were not quick enough, taking only one prisoner, a terrified sentry of the 4th Infantry.

Another party of warriors, probably the flank guard under Tecumseh, circled round through the woods that covered the ground to the north of the fort. One account by William Hamilton Merritt reported that "Tecumseh extended his men, and marched them three times through an opening [in the woods to the rear of the fort] in full view of the garrison, which induced them to believe that there were at least two or three thousand Indians."[25] This is another story that has gained popular credence, although Merritt could not have seen the event and there is no American account to verify it. What we do know is that Hull believed that "The bands of savages which had then joined the British forces, were numerous beyond any former example."[26]

Meanwhile the main force had continued its march. Approaching Claude Creek, the troops received a nasty shock, as John Richardson reported. For there, pointing straight at them, "planted in the road,"[27] was the advanced battery of three guns, loaded ball over canister, with the smoke of the gunners' slow-match drifting in the air. Richardson said afterwards that:

At each moment we expected that they would be fired, yet although it was evident the discharge must literally have swept our small, but dense column, there was neither halt nor indecision perceptible. This was fortunate. Had there been the slightest wavering, or appearance of confusion in the men, the enemy, who were closely watching us, and who seemed intimidated by the confidence of our advance, would not have failed to profit by the discovery.[28]

It is said that Robert Nichol remonstrated with Brock that he should not expose himself at the head of the column and that Brock replied, "I appreciate the advice you give me, but I feel that in addition to their sense of loyalty and duty, many here follow me from a sense of personal regard, and I will never ask them to go where I do not lead them."[29] This smacks of the very worst sort of Victorian sentimentality and may well be a later invention; but even if he did not use the words, Brock's sense of honour as an officer would certainly have obliged him to place himself at the point of greatest danger. The troops would have expected no less. He did not know that Hull had, or so it seems, given orders that the guns were not to be fired.

The approach to the guns was confined by the river on one side and houses and fences on the other, so that there was no possibility of deploying off the line of march. Before the range closed, Brock directed the head of the column into a covered approach. This cannot have been the same ravine that Norton used, for that ran too close to the American battery, and only a detailed examination of the ground can unravel this. Fortunately there is an excellent map available, drawn by the French cartographer Leeseman in 1796, after the new fort was constructed.[30] As well as the Savoyard, running gradually down into the Claude Creek, there was a second watercourse running northeast from the mouth of the creek to the rear of the fort, which some sources call the Huron Creek. This seems the most likely covered approach and ties in with the general theme that the whole thrust of the advance was to the left, that is, to get round to the rear of the fort, underlining the possibility that the fort was vulnerable from the inland flank. The final proof that this was the line of approach is an annotated sketch map of the attack sent by Brock himself to John Hale, the receiver-general of Lower Canada, after the operation.[31] On this sketch, Brock in his own handwriting marked the creek as the "Ravine where the Column halted, and took a position, a mile and a quarter from the fort."

Assistant Surgeon William Faulkner of the 41st Regiment, about 1810. Faulkner would have been known to Brock; the illustration is a valuable contemporary description of the uniform of the 41st. (By permission of the owner, Mr Nick Saint)

A contemporary French image of a captain of the 41st Foot around 1811, previously unpublished. (By permission of Mr Dan Laroche and Fort George, Niagara-on-the-Lake)

From other accounts too, it appears that the area was planted with corn, which at that time of the year would have been green, between four and six feet tall, and this would have helped to conceal movement.[32] Again, it is said that Brock stood in the road with his back to the American battery while the column filed into the covered approach, but this may be yet more myth-making from a later date.

Beyond the covered approach, while Procter and his officers deployed the troops from column into line, Brock went forward to reconnoitre the fort. The deployment position was, according to John Richardson, "through an open field and orchard, leading to a house about three hundred yards off the road which he [Brock] selected as his Head Quarters. In this position we were covered."[33] The British and Canadian troops paused and rapidly ate a cold breakfast, accompanied by some heroic rum-drinking,[34] it being a matter of pride that British troops never went into action on empty stomachs. The guns were manoeuvred into a position from which they could support the assault from a flank and "a company of riflemen from York" dressed in green, who "were most all painted as Indians,"[35] was sent further left to make contact with Tecumseh's warriors in the woods. The sight of them was too much for the Michigan militia, who began to leave their posts; at least half refused to take part in any fighting. When Hull's son Abraham* ordered a company of Ohio militiamen to the ramparts, they refused.

At 10.00 a.m. the British and Canadian soldiers, waiting for the order to begin the assault, were puzzled by the sight of a white bed-sheet hung over the southwestern bastion. At the same time, the American guns in the fort ceased firing across the river, and the crews of the advanced battery limbered up the guns and withdrew into the fort. Clearly the Americans wanted to parley. Expecting Brock to be at his headquarters in Amherstburg, Hull sent a boat across the river under a flag of truce, proposing a ceasefire of one hour to open negotiations for the surrender of Detroit. Obviously he did not expect the British commanding general to be at the head of the attack, which says as much about Hull himself as about Brock. Captain Hall sent the party back, telling them to look closer to home. In preparation for the negotiations, Hull's aides erected a marquee, decked out in the red and blue

---

* Abraham Fulton Hull, whose wife was a Canadian, was killed at Lundy's Lane in 1814.

colours of the republic – and incidentally of Britain – outside the front gate, under the curious eyes of the attacking army.

Brock allowed a pause for the Americans to complete their arrangements, so that his messengers would not arrive in the midst of an embarrassing and unseemly mess of preparations, and during this pause, Hull's message was delivered. Once he felt that sufficient time had elapsed Brock sent his aides, John Macdonell and John Glegg, forward to the fort, also under a flag of truce, with instructions to arrange the surrender of the fort in no more than three hours or the assault would commence. The two men were stopped short of the fort and conducted to Hull. They reported back to Brock an hour later. Hull had not made a good impression. Like many Americans, and indeed Canadians, he chewed tobacco and either nerves or carelessness in spitting out the juice had left trails of nicotine-coloured spittle over his face and his neck-cloth. His hands trembled and his voice faltered; all in all, he appeared to be in the grip of a great fear: fear of the hordes of native warriors who would surely massacre his men, his women, his children and himself. There has been speculation that Hull had been taking laudanum – the alcoholic tincture of opium – or some other drug, but there is no hard evidence for this. Lewis Cass, although not himself present, said that, as far as he knew, Hull had not at any time discussed surrender with his officers and that it came as a surprise to all.[36] Hull's one honourable action had been to try to gain protection for the Canadian deserters in his ranks; not unnaturally, this was angrily refused by Macdonell.

The terms of surrender were to all effects unconditional. Hull surrendered the fort, the garrison, all its stores and equipment, the town and, unbelievably, the detachments of militia under Cass and McArthur. The 1st Regiment of Michigan Militia was exempted, for this regiment had turned its coat and gone over to the British as soon as Brock's force had appeared on the American shore. Hull asked for the honours of war – that is, for the garrison to march out with its Colours flying, drums beating and bayonets fixed. This was a mark of respect accorded to a gallant foe after an honourable resistance. Brock, quite rightly under the code of the time, refused to grant this. It is easy to be scornful of Hull's apparent cowardice, and there are plenty of conspiracy theories suggesting that the attack was a sham. Hull was an old soldier – too old for war in the wilderness, which was a young man's affair. An old soldier is often a careful soldier and the most likely answer is that Brock had correctly understood the psychological weakness of his opponent from the tone of his correspondence: Hull surrendered out of concern for the fate of the civilian population, and indeed his soldiers, at the hands of what he believed to be an overwhelming number of savage natives. There were, after all, plenty of recent precedents for his concern.[37]

The soldiers of the British army had wound themselves up to a pitch, no doubt fortified by the rum ration with their cold breakfast, ready for the assault. The feelings of anti-climax, followed by relief, followed by elation, must have been intense. In a daze, the British and Canadian soldiers marched into the town and formed two lines on either side of the fort's gates. The American regulars and militiamen, rather dishevelled and themselves also no doubt the worse for rum, marched out of the fort and stacked their arms on the esplanade between the fort and the town. Charles Askin described the American soldiers in less than glowing terms: "the whole of their army were ill dressed, and few of them appeared healthy or well, indeed they seemed to me the poorest looking sett of men I have seen for a long time...."[38]

Just after midday Lieutenant Richard Bullock led the grenadier company of the 41st Foot into the fort, followed by the light company. One account says that they made their first attempt to enter before the time agreed and had to withdraw.[39] The second entry went according to plan, however, as the fifes and drums played "The British Grenadiers" – they were the first British soldiers to enter since the fort had been handed over to the Americans sixteen years before. The Stars and Stripes was lowered and the Union raised, while the fifes played "God Save the King." According to John Richardson, the flag was not the Great Union but a smaller jack, meant to fly from a ship.[40] Troughton's gunners manned several of the captured artillery pieces on the ramparts and fired a general salute of seventeen guns, to the hurrahs of the British and Canadian soldiers, while Tecumseh's warriors fired their muskets and danced with savage glee, gloating over the vanquished Americans and doing nothing to allay Hull's fright. The sullen United States regulars, and indeed the stouter hearts among the Ohio militia, could scarcely believe what had happened. Some smashed their muskets and rifles rather than surrender them; one American soldier, it is said, attempted to burn the Colours of the 4th U.S. Infantry and was physically restrained only in the nick of time. John Richardson said that the Colours had not been handed

over with the usual formalities, so that Brock ordered Lieutenant Richard
Bullock to have them taken down to the Americans assembled on the esplanade to be formally handed over.[41] This was done by Captain Crook of
the 4th Infantry, who "felt much chagrin … presented them saying 'Sir the
fortune of war has placed these in your hands.…'"[42] Either way, the Colours were taken into British custody and placed under guard by the 41st.
But there was one inmate of Fort Detroit who was neither American nor
French-Canadian. This was Private John Dean of the 41st, who had been
taken at the first skirmish on the Aux Canards – his companion Private
James Hancock had died of his wounds. Brock released Dean with his own
hands and returned him to his comrades.

Brock immediately sent off a hasty despatch to Prevost:

> I hasten to apprize Your Excellency of the capture of this very impor-
> tant Post – 2,500 troops have this day surrendered Prisoners of war, and
> about 25 pieces of Ordnance have been taken, without the sacrifice of a
> drop of British blood.
>
> I had not more than 700 troops including Militia and about 600
> Indians to accomplish this service – When I detail my good fortune
> Your Excellency will be astonished – I have been admirably supported
> by Colonel Procter, the whole of my staff and I may justly say every
> individual under my Command.[43]

He also found time to write a short note to his brothers: "My dear
Brothers and Friends, Rejoice at my good fortune, and join me in prayers
to heaven. I send you a copy of my hasty note to Sir George. Let me hear
that you are all united and happy."[44] This letter, it seems, addressed to Irving
in London, arrived on 13 October 1812, the day of the battle of Queenston
Heights. In fact, news of the victory at Detroit had reached London on 6
October; the church bells were rung and Brock's full report had received a
Gazette all to itself.[45]

Brock's estimate of prisoners was slightly adrift: 520 regulars were embarked in ships or held in barracks to be sent to Quebec, from where they
would be exchanged or paroled. The 2,200 militia were embarked in smaller
craft and sent home on parole.[46] Hull was imprisoned at Montreal and later
returned to the United States, where he stood trial by court-martial. As well
as his own failings, he was without doubt the scapegoat for an unprepared

and over-confident U.S. administration. He was found guilty as charged and sentenced to death, a sentence that was later commuted in recognition of his honourable service during the Revolutionary War. He died a broken man.

The captured ordnance and stores in the fort included thirty-five guns and mortars of various calibres up to 24-pdrs, along with enough field and garrison carriages to mount all the guns for either contingency. Among these guns, received with the greatest satisfaction, were nine 24-pdrs and four brass pieces that had been taken from Major-General John Burgoyne's British army after the surrender at Saratoga in August 1777. The ammunition amounted to 11,000 rounds of shot, 4,600 mortar shells and 69 barrels of powder. Turning to small arms, there were 2,500 muskets with bayonets and accoutrements and 500 rifles, along with half a ton of ball ammunition.[47] Finally, the brig *Adams* was added to the Provincial Marine and renamed the *Detroit*. These seizures immediately solved all Brock's shortages of arms and ammunition, but quite apart from that, the value of the haul, which also included food, drink and garrison stores, amounted to around £40,000, or $200,000 U.S.;[48] £3.5 million at today's rates.

Then there was McArthur's detachment. Captain William Elliott was despatched with an escort of militiamen under Major Matthew Dixon to find them, bearing a letter from Hull.[49] He found the detachment late on 16 August at the Rouge River crossing and took their surrender. Brush's detachment was not with them and so, leaving Dixon to escort McArthur's men back to Detroit, Elliott went on to the River Raisin, carrying a note from McArthur to Brush scribbled on the back of Hull's letter. Elliott arrived two days later but was roughly handled by the Americans and taken prisoner – and at one point, threatened with summary execution. However, early the next morning, 20 August, he awoke to the sound of Brush and some of his men making off with what stores they could carry, in defiance of Hull's order. Elliott was released by Lieutenant-Colonel William Anderson of the 1st Michigan Militia, who asked that his command at the River Raisin be treated in the same way as the rest of that regiment – in other words, to come under British command. Elliott undertook to arrange this and the fort was duly handed over at 2.00 p.m. that day. The captured stores and ordnance included 121 muskets and rifles with their ancillaries, a 2½-inch howitzer and ammunition, three wagons and a store of flour, whiskey and salted pork.[50] More stores were later picked up at the abandoned U.S. base at the Miami River rapids, which had been ravaged by the native people, by Captain Peter Chambers, who was sent with a detachment of regular troops to follow Elliott and take charge of all government property.

Under the Prize Regulations then in force,[51] all the captured ordnance and stores would be taken into government service and those who had taken part in the capture would be rewarded by sharing the equivalent cash value – the logic being that the government would anyway have been obliged to buy materiel of war. Prize money was more often a feature of war at sea but applied equally on land and was a significant factor in boosting morale. The share system was applied strictly according to rank: Brock's share under these regulations would have been one-eighth, or £5,000, and had he lived to receive it, it would have more than cleared the outstanding debt to William's creditors. However, new regulations appeared in 1813 in General Orders which appear to have been backdated.[52] These gave each rank a number of shares – a private having one, up to a general officer having eighty, or if commanding a division, 160. The value of one share for Detroit was set at £3, so that by this system, if applied, Brock would have received a mere £480.

The campaign on the Detroit frontier was decided by superior generalship as well as by moral factors. Both sides had to struggle with the same physical factors: the effects of climate, terrain and distance on supply, communications and the size of forces available. On both sides, a small army was lost in the vastness of the continent but a large army would have starved. But on the British side there were Charles Roberts at St Joseph's, Tecumseh, Henry Procter and Isaac Brock, all of whom were willing to take risks to secure and maintain the initiative. Brock in particular had to balance the competing needs of two fronts – the Niagara and Detroit – as well as the need to deal with both civil and military administration. By deciding to treat the Niagara as an economy of force sector in order to generate enough strength to go on the offensive at Detroit, and by accurately analyzing the psychological state of his enemy, he had triumphed. Contrast this with Lewis Cass and Duncan McArthur, who rather than march to the sound of the guns, had sat down and roasted an ox; and William Hull, who had twice made capable subordinates withdraw and lose the advantage they held and who had magnified every difficulty until he was overcome by his own fears. These men had begun with the initiative in their hands at the strategic, operational and tactical levels of war. They had allowed their enemy, and events, to dictate to them and by doing so had thrown victory away.

The news hit Washington, literally, like a bolt from the blue. At first the accounts were disbelieved but when Hull's despatch arrived there was outrage. What made it worse was that Hull was also governor of the Michigan territory, and with his surrender, this vast area was given up to the British. In the Canadas the effect was electrifying. Gone was the sullen feeling of inevitable defeat, for the greater part of the attacking force had, after all, been Canadian militiamen. When Brock returned to York on 27 August, he received a hero's welcome, and from this time on the idolisation of Brock as the saviour of Canada began. With some cause: in the space of nineteen days he had settled matters in the Assembly, travelled 300 miles, repulsed an invading force twice the size of his own available army, taken the whole lot prisoner without the loss of a single life and added the entire Michigan territory to the British dominions. An account of the arrival of Hull and his men at Montreal dated 12 September 1812, where he was met by Prevost, was both scornful and triumphant:

> That General Hull should have entered into our city so soon, at the head of his troops, rather exceeded our expectations. We were, however, very happy to see him, and received him with all the honours due to his high rank and importance as a public character....
>
> It unfortunately proved rather late in the evening for the vast concourse of spectators assembled to experience that gratification they so anxiously looked for. This inconvenience was, however, in great measure remedied by the illuminations of the streets through which the line of march passed.[53]

It was the fall of Detroit that convinced the people of Upper Canada that they could preserve their way of life and that surrender to the Americans was not inevitable. This must be held as a massively important factor in sustaining Canadian belief in victory through the difficult times that followed in 1813 and 1814.

The effect was just as dramatic – more so perhaps – on the aboriginal people and in particular on the nations of the Grand River, who at last began to rally in numbers as Brock's and Tecumseh's stock rose very high indeed. In the immediate aftermath the native people celebrated and there was a fair amount of drinking and looting – but no atrocities. The aboriginal warriors did not, of course, share the same cultural values as the British and the notion of chivalry to a vanquished enemy was highly puzzling to them. If your enemy had surrendered, in the aboriginal view, he accepted whatever fate his conquerors decided upon. Tecumseh's moral force, however, was strong enough to prevent his followers harming their captives.

Brock and Tecumseh made their Detroit headquarters in a vacant house in either St Ann Street or St Honore Street, where the captured American officer Robert Wallace remembered being introduced to Tecumseh, who was wearing a red morocco leather sword belt over his deerskins:

> As soon as Brock presented me to Tecumseh, the interpreter stood at once on one side, and with great promptness conveyed what I said to the Indian. For though he could speak some English, yet he was unwilling to be exposed, in the formalities of intercourse, from using bad English.… He was tall and commanding, and straight as an arrow.[54]

Tecumseh had returned Wallace's greetings by saying, "Well, you are a prisoner; but it is the fortune of war; and you are in very good hands." It is also fairly reliably reported that as a mark of respect Brock took off his red general's sash and presented it to Tecumseh, who received it with every sign of satisfaction. When a while later Tecumseh was seen without the sash and was asked where it was, he replied that he had given it to Chief Roundhead, for it would not be right for him to be seen wearing such a mark of honour in the presence of a much older and distinguished chief.[55] Later stories that Tecumseh responded with an embroidered or woven native belt seem to be invention.[56]

When Prevost received Brock's despatch, he at once published it in full and then, although privately he was probably furious with Brock for having exceeded his instructions, he sent it on to London under cover of some warm words of praise:

> I cannot withhold from Major-General Brock the tribute of applause so justly due to him for his distinguished conduct on this occasion; or omit to recommend him, through your lordship, to the favourable consideration of his royal highness the prince regent, for the great ability and judgement with which he planned, and the promptitude, energy, and fortitude with

which he has effected, the preservation of Upper Canada, with the sacrifice of so little British blood in accomplishing so important a service.[57]

In London there was jubilation. In due course, the Colours of the 4th U.S. Infantry Regiment were laid before the Prince Regent; subsequently they were deposited at the Royal Hospital in Chelsea, where they were recorded in watercolour for the archives. In the 1950s, during a major clear-out, these Colours were returned to the 41st Foot, by then the Welch Regiment, who put them into their museum in Cardiff Castle, where they can still be seen.

Brock received a large number of congratulatory letters, most of which did not arrive for several months. Among them was one that would have given him especial pleasure as it was from General Maitland, the Colonel of the 49th Foot:

> ... allow me, Sir, with the warmest feelings of an old friend to congratulate you, as do the public, on the essential service you have done the country.... I cannot help now observing how prophetic I was in what I wrote to General Vincent yesterday concerning you, which was, that if you were properly supported, I thought the enemy would never cross the line of your command, a proof of which I had a few hours afterwards.[58]

The Duke of York wrote to Prevost that:

> An occurrence which so gloriously terminates a Campaign, commenced under the declared Confidence of Success on the part of an arrogant Enemy, cannot fail of being most acceptable to the Prince Regent and gratifying to the Country in general.... His Royal Highness ... highly approves the judicious and prompt arrangements which you adopted throughout the Province generally, for repelling the Progress of the Invasion: and Major General Brock's exertions in The Country which was the more immediate object of the Enemy's attack....[59]

These happy messages of congratulation were tempered by sad news from the wider world and the war against Napoleon. Isaac's nephew Lieutenant Henry Brock of the Royal Navy had been killed in action; a cousin, Henry Frederick Brock, had died in Guernsey; another nephew, John Tupper, was lost at sea in the Mediterranean, of whom Brock wrote that "I could not have loved a son of my own more ardently."[60] Brock also recorded the

The Colours of the 4th U.S. Infantry Regiment captured at Detroit, presented to the Prince Regent and deposited at the Royal Hospital, Chelsea, where they were recorded in watercolour; reproduced for the first time by permission of the Governor of the Royal Hospital. The original Colours are fragile and are held by the successor regiment to the 41st in Cardiff Castle.

death of Thomas Leggatt of the 10th Royal Veterans, who "has left his family in the most distressing circumstances," and the loss of two valuable military friends.* "I begin to be too old to form new friendships," he wrote, "and those of my youth are dropping off fast."[61]

But there was also relief at home; Lord Bathurst wrote to Wellington, who had just won the victory of Salamanca, that not only secured Portugal against further invasion but laid the ground for the following year's decisive advance to Vitoria in Spain, that: "After the strong representations which I had received of the inadequacy of the force in those American settlements I know not how I should have withstood the attacks against me for having sent reinforcements to Spain instead of sending them to the defence of British possessions."[62] When the Prince Regent heard the news, and received the Colours of the U.S. 4th Infantry Regiment, he ordered John Glegg to be promoted to major and immediately bestowed on Brock a knighthood:

---

* Almost certainly Major-General Barnard Foord Bowes and Major-General John Gaspard Le Marchant, both killed at Salamanca.

I am commanded by his royal highness to desire you to take the earliest opportunity of conveying his ... approbation of the able, judicious, and decisive conduct of Major-General Brock, of the zeal and spirit manifested by Colonel Procter and the other officers, as well as the intrepidity of the troops....

... the enterprise of the American army has been defeated; the territories of his majesty in Upper Canada have been secured; and on the enemy's fort of Detroit, important to that security, the British standard has been happily placed.

You will inform Major-General Brock that his royal highness ... has been pleased to appoint him an extra knight of the most honourable order of the bath.[63]

CHAPTER FOURTEEN

"To Improve and Augment My Resources"

AUGUST–OCTOBER 1812

olonel Henry Procter was immediately installed as the new British
governor of the Michigan territory; Brock himself lost no time in issuing a proclamation to the inhabitants, announcing that they were
once again subjects of his Majesty King George III. Although the militia
were to be disarmed, the tone of the document, in sharp contrast to that issued by Hull at Sandwich on 13 July, was conciliatory, assuring them that for
the time being the extant laws and religious freedoms would stand:

> Whereas the Territory of Michigan was this day by Capitulation ceded to
> the Arms of His Britannic Majesty without any other condition than the
> protection of private property – And wishing to give an early proof of the
> moderation and justice of the Government, I do hereby announce to all
> the Inhabitants … that the Laws heretofore in existence shall continue in
> force until His Majesty's pleasure be known, or so long as the peace and
> security of the said territory will admit thereof. – And I do hereby also
> declare … that they shall be protected in the full exercise and enjoyment
> of their Religion, of which all persons both Civil and Military will take
> notice.[1]

What did not become apparent for a while was the unintended consequence of the victory: taking the Michigan territory strained the line of
communication from the Atlantic and increased the threat to British troops
at Detroit and Amherstburg, for Detroit was as far from Halifax as Moscow
was from Paris. The key to victory was the control of the waterways that
linked this long and thinly held line, threatened as it was at many points.

At the far end of this line Henry Procter was soon, like Brock, grappling
with the complexities of both civil and military government, engaging in

correspondence with Augustus Woodward, the chief justice of the territory, whom Procter appointed as civil secretary, on the geographical extent of the territory, its population, its administration, the payment of its officials and the collection of revenue. One group of people for whom there would be no toleration or moderate treatment was captured deserters from the British army. Writing to Brock on 26 August, Henry Procter gave a list of those captured thus far and found in arms against their country in the service of the Americans:

> My Wish was to have made an Example of them summarily, and would have done so, but that I recollected that deserters, similarly circumstanced were sent Home, from the Isle of France I think, were tried & suffered.[2]

With the threat of Hull's army removed from the Northwest, Brock himself was anxious to keep up the tempo of operations elsewhere in order not to allow the Americans any respite. Now was the time to clear the U.S. army and naval forces from their bases along the vulnerable Niagara frontier. He also intended an early move on the American naval base at Sackets Harbor: "Attack Sackett's Harbour from hence," he is reported to have said while in Kingston, "with our present superiority it must fall. The [U.S.] troops will be recalled for its protection. While they march we sail, and before they can return the whole Niagara frontier will be ours."[3] In campaign terms, this made good sense – Brock intended to maintain the initiative he had seized, keep up a superior tempo of operations by using his greater mobility, and thus force the enemy to react; whether it made strategic sense is another matter. Having despatched the American prisoners, a good deal of captured munitions, and the York Militia and as many of the 41st Foot as he could spare to reinforce Niagara, he himself embarked on the schooner *Chippawa* on 18 August and set off for Fort Erie. On the morning of 23 August the ship met the *Lady Prevost*, which hove to and fired a general officer's salute of seventeen guns before lowering its cutter and passing Brock a despatch containing interesting news.

The news was that Prevost had other ideas. His adjutant-general, Colonel Edward Baynes, had struck a deal for a cessation of hostilities with General Henry Dearborn, the senior American general on the northern frontier, just before the fall of Detroit, as has already been noted. In a subsequent letter, Prevost enlarged on his reasons for doing so, saying that "It was in consequence of an earnest desire not to widen the breach existing between the two countries, the revocation of the Orders-in-Council having removed the plea used in Congress for a declaration of war...."[4] When set against Prevost's declared intent to conduct a war of strict defence and non-aggression, his position is understandable. The arrangements for the truce stated that no offensive measures were to be undertaken, but that routine troop movements, resupply and defensive operations would continue. Whether or not Madison agreed to this, there were advantages, as Prevost explained to Lord Bathurst in a letter of 24 August 1812:

> A suspension of hostilities therefore on a considerable portion of the extremely extensive line of Frontier which I have to defend has enabled me rapidly to strengthen the Flank attacked. The decided superiority I have obtained on the lakes in consequence of the precautionary measures adopted during the last winter has permitted me to move without interruption, independently of the arrangement, both Troops and supplies of every description towards Amherstburg.... His Majesty's Subjects in both Provinces are beginning to feel an increased confidence in the government protecting them.... In the mean time from a partial suspension of hostilities I am enabled to improve & augment my resources against an Invasion....[5]

Brock's forward-leaning posture was not at all what Prevost wished to see just now, and he must have appeared, at times, to be rash. Brock himself seems to have been aware of his tendency to impulsive behaviour. Writing to his brothers after Detroit, he said that the plan he devised for attacking the fort "proceeded from a cool calculation of *pours* and *contres*," but he also said that "the state of the province admitted of nothing but desperate remedies."[6] Another account has him opening up to John Beverley Robinson, serving as a Volunteer with the 41st, during the voyage in the *Chippawa*: "If this war lasts, I am afraid that I shall do some foolish thing, for if I know myself there is no want of courage in my nature – I hope I shall not get into a scrape."[7] For Brock, buoyed up as he was with the elation of his victory, he was in all probability aghast at the loss of opportunity. His official correspondence, however, was moderate in tone. On 29 August he wrote to Lord Bathurst himself, warning of the potential consequences:

However wise and politic the measure must be admitted to be, the Indians, who cannot enter into our views, will naturally feel disheartened and suspicious of our intentions. Should hostilities recommence I much fear the influence the British possess over them will be found diminished.[8]

Brock's private correspondence to his brothers was rather more forthright: "Should peace follow, the measure will be well; if hostilities recommence, nothing could be more unfortunate than this pause."[9]

During the latter part of the passage to Erie, it is recorded that Brock's small ship was becalmed in a fog during the night, and as day broke, it was found that the ship had drifted close to the American shore near the village of Buffalo. Given that the *Chippawa* was also carrying American prisoners and a very small guard, it was vulnerable to capture. When told of the state of affairs, Brock grew angry, again perhaps displaying the impulsive side of his character, telling the master, "You scoundrel, you have betrayed me! Let but one shot be fired from the [American] shore, and I will run you up on the instant to that yard-arm!"[10] The ship's boat was immediately lowered to tow the ship clear, while shots were fired and a signal hoisted to attract help from the nearby, and more powerful, *Queen Charlotte*. With a light breeze now springing up, the *Queen Charlotte* took the *Chippawa* in tow, bringing the ship and Brock safely under the guns of Fort Erie.

When he reached Fort George two days later after a further boat journey and portage round Niagara Falls, Brock found to his irritation that Roger Sheaffe had taken the truce a step further, making his own additional agreement with the American commander on the Niagara frontier, Major-General Stephen Van Rensselaer.* General Van Rensselaer had suggested that no reinforcements of troops or munitions should be sent higher up-river than Fort Erie and that no troops should be moved to any location further west unless four days' notice had been provided.[11] Sheaffe had agreed to this since he knew that Brock had captured Detroit while Van Rensselaer did not, and there was little need, therefore, for the British to shift forces westwards. It also meant that ordnance and munitions

---

* Major-General of Militia Stephen Van Rensselaer (1764–1839) was a federalist and lieutenant-governor of New York. He appointed his more militarily able second cousin Solomon, who later published an account of the general's command cited in this work, as his aide-de-camp in the hope of overcoming his own shortcomings as a military commander.

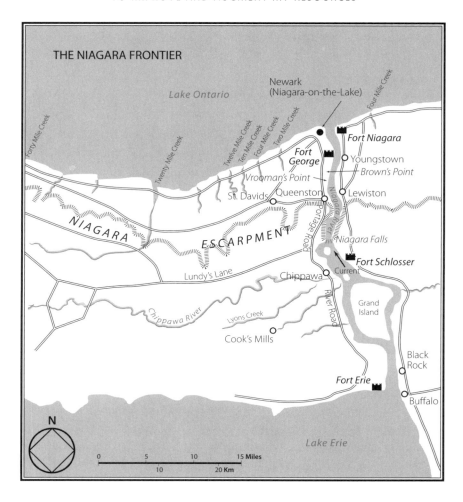

being collected by the Americans at Oswego would not reach them on the Niagara frontier while the truce lasted,[12] or would not have done had Van Rensselaer not outwitted Sheaffe and had water transport excepted from these provisions. Prevost was furious that his instructions had been ignored, although it would be highly embarrassing to disavow Sheaffe's deal. As he wrote to Brock on 30 August: "… it had been expressly stated to General Dearborn and clearly understood by him, that our mutual supplies and reinforcements should move unmolested, with the contemplation of succouring Amherstburg."[13]

Brock was not alone in feeling that Prevost's ceasefire was a mistake, for the fall of Mackinac and then Detroit, and the sight of American prisoners

Niagara Falls from the Canadian side. This view of the falls gives a striking impression of the power of the water. On the left are the American falls and on the right the Canadian, the two divided by Goat Island. Here begins the deep gorge that continues northward to Queenston. (Drawn by Captain James Graham in 1840 and engraved by F. C. Lewis. Library of Congress)

being marched through the streets of York, had done wonders for the fighting spirit of the inhabitants of Upper Canada. According to one witness:

> The surrender of the fort at Detroit and all the Michigan Territory, were events which the people of Canada could scarcely believe, even after they were known to be true…. After this event, the people of Canada became fearful of disobeying the government – some that had fled to the wilderness returned home – and the friends of the United States were discouraged, and those of the King encouraged….
>
> The army now became respectable, and a dread fell on those who had opposed the government. The people now saw that it was as much as their property and lives were worth to disobey orders, and now what they had been compelled to do, after a while they did from choice.[14]

These were the words of an avowed American sympathizer and allowance has to be made for the tone and the assumption of tyranny, but even so the picture is clear. Nevertheless Prevost had a point, for Brock faced even heavier odds on the Niagara than he had done at Detroit, with no certainty that the quality of generalship on the opposite side matched that of Hull. Brock's total force on the Niagara frontier amounted to about 1,200 men, of whom half were militia, against more than 6,000 U.S. troops. Ideally, Brock might have wished to attack and seize Fort Niagara but with these force ratios, this would be impossible. Niagara was much more heavily fortified and gunned than Detroit and could be attacked from one direction only – a far harder nut to crack. Even if he had seized the fort, its possession would not have stopped an American assault across the Niagara River above the falls, between Chippawa and Fort Erie, or indeed in the Lewiston–Queenston area where the gorge petered out.

Brock went straight on to York, where he was greeted with a loyal address from the people, expressing their admiration and delight at the fall of Detroit. In his reply Brock tactfully glossed over earlier difficulties and defeatist attitudes to make the people think well of themselves, as well as to remind them of their responsibilities in sharing the burden of their own defence:

> I cannot but feel highly gratified by this expression of your esteem for myself; but in justice to the brave men at whose head I marched against the enemy, I must beg leave to direct your attention to them as the proper objects for your gratitude…. Allow me to congratulate you, gentlemen, at having sent out from yourselves a large portion of that gallant band, and that at such a period a spirit had manifested itself on which you may confidently repose your hopes of future security.[15]

Everywhere, the evidence of the U.S. forces' build-up on land and water was apparent. Edward Baynes described at some length the preparations he had seen on his journey into the United States to meet Dearborn and negotiate the armistice and his impression that the best of the available American troops were on the Niagara frontier.[16] Brock himself told Prevost that "The enemy was very busy upon Fort Niagara, and indeed appeared inclined to erect additional batteries,"[17] and later that:

> The enemy has evidently assumed defensive measures along the strait of Niagara. His force, I apprehend, is not equal to the attempt, with any probability of success, of an expedition across the river. It is, however, currently reported that large reinforcements are on the march; should they arrive, an attack cannot be long delayed.[18]

Brock's instincts about Sackets Harbor were borne out when the American naval commander, Commodore Isaac Chauncey,* used the ceasefire and the

---

* Isaac Chauncey (1779–1840) saw extensive service in the West Indies and the Mediterranean. He ended his career as president of the Navy Board.

exemption of water transport to good effect, rescuing the schooner *Julia* from Ogdensburg and arming six smaller craft that would certainly pose a threat to the British line of communication along the St Lawrence. Brock could do little more than order work to strengthen defences and train the militia; he therefore returned to Fort George, which itself was undergoing considerable works, as Captain and Adjutant Joseph Smith of the 41st Foot wrote to his colonel, Henry Procter:

> We have made very strong Sod ... along the two Curtains on the Right and Left of the East Gate which saved us from the Enemies Fire ... and I wish that it was completed round the Fort. Under the Right Curtain as you enter from Navy Hall [i.e., on the river bank] is Built a very fine Store for the Ordnance Department & that which was occupied before by them is *at last* fitting up for Barracks which will contain *100 men*....The North Bastion is made a Cavalier Battery & is raised very high & mounts one 24 Pounder (from Detroit) on a Traversing Carriage and will fire almost in every direction....[19]

From Fort George, Brock directed a constant stream of General Orders, shifting his limited numbers of troops between the threatened areas and building up the garrisons of Forts George and Erie and at Chippawa, as well as the encampments at Brown's Point, Queenston and Navy Island,[20] even sending a reinforcement of the 10th Royal Veterans to Mackinac.

As things turned out, President James Madison angrily rejected Henry Dearborn's proposal, despite the obvious and growing anti-war feeling in many of the northeastern states. Despite the shame at the loss of Detroit, resolutions condemning the war were passed, for example, in Connecticut on 25 August and New York on 18 September 1812.[21] The repeal of the Orders-in-Council had addressed only one of Madison's grievances and they might in any case be reinstated at some future date. The impressment of seamen from American ships was not mentioned, and even if it had been, the loss of face caused by the fall of Mackinac and Detroit was unbearable. Even though it was unlikely that General Henry Dearborn had enough forces to carry out the agreed plan of simultaneous attacks on Kingston, Montreal and the Niagara, he was instructed to make a demonstration against Montreal to fix Prevost's attention and prevent the redeployment of troops, while making a determined effort against Kingston and the Niagara. The

Secretary of War therefore notified him that: "After the receipt of this letter and allowing a reasonable time in which you will inform Sir George Prevost thereof, you will proceed with the utmost vigour in your operations."[22]

General Dearborn duly notified Prevost and hostilities recommenced on 4 September 1812. Brock had left Fort George at the tail end of August and gone to Kingston to inspect the defences and the militia units there and to review the four companies of his old regiment, the 49th, under Vincent. It was here that he received Sir George Prevost's despatch telling him that war had been renewed. He therefore returned to Fort George on 6 September. However, General Dearborn did not mount an immediate attack. After garrisoning his posts and securing his line of communications, he had few troops to spare and most of these were militia, who had little incentive to fight and wanted nothing more than to return to their farms, for the harvest was in progress, or to their well-paid jobs. Nor did it seem possible that the British possessed the means to be a threat. For many Americans, it seemed best to let sleeping dogs lie – at least until spring.

Brock had warned of the consequences of a ceasefire to relations with the aboriginal people, but despite his personal feelings he had to follow orders. He had been obliged to rein back Henry Procter, underlining his misgivings about the effects of a ceasefire on native opinion, telling him to:

> … postpone any attempt upon Fort Wayne, or any other post of the enemy. I consider the present forbearance may lead to such consequences that I cannot refrain from sending a second express, to urge you to restrain the Indians likewise in their predatory excursions: this, however, ought to be done with the utmost caution, and on grounds foreign from the present considerations.[23]

There is no record of the talks between Brock and Tecumseh after Detroit, but their content can be inferred from later correspondence. Brock seems to have made a promise that Britain would not desert her native allies; he believed that the aboriginal people were vital to the war effort and moreover he was firmly of the view that trusting to aboriginal fears of the Americans was not enough to engage them firmly in the defence of the Canadas – a concept that meant nothing to the aboriginal mind. As he wrote to Prevost, the native people would have to be tied in to the future of the country; their war aims would have to be part of any settlement with the United States: "Should negotiations for peace be opened, I cannot be too earnest with Your Excellency to represent to the King's Ministers the expediency of including the Indians as allies, and not leave them exposed to the unrelenting fury of their enemies."[24] Any treaty to end the war must include the restoration of "an extensive tract of country, fraudulently usurped from them."[25] The fur traders were also supporters of native claims since if the aboriginal people were driven out by the Americans, their trade would be dead. Sir George Prevost and the British government concurred, but there was no general agreement on what size and shape any package of measures for the benefit of the aboriginal people might take – although the fur traders were probably closest to native aspirations.

Some native people, including Tecumseh, probably wanted far more than could be delivered: the re-conquest of the whole of the Old Northwest. The British, although they might undertake tactical offensives, were committed through lack of resources to an operational and strategic defensive. Without the aid of regular British troops, especially artillery, native warriors could never hope to drive the United States' military from its strongholds, especially as the numbers were against them in the long run. Tecumseh's immediate ambition was the conquest of Fort Wayne on the Maumee River, which had been besieged by warriors sympathetic to the British and for which he needed the support of British troops from Amherstburg or Detroit – but without orders, Henry Procter, who was in command of the western district, was not prepared to commit any forces across the border.

It was not until 12 September, after the expiry of the truce, that Henry Procter moved. The expedition against Fort Wayne consisted of 600 warriors led by Tecumseh himself, Chief Roundhead and Matthew Elliott; another 200 Algonkian warriors from the Mackinac area followed on 15 September. Backing them up were 150 men of the 41st Foot under Captain Adam Muir, 100 militia and two guns, embarked at Amherstburg in schooners of the Provincial Marine for the voyage up the Maumee. However on reaching a point about forty miles from the fort, the hopes of the native people were dashed when news reached them that the siege had been broken by the arrival of Brigadier-General William Harrison with 2,000 U.S. troops, and that this powerful force was heading towards them. Muir decided on discretion and ordered a withdrawal.[26] Brock subsequently

wrote to Sir George Prevost justifying the expedition, which he had authorized and which was, quite clearly, contrary to Prevost's instructions to
maintain a defensive:

> I gave orders for it previous to my leaving Amherstburg, which must have
> induced Colonel Procter to proceed, upon receiving intelligence of the
> recommencement of hostilities, without waiting for further directions. I
> regret exceedingly that this service should be undertaken contrary to your
> excellency's wishes; but I beg leave to assure you, that the principal object
> in sending a British force to Fort Wayne is with the hope of preserving
> the lives of the garrison ... the place was invested by a numerous body of
> Indians, with very little prospect of being relieved.[27]

This was, again, sailing close to the wind in terms of loyalty to his superior.
Brock had certainly approved the expedition but he had issued contradic-
tory instructions, telling Henry Procter that he was not "to resort to offensive warfare for purposes of conquest. Your operations are to be confined to
measures of defence and security."[28]

Major-General Stephen Van Rensselaer, the senior American officer on
the Niagara frontier, was in an uncomfortable situation. When he
arrived at his headquarters in the village of Lewiston to take command,
he found no more than 1,000 U.S. troops, with little in the way of artillery,
camp stores, medicines – or even clothes and shoes. The majority of the
men were from the militia of Ohio and New York and few of them wanted
to be there. Most were farmers, who wanted to get back to their farms before
winter, especially as their pay was well in arrears. Discipline was unsurprisingly poor and things were made worse by the sight of prisoners from
Detroit being marched along the portage road on the Canadian side of the
Niagara River. The general view was that General Van Rensselaer would end
the same way, by having his army "Hulled."[29] The American view of the British, even allowing for exaggeration to justify their defeat, is interesting. The
general's chief of staff and cousin, Colonel Solomon Van Rensselaer, wrote
in his account of the campaign that:

> The condition of the forces on the opposite bank of the river, was in con-
> trast with ours in every particular. There was a well appointed, and well
> found army, under the most exact discipline, and commanded by skilful

Major-General of Militia Stephen Van Rensselaer (1764–1839). He owed his position more to politics and his prominence as a member of one of New York State's wealthiest families than to his military expertise. (Rensselaer Polytechnic Institute)

and experienced officers. Every important post, from Fort Erie to Fort George, was in a defensible state, and the enemy had possessed himself of a very commanding position on the heights of Queenstown, which he was rendering every day more secure and formidable. He had, moreover, the mastery of the Lakes, and was at that moment industriously employed in using that advantage to increase his numbers, and add to his supplies at Niagara.[30]

In fact, the Americans' situation had already substantially improved from the state of affairs even three months before. All along the Niagara frontier at the outbreak of war, U.S. citizens were alarmed by British military activity on the Canadian side of the river. A deputation wrote to New York congress-man and quartermaster-general Peter B. Porter* on 15 April 15 1812 making plain their concern about the lack of arms and ammunition, adding "there is not five muskets that is fit to use in this place & they are not to be had in this quarter." New York Governor Daniel D. Tompkins was also made aware that the New York militia was destitute of arms, camp equipment, blankets and other items, particularly at the settlements of Black Rock (now a part of Buffalo) and Lewiston.

---

* Later Major-General Peter Buell Porter (1773–1844); he was Secretary of War 1828–29.

Colonel Solomon Van Rensselaer, the general's chief of staff, possessed more practical military experience than his cousin Stephen. (Lossing, *Pictorial Field-Book of the War of 1812*)

On 25 June 1812, a week after his promotion and the declaration of war, Governor Tompkins ordered Brigadier-General William Wadsworth,* with his newly formed militia brigade, consisting of the 18th, 19th and 20th Regiments of Detached Militia, to reinforce the 400 regular troops at Black Rock and to take command on the Niagara frontier. The governor's instruction made it clear Wadsworth was "at liberty to act offensively as well as defensively" according to the circumstances he found along the river. William Wadsworth, however, known to history as "the reluctant general," confessed to the governor that he lacked any real military experience and was "ignorant of even the minor duties of the duty to which you have assigned me." He asked to have an experienced military secretary assigned to him;[31] the governor agreed, but on 28 July Tompkins, obviously having second thoughts, assigned the more experienced Major-General Amos Hall to command the Niagara frontier militia, until Major-General Stephen Van Rensselaer could assume the command.

William Wadsworth marched his 900 men from their assembly point at Canandaigua, reaching Batavia on 1 July and picking up regular U.S. troops along the way. These consisted of detachments of the 13th Infantry Regiment under Lieutenant-Colonel John Chrystie, the 23rd Infantry Regiment under

---

* William Wadsworth (1765–1833).

Colonel John Chrystie joined the U.S. 6th Infantry in 1808 as a lieutenant, resigning his commission in 1811, but returned to the colours as war with Britain loomed. He died in 1813. (Chartrand, *Uniforms and Equipment of the United States Forces in the War of 1812*, by permission)

Lieutenant-Colonel William Clarke and elements of the 3rd Artillery Regiment under Captain James McKeon. Brigadier-General Wadsworth reached Black Rock on 3 July with about 1,600 men. He immediately dispatched some of the militia to reinforce Fort Schlosser and Lewiston and sent a detachment of regulars on to Fort Niagara. About a week later four more companies of volunteer militia attached to the 20th Regiment arrived, along with twenty mounted couriers. This brought General Wadsworth's strength to nearly 1,900. Wadsworth, to his credit, immediately surveyed the defences between Buffalo and Fort Niagara and found the latter both decayed and undergunned. He asked for heavy ordnance for the fort and for field artillery. He also demanded that Governor Tompkins should dispatch 2,000 more troops and that he should immediately send food, tents, shoes and equipment for the men currently there. In the meantime, General Wadsworth ordered the construction of batteries and defensive works in areas where the British might attempt assault landings, but this work went painfully slowly for want of proper tools.[32] It was this activity, seen by the British over the late summer, which Brock reported at various times to Sir George Prevost as evidence that the U.S. effort on the Niagara at this point was, in the main, defensive.

To answer General Wadsworth's request for an experienced aide, Governor Tompkins dispatched his personal assistant, the engineer and artillery expert Major Nicholas Gray. On arrival on 18 July, Gray reported back to Tompkins that he was impressed with General Wadsworth, whose "camps were in good health and orderly" and that he "had ordered a military school, both for officers and soldiers … and pays unwearied attention to the troops, and is forming a system which has as its objective the organization of the staff and camp duties."[33] Gray supervised the construction of a number of batteries, including one above Lewiston that became known as Fort Gray, which was sited to try to suppress the fire of the British batteries on Queenston Heights and on Queenston wharf. On 24 July Major-General Amos Hall arrived at Buffalo and took command, but this was only a temporary measure as both Generals Wadsworth and Hall knew they were shortly to be replaced. On 13 August 1812 Major-General Stephen Van Rensselaer arrived at Lewiston.

Van Rensselaer approved and continued Wadsworth's institution of proper camp routine and training for the troops, but improvements were slow. In the middle of September, Brock interviewed two U.S. deserters, who complained of "bad usage, bad and scanty food, and a total want of pay" and reported that half the men of their company had already deserted and the rest planned to follow.[34] A few days later he wrote to Prevost that "Sickness prevails all along the line, but principally at Black Rock."[35] The same day he wrote to Savery that:

> The U.S. regiments of the line desert over to us frequently, as the men are tired of the service: opportunities seldom offer, otherwise I have reason to think the greater part would follow the example. The militia, being chiefly composed of enraged democrats, are more ardent and anxious to engage, but they have neither subordination nor discipline. They die very fast.[36]

Nor was General Stephen Van Rensselaer on good terms with his subordinates. His supplies depended on Major-General Peter B. Porter, whom Colonel Solomon Van Rensselaer blamed for the poor logistic situation, almost provoking a duel between the two.[37] Stephen Van Rensselaer's was a militia commission and U.S. regulars were not inclined to defer to civilians in uniform, least of all Van Rensselaer's most significant subordinate, Brigadier-General Alexander Smyth.[*] The latter arrived at Buffalo on 29

---

[*] Brigadier-General Alexander Smyth (1765–1830) had joined the regular army in 1808 to command a rifle regiment then being added to the establishment of the U.S. Army. He had never seen active service. He had however compiled the *Regulations for the Field Exercise, Manoeuvres and Conduct of the Infantry* in 1811.

"Soldiers on the march to Buffalo." A rather cynical contemporary cartoon of American troops and their camp followers based on Thomas Rowlandson's "Women and Children on the March. Old Buffs 1808." (William L. Clements Library, University of Michigan)

September with a brigade of four regular regiments – the 5th, 12th, 13th and 14th Infantry Regiments – but never even reported to General Van Rensselaer, claiming that he was too busy, and did not attend any of Van Rensselaer's councils of war.[38] Subsequently, Smyth also quarrelled with Peter B. Porter over the conduct of operations and the two did fight a duel; it was a bloodless affair, as both men missed. To cap it all, General Van Rensselaer was being harried by both Henry Dearborn and Governor Tompkins, a political rival. Both men certainly felt the disgrace of Hull's surrender keenly and were eager for revenge.

By late September the situation appeared to be improving. American morale was raised by news of the defeat of HMS *Guerriere*, in action for the second time against a U.S. ship, by the far more powerful USS *Constitution*, commanded by General William Hull's nephew Isaac, giving a new slant on the business of being "Hulled." Troop numbers were also rising: Smyth's

1,200 regulars, green and untried as they were, were eager to fight. General Van Rensselaer's force at Lewiston numbered 900 regulars and 2,270 militia, again raw, with another 1,300 militia close by in Manchester. General Van Rensselaer wrote that even his "best troops are raw; many of them dejected by the distress their families suffer by their absence, and many have not the necessary clothing."[39] When the 1,200 regulars of the 6th, 13th and 23rd Infantry Regiments forming the garrison of Fort Niagara and the 300 gunners at the batteries and other outposts were included, the total force numbered around 6,400,[40] which was the figure generally agreed as being needed successfully to invade Upper Canada and defeat the British there. Henry Dearborn was insistent that the extant strategic and operational plans must be pushed forward, despite all the problems of a raw and improperly coordinated force: "At all events, we must calculate on possessing Upper Canada before winter sets in."[41]

Brock's main concentrations of regular troops, reflected in the organization of his four "divisions,"[42] were at Fort Erie, where there were two companies of the 49th Foot, one company of the Royal Newfoundland Regiment and one company of the Lincoln Militia under Captain Adam Ormsby; Chippawa, where there were three companies of the 41st and one company of the Lincoln Militia under Captain Richard Bullock; Brown's Point, where there were two companies of the York Militia; and Fort George, where there were three companies of the 41st Foot, three companies of militia from Lincoln and York, a troop of the Niagara Dragoons, 300 Grand River warriors and a small company of "men of colour" who had volunteered for active service. These troops were under the direct command of Major Thomas Evans, but above him, commanding the sector, was Colonel William Claus and above him, Major-General Roger Hale Sheaffe. Including the garrison at Queenston, of which more will be said, the total available force was about 1,700 regulars and militia and up to 300 Grand River warriors.[43] Despite their small numbers, Brock was reasonably confident of their capabilities. He was particularly pleased to have his old regiment back under command, writing to Savery that:

> I now have officers in whom I can confide: when the war commenced, I was really obliged to seek assistance among the militia. The 41st is an

uncommonly fine regiment, but wretchedly officered [i.e., there were insufficient officers].[44] Six companies of the 49th are with me here, and the
remaining four at Kingston, under Vincent. Although the regiment has
been ten years in this country, drinking rum without bounds, it is still
respectable, and apparently ardent for an opportunity to acquire distinction: it has five captains in England, and two on the staff in this country,
which leaves it bare of experienced officers.

He added rather forlornly that "I am anxious for this state of warfare to end,
as I wish much to join Lord Wellington, and to see you all."[45]

Discipline seemed to be holding up well, perhaps under the spur of danger. Captain and Adjutant Joseph Smith of the 41st Foot, writing to Procter,
remarked that "The behaviour of our men here does Credit to the Regt –
We have not had a Corporal Punishment since you left this nor none to my
opinion had deserved it."[46] Smith also commented on the field dress of the
army: "With respect to the Dress of Officers every one dresses as he thinks
proper (Most of them ... found in Round Hatts) from the general to the
Subn* Most of them wear Sabers which in my opinion, like the Round Hatts
answers best at present...."

Brock could read the signs of activity on the American shore well
enough; he was particularly concerned about Fort George, which although
it was his headquarters, was more of a protected depot than a serious fortification on the lines of Fort Niagara. On 18 September 1812 he warned Sir
George Prevost that "It is currently reported that the enemy's force is to be
increased to 7,000, and that on their arrival an attack is immediately to be
made ... nor do I think the attempt can be long deferred."[47] He accordingly
issued detailed guidance to his subordinates along the Niagara, explaining
where he thought the enemy would cross – and this would be where a major
engagement could be avoided. The enemy's likely course of action would be
to "turn our flanks" and this would be "extremely dangerous." He warned
his subordinates that:

> ... it appears likely to me – that his principal attack will be made between
> Fort Erie and Palmers [a tavern opposite Grand Island].... If we weigh
> well the character of our enemy, we shall find him more disposed to brave
> the impediments of nature, when they afford him a probability of accom-

---

* i.e., subalterns; that is, ensigns and lieutenants.

plishing his end by surprise, in preference to the certainty of encountering British troops ready formed for his reception.[48]

On 14 September 1812 Sir George Prevost wrote to Brock, having received from him a letter warning of the probable approach of Brigadier-General William Harrison from the Maumee and a second attack on Amherstburg, ordering Brock to evacuate Detroit and the Michigan territory, adding that he could spare no reinforcements for the upper province above what he had already sent, "unless the operations of the enemy on the Niagara frontier bear a character less indicative of determined hostile measures against your line in their front than they did when you last reported to me."[49] This was probably on account of having received from Colonel Henry Procter some fearful reports drawn from intelligence received in the Michigan territory, that "General Wells with Three Thousand Kentucky Men are on the Route to this place...."[50] Brock replied on 28 September that since he had been allowed some latitude, he would not yet abandon Detroit. To do so would enrage the native people and encourage them to destroy the white population on the American side of the river entirely.

The failure to deal with Sackets Harbor had further consequences with the arrival of a new and energetic American commander, Brigadier-General Jacob Brown[*] of the New York Militia, who had been appointed by Governor Tompkins in June 1812. Tompkins assembled 2,000 New York Militia in and around Sackets Harbor to protect the post. Brown gave orders to the U.S. artillery batteries along the St Lawrence to fire on British shipping and to the garrisons to seize whatever they could through cutting-out operations and raiding across the river. Prevost believed that this increase in activity followed directly from the weakening of the regular garrison of Kingston to strengthen Niagara. Writing to Brock, he observed bitingly that "In consequence of your having weakened the line of communication between Cornwall and Kingston, a predatory warfare is carrying on there very prejudicial to the intercourse from hence to Upper Canada."[51] He despatched two companies of the Glengarry Light Infantry, extra weapons for the militia and two gunboats to increase the small garrison at Prescott under Colonel Robert Lethbridge. Lethbridge had already made a number

* Later Major-General Jacob Brown (1775–1828), who transferred to the regular army in 1813 and was probably the most able and consistently successful U.S. general of the war.

of improvements to the defensive system on the border, fortifying many posts and placing troops at vulnerable points, forming a flying column of artillery and instigating a convoy system for bateaux, protected by soldiers of the Royal Newfoundland Regiment. These measures strengthened the infrastructure, communications and militia organization on the Canadian shore, which was already superior to that on the American side. Although there were relatively few regular troops, superior mobility and protection meant that the British could respond swiftly to American raids, so that although Brown did conduct several attacks across the river, he was never able to disrupt seriously the movement of the 1,300 bateaux running between Kingston and Montreal by July 1812.

However, Prevost did not add his usual rider to refrain from initiating offensive operations in his instructions to Lethbridge. Lethbridge, having been reinforced, suffered a rush of blood to the brain, ordered the available militia to concentrate at Prescott and began very obvious preparations for an attack on the American village of Ogdensburg. Brown observed the whole affair and laid his plans accordingly. When on the morning of Sunday 3 October 1812 the two companies of Glengarries and 600 militiamen set out across the river in boats, they were met with well prepared artillery fire and turned back. Lethbridge was recalled to Montreal and replaced by the younger but far more experienced Colonel Thomas Pearson.[52]

The 6th of October 1812 was Brock's forty-third birthday. A year before, the news of John's bankruptcy had arrived. This year, the prospect seemed to be of battle. It did not however stop all the available officers and prominent civilians in Fort George and Newark from celebrating the general's birthday with a good dinner. Shortly afterwards, at about 3.00 a.m. on the morning of 9 October, a U.S. cutting-out party of fifty seamen under Lieutenant Jesse D. Elliott, and about the same number of soldiers under Lieutenant Nathan Towson, slipped out of Black Rock and boarded the captured *Detroit* and the *Caledonia*, both moored under the guns of Fort Erie. The ships were carrying a detachment of at least fifty British regulars and Canadian militia, American prisoners from Detroit and a quantity of ordnance, arms and ammunition. The *Caledonia* also carried a large number of furs worth around $200,000. The raiders boldly unmoored and sailed the two ships out into the river. *Caledonia* made it safely to the temporary U.S. base at Black Rock but *Detroit*, owing to light wind, was swept away by the strong current and forced to anchor within range of the British guns, and an artillery duel ensued. Lieutenant Elliott brought all his guns to his engaged side and continued the cannonade until his ammunition was exhausted. He then cut the mooring cable and the brig drifted down the river until she grounded on Squaw Island within range of both British and U.S. batteries. Elliott and his men then abandoned her, and almost immediately forty soldiers from the detachment of the 49th Foot under Major Adam Ormsby took brief possession of the brig. U.S. guns soon drove them out with great loss and both sides began pounding the *Detroit* with artillery fire until the Americans finally set fire to and destroyed the battered hulk. The *Caledonia* was taken into American service against her former owners. Brock, furious, rode to Fort Erie, arriving soon after sunset that day just as the *Detroit* burst into flames, but he was too late to save either ship. Lieutenant-Colonel Christopher Myers of the 70th, one of the deputy assistant quartermasters-general, was despatched to take charge of the fort. Writing of the affair to Sir George Prevost, Brock described the action in detail and then summed up the consequences:

> The event is particularly unfortunate and may reduce us to incalculable distress. The enemy is making every exertion to gain a naval superiority on both lakes, which if they accomplish I do not see how we can retain the country. More vessels are fitting out for war on the other side of Squaw Island, which I should have attempted to destroy but for your excellency's repeated instructions to forbear. Now such a force is collected for their protection as will render every operation against them very hazardous.[53]

Despite all the signs of impending attack, Prevost was still urging restraint.[54] Brock replied that "I shall refrain as long as possible, under your excellency's positive injunctions, from every hostile act, although sensible that each day's delay gives a positive advantage."[55] Privately to Savery, Brock did admit that Sir George had a point, saying that "I could at this moment sweep everything before me from Fort Niagara to Buffalo – but my success would be transient."[56] To Henry Procter at Amherstburg he was forthright, verging on disloyalty:

> The fate of the Province is in your hands.... Were it not for the positive injunctions of the commander of the forces I should have acted with greater decision. This forbearance may be productive of ultimate good, but I doubt its policy – but perhaps we have not the means of judging

correctly. You will of course adopt a very different line of conduct. The enemy must be kept in a state of constant ferment.[57]

In the same letter, Brock further urged Procter to strengthen his defences ready for an American move to re-take Detroit, including measures to clear the fields of fire for the guns around the fort. This meant destroying all the government buildings close to the fort, but not private dwellings.

Sir George Prevost might incline to inaction, but not Brock. By remaining purely on the defensive, even though want of activity might make strategic good sense, Prevost had surrendered the operational and tactical initiative that Brock had seized when William Hull withdrew across the Detroit River and had maintained by the capture of Detroit. The Americans' ability to sustain protracted operations was shaky, but on the Niagara and St Lawrence they now held control over the other four factors: the will, the means, the ability to mount offensive operations and the opportunity. Offensive action is a principle of war, and although Prevost would not have thought in such modern terms, he might have reflected upon Napoleon's comment that the logical outcome of defensive warfare is surrender.

CHAPTER FIFTEEN

"Proof of their Loyalty and Courage"

THE ATTACK ON QUEENSTON, 13 OCTOBER 1812

Major-General Stephen Van Rensselaer's daily councils of war had led him to believe that the place to cross the Niagara River was at Queenston, the original site of the falls, where the great gorge of the Niagara runs out in a tumble of rocks. It was opposite Lewiston, had a good landing site with well developed wharves and was covered by the American battery on the high ground above the village. On both sides of the Niagara, a good portage road ran along the river that would allow the movement of troops, guns, vehicles and boats down to the river, across it and up the other side. On the other hand, the current was strong and the large British garrison of Fort George was within easy reach. The British, too, had the area well covered by gun batteries. Brigadier-General Alexander Smyth, however inexperienced, correctly identified a far better crossing site above the falls, where the banks were low, the current less strong and the British less numerous. He told General Van Rensselaer that he felt it "proper to encamp the U.S. troops near Buffalo, there to prepare for offensive operations."[1] General Van Rensselaer's plan, however, was based on deception; it was almost certainly the work of his cousin Colonel Solomon Van Rensselaer and could well have worked if Smyth had played his part. Indeed a very similar operation resulted in success in May 1813 – but General Van Rensselaer never stamped on Smyth, who continued to go his own way.

During the preceding weeks, the Americans had cut a road through the woods, out of sight of the watching British, from Lewiston to Four-Mile Creek, which lies to the east of Fort Niagara on the southern shore of Lake Ontario, and thus out of sight of Fort George and Newark – around the corner, as it were, since Fort Mississauga had not yet been built to the northwest of Newark on a point of land that overlooked U.S. territory on the southern side of the lake. Here sixty bateaux had been assembled. General Van Rensselaer's plan called for Alexander Smyth to march his force down this road to the boats and wait there for orders. General Van Rensselaer's force would then attack Queenston, which would draw the British force from Fort George to halt the invasion. Once this move was observed, a courier would be sent to Smyth, who would attack and seize the undefended Fort George. The whole British line along the Niagara frontier could then we rolled up.[2]

It has often been suggested that the invasion of the Niagara was planned and executed not as a determined attempt to seize the whole of Upper Canada, but as a move to obtain better quarters and rations for the American troops before the bitter winter arrived; they would then exploit their bridgehead in the spring. If so, it was poorly thought out at the operational and tactical levels, as Robert Malcomson has pointed out in his excellent account of Queenston Heights, which is unlikely ever to be bettered.[3] Brock had crossed the Detroit River in August with a small force, but he did so confident that his bridgehead could be secured and that he had enough forces to achieve a breakout and attain his objective; he was morally certain that his enemy would not fight – at least not with his heart and soul in the matter. On the Niagara the situation was entirely different. The British regulars were not raw, dejected men missing their families, but long-service professionals. The Canadian regulars and the militia were not as experienced but the victories in the Northwest had put heart into them. Nor did they have to be supermen – they simply had to be better than their opponents. Even if the Americans had successfully established a bridgehead, they lacked the forces to break out and secure enough territory to accommodate their force; and they lacked the capability to defeat the British army in the field in open combat. Had they confined themselves to a smaller bridgehead they would be attacked without respite, for they were opposed not by a William Hull, but by Isaac Brock. With the benefit of hindsight, therefore, we can say that this was an operation that was doomed to failure long before it started.

On 4 October 1812 an American spy reported wrongly that Brock had gone to Detroit, taking with him as many of the troops as could be spared. Thus encouraged – and more so after the affair of the *Detroit* and the *Caledonia* – General Stephen Van Rensselaer set the date for the attack as 11

Queenston between 1803 and 1807. The buildings of the village, including the Hamilton house with its several chimneys in the middle foreground, are clearly shown, as is the state of the road leading to Fort George. The wharf can be glimpsed but the road up the heights, which at this early date were largely clear of vegetation, can be made out plainly. Most of the remaining vegetation was cleared at the outbreak of war in 1812. (Watercolour by Edward Walsh. Library of Congress)

October and the objective as Queenston. This village was the downstream terminus of the portage road on the Canadian side of the Niagara that carried traffic round the falls. It had been founded in the 1770s around the landing and the large stone house of Robert Hamilton, one of the merchants who had won the first contract to operate the portage. This house was now owned by Archibald Hamilton, a captain of militia. During the Revolutionary War, the then very small village had been garrisoned by a detachment of the Queen's Rangers, and thus had earned its name. In 1812 the village had around twenty mostly stone houses, an inn which provided livery for the coach service between Newark and Fort Erie, several stores and warehouses, a distillery, tannery and blacksmith, all surrounded by peach and apple orchards. Below the buildings of the village was the waterfront, with its wharf. The shoreline downstream from the gorge was marked by a narrow beach

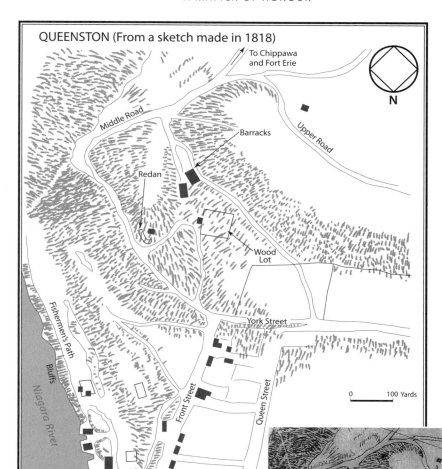

QUEENSTON (From a sketch made in 1818)

A map showing the village of Queenston and the surrounding area shortly after the end of the War of 1812, when all the features of the battle were still intact. It has been drawn from a contemporary sketch (right) at Library and Archives Canada. The village, road layout and redan battery can all be clearly seen. The American landing site is just off the map to the left. In the map and the sketch, north is at the bottom.

PROOF OF THEIR LOYALTY AND COURAGE

of shale, below bluffs about thirty feet high. Lewiston, 200 yards across the fast-flowing river and connected to Queenston in peacetime by a regular ferry service, was in many ways the mirror image, although smaller – the terminus of the portage road on the American side of the Niagara River where in 1807 a dock had been built that took trade away from the Canadian portage road. Immediately above Queenston, the ground rose steeply 300 feet in what was locally termed "the Mountain," or more properly, Queenston Heights, which was part of the Niagara escarpment and the beginning of the gorge of the Niagara River.

The attacking U.S. force, drawn from the troops at Lewiston, was to be augmented by infantry and artillery from Fort Niagara, who were to move after dark on the night of 10 October to avoid detection. Alexander Smyth too was ordered to bring his troops to Lewiston.[4] Covering the attack was the strong battery at Fort Gray above Lewiston, consisting of two 18-pdr and two 6-pdr guns. To transport the troops, the Americans brought thirteen bateaux, each big enough to take up to thirty-five men, to Lewiston from Fort Schlosser by wagon along the portage road. These had been launched at the Lewiston dock and were to be brought to the old portage landing at the foot of a small ravine about half a mile upstream to pick up the first wave of troops. This was not nearly enough boats for the job. Even if no losses were incurred, these boats would have to make repeated trips to and fro across the river to bring following waves of assaulting troops, and while they did so, the first wave would be isolated and the boats vulnerable to the fire of the British batteries.

On the other side, the garrison of Queenston comprised just over 420 all told: the light company of the 49th Foot with a few men of the 41st and some regular gunners under Captain James Dennis* (who was in overall command), located in a barracks on Queenston Heights, and the grenadier company of the 49th under Captain John Williams in the village itself with 200 militiamen from the flank companies of the 5th Lincolns under Captains Samuel Hatt and James Durand, along with two 3-pdr guns and some militia gunners. Also present were a flank company of the 2nd York Militia under Captain John Chisholm and a line company of the same regiment under Captain William Applegarth. Many of these men, as at Detroit, were

---

* Later Major-General Sir James Dennis, K.C.B. (1778–1855).

A view from the redan battery on Queenston Heights. The soldiers sitting on the earthwork are looking down the river from the end of the gorge towards Fort George. Lewiston and its wharf are on the right – the American – bank; Gray's battery would have been just out of sight to the right of the picture. The American embarkation point on the morning of 13 October would have been directly opposite where the soldiers are sitting and the climb up the side of the heights made by Wool and his men, to their right. On the left – Canadian – bank the cleared ground from the battery to the village is very obvious, as is the portage road leading past the Hamilton House and Hamilton Cove, Vrooman's Point and Brown's Point. Brock was probably shot dead about 100 yards below where the two soldiers are sitting admiring the view. (Watercolour by Thomas L. Smith. William L. Clements Library, University of Michigan)

wearing cast-off red coats of the 41st Foot, which probably made Dennis's force look more formidable than it really was. Close by at Brown's Point was a contingent of the two companies from the 2nd and 3rd York Militias.[5] Brock had also placed batteries covering the likely American crossing site from Lewiston. On Queenston Heights was a redan, or V-shaped earthwork, housing an 18-pdr gun firing downstream towards the commercial wharf on the American side and a mortar, probably 8-inch, which was a standard calibre. Lower down, covering the Queenston waterfront, was another battery of a single 9-pdr on a garrison carriage, positioned near the stone guard-house. About 1,000 yards downstream, at Vrooman's, or Froman's, Point was a battery with a 12-pdr gun and an 18-pdr carronade firing upstream and covering the dead ground immediately below the redan. The number and calibre of these guns varies in different accounts and the distribution given here is the most likely given the ranges and availability of guns, mortars and carronades. Finally there was a single 9-pdr at Two Mile Point, mentioned by Joseph Smith. Lieutenant John Ball's detachment of the 1st Lincoln Artillery Company was serving the guns along with a few regular artillerymen. Thus the various batteries effectively covered the entire stretch of river with interlocking arcs of fire, making good use of the few guns available. Although there was some danger of counter-battery fire from the American side, the positioning of the British guns effectively shielded them from the worst of this.

The weather on the night of 10 October 1812 was wet and miserable and the troops were embarked so noisily that the garrison opposite could make out every move; it seemed that the American troops had received no training in boat drill. Things went from bad to worse when it was found that the leading boat, commanded by Lieutenant John Simms, had disappeared, or so the rather unconvincing story went, and this boat contained all the oars. In the wake of this chaotic attempt, General Van Rensselaer postponed the attack by forty-eight hours. Alexander Smyth's brigade never made it at all. Smyth had received the order to march and had obeyed it, but the road was so bad that they were still on the road at 10.00 a.m. the following morning when a courier arrived telling Smyth that the attack was off.[6] Smyth turned his men round and slogged back for another ten hours. He wrote to Stephen Van Rensselaer that he would need time to rest and refit but that he would march again on 14 October.

Brock, however, saw conspiracy rather than chaos. He arrived in Queenston at noon on 11 October on the return journey from Fort Erie, where Captain James Dennis of the 49th's grenadier company gave him an account of what had passed and pointed out the terrain: such a clumsy demonstration could be no more than an attempt to deceive and distract him from the real assault, at Fort George. Accordingly, Brock did not reinforce Queenston.

Over the next twenty-four hours Brock began to revise his opinion, writing to Sir George Prevost that he thought an attack imminent – a despatch that Prevost did not receive until much later – saying that "The vast number of troops which have been this day added to the strong force previously collected on the opposite side convinces me, with other indications, that an attack is not far distant."[7] The catalyst for this change of opinion was an outbreak of mutiny among the soldiers of the flank companies of the 49th Foot. Fed up with detached duty in this isolated village, a number of men had broken into the spirit store and then, fired up by strong drink, had wrecked the guard-house on the dock and threatened violence against their officers. Only a firm stand by James Dennis and some of the troops who had remained sober contained the outbreak. A courier took news of the episode to Brock on the evening of 11 October, in a letter from Dennis; Brock immediately sent the brigade major, Thomas Evans, to bring back the "most culpable," who were confined under arrest for summary dealing.[8] In addition, Evans was to cross the Niagara River under a flag of truce to arrange for the exchange of prisoners captured during the affair of the *Detroit* and the *Caledonia*. Evans arrived early on 12 October and conferred with Dennis, noting that the volume of musketry fire from the far bank had increased considerably. He then made his way over the river in a canoe, carrying a white flag made from a large handkerchief borrowed from Thomas Dickson's wife. Under a deal of harassing fire, Evans and Dickson himself made it to the landing dock at Lewiston, where Evans had been a number of times before. But instead of being conveyed, as was customary, to General Van Rensselaer's headquarters, Evans was kept waiting for two hours while his message was conveyed to the general. Eventually the reply came back, repeated emphatically several times, that nothing could be done until the day after tomorrow. While sitting waiting, Evans noted the line of bateaux drawn up along the beach and concealed with branches; and being in a state of considerable concern he reported, wrongly, that the American force "had been prodigiously swelled by a horde of half-savage troops from Kentucky, Ohio and Tennessee...."[9]

Evans returned, thoroughly alarmed and convinced that an attack was imminent. After conferring with James Dennis, they decided that this was no time to reduce the combat strength of the garrison and Evans therefore ordered the release of the soldiers in detention on "the specious plea that their offence proceeding from too free indulgence in drink" and clearly took the men into his confidence by "appealing to them for proof of their loyalty and courage, which they were assured would be severely tested ere another day dawned."[10] On his way back to Fort George, Major Evans stopped at Vrooman's Point, Brown's Point and Two Mile Point to alert the officers there to the need for vigilance. It was perhaps this that ensured that when the American attack did develop, it was rapidly observed and brought under fire.

Because of the chaos of 10 October, General Van Rensselaer had postponed his attack to 13 October and it was the preparations for this second attempt that Evans had seen. It seems that, despite the evident unwillingness of Smyth to act, Van Rensselaer did not dare delay any further lest he fall under suspicion of conduct similar to that of William Hull: "… such was the pressure upon me from all quarters, that I became satisfied that my refusal to act, might involve me in suspicion, and the service in disgrace."[11] The tensions over command and status that had bedevilled the U.S. force continued right up to the last minute, with Colonel Solomon Van Rensselaer being given command of the militia in the first wave and Lieutenant-Colonel John Chrystie leading the regular troops.

When Evans returned to Fort George, supper was under way and he described to the assembled officers all that he had seen. Evans was not, it seems, believed by Roger Sheaffe and others, but Brock took him on one side and questioned him closely. Afterwards, Brock returned to the dining room, "called his staff together, and gave to each the necessary instructions."[12] Even so, he still gave no orders to reinforce Queenston and went to bed.

There are many accounts, all of which are conflicting to some degree, concerning the events surrounding Brock's final few hours on this earth. These have been confused by a good deal of myth and wishful thinking after the event. By far the best account of the battle on Queenston Heights is that of Malcomson.[13] This book is, however, a biography, not a history and so, with the benefit of Malcomson's work, it can skate over some details while concentrating on Brock's role and decision-making during the early stages of the battle.

Brock's first biographer, Ferdinand Brock Tupper, believed that Brock was an early riser. On the morning of 13 October 1812, he wrote that "Agree-

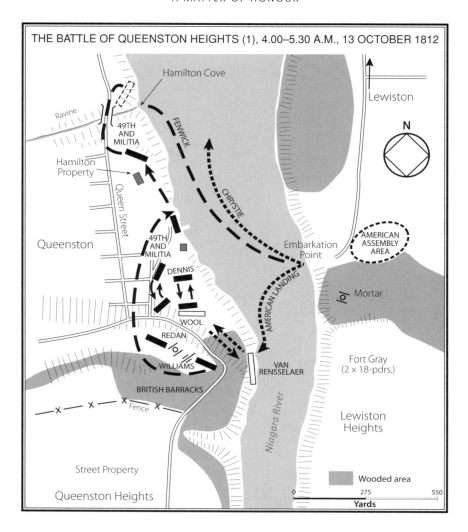

THE BATTLE OF QUEENSTON HEIGHTS (1), 4.00–5.30 A.M., 13 OCTOBER 1812

ably to his usual custom, he rose before daylight...."[14] Once awake, it is said, he immediately became aware of cannon fire from the direction of Queenston. This, however, is unlikely. The weather that morning was "one of those cold stormy days that at this season of the year so strongly ... mark the changes of the season ... so strong was the gale from the Lake ... little was known of what had been going on at Queenston in the night."[15] The wind was blowing from the north – "from the Lake" – so it is unlikely that Brock would have been able to hear gunfire from Queenston, to the south. John Norton, who was with the Grand River warriors close by, recalled that

"A firing was heard from Queenstown, although barely distinguishable from the high Wind blowing."[16] Nor did Lieutenant William Hamilton Merritt, sleeping soundly in Newark, hear it. It seems far more likely that a dispatch rider arrived with the news, as Merritt recorded in his later memoir.

Brock dressed with the assistance of his servant, Private Thomas Porter, putting on an old coat that he had worn as a brigadier and a cocked hat, and walked out into the still-dark early morning. He did not wake either Glegg or Macdonell but left orders that they were to be got up and told to follow directly. Once again, he gave no orders for troops to be stood-to or moved, which suggests that Brigade Major Evans was right when he recorded that "the impression on General Brock's mind ... that the attempt on Queenston would prove only a feint to disguise his real object from the creek in the rear of Fort Niagara."[17] Brock was therefore obviously aware of the concentration of troops and boats at Four Mile Creek and the threat it posed to Fort George. The objection to this view is that in such circumstances, Brock, as the commanding general, should have remained at the point of main effort and most danger, not gone off alone to look at a diversion which, if it proved to be such, would leave him dislocated from the decisive act. Malcomson suggests that perhaps Brock thought that he could make the round trip before anything serious developed at Fort George, which is a fair point; however Brock knew the distance – it was a sixteen-mile return trip – and he also knew the state of the road: it was an unmade, country lane crossing many ravines and marshy creeks; such a return journey would take two and a half to three hours of hard riding, without mishap. We know that Brock was impulsive and the most likely explanation is that he was led purely by the urge to find out what was going on, rather than send a junior officer or a detachment of dragoons to reconnoitre.

Mythology says that he rode to Queenston on the horse Alfred given to him by Sir James Craig. There is, however, no evidence, as already noted, that the horse ever made it farther west than York and this claim is therefore highly dubious. Other wishful thinking says that he diverted from his ride nearly four miles from Niagara to the house of Captain John Powell to see his supposed fiancée, Sophie Shaw:[18] this at between 4.00 and 5.00 a.m. with a battle raging, where the young woman was waiting fully dressed with a hot cup of coffee. How she knew he was coming remains a mystery, so that this too can be dismissed as fantasy.

The gunfire had also alerted the men of the York Militia at Brown's Point and they too began to march towards the battle. According to John Beverley Robinson,* a lieutenant of the regiment, "On our road, General Brock passed us. He had galloped from Niagara in great haste, unaccompanied by his aide-de-camp or a single attendant. He waved his hand to us, and desired us to follow with expedition, and galloped on with full speed to the mountain. Lieutenant-Colonel Macdonell and Captain Glegg passed immediately after."[19] As they marched up the road, the evidence of battle began to appear in the shape of wounded American prisoners: "The road was lined with miserable wretches suffering under wounds of all descriptions and crawling to our houses for protection and comfort." This encounter is probably the origin of the legend that Brock's last words, as reported in contemporary accounts published in Canadian newspapers just after the battle, were "Push on the York Volunteers," or "Push on, brave York Volunteers." Brock then paused briefly at Vrooman's Point and asked why the 18-pdr carronade was not firing along with the 12-pdr gun. Lieutenant Archibald McLean, commanding the battery, explained that the carronade, which was designed for a heavy, smashing fire at close quarters, did not have the range. "It can't be helped," replied Brock, after which, wrote McLean, he "put his spurs to his horse and galloped away for Queenston. Soon after his ADCs Macdonell and Glegg came up as fast as their horses could carry them, and soon after them my companions of York Militia came trotting up from Brown's Point."[20]

What the firing presaged was that the Americans had begun crossing sometime after 3.00 a.m. on 13 October. The first wave of regulars under Lieutenant-Colonel John Chrystie had been carried too far downstream by the current and had missed the intended landing site, which was a narrow beach 400 yards upstream from the Queenston waterfront and therefore out of sight of the British sentries. A mixed party of regulars and militia under Solomon Van Rensselaer did better, and after ten minutes they ran ashore as planned. They were, however, seen by a sentry, who, rather than firing a shot, ran into the village and roused Captain James Dennis. It is

---

* Later Sir John Beverley Robinson, C.B., 1st Baronet (1791–1863). He prosecuted the Canadian renegades at the Bloody Assize of 1814 and was later Attorney General of Upper Canada, Chief Justice, and a member of the Legislative Assembly.

a reasonable supposition that, with the alarm having been raised the previous afternoon by Thomas Evans, the men of the grenadier company and the militia were sleeping on their arms; District General Orders only a week before had specified that all regular and militia troops were to be "under arms in their quarters at the first break of day … one-third of the men in quarters to be clothed and accoutred during the night with their arms at hand, in readiness to turn out in a moment's notice."[21] Certainly the troops were formed with their light guns between the American landing site and the village before the U.S. troops could complete their landing; Captain Dennis

A brigade major and aide-de-camp in Charles Hamilton Smith's *Costumes of the Army of the British Empire according to the Last Regulations, 1812–1815*. Macdonell and Glegg would have appeared very much like this as they rode after Brock in the early morning of 13 October 1812.

himself was quartered in the Hamilton house and ran down to try to find out where the landing was taking place. In the first volley, Colonel Solomon Van Rensselaer himself was hit. He continued to rally the troops but over the next half-hour he was hit a further five times, and although he survived, he was thereafter out of action. The British, however, did not have things all their own way during this exchange. Solomon Van Rensselaer's account said that after "a severe engagement … with heavy loss on both sides … we were victorious, and the enemy gave way, and fled towards Queenston, on our right."[22] A touch exaggerated perhaps, and probably written to justify himself after the event, but Captain John E. Wool,* commanding a detachment of regulars with Solomon Van Rensselaer, also recalled that "The enemy was repulsed."[23] The account from Lieutenant and acting Adjutant Joseph Smith of the 41st Foot, who was not actually present but clearly heard the story immediately after the action, writing from Fort George on 18 October,[24] said that:

> On the Morning of the 13th Inst between 3 & 4 o Clock the Enemy under the Command of GENERAL Wadsworth amounting to about 16 or 1800 Men – attempted to Cross the River in 2 Divisions the first at the fishing ground above the Landing [i.e., Van Rensselaer's party] and the 2nd at the Barr & in the bottom, which they made good, after meeting with a very gallant resistance (which destroy'd numbers of them) made by the Fk Companies of the 49th Regt and some Militia. …[25]

John Beverley Robinson also reported these events, saying that: "At the time the enemy began to cross there were two companies of the 49th Regiment (the Grenadier and Light Company) and, I believe, three small companies of Militia to oppose them."[26]

What is certain is that effective American fire forced Captain Dennis's men back into the buildings of the village – Dennis himself seems also to have been wounded – but British fire also obliged Solomon Van Rensselaer to order his men back to the shelter of the beach, until John Chrystie's troops should arrive. With Colonel Van Rensselaer disabled, command of this part of the landing force devolved on to John Wool. Neither Solomon

---

* Later Brigadier-General John Ellis Wool (1784–1869). Wool served with distinction in the War of 1812, the Mexican-American War and the American Civil War.

Van Rensselaer nor his cousin ever wrote down any detailed plan for the operation, and so as with Brock at Detroit, this account is a reconstruction. It seems highly likely however that he always intended to take the redan battery and control the heights by making an attack from the rear. Wool's account, which differs from that of Solomon Van Rensselaer in many respects, supports this:

> Being the senior officer in the absence of Lt. Col. Chrystie I took command of the detachment. At this moment judge Advocate Lush* arrived and informed me of the landing of Colonel Van Rensselaer and his party, with orders from the Colonel to "prepare for storming Queenstown Heights." … In a few minutes he returned with the order to march. We proceeded a few rods when I received an order to halt. This was at the foot or base of the heights – our right extending towards the village of Queenstown.[27]

It was at this point that the right flank of John Wool's detachment came under fire from Captain James Dennis's grenadiers. Even though Wool's men were in dead ground from the redan, they could be fired at by the 9-pdr in the village and by the British regulars and the militia. Wool himself was wounded by a musket ball that scored excruciatingly across both buttocks; seven other American officers were killed and wounded out of a total of eleven known to have been present in the first hour of the landings.[28]

The firing on the beach had alerted the batteries on both sides of the river and those at Fort Gray, the redan, Queenston wharf and Vrooman's Point were all soon in action. Smith reported that "we had a very fine Battery at Fromans Point in which was a 9 Pounder and another at a Point further on called Scotts Bay which annoyed them very much while crossing & recrossing the River which they did during the whole of the Action…."[29] The fire from the British batteries was especially effective against Chrystie's boats. What Chrystie's force did do, or so it seems, was to induce Captain Dennis to detach part of his force to Hamilton Cove, where he believed an American landing was being attempted. Nothing, however, would induce the crews of Chrystie's boats to approach the shore and, to that command-

---

* Stephen Lush Jr was the son of a prominent American Revolutionary War lawyer and congressman, Stephen Lush (1753–1825). Lush Jr was not actually appointed as judge advocate until 5 October 1813.

er's mortification, they returned to the embarkation point. Here there was total chaos, for the British 9-pdr on Queenston wharf (the only gun in range and with a direct line of sight) had identified the embarkation point and fired ball on to the site and case-shot at the boats as they came within range, rapidly and effectively. Order soon disappeared and the following waves of reinforcing troops never materialised as the plan had determined. All soldiers know Murphy's first law of combat – anything that can go wrong, will go wrong. However on occasions like this, there is also Riley's corollary to be considered – that Murphy was being hopelessly over-optimistic.

Some of the bateaux that had taken the first wave of assault troops across had also, like Chrystie's boats, returned to the embarkation point. These were manned by crews with their hearts rather more in the business, and they picked up more of the 13th Infantry, who joined the remnants of the first wave in the relative shelter of the beach under the bluffs above Queenston village. Solomon Van Rensselaer was out of action, John Chrystie was nowhere to be found and Captain John Wool, despite being wounded, was the senior officer and still on his feet. He asked Solomon Van Rensselaer what to do lest they all be taken prisoner. The colonel replied that "he knew of nothing unless we could take Queenston heights."[30] Solomon Van Rensselaer's own recollection was that he gave his directions to Wool and Captain Peter Ogilvie of the 13th Regiment, who had just come ashore with the second wave, "very young men, not six months in service." They were to follow the fisherman's path upstream along the top of the bluffs – it is still there – "and ascend the heights by the point of the rock, and storm the battery." As neither of these officers knew the ground, Lieutenant John Gansevoort, who had been with the artillery in the area for some months, was detailed off as guide. Lush was also attached to the party, which numbered about 160 men all told, with orders to bring up the rear and "to shoot down the first man who offered to give way."[31]

The party comprised men from a number of units, chiefly the 13th Infantry but also some artillerymen. There has been much discussion about whether or not the party included riflemen: the U.S. Army had added a rifle regiment to its establishment in 1808 – indeed Brigadier-General Smyth, then a colonel, had commanded it. They were armed with the Harper's Ferry-made Model 1803 rifle with an effective range of 200 yards; although in skilled hands it could achieve 400 yards.[32] The U.S. order of battle on the

Niagara as listed by Malcomson shows four companies of riflemen, 180 men, at Lewiston.[33] It is therefore entirely possible that the regular troops under Wool included some riflemen. Otherwise the standard weapon of the U.S. Infantry was the Model 1796 0.69-inch musket, based on the French 1777 pattern Charleville musket. A new pattern was in production in 1812 but the capabilities were much the same, giving the infantry soldier an effective range of 100 yards.

It was now about 6.30 a.m. and at that time of year by no means properly light. Assuming that Brock's ride had taken him over an hour, it was at this point that he arrived in Queenston. Brock rode straight into the village, probably meeting Captain James Dennis at Hamilton Cove, where the road crossed a small ravine. By this time John Glegg and John Macdonell had caught up and the three dismounted to get a view of the situation, which seemed favourable. Brock could make out large bodies of American infantry drawn up at Lewiston, where twenty-four guns were in position. He could see boats crossing over and the musket flashes of several hundred men lining the bank beside Queenston, where about half their number of British troops was keeping them back. So far, the British seemed to be holding their own. However the U.S. battery at Fort Gray had also found the range and within a short time it had put the British 9-pdr out of action, thus taking the pressure off the embarkation point. Once the British fire had ceased, Lieutenant-Colonel John Fenwick* gathered a detachment of regular troops and took them down to the embarkation site to board four of the bateaux that had made it back. Fenwick's party ran into the same problems with the current that had bedevilled John Chrystie, but managed to get ashore at Hamilton Cove, where perhaps a platoon of the grenadiers of the 49th Foot and the same number of militia were waiting. As day was now breaking, this landing was observed by the British and, as the first American landing above the village had weakened the garrison in the village, either Brock or James Dennis ordered a drummer to summon Captain John Williams's light company down from the heights to contain Solomon Van Rensselaer's small bridgehead, while Captain Dennis took the rest of his grenadiers to deal with this new threat at Hamilton Cove. No-one was yet aware of the devel-

---

* Fenwick had been in the U.S. Marine Corps, had resigned and later joined the U.S. Artillery.

oping threat to the southern flank from Wool's detachment, and whoever gave the command to order Williams's company down from the heights, the responsibility for what turned out to be a fatal error lay with the senior officer present – Brock himself.

John Fenwick's men, landing at Hamilton Cove, found themselves taking murderous fire from the top of the bluff: "Their reception was such as did honour to the courage and management of our troops. The grape and musket balls, poured upon them at close quarters as they approached the shore, made incredible havoc. A single discharge from a field-piece directed by Captain Dennis himself killed fifteen in one boat."[34] John Beverley Robinson reported that:

> Three of their batteaux landed at the hollow below Mr. Hamilton's garden in Queenston, and were met by a party of Militia, who slaughtered almost the whole of those in them, taking the rest prisoners. Several other boats were so shattered and raked that the men in them threw down their arms, and came on shore merely to deliver themselves up prisoners of war. Thus far, things had proceeded successfully; and the General, on his approach to the spot, was greeted with the happy intelligence that all our aggressors were destroyed or taken.[35]

Before long, all the Americans at Hamilton Cove were dead, wounded or captured, save a small group of eleven men, five of whom were wounded and which included Colonel John Fenwick. These men, with Captain James Mullany, grabbed a drifting bateau and managed to cross back to the American shore. Those who did not get away but survived were the prisoners John Beverley Robinson reported having seen.

Brock meanwhile had taken stock of the situation and come to the conclusion that the American attack at Queenston was no feint, but the real thing. The guns of Fort Niagara had begun to bombard Fort George shortly after Brock left and the batteries in Fort George had opened up in reply, which Brock would have heard as he made his way south. His aides John Glegg and John Macdonell would have been able to assure him that no landing force had appeared from the direction of Four Mile Creek, at least before they had left. At this point Brock probably sent at least one courier back to Fort George to alert General Roger Sheaffe and summon

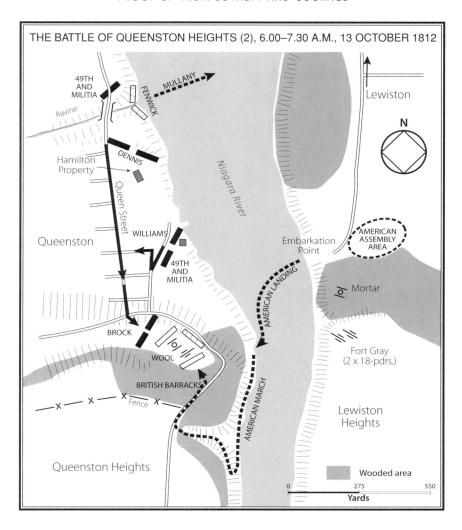

THE BATTLE OF QUEENSTON HEIGHTS (2), 6.00–7.30 A.M., 13 OCTOBER 1812

49TH AND MILITIA

MULLANY

FENWICK

Ravine

DENNIS

Hamilton Property

Queen Street

Niagara River

Queenston

WILLIAMS

49TH AND MILITIA

Embarkation Point

AMERICAN ASSEMBLY AREA

Lewiston

N

AMERICAN LANDING

Mortar

BROCK

WOOL

BRITISH BARRACKS

Fence

AMERICAN MARCH

Fort Gray (2 x 18-pdrs.)

Lewiston Heights

Queenston Heights

Wooded area

0   275   550

Yards

reinforcements and another courier to Chippawa on the same errand. He then appears to have ridden up to the redan with Glegg and Macdonell, to order the gunners to increase the charge of the mortar so as to be able to keep up the fire on the American embarkation point, now that direct fire had been neutralised.[36] But within a very few minutes, the situation changed completely: U.S. infantry appeared on the crest above the redan battery and began firing on the party there.

What had happened to Captain John Wool and his men? They had fol-lowed the fishermen's path along the top of the bluffs immediately above

281

Captain (later Brigadier-General) John Ellis Wool (1784–1869) served with distinction in the War of 1812, the Mexican-American War and the American Civil War. He is shown here in the uniform of a major-general. (Engraving by Alonzo Chappel. 1858, courtesy of the Anne S.K. Brown Collection, Brown University)

the river, guided by Gansevoort, to the beginning of the gorge and had then struck off to their right, up the steep slope. Some accounts speak of a path but there is no sign of this – I, the author, having made the climb. Nor is there any reason why a path should be there: the portage road leads down immediately below the redan battery to the edge of the village, from where it is a simple matter for anyone who wishes to descend to the fishermen's path or to the wharf. The ascent is steep and hard going in modern clothes without the burden of musket, cartridge box, canteen and knapsack, but it is well within the capabilities of fit young men, even in the boots and clothes of 1812. The fact that then, as now, the steep slope was covered with young trees and bushes would have helped, giving the men something they could hold on to while hauling themselves uphill.

Having reached the summit, the men were formed. The ground behind the battery was wooded, giving cover from fire and view, but in contrast to the steep slopes down to the river, the steadier slopes from the battery down to Queenston had been cleared, both to give fields of fire and to provide firewood for the village and the garrison. The contrast in tree cover shows up clearly in Dennis's picture of the battle, one of the illustrations to this chapter. Once John Wool's men moved cautiously to the tree-line, therefore, they would have seen the battery clearly. Brock must have been furious: he knew something of the fisherman's path but had been told the ascent of the mountain was impossible. Had he obeyed his injunction to Fitzgibbon all those years before, he would have reminded himself that for a soldier, nothing should be impossible – and ordered the area either to be denied or guarded. For here, having come up that impassable route, was the enemy. According to Lieutenant Joseph Smith:

> About 200 of the 1ˢᵗ Division of the Enemy by Climbing up the Rocks & by a foot path ascended & were form'd behind the Mountain … as soon as it was found out that the Enemy was in force, in Rear of the Mountain which was not before General Brock had arrived at Queenston from this Post, that he ordered a Party of about 40 Men to Attack. Then the Command of the Party was given to Lt. Col. McDonnell the Generals P.AC – but from the superiority of the Enemy were drove back to the Battery on the Mountain Where the General with a Small Party had stationed himself. The Enemy followed up the pursuit and dislodged the General & his Party all from the Battery & planted the Colours of the U.S. on the Parapet. Private Thomas Haynes 41ˢᵗ Regt who was in the Engineers employ at Queenston with others was killed in the Battery & many taken Prisoners –

From this account it seems that not all the British infantry had left the height; at least some had stayed to protect and help serve the battery, bringing ammunition from the expense magazines to the guns or providing some local defence for the gunners. John Beverley Robinson corroborates this, saying that "General Brock rushed up the mountain on foot with some troops to dislodge them; but they were so advantageously posted, and kept up so tremendous a fire, that the small number ascending were driven back."[37] Sending forty men uphill against 160 was not an act of war and there was nothing for it but flight. Not even pausing to remount, Brock and his aides grabbed their horses' reins and ran down the hill to the village, followed closely by the gunners, who had not waited long enough to knock a spike into the touch-hole to deny the gun to the Americans.

Once in control of the battery, Captain Wool deployed his infantry to give all-round defence towards the village and the rear of the battery. The mortar and the gun were silenced and could no longer impede further crossing operations and, crucially, the Americans controlled the high ground. It would not be long before U.S. artillerymen would be brought up to get the gun back into action and to turn the battery on its former owners. Brock intuitively understood the situation and equally intuitively formed the view that a counter-attack immediately with a platoon might well be better than a counter-attack in two hours' time with a brigade. He did not know the strength of John Wool's detachment and took no care to scout the position. He thus followed the course of action with the highest risk: a frontal counter-attack, uphill over open ground, against an enemy of unknown strength.

Joseph Smith said that "The Enemy having got possession of all the Strong Positions the Genl retreated to the Village where he rallied some of the 49th Regt & Militia in a small Field at the end of McMullins Tavern...."[38] This was at the northern end of the village, and here Brock found part of the light company of the 49th Foot and the flank companies of the 2nd York and 5th Lincoln Militia, perhaps fifty men altogether – the rest were still maintaining their positions above Solomon Van Rensselaer's bridgehead. The troops gave Brock a rousing cheer as he called out to them, "Follow me, boys," and with John Glegg and John Macdonell, he mounted his horse and trotted up the main street to the point where the slope turned into a steeper escarpment, at which point the portage road and the road to the village of St David's diverged. According to the account of George Jarvis, a gentleman volunteer in the 49th Foot,[39] he slowed his horse to a walk and said, "Take breath boys, we shall want it in a few minutes." He dismounted and without hesitation climbed over a stone wall, drew his sword and waved the men forward, taking up a position at the head of the light company of the 49th. The troops probably shook out into line, with their left on the portage road, beyond which the ground fell away sharply. Joseph Smith confirmed this when he wrote that the troops pushed on "by the Old Road tho the Mountain was covered with the Enemy & exposed to a very heavy fire as also a Cross fire from near the Battery...."[40] According to George Jarvis, the advance was under fire from American riflemen from the start, using the cover of the trees that grew thickly on the top and the side of the heights.

To the U.S. soldiers waiting around the battery or in the trees it must have been obvious that the attack was being led by a very senior officer; probably many of them recognized Brock from descriptions but his coat and cocked hat would have picked him out in any case. The sight of him may have inspired awe in the younger soldiers, but to the older men it must have seemed a heaven-sent opportunity. Brock was, even at this late stage, still in front of the men, waving his sword and encouraging them to follow.

An contemporary image of an officer and private man of the 52nd Light Infantry, 1814, from Charles Hamilton Smith's *Costumes of the Army of the British Empire*. Aside from the yellow facings, the light company of the 49th that Brock led up Queenston Heights would have been dressed in very much the same way.

A bullet struck him a glancing blow on the hand but he paid no attention to it. Then, just as he was about to make his final rush, a man stepped out of the trees, took deliberate aim, and shot him.[41] John Beverley Robinson reported that "Several of the 49th assembled round him. One poor fellow was severed in the middle by a ball, and fell across the General. They succeeded, however, in conveying the General's body to Queenston. Just at this instant we reached Queenston."[42]

Brock had been struck in the chest by a low-velocity ball as he half-turned to urge the troops forward,[43] which would have caused enormous trauma and tissue damage, filled his lungs with blood very quickly, and deprived him, through shock, of the ability to speak. Joseph Smith reported this, saying that "he Received a Musket Ball below his Breast that Lodged near his back bone, which put an end to his existence."[44] John Glegg, looking at the body after the battle, realized that the bullet had struck Brock in the right-centre of his chest and, having been fired from above, it had exited his body lower down in the chest and towards the left: analysis of the bullet holes in Brock's uniform, which survives in the Canadian War Museum, corroborates this.[45] Brock would have died within a minute. Several Americans later claimed to have killed Brock, the most persistent being Robert Walcot,[46] who gave details consistent with Brock's wounds, but no claim can be reliably verified and, given the short range of the engagement, it is not possible to say whether the ball was fired from a musket or a rifle.

Where did he fall? Not at the current marker, located on level ground at the south end of Queenston, since this was placed there for the convenience of H.R.H the Prince of Wales when he visited in 1860. Brock was leading the counter-attack, and if he was killed by a musket shot, he was probably no more than 100 yards from the U.S. line around the redan battery. If he was killed by a rifleman, then it could be as far as 200 yards. The ground here, although now reforested, was then cleared for fields of fire and for firewood. The approach for 300 yards to the battery was open and sloping upwards towards the redan. George Jervis's account, corroborated by John Beverley Robinson, says that Brock was shot "as he led the way up the mountain at double quick time."[47]

Many accounts attribute some stirring last words to Brock, even though the nature of his wound would certainly have prevented him from speaking. Joseph Smith, who was not present, said that "He died like a hero for as he fell he said '*never mind me my Boys push on....*'"[48] William Hamilton Merritt later said that Brock cried out, "Push on my boys,"[49] but again this was probably said at an earlier stage of the counter-attack. In any case, Merritt also was not there. John Glegg wrote to Brock's brother William two days after the battle that Brock had said, "My fall must not be noticed or impede my brave companions from advancing to victory."[50] This does not ring true at all and sounds like Glegg trying to talk up Brock's sacrifice for the benefit of the family. The account of George Jervis is the most convincing. Jervis was certainly close to Brock when he was hit and almost certainly the first person to get to him. When he asked Brock if he was much hurt, Brock "placed his hand on his breast and made no reply, and slowly sunk down."[51]

Some accounts, including that of Smith, suggest that after Brock fell, the

Brock's death has inspired many artists to capture the drama of the moment. This watercolour by C.W. Jefferys contains several inaccuracies. No native warriors were present, the militia were wearing red coats and the 49th would not have received the 1812 pattern shako by this date. (Government of Ontario Art Collection, 619871. Archives of Ontario.)

counter-attack was maintained for a while, the troops shouting "Revenge the General!"

> … they gained the Heights attacked the Enemy & drove them to the edge of the Rocks by which they ascended but a fresh Reinforcement of the E[nemy] having got up the Rocks & form'd, they in their turn forced our brave fellows to retire, which I believe was not very Regular.…[52]

Brock's body was taken into the village and left at a stone house belonging to Patrick McCabe (who had voluntarily returned to the U.S.), rented to John Smith and used as a tavern.* Here it remained, untouched, while the battle continued. A second counter-attack was led soon afterwards by John

---

* The stone house was used as a hospital from the beginning of the war under the charge of Doctor Muirhead. It was occasionally thereafter used as a barracks by different detachments in 1813 and 1814 and from then until after the peace by the 96th Regiment. (War Losses claims – War of 1812 Claim No. 233 – Patrick McCabe, Queenston).

Brock's coat is on display at the Canadian War Museum. The arrow indicates the hole made by the bullet that killed him. The presence of the sash, or *ceinture fléchée*, in this photograph is of questionable authenticity. (CWM 19670070-009 © Canadian War Museum)

Brock's hat, the standard cocked hat of a British general officer of the period, made from heavy felt and fringed with white ostrich feathers. The plume is also feather, the lower part dyed red. Brock had an unusually large head, as noted in his letter to his brothers in 1810 on page 110; this is probably the hat refered to then. (Niagara Historical Society Museum)

Macdonell, which almost succeeded in regaining the heights, but Macdonell was seriously wounded and the attack lost momentum as the troops lost heart without their leader. Macdonell was carried from the field; he lived another twenty-four hours in agony before his death. The remaining British and Canadian troops under James Dennis retreated to Vrooman's Point, so that by 10.00 a.m. the Americans were opposed only by the 24-pdr there, which continued firing at long range. The Americans were able to push several hundred fresh troops and a 6-pdr gun across the river. They also turned the 18-pdr in the redan on to Queenston village, but it had a limited field of fire away from the river. American troops entered Queenston village and rescued Lieutenant-Colonel Fenwick and the survivors of his party, but they did not attempt to force Dennis from his position.

Lieutenant-Colonel John Chrystie briefly took charge of the U.S. troops on the Canadian bank but returned to Lewiston to bring up reinforcements and entrenching tools. At about noon General Van Rensselaer and Colonel Chrystie recrossed to the Canadian side of the river. They ordered the position on Queenston Heights to be fortified under the direction of Lieutenant Joseph Totten of the U.S. Army Corps of Engineers.* Because of the level of casualties among his officers during the landing, Van Rensselaer appointed Lieutenant-Colonel Winfield Scott to take charge of the regulars on Queenston Heights, and Brigadier-General William Wadsworth, who as a militia general waived his right to overall command, took charge of the militia. Only just over 1,000 of General Van Rensselaer's men had crossed the Niagara River and few of these men were in orderly units or with sufficient officers to control them.

Meanwhile, British reinforcements had begun to arrive from Fort George. A detachment of gunners under Captain William Holcroft and another of the car brigade under Captain Isaac Swayze with two 6-pdr guns moved into Queenston, supported by what remained of the light company of the 41st under Captain William Derenzy. Archibald Hamilton guided them to a firing position in the courtyard of his own house. When they

---

* Later Brigadier-General Joseph Gilbert Totten (1788–1864). He served throughout the War of 1812 and during the Civil War. He was chief engineer of the U.S. Army, regent of the Smithsonian Institution and co-founder of the National Academy of Sciences. He was a man of great intellectual and professional stature and a major influence on several generations of engineers in the U.S. Army.

The famous composite view of the battle of Queenston Heights by Major James
Dennis of the 49th Foot. The whole action of the battle from the first crossing through
to the American surrender is illustrated but there are some important details: the nature
of the cleared ground and the tree-line on the heights; the route taken by John Wool
and his men; the position of Gray's battery; the positions of the British field guns on

the wharf and later, beside the Hamilton house; the size of the bateaux used by the Americans; and finally the attack in line up the heights during which Brock was shot. This is one of several published colour lithographs based on Dennis's painting. (Library and Archives Canada R13133-387) opened fire at 1.00 p.m., it once again became dangerous for American boats to cross the river, and accurate fire several times silenced the American guns in Lewiston village. At the same time, a large contingent of Iroquois warriors, mainly Mohawks, led by John Norton and John Brant, scaled the heights and suddenly fell on Scott's outposts from the eastern side, away from the river. Although the Mohawks were driven back, their appearance shook the Americans' determination; moreover the war cries of the warriors could be heard in Lewiston, where militiamen waiting to cross the river refused orders to embark.

Roger Sheaffe arrived at Queenston at 2.00 p.m. and took command of all British and Canadian troops. Most of the garrison of Fort George was now closing on Queenston, and when he had consolidated his force, he led the men on a three-mile detour to the east of the heights, on an approach shielded from American artillery fire. Here, he was joined by another column of reinforcements from Chippawa under Captain Richard Bullock of the 41st. In all, Sheaffe now commanded over 800 men. In addition to the original garrison of Queenston, he had five companies of the 41st and seven of militia, with two 3-pdr guns.

Worried that his build-up was stalling, General Van Rensselaer decided to return to Lewiston to push forward reinforcements and ammunition. There he found that all order had vanished. The militia had dissolved into a disorderly crowd and he was unable to persuade any more to cross the river. He then tried to make the civilian boatmen cross the river and recover his force, but they too refused. He therefore sent a message to General Wadsworth that left to him the decision on whether to stand and fight or retreat back across the Niagara by any means possible

This message arrived just as the British and Canadian troops and the native warriors began their advance on to the main position on Queenston Heights. Scott decided to abandon the incomplete defensive works and withdraw. He and his men fell back to the top of the heights, where they attempted to throw up a hasty barricade of fence rails and brushwood to cover the evacuation with the regular U.S. infantry. Scott placed his 6-pdr gun in front of the line and posted some riflemen on the right among the barrack buildings which had been occupied by the light company of the 49th.

It was not until 4.00 p.m., twelve hours after Van Rensselaer had begun his assault, that Sheaffe launched his final attack. The assault was led by the light company of the 41st – who, having been twice pushed off the heights, had a point to make – with a company of militia and some native warriors, against the riflemen on Scott's right. Using tactics that had been tried and tested back in the Revolutionary War, they fired one volley, then charged with the bayonet, forcing the riflemen to flee. Seeing this, Sheaffe immediately ordered a general advance; the entire British and Canadian line fired by platoons, then raised a mixture of loud hurrahs and native war cries – and charged. The American militia, hearing the dreaded whoops from the Mohawks and believing themselves doomed, broke and ran. Cursing the men who would not cross the river, General Wadsworth surrendered at the edge of the precipice with 300 men. Winfield Scott, Joseph Totten and others tumbled down the steep slope and then the bank, to the edge of the river. With no boats arriving to evacuate his men and with the Mohawks furious over the deaths of two chiefs, Scott feared a massacre and surrendered. Thus a second American invasion army ended up, like Hull's men, as prisoners of war:

> A flag of truce from those that remained begging for quarter, ended the day, and General Wadsworth, Colonel Scott and 71 other officers, together with 853 men, were made prisoners of war, the enemy's loss in killed and wounded could not be less than 400 or 500 men, whilst ours, strange to tell, consisted of only 11 killed and 60 wounded, the Indians lost only 5 men and 9 wounded.[53]

CHAPTER SIXTEEN

"The Honourable Bed of a Soldier"

AFTERMATH

Lieutenant Archibald McLean of the York Militia had been wounded in the thigh trying to help John Macdonell after he fell. McLean had spent much of the rest of the day having his injury seen to, but by the evening he felt able to make his way back to Brown's Point. As he limped out onto the road he saw a wagon coming up, driven by Captain Isaac Swayze of the car brigade. As he scrambled aboard, he found that the cart already had one passenger: Isaac Brock.[1]

The general's body was taken to Government House in Newark. John Macdonell died during the morning of Wednesday, 14 October; his body joined Brock's and the two men lay in state until their funeral on Friday, 16 October. This was, it was said, one of the grandest events ever to have taken place in Upper Canada. Around 5,000 people crowded into Newark to watch the procession – a huge number given that the total population of the entire province was no more than 80,000 – but a figure that included military personnel. Two graves had been dug in the northeast bastion of Fort George, known variously as the Cavalier Bastion or the York Battery. The route between Government House and the fort was lined by British and Canadian regulars, militiamen and native warriors. The ceremony had been arranged under the direction of John Glegg, who was well aware of Brock's dislike of fuss or ostentation and who thus made the ceremonial as simple as possible, consistent with the unavoidable requirements of military and state protocol.

At 10.00 a.m. two guards of sixty men from the 41st Foot and sixty from the various regiments of militia present at Fort George stepped off, led by Fort Major Donald Campbell, followed by the regimental band of the 41st Foot and the regiment's corps of fifes and drums, playing a solemn march, as minute guns marked the passage of the cortège. They were followed by Brock's horse – there is no record that this was Alfred – draped in black and led by four grooms, with his personal staff and servants. Then came the two coffins, Macdonell followed by Brock, both on ammunition wagons, each with four supporters and eight pall bearers. Glegg had arranged for a local silversmith to inscribe plates on both coffins, although the details of the inscriptions have not survived.[2] Brock's coffin was supported by James Coffin of the commissary, Brigade-Major Thomas Evans of the 8th, and John Williams and John Glegg. His bearers were the gunner William Holcroft, James Dennis of the 49th, William Derenzy of the 41st, Henry Vigoreaux of the engineers, William Hamilton Merritt, Thomas Clark and Johnson Butler of the Lincoln Militia and William Claus of the Indian Department, all bearing the marks of mourning on their regimentals. The senior mourners and friends of the dead men followed, led by Major-General Roger Hale Sheaffe, now the most senior officer in Upper Canada. Glegg later wrote that "no pen can describe the real scenes of that mournful day. A more solemn and affecting spectacle was perhaps never witnessed."[3] The service was read by the Reverend Mr Robert Addison and as the coffins were lowered into the earth, a salute of twenty-one guns was fired.[4] Shortly afterwards, the guns of Fort Niagara also fired a salute in tribute to their conqueror. The Grand River people held a ceremony in Fort George on 5 November attended by senior military officers and chiefs; on the following day, more warriors from the Six Nations met Claus and Norton at Fort George to honour Brock. Chief Kodeaneyonte gave Roger Sheaffe a present of eight strings of wampum and a large white wampum belt to cover Brock's grave, so that his body would receive no injury.[5] A vessel of the Provincial Marine was named after Brock at this time; however it was destroyed, uncompleted, during the American attack on York in 1813.

Expressions of grief, both private and public, continued for weeks. The *Quebec Gazette* described Brock's death as "a public calamity";[6] the *Niagara Bee* launched an extensive eulogy which captures the general sentiment in the Canadas:

The unfortunate loss of the brave General Brock … for a while seemed to overcloud the brilliant sun of victory, and the people paused to mourn their country's friend ere public rejoicing for the glorious issue of the day could for a moment prevail – the loss is truly great.… General Brock was bold and daring, even to excess – utterly regardless of danger – his country's good – the honor of England – the fame of Britain was his leading star … terrible in Battle – yet a most generous foe – a friend to humanity – he loved the inhabitants of Canada – their interests were his continual study, their rights and priviledges his sacred care to preserve – none suffered under his administration – even the guilty wretch looked confidently to him for mercy – can it be wondered then that he was universally beloved, and that he is, alas! now equally regretted? He died in the honorable bed of a soldier.…[7]

To his family and friends in England and the Channel Islands, Brock was still alive. The news reached Guernsey in the ship *Fame* two days before it was known in London, on 26 November 1812. Less than a month later, William received the gold medal for Detroit that was due to Brock, with a letter from the Duke of York explaining that this mark of esteem had been directed personally by the Prince Regent,[8] who also made a special grant to allow the heraldic supporters that would have been incorporated into Brock's coat of arms as a Knight of the Bath to be retained by his family. When Sir George Prevost's despatch reached London, Lord Bathurst replied to the news that:

> His royal highness the prince regent is fully aware of the severe loss which his majesty's service has experienced in the death of Major-General Sir Isaac Brock. This would have been sufficient to have clouded a victory of much greater importance. His majesty has lost in him not only an able and meritorious officer, but one who, in the exercise of his functions of provisional lieutenant-governor of the province, displayed qualities admirably adapted to awe the disloyal, to reconcile the wavering, and to animate the great mass of the inhabitants against successive attempts of the enemy to invade the province.….[9]

A much reduced version of this letter was published in Prevost's General Orders the following April, once communication with England had re-opened after the winter, which excited a good deal of annoyance in both provinces, the implication being that Prevost wished to denigrate Brock's image in his own interest. If Prevost was wanting in acknowledging Brock's role in seizing the physical and moral initiative in the early stages of the war, he made up for it in his final General Order when ordered home. In this order, although not mentioning any officer by name, he referred to Brock's achievements several times:

> At Detroit, and at the river Raisin two entire armies with their commanding generals were captured; and greatly superior armies were repulsed. – The several battles of Queenstown, Stoney Creek, Chateauguay … will ever immortalise the Heroes who were on those occasions afforded the opportunity of distinguishing themselves. The capture of Michilimackinac … and Niagara by Assault, are trophies of the prowess of British Arms. The names of the respective officers who led his Majesty's Troops to these several achievements … will be transmitted by the faithful historian with glory to a grateful posterity.[10]

As to Brock's effects, the usual military procedure was followed, there being no will. The general's possessions, wine, books, furniture and uniforms were auctioned off on 4 January 1813. An inventory was compiled and is held today in the Toronto Reference Library; Brock's possessions included twenty-seven wine and spirit decanters of various sizes, 250 glasses of various sizes and colours, very large quantities of dried and bottled fruits, pickles and preserves, and a quantity of plate. Roger Sheaffe and John Glegg bought most of the items either at the sale or by private treaty; more than £950 was remitted to his family as a result. Glegg kept back some of Brock's belongings though: one of his swords, a dress tunic, a cravat (which has since disappeared), the undress coatee that he was wearing at the time of his death and probably another coatee which has now largely disintegrated. These mementos were taken back to Guernsey by Thomas Porter in the spring of 1813 and remained in the family until the beginning of the twentieth century, when they were donated to various institutions in Canada and Guernsey.[11]

There was one last unresolved issue. Brock had a history of looking after old soldiers fallen on hard times and the families of men he had known who were in need. It seems that, in keeping with this, there was a young boy living under Brock's roof, probably in the care of his housekeeper,* whom

---

* Unnamed, but mentioned as having survived Brock until at least 1825 when she was reported as having met Mrs Jane Eliot (née McCrea) and shown her a piece of the shirt Brock wore on the day of his death, that she had cut off as a remembrance. Mrs Eliot to her sister in Guernsey dated 12 January 1825 in *Correspondence*, p. 243–244.

John Glegg was at pains to assure William Brock was no illegitimate son of the general.[12] The boy, whose Christian name is not recorded, seems to have been the only son of Captain Hercules Ellis of the 49th; he had been born in Montreal in 1803 and was therefore nine years old. Ellis had transferred to the 73rd Regiment in 1809 to obtain a captaincy but had been drowned at sea in 1810,[13] leaving a widow and this seven-year-old boy. The 73rd was at that time stationed in New South Wales, a desolate, harsh penal settlement unsuited for families, and Ellis probably left his wife and son in the Canadas until he could make arrangements for them at home. Brock had, it seems, taken the boy under his wing; Glegg, in turn, took care of the boy, placed him in "a good school" and made sure he was well looked after.[14] Ellis was an Irishman, probably from Fermanagh, and although it is hard to be completely certain, the Ellis family archives indicate that he may have been a relative of Edward Corry, Brock's opponent in the duel long ago in the Barbadoes. If so, this would be ironic indeed.

Isaac Brock and John Macdonell lay undisturbed throughout the occupation of Fort George by the Americans in 1813. During this time, on 20 July 1813, a marble monument was authorized by the Imperial Parliament, to be placed in St Paul's Cathedral in London. The contract was awarded to Richard Westmacott, a sculptor and officer of the Royal Artillery, who produced a bas-relief at the considerable cost of £1,575. It was mounted on the wall on the west side of the south transept, where it can still be seen along with monuments to Nelson and other Protestant heroes. Twelve thousand acres of land was granted by the Parliament of Upper Canada to Brock's four brothers, along with a pension of £200 a year each for life granted by the Imperial Parliament in Westminster. Savery travelled to Upper Canada in August 1817 to receive the land and was met everywhere by dinners, toasts and speeches in honour of his brother.

After the conclusion of the war, on 14 March 1815, the Provincial Parliament of Upper Canada passed an act, in the form of an address to the King, for the erection of a substantial monument to Brock. This would be supervised by three men who had been close to him in life: Robert Nichol, Thomas Clark and Thomas Dickson. The engineer Francis Hall was engaged and £1,000 voted for the project. On 13 October 1824 the monument, in the form of a tall circular column 135 feet tall, was completed on Queenston Heights.

Brock's memorial in St Paul's Cathedral, London. (Photograph by Robert Malcomson)

The remains of the two men were disinterred from Fort George, carried in solemn procession and reburied in a vault beneath the column. With its spiral internal staircase and viewing platform on the top, this was then the tallest memorial in North America. Here Brock rested undisturbed until Good Friday, 17 April 1840, when the Irish terrorist Benjamin Lett tried to blow up the column. Lett succeeded in blowing off the top of the monument, destroying the stairs and cracking the main structure – but not in dropping it. Francis Hall was adamant that he could repair the monument but official and private opinion was against him – indeed there was universal outrage at the attack. The damaged column remained standing until 1853 when the bodies of Brock and Macdonell were again exhumed and placed in temporary burial in a small private cemetery in Willowbank belonging to the Hamilton family. The damaged monument was demolished then; since it took three attempts with explosive charges to bring the structure down, Hall was probably right in his assessment. Its replacement was even grander: 185 feet tall and capped with a 16-foot-high statue of Brock. It was at that time the second tallest monument of its kind in the world, beaten

Brock's first monument on Queenston Heights. Note how the site was bare of trees. This monument was seriously damaged in a terrorist attack in 1840 and had to be demolished. (Detail of painting by Gardner D. Engleheart. Library and Archives Canada C-100116)

only by Wren's monument to the great fire in the City of London. The bodies of Brock and Macdonell were interred, for the fourth and final time, in the autumn of 1853.

Close by, at the base of the heights and just above Queenston village, a small cenotaph and a statue of the horse Alfred were erected in 1860, on the occasion of a visit by His Royal Highness Edward, Prince of Wales. In theory, these mark the place where Brock was killed, but the cenotaph is too far down the slope and says more about the Prince's ability to climb a steep slope than Brock's; nor is there any record of Alfred having been at Queenston, save a fanciful account published in 1859 claiming that Alfred was ridden by Macdonell.

There were other memorials too: articles, obituaries and laudatory citations in newspapers and journals, and poems by, among others, Ann Bruyères and Arendt DePeyster. In 1816 a private mint issued a memorial halfpenny coin, describing Brock as "The Hero of Upper Canada." To this day Brock's name is in everyday use in Canada: the towns of Brockville and Brock in Ontario, Brock in Saskatchewan; Brock University in St Catharines; General Brock Parkway as the name of Ontario Highway 405; and schools in Toronto, Guelph, Hamilton, London and Windsor are the most obvious examples, but most towns and cities, including the national capital, have their Brock Street or Brock Square. This is not the case in Britain, but on the island of Guernsey he was commemorated by an oak screen erected in the parish church of St Peter Port, dedicated by the Bishop of Winchester and bearing the simple inscription "Sir Isaac Brock, K.B. Who Saved Canada." The Brock house too is marked by a plaque. There at least, he is still remembered and commemorated in the small change of daily life, such as issues of stamps. His name is unknown now to most people in Britain, even in the British army, save among those military and regimental historians with a more than passing knowledge of the Napoleonic Wars.

Brock's second (present) monument on Queenston Heights is shown in a view from the late nineteenth century. There were more trees by this time, and today the site is heavily wooded. The monument, which belongs to Parks Canada, was closed for a number of years for repairs, but it has been reopened in time for the bicentennial of Brock's death, and visitors can once again climb to the top for a view of the battlefield and sweeping panoramas of the Niagara Peninsula. (Library of Congress)

The Brock house in St Peter Port, Guernsey, bears this plaque commemorating the famous Channel Islander who grew up here. (Photos by courtesy of Bob W. Scott)

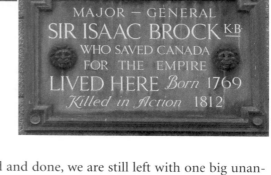

When all has been said and done, we are still left with one big unanswered question: how was it that that the general officer commanding all British and Canadian troops in Upper Canada met his death doing the job of a captain? Caution is always needed when examining judgments and decisions made in the past, with the benefit of hindsight. Whatever decision Brock made, he made according to the available information and exercising his own intuitive judgment. That information was bound to be partial and subjective and coloured by the responsibilities that he held. We, on the other hand, have a complete picture and none of the burden of responsibility. To criticise a commander like Brock is therefore not only futile, it is downright wrong. All that we can do is to examine how and why that decision was made.

This plaque, by the Archaeological and and Historic Sites Board of Ontario, is mounted on the wall of St Peter Port Church, Guernsey. (Photo by courtesy of Bob W. Scott)

In Brock's case he probably felt that there was some doubt over which side would win the race to build up forces fastest. If the Americans won it, they would be very difficult indeed to dislodge and therefore a rapid counter-attack, which might catch them unprepared and evict them, was a risk worth taking. His pride too would have been hurt: having been at one moment master of the situation, as he thought, and the next forced ignominiously to flee down the hillside, would scarcely have been conducive to rational thought. Then there is the matter of impulse. We know that Brock was impulsive and, as a commander, aggressive. He believed in offensive action. Thomas Evans remarked on this in his account of the events of 13 October, saying that "here you will recognize that impetuosity of disposition, that fixed untempered by discretion which characterized our fallen … general what a Pity a Mind so noble and generous had not possessed that prudence which might easily have saved his own valuable life."[15] Moreover, all that he had done that day, 12 October, had been impulsive from the moment he woke. Then, he was also at the head of men from his old regiment, the 49th, which had last gone into battle twelve years before, under his personal command; it would only have been human nature to forget that he was responsible for higher things and descend to a level of comfort.

Finally, there was the eternal need for the British officer to lead by example. As we discussed in the opening chapter of this book, in the British army of the late eighteenth and early nineteenth centuries, little was expected of an officer other than that he cared for the well-being of his men before he took care of himself, that he never lost control of the good order and discipline of those men, and above all that he was brave in the face of the enemy. Even a general was expected to show an example by placing himself at the head of his men: Lieutenant-General Sir John Moore was killed doing it at Corunna and Lieutenant-General Sir Thomas Picton at Waterloo.

It is well to remember that, including Brock, five British generals were killed in action or died of wounds during the year 1812, a total not out of place for the whole period of the Napoleonic War; the others were Major-General Barnard Foord Bowes at Salamanca, Major-General Robert Crauford at Ciudad Rodrigo, Major-General Henry Mackinnon at Ciudad Rodrigo and Major-General John Gaspard Le Marchant at Salamanca. Another nine were wounded in action.[*] Brock was certainly not lacking in courage but on Queenston Heights it may have edged into bravado. But his personal honour – which mattered far more than modern notions of morality in an officer – compelled him to lead the attack in person, rather than hand over the responsibility to a more junior officer. For Isaac Brock this was, therefore, a matter of honour.

---

[*] Brigadier-General William Maundy Harvey at Badajoz, Major-General James Kempt at Badajoz, Lieutenant-General James Leith at Salamanca, Major-General the Hon Galbraith Lowry Cole at Salamanca, Major-General Stapleton Cotton at Salamanca, Major-General John Ormsby Vandeleur at Ciudad Rodrigo, Major-General George Townsend Walker at Ciudad Rodrigo, Lieutenant-General William Carr Beresford at Salamanca and Brigadier-General John Downie while serving with Spanish troops in Seville. See John A. Hall, *A History of the Peninsular War, Volume VIII, The Biographical Dictionary of British Officers Killed and Wounded, 1808–1814* (London, 1998).

Endnotes

Abbreviations

CO	Colonial Office Papers in the National Archives (U.K.).
FO	Foreign Office Papers in the National Archives (U.K.).
LAC	Library and Archives Canada
TNA	The National Archives, Kew.
WO	War Office Papers in the National Archives.

Abbreviations used in references throughout the book. Abbreviations used in only one chapter are not cited here.

Correspondence	Ferdinand Brock Tupper, *The Life and Correspondence of Sir Isaac Brock* (Guernsey, 1845).
Cruikshank, *Documentary History*	*Documentary History of the Campaign upon the Niagara Frontier, 1812–1814*, ed. E.A. Cruikshank, (9 vols, Welland, 1896–1908).
Cruikshank, *Documents*	*Documents Relating to the Invasion of Canada and the Surrender of Detroit 1812*, ed. E.A. Cruikshank, (Ottawa, 1913).
District General Orders	*District General Orders of Maj.Gen. Sir Isaac Brock from June 27th, 1812–Oct. 16th, 1812.* Women's Canadian Historical Society of Toronto, Transaction No. 19.
Fitzgibbon	Mary Agnes Fitzgibbon. *A Veteran of 1812. The Life of James Fitzgibbon* (Toronto, 2000).
Richardson	John Richardson, *Richardson's War of 1812, with Notes and a Life of the Author by A.C. Casselman* (Toronto, 1902).

Chapter 1: "A Remarkable Fine Corps"

1. For more information see John Uttley, *The Story of the Channel Islands* (London, 1966).
2. For example Sir Bernard Burke, *The General Armoury of England, Scotland, Ireland and Wales* (London, 1884).
3. Ferdinand Brock Tupper, *The Life and Correspondence of Sir Isaac Brock* (Guernsey, 1845), p. 9 (hereafter *Correspondence).*
4. Ecclesiastical Court Records of Greffe 5/373 of 1777, Guernsey Museums and Galleries.
5. SPP tax lists cited by Dr Darryl Ogier and Richard Hocart, Guernsey Museums and Galleries.
6. *Correspondence,* op cit.
7. François Bernier (1625–1688), *Voyage dans les Etats du Grand Mogol* (Paris, 1663).
8. Details of the Brock family are set out in J.S. Brock to Lord Bathurst dated 28 November 1812 in TNA CO 43/353, Entry Books for 1812.
9. Quoted by Tupper in *Correspondence* and in "Isaac Brock – Saviour of Canada," *Historica Canadiana,* 27 (November 2006).
10. Prize-fighting was an obsession of British society at this time. For a comprehensive account, see Peter Radford, *The Celebrated Captain Barclay. Sport, Money and Fame in Regency Britain* (London, 2001).
11. Carey and McCance, *Regimental Records of the Royal Welch Fusiliers,* p. 185.
12. Colonel John Davis History *of the Second Queen's Royal Regiment, Vol. III, 1715–1799* (London, 1895) p. 203.

13. TNA WO 27/53–71 (Inspection Returns 1786–1791).
14. J.A. Houlding, *Fit for Service*, p. 124–127.
15. Richard Holmes, *Redcoat. The British Soldier in the Age of Horse and Musket* (London, 2001), p. 59.
16. Conversion rates of money from 1812 to modern day have been worked out using <www.eh.net/ ehresources/howmuch/poundq.php>.
17. Sir John Fortescue, *A History of the British Army. Volume 3, 1763-1793* (London, 1911), p. 522 et seq
18. Graves, *Dragon Rampant*, chapter 1.
19. I am indebted for much information in this section to Donald E. Graves in *Dragon Rampant: The Royal Welch Fusiliers at War, 1793–1815* (London, 2010). For a fuller explanation of the system of purchase see Major-General W.H. Anderson, *Outline of Development of the British Army Up to the commencement of the Great War, 1914: Notes for Four Lectures delivered at the Staff College, Camberley* (London, 1926).
20. J.A. Houlding, *Fit for Service: The Training of the British Army. 1715-1795 (Oxford, 1981) p. 100–102.
21. A.D.L. Carey and Stouppe McCance, *Regimental Records of the Royal Welch Fusiliers, Vol. 1 1689–1815* (London, 1921), appendix 2.
22. Graves, *Dragon Rampant*, chapter 1.
23. See, for example, Charles Dalton, *English Army Lists and Commission Registers, 1661–1714* (London, 1892).
24. Cited by Graves, *Dragon Rampant*, chapter 1, to whom I am obliged for much of the material in this section.
25. J.A. Houlding, *Fit for Service*, chapter I and appendix A,
26. See, for example, Mark Urban, *Fusiliers: Eight Years with the Redcoats in America* (London, 2007), chapters 23 and 24; Matthew H. Spring, *With Zeal and With Bayonets Only. The British Army on Campaign in North America, 1775–1783* (University of Oklahoma, 2008); Fortescue, Vol. III p. 530–533; Roger Lamb (23rd Fusiliers), *An Original and Authentic Journal of Occurrences during the Late American War, from Its Commencement to the Year 1783* (Dublin, 1809, reprinted New York, 1968); David Gates, *The British Light Infantry Arm c.1790–1815* (Batsford, 1987), chapter 1.
27. Mark Urban, *Fusiliers*, p. 308. See also Colonel David Dundas, *Principles of Military Movements, Chiefly Applied to the Infantry* (1788).
28. *The Manual Exercise with Explanations as ordered by His Majesty, 1778.*
29. *New Manual, and Platoon Exercise: with an Explanation. Published by Authority* (Dublin, 1764).
30. The 49th, which Brock joined in 1791, was discovered doing just this when inspected at Waterford in 1786. J.A. Houlding, *Fit for Service*, p. 229.
31. *Rules and regulations for the Field Exercise and Movements of the Army in Ireland* (Dublin, 1789).
32. *Rules and Regulations for the Formations, Field-Exercise, and Movements, of His Majesty's Forces* (1792); Graves, *Dragon Rampant*, chapter 1.
33. The conduct of this is laid down in *A New Manual and Platoon Exercise: With An Explanation. Published by Order of His Majesty: Edward Harvey, Adjutant General. August 1764.*
34. See especially *Rules and Articles For the better Government of His Majesty's Horse and Foot Guards, And all other His Forces in Great Britain and Ireland, Dominions Beyond the Seas, and Foreign Parts, From the 24th of March, 1762.*
35. Richard Holmes, p. 113–115. See also *Cuthbertson's System for the Complete Interior Management and Œconomy of a Battalion of Infantry, a New Edition, with Corrections* (Bristol, 1776).
36. Brendan Morrissey and Adam Hook, *Quebec 1775: The American Invasion of Canada*, (New York, 2003) p. 66-8.
37. *London Gazette* 12627, 5 March 1785.
38. Army Lists; TNA WO 27/56 (Inspection Return for 1795/6). See also the correspondence in WO 28/2, headquarters records of the 8th Foot and Field Officers' letters 1778–1782.
39. Army Lists; TNA WO 27/64 (Inspection Return for 1798).
40. Information supplied by various Masonic sources.
41. TNA WO 27/56 (Inspection Return for 1795/6).
42. The portrait, a miniature by Philip Jean of Jersey (1775–1802), was authenticated by Ludwig Kosche in "Contemporary Portraits of Isaac Brock: An Analysis" in *Archivaria* No. 20, Summer 1985,

p. 24. At that time, the portrait was in the possession of Captain M. H. T. Mellish of Guernsey and is now owned by the Museums and Galleries of Guernsey.

43. *Correspondence*, p. 9.

44. An inventory of Brock's estate survives, which lists his books. This is in the William Allen papers in Toronto Reference Library and is cited in Robert Malcomson, *Burying General Brock* (1996). Most of the books were bought by his successor in command, Major-General Roger Hale Sheaffe. Others were bought by his cousin, Captain James Brock, and his aide-de-camp, Captain John Glegg. See also Patricia Fleming, "The Library of Major-General Sir Isaac Brock" in *The Fife and Drum* (Newsletter of the Friends of Fort York and the Garrison Common), vol. 12 no. 1, March 2008.

45. TNA WO 27/59 (Inspection Return for 1787).

46. TNA WO 27/61 (Inspection Return for 1788).

47. TNA WO 27/64 (Inspection Return for 1789).

48. *London Gazette* 13166, 12 January 1790.

49. Richard Hocart, *Unpublished Notes on the de Havilland Letters*, Guernsey Island Achives.

50. TNA WO 27/63–71 gives the new or resurrected regiments, increases in establishments and the independent companies authorized.

51. TNA WO 27/71.

52. *London Gazette* 13278 dated 29 January 1791.

53. Army Lists 1798–1805.

54. TNA WO 3/10.

Chapter 2: "Be Sober, Be Ready"

1. Army Lists.

2. TNA WO 27/46 (Inspection Returns 1780).

3. Matthew H Spring, *With Zeal and With Bayonets Only*, p. 86; Army Lists.

4. Spring, *With Zeal and With Bayonets Only*, pp. 86, 99–101.

5. Spring, *With Zeal and With Bayonets Only*, p. 239.

6. Thomas Sullivan (49th Foot), *From Redcoat to Rebel: The Thomas Sullivan Journal*. Ed J. L. Boyle (Heritage, 1997).

7. Army Lists.

8. TNA WO 27/53 (Inspection Returns, Irish Establishment, 1784).

9. TNA WO 27/58 (Inspection Returns, Irish Establishment, 1787).

10. J.P. Riley, "Continuity in the English Army, 1658–1668" (Unpublished MA Thesis, Leeds University, 1989).

11. Karl Weston, *Slavery and Economy in Barbados* (B.B.C. on-line website article, 2009).

12. TNA WO 27/71 (Inspection Returns, England and Abroad, 1787).

13. Tupper, p. 9; D. B. Read, *Life and Times of Sir Major-General Sir Isaac Brock* (London, 1894); D. J. Goodspeed, *The Good Soldier. The Story of Isaac Brock* (London, 1965), p. 12.

14. *Rules and Articles For the better Government of His Majesty's Horse and Foot Guards, And all other His Forces in Great Britain and Ireland, Dominions Beyond the Seas, and Foreign Parts, From the 24th of March, 1762, Section VIII.*

15. Army Lists.

16. Edmund Burke, *Reflections on the Revolution in France* (London, 1791).

17. F. Lorraine Petrie, *History of the Royal Berkshire Regiment (Princess Charlotte of Wales's)* (Reading, 1925), p. 51.

18. C. L. R. James, The *Black Jacobins: Toussaint l'Ouverture and the San Domingo Revolution* (London, 1963).

19. Roger Norman Buckley, *The British Army and the West Indies: Society and the Military in the Revolutionary Age* (University of Florida, 1998); Michael Duffy, *Soldiers, Sugar and Seapower: The British Expeditions to the West Indies and the War Against Revolutionary France* (Oxford, 1987).

20. Petrie, *History*, p. 53.

21. Petrie, *History*, p. 59.

22. National Health Service (Great Britain) on-line information on infectious and communicable diseases.

23. Uttley, *Story of the Channel Islands*, p. 154.
24. *London Gazette* 13790, dated 23 June 1795.
25. Petrie, *History*, p. 60–61.
26. Petrie, *History*, p. 61.
27. *London Gazette* 14059, dated 24 October 1797.
28. Ferdinand Brock Tupper, *The Life and Correspondence of Sir Isaac Brock* (Guernsey, 1845), p. 10.
29. TNA WO 17/162.
30. TNA WO 17/162; the monthly return for 1 April 1798 shows Brock as commanding the Regiment for the first time, with Sheaffe as the junior Lieutenant-Colonel.
31. See Conrad Gill, *The Naval Mutinies of 1797* (Manchester, 1913).
32. See, for example, Thomas Bartlett, Kevin Dawson and Daire Keogh, *Rebellion* (Dublin 1998).
33. Pamphlet held in the Archives of the Royal Welch Fusiliers, Caernarfon.
34. *Correspondence*, p. 10.
35. Petrie, *History*, p. 62–64.

Chapter 3: "Ever Glorious to the 49th"

1. A Supplementary Militia Act had been passed in 1795 (26 Geo. III C.107) and in 1798, English and Welsh militiamen were given the option of enlisting into regular regiments with a bounty of £10. In 1799, 15,000 Irish militiamen volunteered for the regular army. See J. R. Western *The English Militia in the Eighteenth Century* (London, 1965), p. 221 *et seq*; and J. E. Cookson *The British Armed Nation 1793–1805* (OUP, 1997).
2. Petrie, *History*, p. 65.
3. For a full account of the campaign see S. Schama, *Patriots and Liberators. Revolution in the Netherlands 1780-1813* (New York, 1977).
4. Mary Agnes Fitzgibbon *A Veteran of 1812. The Life of James Fitzgibbon* (Toronto, 2000), p. 24–25.
5. FitzGibbon, p. 25.
6. *Correspondence*, p. 11.
7. *Correspondence*, p. 12.
8. *Correspondence*, p. 12.
9. *Correspondence*, p. 12–13.
10. *Correspondence*, p. 14.
11. Fitzgibbon, p. 26.
12. *Correspondence*, p. 14.
13. *Correspondence*, p. 14.
14. *Correspondence*, p. 14.
15. Fitzgibbon, p. 31.
16. *Correspondence*, p. 14–15.
17. *The New Annual Register* 1799, p. 143.
18. *Correspondence*, p. 15.
19. *Correspondence*, p. 15.
20. C. R. T. Krayenhoff, *Geschiedkundige Beschouwing van den Oorlog op het grondgebied der Bataafsche Republiek in 1799* (Amsterdam, 1832). Krayenhoff was at this time commanding the Batavian engineers and pioneers and played a substantial part in flooding low-lying areas and preparing defences.
21. Petrie, p. 76.

Chapter 4: "An Immediate and Vigorous Attack"

1. Petrie, p. 76.
2. *Correspondence*, p. 17.
3. Fitzgibbon, p. 33.
4. *Correspondence*, p. 17.
5. Fitzgibbon, p. 36.
6. An excellent account of the battle is in Tom Pocock, *Horatio Nelson* (London, 1987); see also Dudley Pope, *The Great Gamble: Nelson at Copenhagen* (London, 1972).

7. *Correspondence*, p. 18.
8. Memoir of the expedition by Captain Birkenhead Glegg of the 49th, cited in Petrie, *History* p. 78–80.

Chapter 5: "Nothing Should be Impossible for a Soldier"

1. R. B. Mowatt, *The Diplomacy of Napoleon* (London, 1924), p. 88.
2. Felix Markham, *Napoleon* (London, 1963), p. 143; Clive Emsley *State, Economy and Nation in 19th Century Europe* (London, 1996), p. 123-33.
3. Paul Fregosi, *Dreams of Empire: Napoleon and the First World War, 1792–1815* (London, 1991), p. 221.
4. Mason Wade, *The French Canadians* (Toronto, 1975), p. 99.
5. TNA CO 42/98, Milnes to Earl Camden, Secretary for War and the Colonies dated 27 July 1805.
6. An excellent survey of the geography, history and military significance of the St Lawrence system is contained in John Grodzinski, "The Vigilant Superintendence of the Whole District: The War of 1812 on the Upper St Lawrence," Unpublished M.A. Thesis, R.M.C. Canada, 2002.
7. Details of the history and construction of the St Lawrence Seaway are available at the Great Lakes/St Lawrence Seaway System website at <http://www.seaway.ca>.
8. Brock to his brothers dated July 1803 in W. R. Wilson, *Historical Narratives of Early Canada* (2009).
9. Petrie, *History*, p. 83.
10. Ruth Mackenzie, *James Fitzgibbon. Defender of Upper Canada* (Toronto, 1983), p. 19–21.
11. Mackenzie, p 20.
12. Brock to Major James Green dated 2 December 1803 in LAC RG 8 I/922; the charge sheet for their court-martial is dated 1 October 1803 and is in LAC RG 68 I/922.
13. Sheaffe to Major James Green dated 13 August 1803 in LAC RG 68 I/922.
14. Testimony of – Private 49th Regiment dated 14 August 1803 in LAC RG 68 I/922.
15. Read, p. 18.
16. *Correspondence*, p. 21.
17. Petrie, *History*, p. 84; the full details are in Sheaffe's charge sheets and a report from the *Quebec Gazette* in Library and Archives Canada (LAC) RG 68 I/922. There is one man unaccounted for in the total of nineteen, who presumably received a lesser sentence.
18. *Correspondence*, p. 22.
19. Brock to unknown recipient, probably Green, dated 2 April 1804 in LAC RG 88 I/923.
20. Brock to Lieutenant-Colonel James Green dated 8 February 1804 in LAC RG 68 I/923.
21. Brock to Lieutenant-Colonel James Green dated 8 February 1804 in LAC RG 68 I/923.
22. Brock to Lieutenant-Colonel James Green dated 8 February 1804 in LAC RG 68 I/923.
23. Archives of Ontario, F.B. Tupper Papers: Fitzgibbon to Tupper dated 12 September 1846.
24. Tupper Papers: Fitzgibbon to Tupper dated 12 September 1846.
25. Army Lists.
26. FitzGibbon, p. 57.
27. *Dictionary of Canadian Biography*.
28. *London Gazette* 15856 dated 29 October 1805.

Chapter 6: "The Most Volatile and Easily Led Astray"

1. *Correspondence of the Emperor Napoleon*, no. 11281 dated 19.xi.1806 and 11283 dated 21.xi.1806.
2. *Correspondence of the Emperor Napoleon*, no. 13391 dated 17.xii.1807.
3. Markham, p. 143
4. David Chandler, *Dictionary of the Napoleonic Wars* (London, 1979), p. 100.
5. The Orders are printed in *Hansard*, x. pp.126-48.
6. *Correspondence*, p. 23.
7. *Correspondence*, p. 23.
8. TNA WO 27/90 (Inspection Return 1806).
9. Lord Dorchester to Simcoe dated 7 October 1793 in E.A. Cruikshank, ed, *The Correspondence of Lieut. Governor John Graves Simcoe, Vol II, 1794–1795*, E.A. Cruikshank, ed., (Toronto: Ontario Historical Society, 1924), p. 84.

10. Simcoe to Dorchester dated 2 December 1793 in Cruickshank, *Simcoe Papers, Vol II*, p. 112.
11. TNA WO 27/190 (Inspection Return 1806).
12. Army Lists; TNA WO 27/90 (Inspection Return 1806).
13. TNA WO 27/190 (Inspection Return 1806).
14. *Correspondence*, p. 22.
15. *Correspondence*, p. 23.
16. J. Mackay Hitsman, *The Incredible War of 1812* (Toronto, 1999), p. 14.
17. Army Lists.
18. Regimental Standing Orders, 10th Royal Veterans, p. 12–13 from *The Discriminating General* website, 1997.
19. Letter Macdonell to Brock dated 28 January 1807, cited in *Correspondence*, p. 29.
20. TNA CO 42/102, Brock to Windham dated 12 February 1807.
21. TNA CO42/107, Craig to Castlereagh dated 31 May 1808.
22. Grodzinski, chapter 1.
23. Edwin C. Guillet, *Pioneer Travel in Upper Canada* (Toronto, 1933), pp. 133, 134, 162.
24. Guillet, p. 52. The conversion is calculated using the formula in the website http://www.eh.net/ehresources/howmuch/poundq.php.
25. Supplementary Militia Act 1794 passed by Sir George Simcoe, Lieutenant-Governor of Upper Canada. TNA CO 42/318 dated 23 February 1794.
26. Ross Mackenzie to Lieutenant-Colonel James Green, 4 August 1807 in NAC RG 8 C I Volume 725, p. 83.
27. George F. G. Stanley, *The War of 1812. Land Operations* (Toronto, 1983), p. 75.
28. Harry L. Coles *The War of 1812* (Chicago, 1965), p. 110.
29. TNA CO 42/99, Letter from Chatham to Camden dated 5 July 1805. This encloses a report on the defences dated 14 March 1805.
30. TNA CO 42/106-2, Concurrence of the Board of Ordnance to Brock's proposals dated 28 May 1807.
31. TNA CO 42/104, Brock to Dunn dated 17 July 1807.
32. TNA CO 42/104, Report of the Council dated 25 July 1807.
33. The general foot-dragging by Dunn and the council is summed up in Brock's complaint to Castlereagh in CO 42/104 dated 5 August 1807.
34. *Correspondence*, p. 29.
35. TNA CO 42/102, Brock to Dunn dated 8 May 1807; Dunn to Windham dated 10 May 1807.
36. TNA CO 42/104, Dunn to Windham dated 6 June 1807.
37. TNA CO 42/102, Windham to Brock, dated 8 August 1807.
38. TNA CO 42/102, Castlereagh to Dunn, dated 8 August 1807.
39. *Correspondence*, p. 35.
40. *Correspondence*, p. 31.
41. *Correspondence*, p. 31.
42. TNA CO 42/98, 1 August 1805.
43. TNA CO 42/98, Letter from Milnes authorizing the issue of arms from the magazine in Quebec.
44. *Correspondence*, p. 32.
45. TNA CO 42/104, Brock to Dunn dated 18 August 1807.
46. TNA CO 42/104, Order dated 20 August 1807 and additional order in French dated 9 September 1807.
47. *Quebec Mercury*, 31 August 1807.
48. TNA CO 42/104 Dunn to Castlereagh dated 15 September 1807.
49. TNA CO 42/106-1, Craig to Castlereagh dated 9 November 1807.
50. TNA CO 42/104, Dunn to Windham dated 10 May 1807.
51. Craig's commission from Castlereagh appointing him Captain-General and Governor-in-Chief of Upper and Lower Canada is dated 31 August 1807. TNA CO 42/104.

Chapter 7: "Craig's Reign of Terror"

1. *Correspondence*, p. 31.

2. TNA CO 42/106-1, Craig to Castlereagh dated 9 November 1807.

3. Stuart Sutherland, ed, *"A Desire of Serving and Defending my Country": The War of 1812 Journals of William Hamilton Merritt* (Toronto, 2001).

4. *Correspondence*, p. 41.

5. Hitsman, *The Incredible War of 1812*, p. 19.

6. TNA CO 42/106, Craig to Castlereagh dated 9 November 1807.

7. Hitsman, *The Incredible War of 1812*, p. 19.

8. TNA CO 42/107; Tupper, p. 49.

9. Craig to Gore dated 6 December 1807 in TNA CO 42/136, p. 154.

10. TNA, CO 42/136, Craig to Gore dated 6 December 1807 and Gore's reply dated 5 January 1808.

11. TNA CO 42/107, Despatch to Craig dated 22 January 1808.

12. TNA CO 42/107, Harrison to Craig dated 4 February 1808.

13. Gore to Craig dated 5 January 1808 in CO 42/136.

14. *Correspondence*, p. 51.

15. See especially Wade, *The French Canadians*, p. 110.

16. G. Lanctôt, "Les Colonies américains 1760–1820" *in Les Canadiens français et leurs voisins du sud* (Montreal, 1941), p. 131.

17. Brock to Irving dated 19 February 1811 in *Correspondence*, p. 53.

18. *Correspondence*, p. 34.

19. *Correspondence*, p. 34.

20. *Correspondence*, p. 40.

21. TNA WO 27/102 (inspection Return for 1810).

22. Robert Henderson, "Captains of the Canadian Fencibles in 1812," *War of 1812 website* (1997).

23. *Correspondence*, p. 39.

24. Thornton to Brock dated 4 October 1810, in *Correspondence*, p. 45–46.

25. *Correspondence*, p. 41.

26. Michael Smith, *A Geographical View of the Province of Upper Canada and Promiscuous Remarks on the Government etc* (Boston, 1813).

27. Brock to Irving dated 19 February 1811 in *Correspondence*, p. 53.

28. The strength of the garrisons and militia are given in Prevost's despatch to Lord Liverpool dated 18 May 1812, in TNA CO 42/146.

29. *Correspondence*, p. 43.

30. Kempt to Brock dated 17 January 1811 in *Correspondence*, p. 50–51.

31. *Correspondence*, p. 52.

32. Walter R. Nursey, *The Story of Isaac Brock* (Toronto, 1908).

33. See especially Robert Malcomson, "Picturing Isaac Brock" in *The Beaver*, 1 October 2004.

34. Glegg to William Brock dated 14 October 1812 in Cruikshank, *Documentary History,* iv, 83.

35. Vesey to Brock dated 9 April 1811 in *Correspondence,* p. 58.

36. J. R. Robertson, *The History of Freemasonry in Canada from its Introduction in 1749* (Toronto, 1899).

37. *Thornton* to Brock dated 4 October 1810, in *Correspondence*, p. 45.

38. WO 23/147, British Army Pension Records, Colonies.

39. *Correspondence*, p. 44.

40. Baynes to Brock dated 11 October 1810 in *Correspondence*, p. 46.

41. Kempt to Brock dated 17 January 1811 in *Correspondence*, p. 50–51.

42. Vesey to Brock dated 9 May 1811 in *Correspondence*, p. 59.

43. TNA CO 42/107, Gore to Craig dated 8 April 1808.

44. Gore to William Claus, Deputy Superintendant of Indian Affairs dated 20 February 1811 in TNA CO 42/314; see also Craig's "Secret and Confidential Information and Future Guidance" dated 4 February 1811 and cited in Brock to Taylor, *Correspondence*, p. 55.

45. *Correspondence*, p. 54.

46. Craig's "Secret and Confidential Information and Future Guidance".

47. Brock to Craig dated 27 February 1811, in *Correspondence*, p. 54.

48. Brock to Taylor dated 4 March 1811, in *Correspondence* p. 55–56.

49. Baynes to Brock dated 4 March 1811, in *Correspondence* p. 57–58.

50. No *London Gazette* entry for his promotion can be found; however the letter of authority is dated 18 June 1811 in TNA CO 42/30.

Chapter 8: "The Fittest Person"

1. *Annals of Congress: Debates and Proceedings in the Congress of the United States, 1789–1834* (42 vols, Washington, 1834–1836), 12th Congress, Session 11.

2. Gore to Craig dated 13 July 1811 in TNA CO 42/131.

3. The General Order was dated 14 September 1811 in TNA CO 42/1168. This was followed by a set of instructions from the Prince Regent dated 17 September 1811. For confirmation of the implementation see Prevost to Lord Liverpool dated 28 September 1811 in TNA CO 42/172.

4. Prevost to Lord Liverpool dated 24 September 1811 in TNA CO 42/114.

5. Brock to Lord Liverpool dated 9 October 1811 in TNA CO 42/314.

6. Drummond to Brock dated 31 August 1811 in *Correspondence*, p. 64.

7. Army Lists.

8. Brock to Irving dated 30 October 1811 in Correspondence, p. 113. For a full examination of Brock's uniforms see Ludwig Kosche, 'Relics of Brock: An Investigation' in *Archivaria* No 9 (1 January 1979), p. 33–103.

9. Thornton to Baynes dated 2 August 1811 in *Correspondence*, p. 63.

10. Torrens to Brock dated 17 October 1811, in *Correspondence*, p. 65–66.

11. *Dictionary of Canadian Biography Online.*

12. See especially Lanctôt, "Les Colonies américains 1760–1820" in *Les Canadiens français et leurs voisins du sud,* p. 135.

13. Thomas R. Berger, *A Long and Terrible Shadow: White Values, Native Rights in the Americas, 1492–1992* (Vancouver, 1992), p. 62.

14. J. R. Miller, *Skyscrapers Hide the Heavens: A History of Indian-White Relations in* Canada (Toronto, 1989), p. 73.

15. Miller, p. 76.

16. An account of this action is in E. A. Cruikshank, ed., *Documents Relating to the Invasion of Canada and the Surrender of Detroit 1812,* (Ottawa, 1913), p. 6–7.

17. Brock to Lord Liverpool dated 25 May 1812 in Cruikshank, *Documents,* p. 27.

18. For more detail see Carl Benn, *The Iroquois in the War of 1812* (Toronto, 1998), p. 39–42.

19. John Norton, "The Journal of Major John Norton, 1816" in *The Publications of the Champlain Society* (Toronto, 1970), p. 288.

20. "Journal of Major John Norton," p. 290 - 291.

21. D. E. Graves and John Grodzinski, *The War of 1812 in the Niagara Peninsula.* Background study for a battlefield tour, 28–30 June 2007.

22. For a fuller discussion see J. P. Riley, *Napoleon and the World War of 1813* (London, 1998), chapter II and part 5.

23. See Miller, p. 62 for a description of the aboriginal way of war.

24. Gore's fullest explanation for this is in his letter to Castlereagh dated 26 November 1809 in TNA CO 42/312.

25. D. E. Graves, "Joseph Willcocks and the Canadian Volunteers," M.A. Thesis, Carleton University (Ottawa, 1982), p. 22.

26. Brock to Prevost, February 1812, in *Correspondence*, p. 86.

27. Upper Canada Militia Act in Cruikshank *Documents,* p. 27.

28. Brock to Butler dated 8 April 1812, cited in Hitsman, p. 40.

29. Militia General Order dated 12 April 1812 in *York Gazette* dated 8 May 1812.

30. Brock to Baynes dated 12 February 1812 in Cruikshank *Documentary History* II, p. 39.

31. Brock to Lord Liverpool dated 23 March 1812 in TNA CO 42/315.

32. Brock's address cited in Graves, "Joseph Willcocks," p. 23.

33. *Correspondence*, p. 129.

Chapter 9: "A System Strictly Defensive"

1. Economic History Association <www.eh.net/ehresources/howmuch/poundq.php>.
2. For more details see *London Gazette* No 16584 dated 17 March 1812.
3. Brock to Savery dated 7 October 1811 in D. J. Goodspeed, *The Good Soldier*, p. 60.
4. Irving to Brock dated 3 August 1811 in Goodspeed, *The Good Soldier*, p. 60.
5. William to Brock undated in Wood, *Select British Documents*, i, 21.
6. Brock to Irving dated 30 August 1811in Goodspeed, *The Good Soldier*, p. 61.
7. Ridout to unknown recipient dated 18 December 1811 in Lady Matilda Edgar, *General Brock* (Toronto, 1904), p. 168.
8. "Report upon the Provincial Marine Establishment in Upper Canada" by Captain A. Gray, Acting Deputy Quartermaster General, 24 February 1812, NAC RG 8 Volume 728, p. 86 –93.
9. Gray to Prevost, 29 January 1812 in NAC RG 8 I Volume 728, p. 78.
10. Brock to Prevost dated 2 December 1811 in *Correspondence*, p. 67–71.
11. Prevost to Lord Liverpool dated 2 January 1812 in TNA CO 42/117.
12. Baynes to Brock, dated 12 December 1811 in *Correspondence*, p. 73.
13. Baynes to Brock, dated 24 December 1811 in *Correspondence*, p. 74.
14. Brock to Prevost dated 11 December 1811 in *Correspondence*, p. 72 - 73.
15. Evans to Procter dated 22 October 1812 in Malcolmson, *Brilliant Affair*, p. 197–198.
16. TNA CO 42/23, the Prince Regent's Instructions to Prevost dated 22 October 1811.
17. Prevost to Brock, dated 24 December 1811, in *Correspondence*, p. 74–75.
18. Prevost to Lord Liverpool dated 18 May 1812 in TNA CO 42/146, p. 197–202.
19. Prevost to Lord Bathurst dated 27 August 1814 in George F. G. Stanley, *The War of 1812. Land Operations* (Toronto, 1983), p. 240.
20. Prevost to Lord Liverpool dated 18 May 1812 in TNA CO 42/146.
21. Captain Andrew Gray to Prevost dated 13 January 1812 in Cruikshank, *Documents*, p. 9.
22. Gray to Prevost dated 13 January 1812 in Cruikshank, *Documents*, p. 9 - 10; Memoranda on the Defensive Strength and Equipment of the North West Company in Cruikshank, *Documents*, p. 11–12.
23. Prevost to Brock dated 31 March 1812 in TNA CO 42/117.
24. George Raudzens, " 'Red George' Macdonell, Military Savior of Upper Canada?" in *Ontario History*, vol LXII, no. 4, pp. 199, 207.
25. Hitsman, p. 41.
26. For example, 9 March 1812, 20 April 1812, 27 May 1812.
27. "Journal of Major John Norton, 1816" in *Publications of the Champlain Society* (Toronto, 1970), p. 286.
28. Baynes to Brock, dated 23 January 1812 in *Correspondence*, p. 79.
29. Brock to Prevost dated 28 February 1812 in TNA CO 42/1218.
30. Approved by an Order in Council by Prevost and transmitted to London 19 May 1812 in TNA CO 42/315.
31. For example on 25 May 1812. Cruikshank, *Documents*, p. 28.
32. Brock to Prevost dated 25 February 1812 in Cruikshank, *Documents*, p. 17.
33. TNA CO 42/116; 42/1218.
34. TNA CO 42/329.
35. Brock to Prevost, 15 May 1812 in Cruikshank, *Documents*, p. 25.
36. Brock to Prevost in TNA CO 42/315.
37. Prevost to Lord Liverpool dated 3 April 1812 in TNA CO 42/117.
38. Brock to Prevost dated 16 May 1812 in *Correspondence*, p. 99.
39. For a fuller discussion on this see J. P. Riley, *Decisive Battles* (London, 2010), chapter 1 and *Napoleon as a General* (London, 2007), chapter 1.

Chapter 10: "Mr Madison's War"

1. Rory Muir, *Britain and the Defeat of Napoleon, 1807–1815* (Yale, 1996), p. 232–233, provides an excellent and balanced summary of the dispute.
2. "Declaration of War by the United States" in the *Annual Register, or a View of the History, Politics,*

and Literature for the Year 1812, vol 54, p. 342 dated 18 June 1812 (London, 1822–1825).

3. Foster to Castlereagh, 20 June 1812 in TNA FO 5/86.

4. The *Annual Register, or a View of the History, Politics and Literature for the Year 1811*.

5. Stanley, *The War of 1812: Land Operations*. (Toronto, 1983), p. 49.

6. Alan Lloyd, *The Scorching of Washington – The War of 1812* (New York, 1975), p. 30.

7. Graves and Grodzinski, *The War of 1812 in the Niagara Peninsula*. Background study for a battlefield tour, 28–30 June 2007.

8. See William Duane, *Hand Book for Infantry* (Applewood, 2009) for more detail.

9. Muir, *Britain and the Defeat of Napoleon*, p. 234, characterises the U.S. government's decision to go to war as "stark folly."

10. *Dispatches of the Duke of Wellington*, vol ix, p. 525–6.

11. Secretary of State for War to Dearborn dated 26 June 1812 in Cruikshank, *Documents*, p. 40.

12. Cruikshank, *Documentary History*, i, 1–3.

13. Hull to the Secretary of War dated 6 March 1812 in Cruikshank, *Documents*, p. 20.

14. Hull to the Secretary of War dated 6 March 1812 in Cruikshank, *Documents*, p. 21.

15. Cruikshank, *Documents*, p. 1–3.

16. Hull to the Secretary of War dated 6 March 1812 in Cruikshank, *Documents*, p. 22.

17. Carl-Maria von Clausewitz, *Vom Krieg* (*On War*), translated by J.J. Graham (London, 1873), chapter VII – "Friction in War."

Chapter 11: "A Force Which Will Look Down All Opposition"

1. Prevost to Lord Liverpool dated 1 June 1812 in TNA CO 42/117.

2. Prevost to Lord Liverpool dated 29 June 1812 in TNA CO 42/118.

3. Prevost to Brock dated 27 July 1812 in Cruikshank, *Documents*, p. 98.

4. Baynes to Brock dated 21 May 1812 in *Correspondence*, p. 100.

5. Prevost to Lord Liverpool dated 15 July1812 in TNA CO 42/118.

6. Figures are compiled from WO 17/1516, monthly returns for 25 May 1812 and CO 42/118, Prevost to Lord Bathurst dated 24 August 1812.

7. Army Lists 1812.

8. District General Orders dated 2 July 1812 in *District General Orders of Maj.-Gen. Sir Isaac Brock from June 27th, 1812–Oct. 16th, 1812.* (Women's Canadian Historical Society of Toronto, Transaction No. 19).

9. Brock to Prevost undated, in Cruikshank, *Documents*, p. 12–14.

10. Baynes to Brock dated 19 March 1812 in *Correspondence*, p. 90.

11. Brock to Prevost, 3 July 1812 in *Correspondence*, p. 111.

12. District General Orders dated 9 July 1812.

13. District General Orders dated 27 June 1812.

14. Brock to Prevost, 3 July 1812 in *Correspondence*, p. 117.

15. Secretary of War to Hull dated 18 June 1812, in Cruikshank, *Documents*, p. 35.

16. Strength Return dated 27 June 1812 in Cruikshank, *Documents*, p. 39.

17. Cruikshank, *Documents*, p. 39.

18. Brock to Prevost dated 3 July 1812 in *Correspondence*, p. 111; Prevost to Lord Liverpool dated 15 July1812 in TNA CO 42/118.

19. Prevost to Brock dated 10 July 1812, in *Correspondence*, p. 115.

20. Captain M.C. Dixon to Bruyères dated 8 July 1812 in Cruikshank, *Documents*, p. 48.

21. Captain M.C. Dixon to Bruyères dated 8 July 1812 in Cruikshank, Documents, p. 48.

22. The Prince Regent confirmed Macdonell's appointment on 14 October 1812. TNA CO 42/315.

23. Brock to Prevost dated 28 July 1812 in Cruikshank, *Documents*, p. 99.

24. Speech by Brock on opening the Legislature, in Cruikshank, *Documents*, p. 196.

25. Brock to Prevost dated 29 July 1812 in Cruikshank, *Documents*, p. 104.

26. *Upper Canada Guardian*, 9 June 1812.

27. Minutes of the Executive Council of Upper Canada, 3 August 1812, in Cruikshank, *Documents*, p. 196–197.

28. Brock to Baynes dated 29 July 1812 in Cruikshank, *Documents*, p. 106.
29. Hull to the Secretary of War dated 13 July 1812 in Cruikshank, *Documents*, p. 57.
30. St George to Brock dated 15 July 1812 in Cruikshank, *Documents*, p. 61.
31. Proclamation by Brigadier-General Hull, Sandwich, 13 July 1812 in Cruikshank, *Documents*, p. 58–59.
32. St George to Brock dated 21 July 1812 in TNA CO 42/676.
33. John Sugden, *Tecumseh*, p. 283.
34. District General Orders dated 16 July 1812.
35. Brock to Prevost dated 20 July 1812 in TNA CO 42/676.
36. Brock to Lord Bathurst dated 29 August 1812 in Cruikshank, *Documents*, p. 190.
37. Hitsman, *The Incredible War of 1812*, p. 70.
38. Hull to Eustis dated 9 July 1812 in Hitsman, *The Incredible War of 1812*, p. 70.
39. Elliott to Claus dated 15 July 1812 in Cruikshank, *Documents*, p. 61.
40. See the account in Cass's despatch to Hull in Cruikshank, *Documents*, p. 71, and James Baby's account to Glegg in *ibid*, p. 95.
41. Cruikshank, *Documents*, p. 81–83.
42. Militia General Order dated 22 July 1812.
43. Brock to Prevost dated 26 July 1812 in Cruikshank, *Documents*, p. 91.
44. Procter to Brock dated 26 July 1812 in Cruikshank, *Documents*, p. 89.
45. Roberts to Brock dated 27 June 1812 in Cruikshank, Documents, p. 53.
46. Roberts to Glegg dated 29 July 1812 in Cruikshank, Documents, p. 101.
47. See the account by Toussaint Pothier in Cruikshank, *Documents*, p. 214–216.
48. Cruikshank, *Documents*, pp. 17, 53, 54, 55.
49. Roberts to Baynes, 17 July 1812 in Cruikshank, *Documents*, p, 65.
50. Hanks to Hull, 4 August 1812 in Cruikshank, *Documents*, p. 67–68.
51. The Articles of Capitulation are in Cruikshank, *Documents*, p. 63–64 and were transmitted to Brock immediately. He sent them on to Prevost on 29 July 1812.
52. Roberts to Baynes, dated 17 July 1812 in Cruikshank, *Documents*, p. 65.
53. Brock to Prevost dated 29 July 1812 in Cruikshank, *Documents*, p. 103–104.
54. District General Orders dated 31 July 1812 in Cruikshank, *Documents*, p. 112.
55. Prevost to Brock dated 12 August 1812 in *Correspondence*, p. 142.
56. Brock to Prevost dated 26 July 1812 in TNA CO 42/676.
57. D. E. Graves, "Joseph Willcocks and the Canadian Volunteers," p. 28.
58. Willcocks to Macdonell dated 1 September 1812 in Cruikshank, *Documentary History*, i, 209–211.
59. Hull to the Secretary of War dated 4 August 1812 in Cruikshank, *Documents*, p. 116.
60. Procter to Brock dated 11 August 1812 in Cruikshank, *Documents*, p. 136.
61. Hull to the Secretary of War dated 7 August 1812 in Cruikshank, *Documents*, p. 125. See also John Richardson, *War of 1812. First Series* (reprinted Memphis, Tennessee, 2010), p. 6–7.

Chapter 12: "A More Sagacious Warrior"
1. Glegg to Baynes dated 5 August 1812 in Cruikshank, *Documents*, p. 122.
2. Prevost to Brock dated 12 August 1812 in *Correspondence*, p. 141.
3. District General Orders dated 1 August 1812.
4. Prevost to Brock dated 31 July 1812 in Cruikshank, *Documents*, p. 113.
5. Brock to Irving dated 3 September 1812 in *Correspondence*, p. 170.
6. District General Orders dated 19 August 1812.
7. Baynes to Brock dated 1 August 1812 in *Correspondence*, p. 139.
8. WO 17/1516, monthly returns dated 25 May 1812; CO 42/118, Prevost to Lord Bathurst dated 24 August 1812; Return of the Newfoundland Fencibles dated 1 July 1812 in E.A. Cruikshank, "Record of the Services of Canadian Regiments in the War of 1812, No1, The Royal Newfoundland Regiment," in *Canadian Military Institute, Selected Papers, No 5 (1893–1894)*, p. 5–15. These give the strength of the rank and file, without officers, NCOs, drummers and so on, as 2,442.
9. F. Lorraine Petrie, *History*, p. 86.
10. Glenn A. Steppler, "A Duty Troublesome Beyond Measure: Logistical Considerations in the Ca-

nadian War of 1812." Unpublished M.A. Thesis, McGill University, 1974, p. 270.

11. Richard Glover, *Peninsular Preparation: The Reform of the British Army, 1795–1809*, (Cambridge, 1963), Annexes A and B.

12. Adjutant-General Dundas to Simcoe dated 20 June 1794 in Cruikshank, *Simcoe Papers* II, p. 80.

13. Monthly Returns, Return of the General and Staff Officers at Present Serving in British North America dated 25 January 1812 in TNA WO 17/1516, pp. 1, 2.

14. Steppler, pp. 30–33, 40, 41.

15. TNA WO 17/1516, p. 2.

16. Alfred Sayer Mahan, *The Influence of Sea Power upon History 1660–1783* (New York, 1890), vol I, p. 349, cited in Hitsman, *The Incredible War of 1812*, p. 70.

17. Cited in John Sugden, *Tecumseh*, p. 286.

18. Dearborn to the Secretary of War dated 9 August 1812 in Cruikshank, *Documents*, p. 127.

19. Hull to the Secretary of War dated 8 August 1812 in Cruikshank, *Documents*, p. 126.

20. Macdonell to Duncan Cameron dated 10 August 1812 in Cruikshank, *Documents*, p. 130.

21. John Richardson, *Richardson's War of 1812, with Notes and a Life of the Author by A.C. Casselman* (Toronto, 1902), p. 13.

22. Macdonell to Duncan Cameron dated 10 August 1812 in Cruikshank, *Documents*, p. 130. See also the account of the voyage by Richardson, *ibid.*

23. District General Orders dated 11 August 1812.

24. District General Orders dated 14 August 1812.

25. District General Orders dated 14 August 1812.

26. Pay List at the Surrender of Detroit in Cruikshank, *Documents*, p. 148.

27. Richardson, p. 10–11.

28. Ludwig Kosche "Contemporary Portraits of Isaac Brock: An Analysis," in *Archivaria* No 20, (Summer 1985), p. 22–65; and "Relics of Brock: An Investigation," in *Archivaria* No 9 (Winter 1979–1980), p. 33–103.

29. William Stanley Hatch, *A Chapter of the History of the War of 1812 in the Northwest* (Cincinnati, 1872), p. 63.

30. *Cleveland Herald Supplement*, 18 November 1871.

31. *Correspondence*, p. 24.

32. Colonel William Stanley Hatch, *A Chapter of the History of the War of 1812 in the Northwest*, p. 63; John Richardson, *War of 1812, First Series, Containing a Full and Detailed Narrative of the Right Division of the Canadian Army* (Brockville, 1842), p. 68.

33. *Correspondence*, p. 467.

34. *Correspondence*, p. 40.

35. Robert Malcomson, "Picturing Isaac Brock," in *The Beaver*, October 2004.

36. John Andre, *William Berczy, Co-Founder of Toronto, a Sketch* (Toronto, 1967), p. 98–99.

37. This picture, like the earlier miniature of Brock as an ensign in the 8th, was authenticated by Ludwig Kosche in "Contemporary Portraits of Isaac Brock: An Analysis'" in *Archivaria* No 20, (Summer 1985) p. 60–66. It was then also in the possession of Captain H. M. T. Mellish of Guernsey and has since been acquired by the Guernsey Museums.

38. Glegg to William Brock dated 30 December 1812 in Cruikshank, *Documentary History*, iv, 83.

39. *Correspondence*, p. 242–245.

40. Brock to Lord Liverpool dated 29 August 1812 in TNA CO 42/352.

41. Brock to Prevost dated 17 August 1812 in Cruikshank, *Documents*, p. 158.

42. Goodspeed, *The Good Soldier*, p. 97.

43. Fitzgibbon to Tupper, dated 27 September 1845 in the Tupper Papers.

44. *Correspondence*, p. 242–245.

45. This was a considerable property, as Elliott owned 4,000 acres of land a large number of black slaves. See Reginald Horsman, *Matthew Elliott, British Indian Agent* (Detroit, 1964).

46. Brock to Hull dated 15 August 1812 in Cruikshank, *Documents*, p. 144.

Chapter 13: "Intimidated by the Confidence of Our Advance"

1. Cruikshank, *Documents*, p. 4–5.
2. Brian Leigh Dunnigan, *Frontier Metropolis: Picturing Early Detroit* University of Michigan, 2001), p. 136.
3. Information provided by the Ontario Historical Foundation.
4. This account appears in Walter Nursey, *The Story of Isaac Brock* (Toronto, 1908), p. 97, but it has more the ring of embroidery after the event, since it is not mentioned by any contemporary witness.
5. Brock to Prevost dated 17 August 1812 in Cruikshank, *Documents,* p. 158.
6. *Journal of John Norton*, p. 300.
7. Cass to Meigs dated 12 August 1812 in Cruikshank, *Documents,* p. 138.
8. Cruikshank, *Documents*, p. 235–243.
9. Cruikshank, *Documentary History*, iii, 186.
10. "Journal of John Norton," p. 300.
11. D. B. Read, *Life and Times*, p. 156.
12. Brock to Prevost dated 17 August 1812 in Cruikshank, *Documents,* p. 158.
13. Hull to the Secretary of War dated 26 August 1812 in Cruikshank, *Documents,* p. 188.
14. Richardson, *War of 1812, First Series*, p. 14.
15. Lydia Bacon, cited in Dianne Graves, p. 263.
16. Thomas Verchères de Boucherville, cited in Dianne Graves, p. 262.
17. Hull to the Secretary of War dated 26 August 1812 in Cruikshank, *Documents,* p. 188.
18. Mary McCarty, a local resident, cited in Dianne Graves, *In the Midst of Alarms. The Untold Story of Women and the War of 1812* (Toronto, 2007), p. 262.
19. Richardson, *War of 1812, First Series*, p. 14.
20. Brock to Prevost dated 17 August 1812 in Cruikshank, *Documents,* p. 158.
21. Richardson, *War of 1812, First Series*, p. 14.
22. "Journal of John Norton," p. 300.
23. Cruikshank, *Documentary History*, p. 220.
24. Brock to Prevost dated 17 August 1812 in Cruikshank, *Documents,* p. 159.
25. Merritt Papers, MS Group E1-4.
26. Hull to the Secretary of War dated 26 August 1812 in Cruikshank, *Documents,* p. 189.
27. Richardson, *War of 1812: First Series*, p. 14.
28. Richardson, *War of 1812: First Series*, p. 14.
29. Goodspeed, *The Good Soldier*, p. 112.
30. Leeseman, *Plan Topographique du Détroit et les Eaux qui forment la junction du lac Erié avec le lac St Clair* (1796) in Bently Historical Library, University of Michigan.
31. The map is reproduced in Brian Dunnigan, *Frontier Metropolis*, p. 137.
32. Read, *Life and Times*, p. 157.
33. Richardson, *War of 1812: First Series*, p. 14.
34. District General Orders on 14 August 1812 directed a gill of spirits per man per day during the period of the attack on Detroit.
35. "Journal of Charles Askin" in Cruikshank, *Documents*, p. 240.
36. Cruikshank, *Documents*, p. 221–222.
37. Hull's own account and his justification are contained in his letter to the Secretary of War from Fort George dated 26 August 1812 in Cruikshank, *Documents*, p. 184–190.
38. "Journal of Charles Askin" in Cruikshank, *Documents*, p. 242.
39. "Journal of Charles Askin" in Cruikshank, *Documents*, p. 237.
40. Richardson, *War of 1812: First Series*, p. 16.
41. Richardson, *War of 1812: First Series*, p. 16.
42. Richardson, *War of 1812: First Series*, p. 17.
43. Brock to Prevost dated 16 August 1812 in Cruikshank, *Documents,* p. 154.
44. *Correspondence*, p. 168.
45. *London Gazette* No. 16653, dated 6 October 1812.
46. General Return of Prisoners of War Surrendered by Capitulation at Detroit, Aug. 16, 1812 in

Cruikshank, *Documents*, p. 153.

47. Return of Ordnance and Ordnance Stores Taken at Detroit 16th August 1812 in Cruikshank, *Documents*, p. 154.

48. Nichol to Brock dated 25 August 1812 in *Correspondence*, p. 171.

49. Elliott to Procter dated 22 August 1812 in Cruikshank, *Documents*, p. 172.

50. Return of Arms and Stores found at the River Raisin dated 20 August 1812 in Cruikshank, *Documents*, p. 176.

51. These were based on the *1753 Report of the Law Officers* by William Murray, 1st Earl of Mansfield, modified in 1808.

52. General Orders, Quebec, dated 30 December 1813 in L. Humphrey Irving, *Officers of the British Forces in Canada during the War of 1812–1815* (Canadian Military Institute, Welland, 1908), p. 237.

53. *Correspondence*, p. 172.

54. John Sugden, *Tecumseh* p. 304–305.

55. William James, *A Full and Correct Account of the Military Occurrences of the Late War between Great Britain and the United States of America* (London, 1818) vol I p. 291–292.

56. Lugwig Kosche "Relics of Brock," p. 59–61.

57. Prevost to Lord Bathurst dated 26 August 1812 in *Correspondence*, p. 162.

58. Maitland to Brock dated 8 October 1812 in *Correspondence*, p. 167.

59. The Duke of York to Prevost dated 7 October 1812 in Cruikshank, *Documents*, p. 224–225.

60. Brock to his brothers dated 4 September 1812 in *Correspondence*, p. 170–171.

61. Brock to his brothers dated 3 September 1812 in *Correspondence*, p. 169–170.

62. Bathurst to Wellington dated 12 October 1812 cited in John Latimer, *1812. War With America* (London, 2007), p. 71.

63. Bathurst to Prevost dated 10 October 1812 in *Correspondence*, p. 164–165.

Chapter 14: "To Improve and Augment My Resources"

1. Proclamation by Brock dated 16 August 1812 in Cruikshank, *Documents*, p. 155–156.

2. Procter to Brock dated 26 August 1812 in Cruikshank, *Documents*, p. 180–181.

3. Read, p. 197.

4. Prevost to Brock dated 31 August 1812 in D.B. Read, *Life and Times*, p. 194.

5. TNA CO 42/147, Prevost to Lord Bathurst dated 24 August 1812.

6. Read, *Life and Times*, p. 198.

7. Goodspeed, *The Good Soldier*, p. 118.

8. TNA CO 42/352, Brock to Lord Bathurst dated 29 August 1812.

9. Brock to Irving dated 3 September 1812 in *Correspondence*, p. 284.

10. Read, *Life and Times*, p. 207.

11. Stephen Van Rensselaer to Sheaffe dated 20 August 1812 in Cruikshank, *Documentary History*, iii, p. 87.

12. Solomon Van Rensselaer, *A Narrative of the Affair of Queenston in the War of 1812* (New York, 1836), p. 11.

13. TNA CO 42/376, Prevost to Brock dated 30 August 1812.

14. The Rev Michael Smith, cited in Hitsman, *Incredible War of 1812*, p. 86.

15. Read, *Life and Times*, p. 190.

16. Baynes to Brock dated 13 August 1812 in *Correspondence*, p. 177.

17. Brock to Prevost dated 4 September 1812 in *Correspondence*, p. 178.

18. Brock to Prevost dated 28 September 1812 in Wood, *Select British Documents*, i, 596.

19. Smith to Procter dated 18 October 1812, letter supplied by Professor Ray Hobbes.

20. See for example, General Orders dated 27 and 31 August, 1, 3, 5, 8, 9, 13, 17, 19 September 1812.

21. Read, *Life and Times*, p. 192–193.

22. Eustis to Dearborn dated 13 August 1812, cited in Hitsman, *Incredible War of 1812*, p. 87.

23. Brock to Procter dated 25 August 1812 in *Correspondence*, p. 178.

24. Brock to Prevost dated 28 September 1812 in Wood, *Select British Documents*, i, 596.

25. Brock to Prevost dated 28 September 1812 in Wood, *Select British Documents*, i, 596.

26. Muir to Procter dated 26 and 30 September 1812 cited in Jon Latimer, *1812*, p. 68.

27. Brock to Prevost dated 18 September 1812 in *Correspondence*, p. 188.

28. Brock to Procter dated 17 September 1812 in *Correspondence*, p. 184.

29. Jon Latimer, *1812*, p. 74.

30. Solomon Van Rensselaer, *Narrative of the Affair of Queenston*, p. 10.

31. For more details see Charles Whittlesey "General Wadsworth's Division, War of 1812" Cleveland: Western Reserve Historical Society, 1879.

32. Wadsworth to Tompkins, 6 and 8 July 1812 in Cruikshank, *Documentary History*, iii, 101, 116.

33. Gray to Tompkins dated 22 July 1812 in Cruikshank, *Documentary History*, iii, 139; Charles Whittlesey "General Wadsworth's Division".

34. Brock to Prevost dated 13 September 1812 in TNA CO 42/677.

35. Brock to Prevost dated 18 September 1812 in *Correspondence*, p. 189.

36. Brock to Savery dated 18 September 1812 in *Correspondence*, p. 189.

37. Robert Malcomson, *A Very Brilliant Affair. The Battle of Queenston Heights, 1812* (Toronto, 2003), p. 107–109.

38. Solomon Van Rensselaer, *Narrative of the Affair of Queenston*, p. 19–20.

39. Stephen Van Rensselaer to Dearborn dated 8 October 1812 in Cruikshank, *Documentary History*, iv, 40.

40. Malcomson, *Brilliant Affair*, p. 256–258.

41. Dearborn to Stephen Van Rensselaer dated 26 September 1812 in Cruikshank, *Documentary History*, iii, 295.

42. See chapter 10.

43. Malcomson, *Brilliant Affair*, p. 272–273.

44. See the figures of absentee officers quoted in chapter 10.

45. Brock to Savery dated 18 September 1812 in *Correspondence*, p. 189.

46. Smith to Procter dated 18 October 1812, letter supplied by Prof Ray Hobbes.

47. Brock to Prevost dated 18 September 1812 in *Correspondence*, p. 189.

48. "Instructions Sent to Officers Commanding Forts," undated but probably late September 1812; District General Orders dated 6th October 1812.

49. Prevost to Brock dated 14 September 1812 in *Correspondence*, p. 183.

50. Procter to Brock dated 29 August 1812 in Cruikshank, *Documents*, p. 201.

51. Prevost to Brock dated 25 September 1812 in *Correspondence*, p. 190.

52. See his biography by Donald E. Graves, cited in the bibliography.

53. Brock to Prevost dated 11 October 1812 in *Correspondence*, p. 198.

54. Prevost to Brock dated 25 September 1812 *Correspondence*, p. 190.

55. Brock to Prevost dated 28 September 1812 in Wood, *Select British Documents*, i, 596.

56. Brock to Savery dated 18 September 1812 in *Correspondence*, p. 315.

57. Brock to Procter dated 11 October 1812 in *Correspondence*, p. 200.

Chapter 15: "Proof of their Loyalty and Courage"

1. Malcomson, *Brilliant Affair*, p. 111.

2. Malcomson, *Brilliant Affair*, p. 114.

3. Malcomson, *Brilliant Affair*, p. 118.

4. The instructions to the various commanders are outlined in Solomon Van Rensselaer, *Narrative of the Affair of Queenston*, p. 72 et seq.

5. Malcomson, *Brilliant Affair*, p. 274.

6. Smyth to Van Rensselaer in *Narrative of the Affair of Queenston*, p. 72.

7. Brock to Prevost dated 11 October 1812 in TNA CO 42/677.

8. Evans to unknown recipient dated 15 October 1812 in Wood, *Select British Documents*, i, 617.

9. Evans's diary, cited in Malcomson, *Brilliant Affair*, p. 125.

10. Evans to unknown recipient dated 15 October 1812 in Wood, *Select British Documents*, i, 620.

11. Solomon Van Rensselaer, *The Affair of Queenston*, p. 22.

12. *Correspondence*, p. 202.

13. Malcomson, *Brilliant Affair*.

14. *Correspondence*, p. 202.

15. Captain James Crooks, 1st Lincoln Militia, to Thomas Maclear dated 17 March 1853 (Archives of Ontario MU 2144/14).
16. "Journal of John Norton," p. 304.
17. Evans to unknown recipient dated 15 October 1812 in Wood, *Select British Documents*, i, 620.
18. See, for example, Walter Nursey, *The Story of Isaac Brock*, p. 221.
19. Letter from John Beverley Robinson to unknown recipient dated 14 October 1812 in Wood, *Select British Documents*, i, 40–41.
20. McLean's account dated 22 July 1860, cited in Malcomson, *Brilliant Affair*, p. 147–148.
21. District General Orders dated 6 October 1812.
22. Solomon Van Rensselaer, *the Affair of Queenston* p. 25.
23. Malcomson, *Brilliant Affair*, p. 138.
24. Smith to Procter dated 18 October 1812.
25. Smith to Procter dated 18 October 1812.
26. Letter from John Beverley Robinson to unknown recipient dated 14 October 1812 in Wood, *Select British Documents*, i, 40–41.
27. "Major-General John Ellis Wool to W. L. Stone on the Battle of Queenston Heights in October 1812" dated 13 September 1838 in *New York Public Library Bulletin*, 9 (1905).
28. Malcomson, *Brilliant Affair*, p. 138.
29. Smith to Procter dated 18 October 1812.
30. Wool to Stone dated 13 September 1838.
31. Solomon Van Rensselaer, *The Affair of Queenston*, p. 26.
32. Information from Mr Jonathan Ferguson, Curator of Firearms at the Royal Armouries.
33. Malcomson, *Brilliant Affair*, p. 257.
34. Letter from John Beverley Robinson to unknown recipient dated 14 October 1812 in Wood, *Select British Documents*, i, 40–41.
35. Robinson's letter dated 14 October 1812 in Wood, *Select British Documents*, i, 40–41.
36. Smith to Procter dated 18 October 1812 and other sources, including William Hamilton Merritt, all say that he was at the battery, although neither was present. The sequence of events that followed only makes sense, however, if indeed Brock had been there.
37. Robinson's letter dated 14 October 1812 in Wood, *Select British Documents*, i, 613.
38. Smith to Procter dated 18 October 1812.
39. Letter of George S. Jervis narrating the events of the battle in Cruikshank, *Documentary History*, iv, 146.
40. Smith to Procter dated 18 October 1812.
41. Narrative of G. S. Jervis, in Cruikshank, *Documentary History*, iv. 116.
42. Robinson's letter dated 14 October 1812 in Wood, *Select British Documents*, i, 40–41.
43. See the detailed investigation of Brock's coat in Ludwig Kosche "Relics of Brock," p. 33–103.
44. Smith to Procter dated 18 October 1812.
45. Ludwig Kosche "Relics of Brock," p. 48–50.
46. Donald R. Hickey, *Don't Give Up the Ship! Myths of the War of 1812* (Toronto, 2006), p. 59–60; Ludwig Kosche "Relics of Brock," p. 102.
47. Narrative of G. S. Jervis, in Cruikshank, *Documentary History*, iv. 116. See also John Beverley Robinson's letter dated 14 October 1812 in Wood, *Select British Documents*, i, 613.
48. Smith to Procter dated 18 October 1812.
49. William Hamilton Merritt, "Journal of events Principally on the Detroit and Niagara Frontiers" in Wood, *Select British Documents*, iii, 559.
50. Glegg to William Brock dated 14 October 1812 in Cruikshank, *Documentary History*, iv, 83.
51. Narrative of G. S. Jervis, in Cruikshank, *Documentary History*, iv. 116.
52. Smith to Procter dated 18 October 1812.
53. *The Niagara Bee*, 24 October 1812.

Chapter 16: "The Honourable Bed of a Soldier"

1. McLean's account dated 22 July 1860, cited in Malcomson, *Brilliant Affair*, p. 192.
2. Glegg to William Brock dated 30 December 1813 in Cruikshank, *Documentary History*, iv, 83.

3. *Correspondence*, p. 206.
4. District General Orders dated 16 October 1812.
5. For a detailed account of Brock's various burials and memorials see Robert Malcomson, *Burying General Brock. A History of Brock's Monuments* (Niagara, 1996).
6. *Correspondence*, p. 204.
7. *The Niagara Bee*, 24 October 1812.
8. Frederick, Duke of York to William Brock dated December 1815 in *Correspondence*, p. 236.
9. Lord Bathurst to Prevost dated 8 December 1812 in *Correspondence*, p. 205.
10. Prevost's final general order in the *Columbian Centinel* dated 19 April 1815 (Boston Public Library).
11. Malcomson, *Burying General Brock*, p. 6–7; Ludwig Kosche "Relics of Brock," p. 33–103.
12. Glegg to William Brock dated 30 December 1813 in Cruikshank, *Documentary History,* iv, 83. See also Ludwig Kosche "Relics of Brock," p. 79–80.
13. Army List *1811*.
14. Glegg to William dated 30 December 1813 in Cruikshank, *Documentary History,* iv, 83.
15. Evans to Procter dated 22 October 1812 in Malcomson, *Brilliant Affair*, p. 197–198.

Bibliography

PRIMARY SOURCES

The National Archives, Kew

War Office Papers
WO 17, Monthly Returns of Regiments.
WO 23, Pension Records, Colonies.
WO 27, Inspection Returns.
WO 28, Headquarters Records and Field Officers' Letters.

Colonial Office Papers for British North America
CO 42, State Papers, Colonial Office, Canada.
CO 43, Entry Books for 1812.

Foreign Office Papers for British North America
FO 5, State Papers U.S.A.

Library and Archives Canada
RG 8 I vols 725, 728, 922, 923
Brigade Thomas Major Evans's Diary: *Extract from the Diary of General T. Evans while serving as an officer on staff of General Brock at Queenston, War of 1812–1814, Government House, Fort George, 15 October 1812*. National Archives of Canada MG 24.
District General Orders of Maj.-Gen. Sir Isaac Brock from June 27th, 1812–Oct. 16th, 1812. Women's Canadian Historical Society of Toronto, Transaction No. 19.
Documents Relating to the Invasion of Canada and the Surrender of Detroit 1812, E.A. Cruikshank, ed., (Ottawa, 1913).
Documentary History of the Campaigns upon the Niagara Frontier, 1812–1814, E.A. Cruikshank, ed., (9 vols, Welland, 1896–1908).
The Correspondence of Lieut. Governor John Graves Simcoe, Vol II, 1794–1795, E.A. Cruikshank, ed., (Toronto: Ontario Historical Society, 1924).
Crooks, Captain James, 1st Lincoln Militia, to Thomas Maclear dated 17 March 1853 on the Battle of Queenston (Archives of Ontario MU 2144/14).
Merritt Papers in National Archives of Canada, Toronto, MS Group 24, E1-4.
Report on Canadian Archives by Douglas Brymner, Archivist, 1892 (Ottawa, 1893).
Report on Canadian Archives by Douglas Brymner, Archivist, 1893 (Ottawa, 1894).
Report on Canadian Archives by Douglas Brymner, Archivist, 1896 (Ottawa, 1897).
Tupper, Ferdinand Brock, Papers, Archive of Ontario, Toronto.
Wood, William L., *Select British Documents of the War of 1812* (3 vols, Toronto, 1920–1928).
Wool, Major-General John Ellis, to W.L. Stone on the Battle of Queenston Heights in October 1812 dated 13 September 1838 in *New York Public Library Bulletin, 9* (1905).

U.S. Archives
Annals of Congress: Debates and Proceedings in the Congress of the United States, 1789–1834 (42 vols, Washington, 1834–1836).

Annual Register, or a View of the History, Politics, and Literature for the Year 1810–1812 (London, 1822–1825).

London Gazette
12627, 5 March 1785; 13166, 12 January 1790; 13278, 29 January 1791; 13790, 23 June 1795; 14059, 24 October 1797.

Guernsey Archives
Ecclesiastical Court Records of Greffe, Normandy.
Island Archives of Guernsey, Research Pedigrees.
Island Archives of Guernsey, Royal Court Library, Pedigrees of Guernsey Families.
Richard Hocart *Notes on the de Havilland Letters* (Unpublished, Guernsey).

Regulations
Rules and Articles For the Better Government of His Majesty's Horse and Foot Guards, And all other His Forces in Great Britain and Ireland, Dominions Beyond the Seas, and Foreign Parts, From the 24th of March, 1762.
New Manual, and Platoon Exercise: with an Explanation. Published by Authority (Dublin, 1764).
The Manual Exercise with Explanations as ordered by His Majesty, 1778.
Rules and regulations for the Field Exercise and Movements of the Army in Ireland (Dublin, 1789).
Rules and Regulations for the Formations, Field-Exercise, and Movements, of His Majesty's Forces (1792).
Regulations for the Exercise of Riflemen and Light Infantry (Francis, Baron de Rottenburg, 1798).

Contemporary Accounts
Burke, Edmund, *Reflections on the Revolution in France* (London, 1791).
Cuthbertson's System for the Complete Interior Management and Œconomy of a Battalion of Infantry, a New Edition, with Corrections (Bristol, 1776).
DePeyster, Arendt Schuyler, *Miscellanies, by an Officer* (1813; annotated edition, 1888).
Dundas, Colonel David, *Principles of Military Movements, Chiefly Applied to the Infantry* (1788).
Hatch, William Stanley, *A Chapter of the History of the War of 1812 in the Northwest,* (Cincinnati, 1872).
Krayenhoff, C. R. T., *Geschiedkundige Beschouwing van den Oorlog op het grondgebied der Bataafsche Republiek in 1799* (1832).
Lamb, Sergeant Roger (23rd Fusiliers), *An Original and Authentic Journal of Occurrences during the Late American War, from Its Commencement to the Year 1783* (Dublin, 1809, reprinted New York, 1968).
Norton, John, "The Journal of Major John Norton, 1816" in *The Publications of the Champlain Society* (Toronto, 1970).
Richardson, John, *Richardson's War of 1812, with Notes and a Life of the Author by A. C. Casselman* (Toronto, 1902).
Richardson, John, *War of 1812, First Series, Containing a Full and Detailed Narrative of the Right Division of the Canadian Army* (Brockville, 1842).
Sheaffe, Roger H., *Letter Book of General Sir Roger Hale Sheaffe* (University of California, 2007).
Sullivan, Private Thomas, (49th Foot) *From Redcoat to Rebel: The Thomas Sullivan Journal.* J. L. Boyle, ed., (Heritage, 1997).
Smith, Michael, *A Geographical View of the Province of Upper Canada and Promiscuous Remarks on the Government etc (Boston, 1813).*
Rensselaer, Soloman Van, *A Narrative of the Affair of Queenston in the War of 1812* (New York, 1836).
Sutherland, Stuart, ed., *"A Desire of Serving and Defending my Country": The War of 1812 Journals of William Hamilton Merritt* (Toronto, 2001).

Newspapers
Cleveland Herald Supplement, 1871.
Niagara Bee, 24 October 1812.

Quebec Mercury, 1805–1812.
Upper Canada Guardian; or, Freeman's Journal. 1808–1812.
York Gazette, 1811–1812.

Reference Works
Army List, yearly and/or monthly, 1776 to 1812.
Burke, Sir Bernard, *The General Armoury of England, Scotland, Ireland and Wales* (London, 1884).
Chandler, David, *Dictionary of the Napoleonic Wars* (London, 1979).
Clausewitz, Carl-Maria von, *Vom Krieg (On War)*, translated by J. J. Graham, (London, 1873).
Crowder, Norman K., *British Army Pensioners Abroad 1772–1899* (Baltimore, 1995).
Duane, William, *Hand Book for Infantry* (Applewood, 2009).
Dunnigan, Brian Leigh, *Frontier Metropolis: Picturing Early Detroit* (Detroit, 2001).
Hansard's *Parliamentary Debates*, vols vi–xiii (London, 1805–1814).
Irving, L. Homfray, *Officers of the British Forces in Canada during the War of 1812–1815* (Canadian Military Institute, Welland, 1908).
Malcomson, Robert, *Burying General Brock. A History of Brock's Monuments* (Niagara, 1996).
John Brannan, ed., *Official Letters of the Military and Naval Officers of the United States During the War with Great Britain in the Years 1812, 1813, 1814, 1815.* (Washington D.C., 1823).
Petrie, F. Lorraine, *History of the Royal Berkshire Regiment (Princess Charlotte of Wales's)* (Reading, 1925).
Robertson, J. R., *The History of Freemasonry in Canada from its Introduction in 1749* (Toronto, 1899).
Some Account of the Public Life of the late Sir George Prevost, Bart (Quarterly Review, London, 1823).
Tupper, Ferdinand Brock, *The History of Guernsey and its Bailiwick; with occasional notices of Jersey* (2nd edition, London, 1876).
Uttley, John, *The Story of the Channel Islands* (London, 1966).
Wood, William L., ed., *Select British Documents of the War of 1812*, 4 vols (Toronto 1920–1928).

Earlier Biographies
Edgar, Lady Matilda, *General Brock* (Toronto, 1904).
Goodspeed, D. J., *The Good Soldier. The Story of Isaac Brock* (London, 1965).
Nursey, Walter R., *The Story of Isaac Brock* (Toronto, 1908).
Read, D. B., *Life and Times of Major-General Sir Isaac Brock* (London, 1894).
Tupper, Ferdinand Brock, *The Life and Correspondence of Sir Isaac Brock* (Guernsey, 1845).

MODERN SECONDARY SOURCES

Books
Allen, R. S., *Her Majesty's Indian Allies. British Indian Policy in the Defence of Canada, 1774–181* (Toronto, 1992).
Andre, John, *William Berczy, Co-Founder of Toronto, a Sketch* (Toronto, 1967).
Benn, Carl, *The Iroquois in the War of 1812* (University of Toronto, 1998).
Berger, Thomas R., *A Long and Terrible Shadow: White Values, Native Rights in the Americas, 1492–1992* (Vancouver, 1992).
Buckley, Roger Norman, *The British Army and the West Indies: Society and the Military in the Revolutionary Age* (University of Florida, 1998).
Carey, A. D. L., and Stouppe McCance, *Regimental Records of the Royal Welch Fusiliers, Vol I 1689–1815* (London, 1921).
Coles, Harry L., *The War of 1812* (Chicago, 1965).
Cookson, J. E., *The British Armed Nation 1793–1805* (OUP, 1997).
Craig, Gerald M., *Upper Canada, the Formative Years 1784–1841* (Toronto, 1963).
Davis, Colonel John, History *of the Second Queen's Royal Regiment, Vol III, 1715–1799* (London, 1895).
Duffy, Michael, *Soldiers, Sugar and Seapower: The British Expeditions to the West Indies and the War Against Revolutionary France* (Oxford, 1987).

Emsley, Clive, *State, Economy and Nation in 19th Century Europe* (London, 1996).

FitzGibbon, Mary Agnes, *A Veteran of 1812: The Life of James FitzGibbon* (Toronto, 2000).

Fortescue, Sir John, *A History of the British Army. Volume 3, 1763-1793* (London, 1911).

Fregosi, Paul, *Dreams of Empire: Napoleon and the First World War, 1792–1815* (London, 1991).

Gates, David, *The British Light Infantry Arm c1790–1815* (Batsford, 1987).

Gill, Conrad, *The Naval Mutinies of 1797* (Manchester, 1913).

Glover, Richard, *Peninsular Preparation: The Reform of the British Army, 1795–1809* (Cambridge, 1963).

Graves, Dianne, *In the Midst of Alarms: The Untold Story of Women and the War of 1812* (Toronto, 2007).

Graves, Donald E., *Fix Bayonets! A Royal Welch Fusilier at War, 1792–1815* (Toronto, 2005).

Graves, Donald E., *Dragon Rampant: The Royal Welch Fusiliers at War, 1793–1815* (London, 2010).

Guillet, Edwin C., *Pioneer Travel in Upper Canada* (Toronto, 1933).

Hickey, Donald R., *Don't Give Up the Ship! Myths of the War of 1812* (Toronto, 2006).

Hitsman, J. Mackay, *The Incredible War of 1812: A Military History* Updated by Donald E. Graves (Toronto, 1999).

Holmes, Richard, *Redcoat: The British Soldier in the Age of Horse and Musket* (London, 2001).

Horsman, Reginald, *Matthew Elliott, British Indian Agent* (Detroit, 1964).

Houlding, J. A., *Fit for Service: The Training of the British Army. 1715-1795* (Oxford, 1981).

James, C. L. R., The *Black Jacobins: Toussaint l'Ouverture and the San Domingo Revolution* (London, 1963).

Latimer, Jon, *1812: War with America* (London, 2007).

Lloyd, Alan *The Scorching of Washington–The War of 1812* (New York, 1975).

Mackenzie, Ruth, *James Fitzgibbon: Defender of Upper Canada* (Toronto, 1983).

Malcomson, Robert, *A Very Brilliant Affair: The Battle of Queenston Heights, 1812* (Toronto, 2003).

Markham, Felix, *Napoleon* (London, 1963).

Miller, J. R., *Skyscrapers Hide the Heavens: A History of Indian-White Relations in* Canada (Toronto, 1989).

Morrissey, Brendan, and Adam Hook, *Quebec 1775: The American Invasion of Canada*, (New York, 2003).

Mowatt, R. B., *The Diplomacy of Napoleon*, (London, 1924).

Muir, Rory, *Britain and the Defeat of Napoleon, 1807–1815* (Yale, 1996).

Radford, Peter, *The Celebrated Captain Barclay: Sport, Money and Fame in Regency Britain* (London, 2001).

Riley, Jonathon, *Napoleon as a General* (London, 2007).

Riley, Jonathon, *Decisive Battles* (London, 2010).

Schama, S., *Patriots and Liberators: Revolution in the Netherlands 1780-1813* (New York, 1977).

Sheppard, George, *Plunder, Profit and Paroles: A Social Hisotry of the War of 1812 in Upper Canada* (Montreal, 1994).

Spring, Matthew H., *With Zeal and with Bayonets Only: The British Army on Campaign in North America, 1775–1783* (University of Oklahoma, 2008).

Stanley, George F. G., *The War of 1812, Land Operations* (Toronto, 1983).

Urban, Mark, *Fusiliers: Eight Years with the Redcoats in America* (London, 2007).

Wade, Mason, *The French Canadians* (Toronto, 1975).

Western, J. R., *The English Militia in the Eighteenth Century* (London, 1965).

Articles

Anderson, Major-General W. H., "Outline of Development of the British Army Up to the commencement of the Great War, 1914: Notes for Four Lectures delivered at the Staff College, Camberley" (London, 1926).

Carman, W. Y., "Infantry Clothing Regulations, 1802" in *Journal of the Society for Army Historical Research*, no. 19 (1940), p 200–235.

Cruikshank, E. A., "Record of the Services of Canadian Regiments in the War of 1812" in *Canadian Military Institute, Selected Papers* (1893 et seq).

Fleming, Patricia, "The Library of Major-General Sir Isaac Brock" in *The Fife and Drum* (The Newsletter of the Friends of Fort York and the Garrison Common), vol 12 no. 1, March 2008.

"Isaac Brock – Saviour of Canada" in *Historica Canadiana*, 27, November 2006.

Kosche, Ludwig, "Contemporary Portraits of Isaac Brock: An Analysis" in *Archivaria*, no. 20, (Summer 1985).

Kosche, Ludwig, "Relics of Brock: An Investigation" in *Archivaria*, no. 9, (1 January 1979).

Lanctôt, G., "Les Colonies Américains 1760–1820" *in Les Canadiens français et leurs voisins du sud* (Montreal, 1941).

Malcomson, Robert, "Picturing Isaac Brock" in *The Beaver* (October 2004).

Marshall-Fraser, W., "History of Banking in the Channel Islands and a record of bank-note issue" in *Transactions of La Société Guernesiaise*, 1949, 378–443.

Raudzens, George, "'Red George' Macdonell, Military Savior of Upper Canada?" in *Ontario History*, vol LXII, no. 4

Stacey, C. P., "Sir Isaac Brock" in *Dictionary of Canadian Biography Online* (University of Toronto, 2000).

Whittlesey, Charles, "General Wadsworth's Division, War of 1812" in Cleveland: Western Reserve Historical Society, 1879.

Unpublished Academic Theses

Graves, Donald E., "Joseph Willcocks and the Canadian Volunteers: An Account of Political Disaffection in Upper Canada during the War of 1812." Unpublished M.A. Thesis, Carleton University, Ottawa, 1982.

Grodzinski, John, "The Vigilant Superintendence of the Whole District: The War of 1812 on the Upper St Lawrence." Unpublished M.A. Thesis, Royal Military College of Canada, Kingston, 2002.

Steppler, Glenn A., "A Duty Troublesome Beyond Measure: Logistical Considerations in the Canadian War of 1812." Unpublished M.A. Thesis, McGill University, Montreal, 1974.

Internet

Conversion rates of money from 1812 to modern day have been worked out using <www.eh.net/ehresources/howmuch/poundq.php>.

Details of the history and construction of the St Lawrence Seaway are available at the Great Lakes/St Lawrence Seaway System website at <www.seaway.ca>.

Dictionary of Canadian Biography Online.

Henderson, Robert, "Captains of the Canadian Fencibles in 1812" on the *War of 1812 website* (1997).

National Health Service (Great Britain) on-line information on infectious and communicable diseases.

Weston, Karl, "Slavery and Economy in Barbados" on BBC broadcasts website, 2009.

Index